BABEL

Samuel L. Boyd

BABEL

*Political Rhetoric
of a Confused Legacy*

FORTRESS PRESS
MINNEAPOLIS

Dedicated to the memory of David Shneer (z"l). You believed in this project. You believed in me. And you believed that we could make the world better. It's our responsibility to carry on your legacy.

Contents

Acknowledgments

In many ways, this is a book about words, what they mean, how to interpret them, and how a new reading of the Tower of Babel reframes our understanding of one of the most famous stories from the Bible. Yet my own words fail to thank adequately the many people responsible for supporting me and my work. All faults in this book are my own responsibility, though I am immensely grateful for the rich and caring academic community that has honed my thought and allowed me to bring this task to completion.

I have dedicated this book to the memory of David Shneer. He, along with John Cumalat, is why I have the position I have at the University of Colorado Boulder. David also inspired me with his vision for how academic work could make the world a better place. He encouraged me in this project, and his untimely passing left for many of us a gaping hole in the world. I hope that this book is a small testament to his legacy.

The initial planning of this book happened at a faculty retreat through the Research and Innovation Office faculty fellowship at the University of Colorado Boulder. I am extremely indebted to the wonderful colleagues and mentors from around the university who were a part of that fellowship. In particular, I want to thank Alan Townsend, Kirsten Rowell, and Terri Fiez for creating such a warm and stimulating program. It was an honor to be a part of it.

Additionally, my colleagues at the University of Colorado Boulder have been an ever-present support network for me and my work. I would like to thank especially Brian Catlos and the Mediterranean Studies Seminar for providing a platform to workshop ideas from this book. My chairs during the writing of the book, Susan Kent and Deborah Whitehead, have been more encouraging than I can express. Eli Sacks, the director of the Program in Jewish Studies, has always been an avid promoter of my work and a wonderful friend. I would also like to thank Aun Ali, Loriliai Biernacki, Holly Gayley,

Nan Goodman, Terry Kleeman, and Samira Mehta. Hilary Kalisman read versions of chapters one and six, and her input was invaluable.

I would also like to thank my friends and colleagues in the field and in the Boulder community for discussing ideas and reading portions of the arguments in this book. In particular, I am grateful for the enduring mentorship of Jeff Stackert, whose influence on my work is notable and likely obvious to most. Thank you, Jeff! Seth Sanders very graciously read parts of the book, pushed me to make my arguments and voice sharper, and, in all ways, has been a constant advocate for me and my scholarship. I am very thankful for his input and our wonderful conversations. Elaine Pagels offered me space in her "God and Satan, Goddesses and Monsters" undergraduate seminar at Princeton in 2021 to present my ideas. The engagement with the undergraduates was more stimulating than I can express, and it is an honor to have been able to be a part of the classroom with such a wonderful group of students. I am thankful to Elaine for this opportunity and for our friendship over the years. Cathleen Chopra-McGowan and Chloe Blackshear provided a stimulating environment to discuss this project in their panel on the Bible and nationalism at the Association for Jewish Studies conference in 2021. The contributions from the organizers and other panelists greatly enriched my thoughts on this timely and important topic. I would also like to thank Joel Baden, David Carr, Joel Casavant, Simi Chavel, John Chavis, Michael D. Coogan, Liane Feldman, Bradley Gregory, Chip Hardy, Charles Huff, David Ilan, Nate Klemp, Nathan Mastjnak, and Jacqueline Vayntrub. All errors are mine alone, but much of the good in my work can be ascribed to the (collective and/or individual) influence of these amazing colleagues. Yet again, I am very much indebted to the incredible copy-editing work, and overall insights, of Lark Lundberg. Thank you!

Carey Newman deserves special thanks for his work as editor. Our conversations reworked how I thought about writing and editing this book, as well as writing in general. He displayed the patience of Job as I finished the draft of the manuscript and was always prompt in his feedback and keen insights. I cannot thank him enough for taking a chance on this project, for inspiring me with his wisdom on the craft of writing, and for seeing it through to completion. Steven Hall and the amazing production team at eVC-Tech as well as Paul at HK Scriptorium, who graciously produced the indexes, deserve major credit for making this book much better than it would have been otherwise.

I would like to thank the editors of the *Journal of Near Eastern Studies*, particularly Seth Richardson, who was also instrumental in directing me to idioms in Akkadian that appear in chapter 2 and that are relevant for the thesis of this book. Parts of chapters 2 and 3 appeared as a journal article.[1] Though it has been heavily edited and adapted to this book, I am thankful for their permission to include that material here, which provided the nucleus of the ideas now fleshed out in book form.

As always, my family, my favorite people in the world, provide enduring support, motivation, and love without limit in ways that I am still grasping to understand. Kim, you are the love of my life, and you challenge me to think creatively and constructively about my work. Thank you for everything. Skip and Anna, my kids, are the joys of my life, and I love every second that I get to be your dad. I really love you!

---

1 Samuel Boyd, "Sargon's Dūr-Šarrukīn Cylinder Inscription and Language Ideology: A Reconsideration and Connection to Genesis 11:1–9," *JNES* 78 (2019): 87–111, DOI: https://doi.org/10.1086/702011.

Preface

While it may strike many people as odd, counterintuitive, or simply wrong, the Tower of Babel story in Genesis 11:1–9 is not an account explaining the origin of the diversity of languages. At least it was not about this in the form of the narrative immediately prior to the editing of the Torah, or the first five books of the Bible, despite this image immortalized in art, popular imagination, and political rhetoric.[1] The placement of the passage in the Hebrew Bible, or Old Testament, lends itself toward the interpretation that the episode at

---

1 At least three levels of analyzing a biblical text exist, and the Tower of Babel story has been studied at all three. One level involves the oral prehistory, or the pre-literary composition of the text, as exemplified in Hermann Gunkel's commentary on Genesis, in which he divides Genesis 11:1–9 into two stories, one about a tower, another about a city. See Gunkel, *Genesis*, trans. Mark E. Biddle, 3rd ed. (Macon, GA: Mercer University Press, 1997), 94–102. The Tower of Babel has also been examined as part of a precompilation strand of the Pentateuch called J. For this type of analysis, in conversation with both Gunkel and modern literary critics, see Joel S. Baden, "The Tower of Babel: A Case Study in the Competing Methods of Historical and Modern Literary Criticism," *JBL* 128 (2009): 209–224. A third approach is to interpret Genesis 11:1–9 in its canonical context, taking into account historical criticism and reception history but attempting to elucidate, ultimately, the Tower of Babel in its current shape, form, and placement in the book of Genesis. See Richard S. Briggs, "The Book of Genesis," in *A Theological Introduction to the Pentateuch: Interpreting the Torah as Christian Scripture*, ed. Richard S. Briggs and Joel N. Lohr (Grand Rapids, MI: Baker Academic, 2012), 19–50. In this book, I focus on the second and third levels. Whatever value the study of orality may have for understanding a biblical passage, the chapters that follow are concerned with the literary (in the sense of written) presentation of the story, both in the sense of a reconstructed and hypothetical non-P (or J) and in the sense of the canonical placement and interpretation of Genesis 11:1–9. The term "hypothetical" refers to the fact that no manuscript of non-P/J exists, or likely will ever be discovered. Nonetheless, as I argue below, such diachronic approaches to the text explain much of the literary phenomena in the Hebrew Bible and provide the most convincing frameworks for understanding the precompilation state of the literature that was woven together to form the Pentateuch as it exists. See the seven points regarding the methodological concerns in the Neo-Documentary

Babel is about the beginnings of multilingualism; however, even in a canonical reading, or a reading of the Bible as it now appears, a better interpretation exists than the traditional explanation.

In fact, the Tower of Babel is a story that is not primarily about a tower, nor was its composition in Babylon. The combination of setting Genesis 11:1–9 in the context of events in the Assyrian empire, decades if not over a century prior to the Neo-Babylonian period, and the results of other critical analyses reveal that the Tower of Babel story is not about the origins of polyglossia, not about a massive ziggurat (though that feature is a part of the story), and not about the evils of Babylon.[2] Naturally, it is not very inspiring simply to argue what a story is not, namely the traditional understanding of the passage as the initial appearance of many languages on earth. There is a more satisfying, and interesting, alternative when Genesis 11:1–9 is seen as a drama navigating who has the authority to unify or fragment political entities.

Challenging millennia of commentaries on the passage involves methods and data used to support this thesis, which could be phrased both negatively (the story is not about language) and positively (it is about politics). A new analysis of Genesis 11:1–9 not only brings clarity to this passage but also allows for a better understanding of some of the features (or lack thereof) in the call of Abram story in Genesis 12:1–3. In other words, there is a lot of payoff in rereading the Tower of Babel.[3] Perhaps more interestingly, exploring

---

Hypothesis, particularly point five, in Jeffrey Stackert, *A Prophet Like Moses: Prophecy, Law, and Israelite Religion* (New York: Oxford University Press, 2014), 20–22.

2 Others have also come to the conclusion that Genesis 11:1–9 is not principally concerned with this topic. See Christoph Uehlinger, *Weltreich und "eine Rede": Eine neue Deutung der sogenannten Turmbauerzählung (Gen 11, 1–9)*, OBO 101 (Göttingen: Vandenhoeck & Ruprecht, 1990). Though I agree with Uehlinger in the use of Neo-Assyrian rhetoric to demonstrate that Genesis 11:1–9 is not about the origins of multilingualism, I employ a distinct framework for the development of the Bible, which also creates more insights into the meaning and development of the text. Moreover, my use of interpretive traditions is also to a different end than Uehlinger's use of ancient interpreters.

3 The idea for this book began as an article. The thesis of the article was that some biblical scholars are imprecise when discussing Assyrian rhetoric as it pertained to language and bilingualism in Mesopotamia during the eighth and seventh centuries BCE. They do not reflect accurately the linguistic situation on the ground, nor do they analyze sufficiently the nuances of Assyrian rhetoric. Moreover, the heart of the article concerned the role that a reanalysis of Assyrian rhetoric would have for the interpretation of Genesis 11:1–9, or the episode of the Tower of Babel. That article appeared in the *Journal for Near Eastern Studies*, and the following pages represent a significant expansion of the ideas that originally appeared in article form. Indeed,

the passage anew can also explain how it became possible to read it as a myth describing the advent of multilingualism.

A major payoff of any attempt to reread parts of the Bible is the inevitable effect that it can have on society. The critical study of the Bible has often served as a corrective to the manner in which Scripture has functioned in society, beginning with Baruch Spinoza. Putting such a study into conversation with the way Genesis 11:1–9 has influenced political rhetoric and policy, particularly in America, can offer insights into both how people shape the Bible and how the Bible shapes people.[4] For example, Rastafarian readings of the Tower of Babel display how enslaved communities in Jamaica found an explanation for why so many displaced people brought there had common roots yet spoke different languages. Babel still represents a problem entailing the advent of multilingualism, but Rastafarians utilize the narrative to provide an explanatory foundation for a nondominant situation.[5] In other religious communities, Genesis 11:1–9 portrays divine judgment, but in that judgment the deity ordains the existence of multilingualism. In Acts 2 the Pentecost event does not invalidate polyglossia but instead shows how the workings of the Holy Spirit in Christian thought overcomes the potential for miscommunication without eradicating the existence of different languages. Despite the divine displeasure at the Tower of Babel in the Bible itself, readings exist

---

the Assyrian background and the relevance of imperial rhetoric for understanding Genesis 11:1–9 still animates this book. These issues form the central themes around which the following chapters are grouped, with the inclusion of a chapter on the reception history of Genesis 11:1–9 and the manner in which the interpretation of that passage explains the role of Abram as a reversal of the Tower of Babel.

4 The Tower of Babel provided a framework of sorts through which to envision American history already by the centennial celebration of America in 1876. See, for example, Erastus Salisbury Field's painting *Historical Monument of the American Republic*, a canvas that conveys important moments of American history as a series of towers constructed, each of which resembles closely contemporaneous depictions of the Tower of Babel. Mark A. Noll, *America's Book: The Rise and Decline of a Bible Civilization, 1794–1911* (New York: Oxford University Press, 2022), 613.

5 Similarly from the perspective of a nondominant author, for Robert Benjamin Lewis, the "son of a Native American father and an African mother," the Tower of Babel demonstrated that all humanity had originally descended from dark-skinned ancestors, and, as a result, the story provided the basis for antislavery argumentation. See a discussion of the reprint of his 1836 publication in 1844, the same year that William Graham published a proslavery argument based on Leviticus 25, in Noll, *America's Book*, 333–334.

in which the result according to the traditional interpretation (polyglossia) is still a positive trait.[6]

Important as these interpretations of Genesis 11:1–9 are, a specific strain of utilization of the Tower of Babel merits further consideration, specifically the manner in which the story has functioned in the context of modernity and the nation-state. These are employments of the passage from often upper-class, often white, communities seeking to define how language and land interact. A juxtaposition of a new examination of the passage with the history of this specific mode of interpretation into the current era also throws into sharp relief a historical oddity: how originally nondominant stories from oppressed communities (such as Judah) containing anti-imperial rhetoric (as in the Tower of Babel) transformed over time seemingly to give voice to (and offer support for) the fears of those in power seeking to maintain a certain kind of link between nationalism, identity (in language), and the Bible. Unlocking this puzzle in terms of the Tower of Babel can shed light on how the story not only became a narrative about multilingualism but then how that interpretation served the particular concerns of the modern nation-state, linking the emphases of people, land, and language.

Even in colonial America, the Tower of Babel was a powerful metaphor in politics, bringing to mind the dangers of disagreement and dissension at a time when unified action was essential. The story also functioned as a cultural metaphor, pointing to the threats of multilingualism for national identity and coherence in enacting policy. Often (though not always) in American politics, Babel represents a curse to be overcome.[7] The understanding of Genesis 11:1–9 as a story of multilingualism founded on divine displeasure has especially haunted legislative discourse in America in the twentieth and twenty-first

---

6 Such readings are not always in service of social equality. For a discussion of white, southern, postbellum Christian apologetics that leveraged this story to see a common language as "miscegenation" and to provide an argument against a strong, federal government, see Noll, *America's Book*, 484. In this interpretation, the story justifies national, and also racial (defined as phenotype), distinctions through supposedly biblical groundings of polygenesis.

7 See, however, an alternate use of the Tower of Babel in the Toronto sculpture titled "Mirrors of Babel," in which the sculptor (eL Seed) reproduced a poem by an Indigenous, Mohawk artist (E. Pauline Johnson, Tekahionwake) in Arabic calligraphy using a metalwork tower-shaped structure. The effect is to evoke the story in Genesis 11:1–9 as a celebration of multilingualism and diversity.

centuries.[8] More recently, it has been used to create a sense of panic, particularly in debates pertaining to immigration reform. A new, historically and literarily sensitive reading can delegitimize the use of the Tower of Babel in these debates regarding language policy and immigration, though there are other passages that might serve these purposes (unfortunately, there are). Understanding this passage as accurately as possible, therefore, is important, and provides a testing ground where scholarship and real-world issues merge. If the thesis that Genesis 11:1–9 is not actually about the origins of multiple languages in history is correct, then this narrative cannot be used as biblical grounding for seeing multilingualism as a sign of divine curse, even if other passages, such as Nehemiah 13:23–25, still can. Such arguments should be constructed with the tools of biblical scholarship, such as the study of language and history. Even more, though, a new reading of this passage could also make a practical contribution to how the Bible, politics, and culture relate to one another.

---

8 Note how the diversity resulting from divine action in Genesis 11:1–9 has also been seen as a positive development in ancient interpretation as well as in some aspects of modern political debate. See more in chapters 5 and 6 of this book.

A New Translation of Genesis 11:1–9

All the world was unified (or, had the same plan) and had the same custom. As they migrated from the east, they found a plain in the land of Shinar and they dwelt there. They said to one another, "Come, let us make bricks, and let us burn them thoroughly." They had brick for stone, and bitumen for mortar. They said, "Come, let us build for ourselves a city and a tower with its top in the heavens, and let us make a name for ourselves lest we be dispersed over the face of all the earth." Yahweh came down to see the city, as well as the tower that the children of humankind had built. Yahweh said, "Look, they are one people and have the same plan! This is the beginning of what they will do. And now, nothing they propose to do will be withheld from them! Come, let us go down that we might confuse there their plan, that no one will heed the plan of his companion." So Yahweh dispersed them from there over all the face of the earth, and they stopped building the city. Therefore, its name was called Babel, because there Yahweh confused the plan of all the earth, and from there Yahweh dispersed them over the face of all the earth.[1]

---

1 For a discussion and defense of this translation, see chapter 3 of this book.

CHAPTER 1

The Political in Babel

THE IMPORTANCE OF BABEL:
Reading Strategies, Politics, and the Cultivation of Identity

Examining the Tower of Babel narrative involves exploring many facets of human inquiry into who we are and why we are the way we are. So enduring and striking are the classic scenes and images of this short passage in literature and art that few people bother to ask if we really understand these verses. As a result, many of the interpretations that arise from reading Genesis 11:1–9 tend to conform to pervasive perceptions of this iconic text from the Hebrew Bible. These perceptions, because of the way that biblical stories have shaped much of human history and consciousness, blur the distinction between an ancient "them" and a modern "us."[1] The meaning of the Tower of Babel exists as a symbol, whether the interpreter believes the story to be historical or not, and guides sensibilities in the present. For both ancient interpreters like the community responsible for the Dead Sea Scrolls and modern intellectuals (either religious or not), stories like the Tower of Babel reveal how humanity can go wrong and civilizations crumble under the weight of the just deserts of hubris. For example, Saul Bellow, the famed twentieth-century writer, is reported as having stated that America's goal as far as diversity, culture, and language are concerned should adhere to a fine line: "a melting pot, yes. A

---

1   For an insightful examination on the "us" of modernity and "them" of antiquity, see Seth L. Sanders, *The Invention of Hebrew*, Traditions (Urbana: University of Illinois Press, 2009), 14–17.

tower of Babel, no."[2] Interpreters in the medieval and modern West generally and America specifically have drawn on the Tower of Babel episode in Genesis 11:1–9 as a passage on which (or into which) to project their own identities. Leaders often fear that the communities they oversee could become Babel, and Genesis 11:1–9 functions as a warning text through which negative associations with pride, judgment, and the dangers of diversity find a public hearing. The story, or at least some version of it, is widely known, and invoking the Tower of Babel caters to a host of political and religious anxieties.

If we have fundamentally misunderstood this story, if the Tower of Babel is not a story about languages at all, then a reanalysis of the passage could provide a means through which biblical texts and self-perception are re-evaluated as well. The result, at least in this example of a biblical story and its modern applications, is that multilingualism and multiculturalism are not a result of divine disfavor, at least not due to the narrative in Genesis 11:1–9.[3] Comparison with ancient Near Eastern texts and imperial rhetoric from the Neo-Assyrian and Neo-Babylonian empires, involving examinations of texts written in Akkadian (and, to a lesser degree, Sumerian and Aramaic), reveals different concerns that lie behind the passage than those traditionally attributed to it. This approach opens up historical backgrounds that offer a better way to interpret the story. Additionally, a closer look at the words of the narrative and the history of the biblical text of the Primeval History, or Genesis 1–11, demonstrate that Genesis 11:1–9 is not about languages. Even more, a new understanding of the Tower of Babel not only makes sense of the story itself but also of many of the puzzles contained in the call of Abram in Genesis 12, as well as key points of the plot of parts of Genesis beyond the Primeval History.

---

2   See the quote and the analysis of language policy in America in Jeehyum Lim, *Bilingual Brokers: Race, Literature, and Language as Human Capital* (New York: Fordham University Press, 2017), 77.

3   The events recorded in the books of Ezra and Nehemiah, in which Judeans are commanded to get rid of their foreign wives and any children that result from such mixed unions, do not have the popular currency of Genesis 11:1–9 in this regard, but perhaps speak more starkly, and darkly, about multilingualism and diversity. See especially Nehemiah 13:23–25. The historical situation of fifth century BCE Judaism was much more complex than this biblical passage would indicate, particularly by comparison with the Jewish garrison at Elephantine. For an accessible juxtaposition of these two sources in Judaism and how they compete with respect to multilingualism and multiculturalism, see Simon Schama, *The Story of the Jews: Finding the Words, 1000 BC–1492 AD* (New York: Ecco, 2014), 35–36.

In other words, the Tower of Babel is an important story in the Bible. Interpreting it better and more rigorously unlocks many aspects of other foundational biblical narratives. The argument that, with a few exceptions, interpretations of this story have been incorrect for hundreds if not thousands of years necessarily involves examinations of languages and literatures, as well as critical frameworks for studying the Bible, that may not be immediately familiar to all readers. Nonetheless, the payoff for reexamining Genesis 11:1–9 is a practical one. This practical payoff exists in the ways in which the Tower of Babel, understood as a story about imperial hubris, divine judgment, and the resulting diversity, has shaped religious and political identities. Perhaps even more than identity, the traditional understanding of this story has had a dramatic impact on political policy, particularly in America. The reading of Genesis 11:1–9 involving divine judgment and multilingualism is not only the result of misunderstanding certain idioms in the biblical text but also a result of reading Genesis 10–11 as a whole, the latter chapter in some sense representing a case-in-point of the earlier chapter in a synchronic, canonical reading. This reading falls apart when the distinct plotlines, apparent at the very start of the Bible, are explored (and even in light of a synchronic reading of the passage).

Indeed, the episode of the Tower of Babel has always been an object of reflection, combining politics and biblical interpretation, even when the tower was thought to reside outside of Babylon. For centuries Jewish traditions and local populations connected the story in Genesis 11:1–9 to Birs Nimrud, a site eleven miles south of Babylon and called Borsippa in ancient Akkadian texts, and to its ziggurat, called Ezida in ancient sources.[4] The association between Babylon and Nimrud was well established in Babylonian politics and religion, as Borsippa was considered a smaller sibling city to Babylon. In the latter, Marduk, the high god of Babylonian religion, dwelled, whereas Nabu, the son of Marduk, dwelt in the former. The association was so close, however, that evidence exists that Nabu at times was even considered to be the supreme god of Babylon along with Marduk.[5]

---

4   For a twentieth-century scholar who also argued for this connection, see J. P. Peters, "Tower of Babel at Borsippa," *JAOS* 41 (1921): 157–159. For more, see Day, "The Tower and City of Babel Story (Genesis 11.1–9): Problems of Interpretation and Background," in *From Creation to Babel: Studies in Genesis 1–11*, LHBOTS 592 (New York: Bloomsbury, 2013), 172.

5   Tammy Schneider, *An Introduction to Ancient Mesopotamian Religion* (Grand Rapids, MI: Eerdmans, 2011), 56–57.

For interpretive traditions, associating the Tower of Babel structure outside of Babylon proper also made sense given the relationship between Genesis 10 and the so-called "Table of Nations," on the one hand, and Genesis 11:1–9, on the other. The juxtaposition of these two chapters together has created a variety of reading strategies that have influenced the interpretation of the Tower of Babel narrative, reading strategies that change the meaning of the text when portions of Genesis 10 (as well as parts of Genesis 11) are identified as sources distinct from Genesis 11:1–9. In the final version of the Bible (or, the form that we read), and in a reading that assumes that both Genesis 10 and 11 function as a unified story, clues exist that have allowed Jewish traditions and some modern scholars to identify Birs Nimrud as the location for the Tower of Babel. This interpretation prevailed, even if a surface reading of Genesis 11:1–9 indicates that the city eleven miles north is the more obvious candidate. For example, Genesis 10:8–12 is as follows:

"Cush begat Nimrod. He was the first to become a mighty man on earth. He was a mighty hunter before the LORD. Therefore it is said 'Like Nimrod, a mighty hunter before the LORD.' The beginning of his kingdom was Babel, Erech, Accad, and Calneh, in the land of Shinar. From that land he went into Ashur, and he built Nineveh, Rehoboth-Ir, Calah, and Resen between Nineveh and between Calah. That is the great city."[6]

Nimrod would become the archetypal evil king of Mesopotamia in both Jewish and Islamic interpretive history, attempting to kill Abram for his monotheistic vision.[7] In Genesis 10:8–12 his connection with the evils of Mesopotamia and the building of cities created a natural connection to Genesis 11:1–9. These particular passages (Genesis 10:8–12 and Genesis 11:1–9) derive from the same literary strand, or source, one of four that were woven together to form the Pentateuch.[8] From Nimrod came Babel and Ashur, two cities that were the capitals of empires that would later conquer Judah and Israel. The association with Babel and Shinar in Genesis 10:10 would also link

---

6 For more on this passage and the history of the character Nimrod, see K. van der Toorn and P. W. van der Horst, "Nimrod Before and After the Bible," *HTR* 83 (1990): 1–29.

7 For more, see chapter 5 of this book and the bibliography cited therein.

8 The verses in Genesis 10 that include a notice regarding language, לשׁון, however, are not from the same literary strand as Genesis 10:8–12 and Genesis 11:1–9, an issue explored in more depth in chapters 3 and 4.

the most famous episode of hubris from southern Mesopotamia, the Tower of Babel, with the site that bore a name reminiscent of Nimrod, namely Birs Nimrud.[9]

This link between Nimrod, Genesis 10:10, and Genesis 11:1–9 appears even in translation. Both passages use the Hebrew word *bābel* for Babylon, a common name for this southern Mesopotamian city and capital that occurs more than two hundred times in the Hebrew Bible. Yet in English translations of the Bible (except the New International Version), only in Genesis 10:10 and Genesis 11:1–9 is the lexeme effectively transliterated as a translation, "Babel." Every other occurrence of *bābel* is translated as "Babylon." This pattern appears in English at least as far back as the Wycliffe Bible (fourteenth century CE) and happens in many other languages.[10]

As additional evidence for dislocating the tower and placing it in Borsippa, the ruins of the ziggurat in Birs Nimrud were larger than those in Babylon, providing further reason for locating such a monumental story eleven miles south of Babylon.[11] While the comparative size of the ruins of the temple complexes in Babylon relative to those in Birs Nimrud were the product of conquest and deterioration from natural processes, these factors were unknown to the local population and Jewish interpretative traditions connecting Birs Nimrud to the location of Genesis 11:1–9. It makes sense that such a larger-than-life figure as Nimrod (at times suggested to be a giant) would have been responsible for the bigger structure. This example displays the ways in

---

9   On the connection between the Tower of Babel and Birs Nimrud, see Day, "The Tower and City of Babel Story (Genesis 11.1–9)," 166.

10   Except for those "for which Babel is the regular term for Babylon anyway." Day, "The Tower and City of Babel Story (Genesis 11.1–9)," 166.

11   For the shift to Birs Nimrud as the focus of research for those attempting to "confirm the biblical tradition of the Tower of Babel and the accounts of Herodotus and other classical authors" in light of "better-preserved remains" at Birs Nimrud, see Andrew George, "The Tower of Babel: Archaeology, History and Cuneiform Texts," *AfO* 51 (2005/2006): 92. See Brian Doak for a discussion of Nimrod as the first גִּבּוֹר in interpretive history, as well as the connection in the *Genesis Rabbah* between Genesis 6:1–4, Genesis 10:8, and Genesis 11:6 via a secondary meaning of חלל as not "to begin" but "to desecrate" in each verse (*The Last of the Rephaim: Conquest and Cataclysm in the Heroic Ages of Ancient Israel*, Ilex 7 [Boston: Ilex Foundation, 2012], 58, 67–70). Since Nimrod was thought to be a giant, it made sense that the ruins of his tower should be the largest observable structures, providing further reason to locate the Tower of Babel at Birs Nimrud. For the Jewish and Christian interpretations of Nimrod as a giant, see Haynes, *Noah's Curse: The Biblical Justification of American Slavery* (New York: Oxford University Press, 2002), 46.

which text, interpretation, place, and politics merge. The convergence of text, place, and identity allows for the story of the Tower of Babel to be dislodged from Babylon and applied to communities through interpretation, even to modern-day America.[12]

REVERSING THE CURSE OF BABEL:
The Rise of Biblical Criticism, Athanasius Kircher, and the Problem of Many Languages

The same reading strategy that identifies narrative continuity between Genesis 10 and 11 as a whole, in which each chapter in its entirety is understood as part of a unified composition, forms the means through which to interpret these passages as an origin story regarding the spread of languages. Perhaps more than any other thinker in the intellectual history of analysis of Genesis 11:1–9, Athanasius Kircher (1602–1680 CE) provided a systematic and rigorous framework to interpret Genesis 10 and 11, on the one hand, and to examine facets of multilingualism, politics, and historicity of the text, on the other. A discussion of his study of the Tower of Babel highlights issues that will be important for exploring the legacy of this narrative well into modernity.

In a variety of realms of research, Kircher proved himself to be a genius, even if at times in unorthodox ways and by the law of unintended consequences.[13] Shortly before his death in 1680, Kircher published his second major work

---

12   The mobility of Babel in association with political concerns contemporaneous to interpreters of Genesis 11:1–9 has ancient pedigree. For example, in the *Caves of Treasure*, a likely sixth-century CE text in its final form, Nimrod not only builds Babel but also Ctesiphon, the capital of the Sassanian Empire until the seventh century CE. See Alexander Toepel, "The Cave of Treasures," in *Old Testament Pseudepigrapha: More Noncanonical Scriptures, Volume 1*, ed. Richard Bauckham, James R. Davila, and Alexander Panayotov (Grand Rapids, MI: Eerdmans, 2013), 561.

13   His unorthodox creativity appears in his description of the *Katzenklavier*, a musical instrument that consisted of cats arranged in stalls according to the pitch of their meow. A string connected their tail to a key on the keyboard. When the keys were depressed, it would prod the cat to meow, allowing for the musician to construct melodies based on these noises. This instrument may have been purely hypothetical, used as an imaginary foil to describe the extravagances and cruelties of the upper class. Prints of this type of instrument preceded Kircher, however, in Johann Theodor de Bry's 1596 book *Emblemata Saecularia Mira et Lucunda*.
       An example of the unintended consequences in his research appears in Kircher's study of the deluge recorded in Genesis 6–9, one of his two major works on the

on the Bible, *Turris Babel*, which focused on the narrative in Genesis 11:1–9. This work, likely begun already as early as 1670 but not brought to completion until nine years later, applied the same systematic and scientific analysis he used in an earlier examination of Noah's ark to the episode of the Tower of Babel.[14] He searched for clues in the canonical text, like many interpreters before him, to allow him to reconstruct the historical context for the episode in Genesis 11:1–9.[15] The mention of Nimrod as king of Babel in Genesis 10:8,

---

Bible. The rigor and depth of analysis he displayed regarding the biblical account of the flood in his *Arca Noae* in 1675 CE reflected a new intellectual movement in the wake of the Counter-Reformation in which Jesuit readings of the biblical text, in an attempt to keep pace with advances in scientific thought, turned to increasingly literalistic interpretations. See Ingrid D. Rowland, *The Ecstatic Journey: Athanasius Kircher in Baroque Rome* (Chicago: University of Chicago Press, 2000). Indeed, Kircher's Arca Noae was part of a larger project that included his examination of the Tower of Babel, published in 1679. Both the *Arca Noae* and *Turris Babel* formed the basis for a comprehensive view of ancient human history as it related to contemporary scientific realities. In *Arca Noae*, Kircher provided an apologetic for the biblical account of the flood. In doing so, he attempted to explain the historical feasibility of the deluge as described in the Bible, focusing specifically on the capacity for the ark to hold all of the land animals that would have existed during Noah's time.

He also theorized the manner in which the number of species that lived in Noah's day, all surviving the flood, then cross-bred, migrated, and adapted to new environments, resulting in the diversity of species known in Kircher's time. For example, Noah would not have needed to bring a giraffe onboard the ark, as they did not yet exist. Instead, after the flood a camel and a leopard mated, producing an animal with spots (from the leopard) and an elongated neck (from the camel) that grew longer through adaptation to stretch for food. Similarly, deer would become reindeer through migration and adaptation to colder climates after the flood. In this manner, and as an unintended consequence, Kircher offered an explanation of adaptation and speciation that preceded Jean-Baptiste Lamarck and Charles Darwin by over one hundred and eighty years, though Kircher's version of the theory was the result of a defense of the literal reading of the Hebrew Bible. Olaf Breidbach and Michael T. Ghiselin, "Athanasius Kircher (1602–1680) on Noah's Ark: Baroque 'Intelligent Design' Theory," *Proceedings of the California Academy of Sciences* 57 (2006): 991–1002. See also Irving Finkel's discussion of Kircher, *The Ark before Noah: Decoding the Story of the Flood* (London: Hodder & Stoughton, 2014), 203–205.

14 Joscelyn Godwin, *Athanasius Kircher: A Renaissance Man and the Quest for Lost Knowledge* (London: Thames & Hudson, 1979), 34. Much of book 1 of *Turris Babel* concerns the history between Noah's ark and the Tower of Babel narrative, particularly regarding the spread of humanity from the regions of Ararat to Shinar.

15 For the history of interpretation connecting Nimrod to the building of the Tower of Babel, see James Kugel, *Traditions of the Bible: A Guide to the Bible as It Was at the Start of the Common Era* (Cambridge, MA; Harvard University Press, 1998), 229–232.

located in the land of Shinar (as in the geographical description of Genesis 11:2), creates a natural association between Genesis 10 and the narrative of the Tower of Babel in Genesis 11:1–9.[16] Reading the two chapters not simply as contiguous parts of biblical narrative but as chronologically overlapping invites the interpretation that Nimrod was the king of Babylon who orchestrated the construction of tower and city in Genesis 11:1–9, despite the fact that Nimrod is not mentioned at all in the latter passage. The conflation of Genesis 10 through 11 as part of the same chronology is also made possible in a canonical reading by the genealogy in Genesis 11:10, which mentions Shem, who fathered Arpachshad two years after the flood.[17] This verse envelops both Genesis 10 and the Tower of Babel around notices of the deluge, which ended in Genesis 9.

With the king of Babel established as Nimrod, the archetypal enemy of Abraham in reception history, Kircher was able to examine more fully the nature of the ruler's folly.[18] Nimrod wanted to invade the heavens. In order to arrive at the first tier of the celestial realm, Kircher claimed that Nimrod needed to build a tower to reach the moon. The problem was that, according to Kircher, in order to build a tower stretching toward a lunar destination, Nimrod would need so much material aligned in one spot on earth that it would actually move the earth itself, meaning that the project was impossible and doomed to fail.[19] Kircher made such futility remarkably tangible with calculations as well as an illustration displaying the failed experiment of the

---

16 See Kircher, *Turris Babel*, chapter 2 of book 2: *ex hisce verbis colligimus, unum alterum ad grande quoddam moliminis specimen monstrandum follicitasse, quod sine capite praestare non poterant, utique ipso Nembrod, qui astutia fua, et simul à natura sibi insita facundia, non dicam instimulabat, fed et eos miris verborum illiciis veluti fascinabat; juxta illud Gen 10 vers 8, 10.* See also chapter 8 of book 1, in which Kircher uses the mention of Amraphel, a king of Shinar in Genesis 14:1, and biblical genealogies beginning in Genesis 4, to establish when Nimrod would have built the tower.

17 See the chronology of Noah, Japheth, Ham, and Shem in chapter 12 of book 2 of *Turris Babel*.

18 On the rabbinic connection between Nimrod in Genesis 10 and the building of the tower in Genesis 11, see Ronald Hendel, "Genesis 1–11 and Its Mesopotamian Problem," in *Cultural Borrowings and Ethnic Appropriations in Antiquity. Oriens et Occidens*, ed. Erich S. Gruen, Studien zu antiken Kulturkontakten und ihrem Nachleben 8 (Stuttgart: F. Steiner, 2005), 30.

19 Kircher calculated that the tower would need to be 178,682 miles high and would require three million tons of material. Joscelyn Godwin, *Athanasius Kircher*, 35.

Babylonian king, along with the languages that resulted from the disaster (all citing Genesis 11:4).[20]

The Tower of Babel narrative also brought to the fore the issue of the multiplicity of languages for Kircher.[21] Kircher's acumen with languages was on full display in a variety of his writings, as was his belief (which was common at that time) that Hebrew represented the original, perfect, Adamic language.[22] This belief, combined with the view that such Adamic language contained esoteric knowledge about the world, led Kircher to study with Kabbalists. He did so in order to unlock information that would allow him to understand the created realm better, particularly the manner in which Adam named things and how these names, transmitted in Hebrew, unlock something of the essence of each animal or object.[23]

Yet this perfect language was lost, aspects of its essence preserved only in Kabbalistic interpretations and in Egyptian hieroglyphs, an ancient writing system that Kircher believed was able to convey hidden knowledge through symbols in a much deeper and more profound manner than ordinary language

---

20 So Kircher in his *demonstratio* in chapter 3 of book 2: *De Turris ad Lunae Caelum exaltandae*, αδυναμια *sive impossibilitate*.

21 See especially book 3 of *Turris Babel*, titled *Prodromus in Atlantem Polyglossum, quo per praelusiones quasdam de varietate linguarum & idiomatum disparatissima genera, quae unà cum idololatria in orbem terrarum occasione primaevae confusionis irrepserunt, potissiumum agitur*. The connection between multilingualism and polytheism is apparent in the title, revealing, as discussed below, the negative association with multiple languages.

22 See Kircher: *Prima igitur omnium lingua est Hebraïca; quae lingua sancta dicitur, quia hac DEUS mundi opifex primus omnium Adamum & Evam appropriatis nominibus allocutus est, cui eadem Protoplastus & Eva, DEO interroganti de lapsu respondere. Haec est prima lingua, qua primi patriarchae ab Adamo ad Noëmum, continua successione usi funt, uti ex nominibus, Adam, Eva, Caïn, Seth, Enos, Caïnan, Melalael, Jared, Enoch, Methusalem, Lamech, Noë, quae omnia purè Hebraïca nomina sunt, patet.* Joscelyn Godwin, *Athanasius Kircher's Theatre of the World: The Life and Work of the Last Man to Search for Universal Knowledge* (Rochester, VT: Inner Traditions, 2009), 21; Umberto Eco, *The Search for the Perfect Language*, Making of Europe (Cambridge, MA: Blackwell, 1994), 84. See also the discussion of Franciscus van Helmont (d. 1699) in Eco: "not only did the Hebrew sounds reflect the inherent nature of things themselves, but the very mud from which the human vocal organs were formed had been especially sculpted to emit a perfect language that God pressed on Adam in not only its spoken but evidently in its written form as well" (*The Search for the Perfect Language*, 83). See Eco for one of van Helmont's woodcut images in which he correlates parts of the human mouth with the Hebrew alphabet (*The Search for the Perfect Language*, 84).

23 Eco, *The Search for the Perfect Language*, 84–85.

and script.[24] As such, he exerted his intellect on the task of deciphering hieroglyphs. Despite his failure to do so, Kircher has been remembered not only as the author of three impressively erudite, if incorrect, volumes on Egyptology titled *Oedipus Aegyptiacus*; additionally, he was the first in modern times to argue that Coptic was related to ancient Egyptian.[25] There is no indication that Kircher wanted to resurrect these ancient languages as an antidote to the curse of Babel. In fact, his own language in the sense of his own prose was less of interest to him in his writings than the illustrations published with his volumes.

Here lies a key for Kircher's understanding of Babel and the problem of multilingualism. Like many of his contemporaries, and like many subsequent thinkers, he believed that the situation resulting from Genesis 11:1–9 represented an abiding curse. For Kircher, such multilingualism also made humanity correspondingly susceptible toward the worship of multiple gods.[26]

---

24 See Findlen for a discussion regarding how Kircher viewed the ancient wisdom and knowledge of Hebrew and Egyptian as closely related: "According to Kircher, the true Kabbalah preserved the same Adamic wisdom that Hermes Trismegistus encoded in the hieroglyphs, while the 'Rabbinic superstitions' found in many kabbalistic treatises were closely related to Egyptian idolatry" *Athanasius Kircher: The Last Man Who Knew Everything* (New York: Routledge Press, 2004), 149.

25 Kircher's work in this regard made possible much of Champollion's decipherment of hieroglyphs in 1822. Champollion became fluent in Coptic. Kircher's hypothesis about Coptic and ancient Egyptian allowed Champollion to make connections phonologically in the decipherment of hieroglyphs (with the aid of Thomas Young's consideration that hieroglyphs could be phonetic as well as pictographic), connections that might not have been observed if the relationship between Coptic and Egyptian had not been made. For Kircher's grammar, the first of its kind in Europe, in 1636, see Andrew Robinson, *Cracking the Egyptian Code: The Revolutionary Life of Jean-François Champollion* (New York: Oxford University Press, 2012), 21. For Kircher's Coptic grammar and its influence on Champollion, see Robinson, *Cracking the Egyptian Code*, 54. Though Robinson claims that Kircher connected Coptic only to the ancient Egyptian Christian language (and not to hieroglyphs), Finkel states that Kircher recognized Coptic as the last part of the Egyptian language that was also encoded in hieroglyphs (*Ark before Noah*, 205). Finkel's estimation is more accurate. See Kircher's title for chapter 8 of book 3 in *Turris Babel: De lingua Aegyptiaca, seu Copta, quam & veterem Pharaonicam appellamus*.

26 "The latter part of *Turris Babel* is entirely linguistic, and of interest mainly to specialists in the history of language. Among the digressions is an important one on polytheism, which is blamed almost entirely on the division of tongues. Kircher argues that the classical deities are basically only different aspects of the Sun and the Moon" (Godwin, *Athanasius Kircher*, 35). See also the connection between multilingualism and heterodoxy in many Christian thinkers in Late Antiquity (Tim Denecker, *Ideas*

As, for example, the words for sun and moon multiplied with the division of languages, so also these terms and the various aspects of these celestial bodies came to represent many gods.

In order to reverse the curse, many intellectuals in the seventeenth century proposed to resurrect Hebrew as a spoken language.[27] For Kircher, however, it was as though the illustrations in his book served to transform the mess of linguistic diversity.[28] Indeed, one of the motivating theories for Kircher and his contemporaries for deciphering ancient Egyptian was the belief that hieroglyphs contained an elusive, ancient mystery. It was thought that they communicated ideas, not sounds, part of a recurring theme in interpretation that "truth can only be expressed in emblems or symbols."[29] According to a commonly held belief, criticized only decades before Kircher wrote his major works, these symbols were invented by Hermes Trismegistus shortly after the biblical flood, who used hieroglyphs to preserve the perfect wisdom of Adam.[30] Understanding the ancient symbols of Egypt, therefore, would get Kircher closer to understanding what was lost in the aftermath of Babel; however, the hieroglyphs were themselves expressions of the deeper value of emblems and illustrations. Kircher's illustrations in *Turris Babel*, then, functioned as an initial stepping-stone for overcoming the confusion of multilingualism

---

on *Language in Early Latin Christianity*, Supplements to Vigiliae Christianaes 142 [Boston: Brill, 2017], 136–138).

27 The idea to resurrect Hebrew was no less a possibility a century later in post-revolutionary America. English was not an obvious candidate to be the spoken medium for the new country, which had just rebelled against the nation that invented it. In the 1780s, a visitor from France said that "the Americans have carried [their anti-British aversion] so far, as seriously to propose introducing a new language; and some persons were desirous, for the convenience of the public, that the *Hebrew* should be substituted for the English. The proposal was, that it should be taught in schools, and made use of in all published acts" (Marc Shell, "Babel in America: Or, the Politics of Language Diversity in the United States," *Critical Inquiry* 20 [1993]: 108).

28 Eco, *The Search for the Perfect Language*, 165.

29 Eco, *The Search for the Perfect Language*, 15. The recognition of Thomas Young and Jean François Champollion that hieroglyphs convey ideas as well as sounds would be key, over a century after Kircher, to the decipherment of ancient Egyptian.

30 Daniel Stolzenberg, "Four Trees, Some Amulets, and the Seventy-two Names of God: Kircher Reveals the Kabbalah," in *Athanasius Kircher: The Last Man Who Knew Everything*, ed. Paula Findlen (New York: Routledge, 2004), 149–151; Noel Malcolm, "Private and Public Knowledge: Kircher, Esotericism, and the Republic of Letters," in *Athanasius Kircher: The Last Man Who Knew Everything*, ed. Paula Findlen (New York: Routledge, 2004), 303–304.

through the medium of pictures and symbols, capable of conveying deep truths across languages.[31]

Thus, for all his attempts to learn Hebrew and decipher the hieroglyphic code, thereby educating himself on pre-Babel wisdom and language, Kircher made no attempt to argue that these languages should be resurrected as an antidote to the curse of the Tower of Babel. His illustrations served this role to relieve the effects of Genesis 11:1–9. Even in these his concern was, in the manner of Galileo, to construct thought experiments, such as his attempt to display the folly of Nimrod, combining mathematical calculation, ancient historical thought, and illustrations to show how Nimrod might have actually attempted to reach the heavens, but would have never been able to do so.[32] Much of the second half of *Turris Babel*, particularly in the third book of this three-volume work, contains an exposition of how all the languages of the world derived from Hebrew. Kircher's illustration of the futility of Nimrod's enterprise contained a quote from Genesis 11:4 (prior to the confusion of tongues) in a sampling of the languages that resulted from the post-Babel situation: Hebrew still enjoyed the position of being employed by the elect, but it existed alongside Latin, Greek, Syriac, Arabic, and Samaritan. With the addition of Ethiopic (which is not displayed in the illustration), from these languages all other languages of the world were thought to originate. The closer Kircher gets to his contemporaneous situation, the more realistic his analysis becomes.[33] In this manner, even if Kircher's reconstruction of the events of Genesis 11:1–9 strikes a modern reader as fantastical, he attempted to provide a realistic scenario (with calculations) in interpreting the Tower

---

31   This theory stands in contrast to the work of other Jesuit priests at the time. Indeed, some scholars have argued that Kircher viewed the solution to overcoming the confusion of Babel as the spread of Latin with Jesuit missions. Instead, the prominence of images and symbols, revealing the belief in the hermetic value of signs such as hieroglyphs, means that the illustrations, central in many of Kircher's works, may have been his method to overcome the curse of Babel.

32   For such thought experiments, see Anthony Grafton, "Kircher's Chronology," in *Athanasius Kircher: The Last Man Who Knew Everything*, ed. Paula Findlen (New York: Routledge, 2004), 174. On Kircher as Galileo's heir, see Chunglin Kwa, *Styles of Knowing: A New History of Science from Ancient Times to the Present*, trans. David McKay (Pittsburgh: University of Pittsburgh Press, 2011), 71. See also Paula Findlen, "The Janus Faces of Science in the Seventeenth Century: Athanasius Kircher and Isaac Newton," in *Rethinking the Scientific Revolution*, ed. M. J. Osler (New York: Cambridge University Press, 2000), 221–246.

33   Eco, *The Search for the Perfect Language*, 85.

of Babel episode in order to explain the development of languages leading up to his own day. While such realism projected onto the biblical narrative led to fanciful speculation, this analytic thought applied to events and observations closer to his own day became the basis for perceptive theories on the development of languages.[34]

For Kircher, as for contemporaneous thinkers, this development of multilingualism had a strongly political dimension. He claimed that such polyglossia occured as languages continued to diversify after Babel with the rise and fall of empires, a process that even explained contemporary events in the seventeenth century CE. Politics and empire were central in Kircher's view, as cultural and linguistic pressure in light of colonization, war, migrations, and climate all contributed to the spread, mixing, and multiplication of languages.[35] Violence, sin, and the degrading of human life and civilization were catalysts for, and copartners with, the multiplication of languages. Correspondingly, as already indicated, this multiplication of languages, according to Kircher, also resulted in the spread of idolatry. In other words, multilingualism is a patently negative thing, and the linguistic diversity also led to religious syncretism.[36] Indeed, even the hermetic hieroglyphs, contained in the system of Hermes Trismegistus, were corrupted due to contact with other cultures.[37] Creolization, contact, and the creation of new languages moved humanity further and further from pure religion, particularly as the names of God and the gods multiplied, increasing idolatrous worship.

This presentation of the sustained thought that Kircher gave to the story in Genesis 11:1–9 highlights three facets to the interpretation of this biblical text that would become central to its enduring significance. His attention to the details of the Tower of Babel foregrounds the aspects of the story that beg to be explained in light of their historical background, especially in light of Mesopotamian sources. Additionally, his focus on Nimrod as the ruler behind the construction of the tower demonstrates the ways in which Genesis 10–11 have been read together, and how the details in Genesis 10 invite the reader to understand Genesis 11 as part of the same chronology. Finally, Kircher's perception of the connection between multilingualism, violence, and idolatry underscores the manner in which polyglossia was viewed as a curse. Such an

---

34   For more on the intellectual legacy of Kircher, see http://kircher.stanford.edu/.
35   Eco, *The Search for the Perfect Language*, 85.
36   Eco, *The Search for the Perfect Language*, 85.
37   Noel Malcolm, "Private and Public Knowledge," 305.

estimation is present even in modern discussions of this passage: the curse of the Babel story, as evidenced in multilingualism and diversity (however defined), is something to be overcome (if necessary, even by political measures).

Kircher's extensive analysis of the biblical text also reveals the extent to which, already in the seventeenth century, elaborate explanatory edifices could be built to protect the Bible from rising biblical criticism, an approach that puts these three facets in a different perspective. *Turris Babel* was part of a larger project of showing how the details of the Bible could be explored and examined from their ancient pasts to Kircher's present, from biblical histories to the seventeenth-century world. Kircher existed in a century in which profound questions and debates arose regarding the authority of texts like the Bible as well as the authority of texts used to trace the transmission and accuracy of biblical stories over time.[38] In 1822, around 142 years after Kircher's death, Egyptian hieroglyphs were deciphered with the help of the Rosetta Stone, an aid not available in Kircher's own time. As a testament to the genius of Kircher, Champollion consulted his works in the decipherment process, though Champollion rightly rejected many of Kircher's fanciful theories about Egypt.[39] In 1857 the British Royal Academy announced the decipherment of Akkadian, a Semitic language written in cuneiform (or wedge-shaped) script.[40] The language of Babylon could be read, heard, and understood, and the kings of Babel were finally able to speak for themselves

---

38   As Nellen and Steenbakkers argue:

> Attempts to chart the complex transmission process of biblical as well as patristic texts were often thwarted and even diverted in the wrong direction if research was based on spurious sources. It took a long time before the status of the Sibylline oracles, the Orphic hymns and Hermes Trismegistus, supposed author of the famous *Corpus Hermeticum*, went down from genuine relics of the past to forgeries that created an illusion of Christianity before Christ. As late as 1650, Athanasius Kircher simply ignored Isaac Casaubon's demolishment of the authenticity of the *Corpus Hermeticum* of 1614, but nevertheless the English philosopher Ralph Cudworth, who mocked Kircher for that, continued to accept most of the *Corpus* as late as 1678.

Henk Nellen and Piet Steenbakkers, "Biblical Philology in the Long Seventeenth Century," in *Scriptural Authority & Biblical Criticism in the Dutch Golden Age: God's Word Questioned*, ed. Dirk van Miert et al. (New York: Oxford University Press, 2017), 22.

39   See Daniel Stolzenberg, *Egyptian Oedipus: Athanasius Kircher and the Secrets of Antiquity* (Chicago: University of Chicago Press, 2013), 226–53.

40   Among many excellent overviews of this intellectual achievement, see Mogens Trolle Larsen, *The Conquest of Assyria: Excavations in an Antique Land, 1840–1860*

by the nineteenth century CE, a century that also witnessed some of the most significant advances in the critical study of the biblical text. Biblical studies in the present day exist only a hundred and sixty years after the world of Assyria, Babylon, and Persia could offer a firsthand account of the culture and history presented secondhand in classical sources and the Hebrew Bible. Along with modern archaeology, the background of Genesis 11:1–9 became more and more transparent, and the confusion of Genesis 11:7 and 11:9 gave way to increasing understanding.

Yet the three issues of interpreting the Tower of Babel story in Genesis 11:1–9 enumerated above in the discussion of Kircher's work remain. Despite the advances in understanding the literary and historical circumstances in which the Bible was produced and edited, and despite the revolutions that such research has caused in the understanding of a variety of passages, in both scholarly publications and in the popular imagination, the Tower of Babel continues to be read as a story about language and the etiology of multilingualism. Yet a more robust comparative analysis in light of Neo-Assyrian sources yields a different result.[41] In fact, such a robust comparison with Neo-Assyrian imperial rhetoric arrives at a different meaning of Genesis 11:1–9 than the standard interpretation of the Tower of Babel narrative.[42] If a comparative study between Neo-Assyrian evidence and the Tower of Babel yields a different interpretation than the traditional one for Genesis 11:1–9, then it should be the case that a study of the words and literary context of the narrative will reach the same conclusion. Close attention to details of plot, or put otherwise, a source-critical study of Genesis 10 and Genesis 11, supports the conclusion that the multiplication of languages in the Table of Nations in Genesis 10 and the divine judgment of the Tower of Babel are from distinct sources. This observation further supports the thesis that, at least in Genesis

---

(New York: Routledge, 1996); Kevin J. Cathcart, "The Earliest Contributions to the Decipherment of Sumerian and Akkadian," *CDLJ* (2011): 1–12.

41   Naturally, it is not the case that such comparative analyses have not been written; rather, I argue that aspects of Neo-Assyrian rhetoric have not been as robustly in-corporated into a comparative reading of Genesis 11:1–9 as could be. See especially Uehlinger's examination of the passage in relation to Sargon II's Dūr-Šarrukīn cylin-der inscription, discussed more in chapter 2.

42   In this manner, the conclusions of Christoph Uehlinger are consistent broadly with those reached in this book; however, I disagree with key elements of Uehlinger and bring different evidence and analysis to a comparative analysis with Genesis 11:1–9 than he did in his volume.

11:1–9, multilingualism does not arise from divine disfavor since the chapter is not about multilingualism at all.

These three approaches—a comparative study of Neo-Assyrian sources, a philological assessment of the idioms in Genesis 11:1–9, and a source-critical analysis of the Primeval History for the purposes of understanding the role and function of the Tower of Babel episode—form the methodological basis for reconceiving the Tower of Babel. Using these methods provides a new understanding of Genesis 11:1–9. Moreover, this new perspective on the Tower of Babel influences the interpretation of the subsequent narrative, the call of Abram. This call has often been seen as the solution to the curse of Babel, though the puzzling feature of how to relate language to the call of Abram proved to be difficult in the history of interpretation of the Bible. It, at times, became an unresolved aspect of the biblical narrative, one about which modern thinkers have obsessed. As a result, the third issue mentioned above in the century after Kircher, namely how this curse was understood in political policy and highlighted cultural fears, deserves more consideration, particularly given American political rhetoric beginning in the eighteenth century CE. The history of this discourse highlights why the interpretation and the use of the Bible in the public sphere matters and how a new interpretation of Genesis 11:1–9 can be a corrective measure against a prominent political metaphor.

THE TOWER OF BABEL AND POLITICAL AUTHORITY BETWEEN THE SEVENTEENTH AND EIGHTEENTH CENTURIES:
Spinoza and Vitringa

If the Tower of Babel narrative represented a curse for Kircher, that curse manifested itself strongly in the political sphere. The violence evident in human history, such as warring nation-states, exists as a symptom of a disease that infected humanity beginning not only in the fall of Genesis 3 but, for Kircher, also in the Tower of Babel narrative. Diagnosing this disease with biblical history in view meant that Kircher ascribed to the commonly held view of Hebrew as the original, perfect language of paradise that was corrupted and exposed to linguistic competition with the advent of multilingualism in Genesis 11:1–9. Yet language, the biblical narratives, and politics were intertwined in different, though informative, ways in the thought of

Kircher's contemporary Baruch Spinoza, as well as the Dutch theologian Campegius Vitringa.

Spinoza's program in his foundational work *Theological-Political Treatise* was not merely a critical look at the Bible for the sake of a contemporaneous, modern political issue (namely, the use of the Bible to justify tyrannical forms of government), despite misconceptions along these lines. Rather, Spinoza sought to divorce any abiding political power inherent in the biblical text at all.[43] The political voice and power of the Bible, according to Spinoza, belonged to the past. Like any other ancient document, understanding the power of the Bible for social organization and governance was a matter of historical context. Any claim for enduring relevance could not be treated as a given but was rather a matter of historical investigation, and in such investigation, real obstacles appear that prevent facile claims to political authority based on the Bible.

Almost twenty years before Spinoza published his *Theological-Political Treatise*, Hobbes made an argument in *Leviathan* that claims to political power based on the Bible were themselves founded on a problematic assumption regarding communication and the concept of revelation. Since the Bible is written in human language and script, no one could demonstrably prove that they have direct access to revelation; such claims cannot be verified beyond the historical realm and circumstances in which the Bible was produced. For Spinoza, the historical uncertainties regarding the grammar of Hebrew, among other factors (such as the ambiguity of Hebrew and the fact that it was originally written without vowels), in many cases prevented anyone from claiming they know for certain what the text means.[44] Spinoza's thesis, therefore, requires some amount of agnosticism about whether or not Hebrew could be considered a "perfect" language at any point in its history (no matter how corrupted it might have become over time). Like Hobbes, Spinoza made

---

43 Sanders, *The Invention of Hebrew*, 13–14, 18, 18–21. As Levinson argues, Spinoza still maintained a sense of authority grounded in the Bible, but simply an autonomous authority relative to theology, philosophy, and politics and one that modeled the tolerance of contradiction in parallel terms to how disagreement and toleration should function in democratic states (*"The Right Chorale": Studies in Biblical Law and Interpretation* [Winona Lake, IN: Eisenbrauns, 2011], 12–13).

44 Benedictus de Spinoza, *Theological-Political Treatise*, ed. Jonathan Israel, trans. Michael Silverthorne and Jonathan Israel, Cambridge Texts in the History of Philosophy (New York: Cambridge University Press, 2007), 106–109.

communication and the historical difficulties of knowing the Bible's meaning in certain passages a central part of his political argument.

As in Kircher, many thinkers in Spinoza's Dutch context not only affirmed the perfection of Hebrew as the paradisical language but they also subscribed to the belief that the structure and sounds of Hebrew corresponded to the natural world. The claim of the connection between Hebrew and the created order on the one hand and Hebrew as a perfect language and the language of revelation contained in the Bible on the other made the debate regarding the Adamic language political. Yet Spinoza's arguments cast doubt on the ability to understand revelation, since the historical nature of Hebrew meant that over time, many idioms, expressions, and grammatical forms in the Bible became obscure. Even more threatening, this chasm between understanding and revelation also undermined a claim to control the created realm, previously assured through the belief in the interconnectedness between the Adamic language and physical things in the world. (This belief was based on the interpretation of Genesis 2:19–20, in which Adam, presumably speaking Hebrew, names all living things, forging a link between language and the nature of living things in the physical realm.)

Spinoza was in stark contrast to Johannes Leusden, a Dutch philologist who not only maintained the view that Hebrew was a perfect, Adamic language but also articulated the importance of this belief in light of the significance of the Tower of Babel narrative.[45] Leusden provided arguments in order to prove the supernatural origins of Hebrew (such as its supposed difficulty to learn yet its apparent simplicity that also testifies to its primeval history).[46] The significance of Genesis 11:1–9 in this matter lay in two observations. According to Leusden, God instantly and miraculously diversified human language through an act with implications for both writing and speech: God mixed the roots of the letters (a nod to script) to prevent people from understanding one another (a nod to speech).[47] Additionally, Hebrew was, naturally, allowed to continue as a marred, though nonetheless elect, language. This allowance was due to Eber, who refused to participate in the building of the tower and whose name itself evoked the term for the perfect language, Hebrew.[48] Devotion to sacred

---

45   Jetze Touber, *Spinoza and Biblical Philology in the Dutch Republic, 1660–1710* (New York: Oxford University Press, 2018), 64–66.

46   Touber, *Spinoza and Biblical Philology in the Dutch Republic, 1660–1710*, 65.

47   Touber, *Spinoza and Biblical Philology in the Dutch Republic, 1660–1710*, 65.

48   Touber, *Spinoza and Biblical Philology in the Dutch Republic, 1660–1710*, 65.

and revelatory texts in Hebrew and ascription to the belief that Hebrew was an elect, perfect language, then, permitted a religious attachment to Eber and his language. To question that Hebrew was the original, perfect language not only severed the link between revelation, language, and the created order but also denied the manner in which it was thought to survive in the election of Eber. To question that the meaning of the Tower of Babel concerned the multiplication of languages and the concomitant survival of Hebrew was to undermine this scheme of judgment, election, and redemption.

Yet in 1683 Campegius Vitringa did just that in his *Sacrarum observationum liber primus*.[49] He argued that Genesis 11:1–9 was not a story explaining the instant dispersal and advent of multilingualism of humanity from a previously unilingual existence. His thesis proceeded from a number of lines of argumentation. He marshalled evidence of parallel idioms through the Hebrew Bible, building on the work of Jean Le Clerc. Le Clerc had already concluded that the obscure phrasing in Genesis 11:1, literally "one lip" (or, *safah akhat* in Hebrew, often incorrectly translated as "one language"), which occurred elsewhere in the Hebrew Bible only in Genesis 11:6, was nothing other than a synonym of idioms like "one voice" in the sense of unanimity (or, *b-qol akhad* in Hebrew).[50] Second, Vitringa arrived at this conclusion (and supported Le Clerc's assessments) based on his general knowledge regarding how languages change, evolve, develop, and diverge from one another.[51] In this manner, the claim that instantaneous multiplication of languages occurred in the destruction of the Tower of Babel, even with the assumption of divine intervention, defied everything Vitringa knew regarding how languages evolve. As part of a larger intellectual environment in which historical factors were important for explaining the development of culture, Vitringa claimed that multilingualism instead developed slowly over time and as different dispersed populations had different historical experiences.[52]

---

49   Touber, *Spinoza and Biblical Philology in the Dutch Republic, 1660–1710*, 214.
50   Samuel David Luzzatto, *The Book of Genesis: A Commentary*, trans. Daniel A. Klein (Northvale, NJ: Jason Aronson, 1998), 113.
51   John Sandys-Wunsch, "Early Old Testament Critics on the Continent," in *Hebrew Bible/Old Testament: The History of Its Interpretation II: From the Renaissance to the Enlightenment*, ed. Magne Sæbø (Göttingen: Vandenhoeck & Ruprecht, 2008), 973.
52   Sandys-Wunsch, "Early Old Testament Critics on the Continent," 972–973. See, however, Charles K. Telfer, who argues that Vitringa was not nearly as bound by historicist explanations as Sandys-Wunsch claims (*Wrestling with Isaiah: The Exegetical Methodology of Campegius Vitringa (1659–1722)*, Reformed Historical Theology 38 [Göttingen: Vandenhoeck & Ruprecht, 2016], 78–79). H. G. M. Williamson

These conclusions did not sit well with the ecclesial governing body of pastors in the Netherlands at the time. The idea that language diversity should happen through historical means and not as a divine moment robbed the story of its traditionally understood divine agency.[53] Perhaps as offensive to the body of authorities, Vitringa argued that the State's Translation of the Bible, commissioned under the authority of the Dutch Republic, was incorrect not only in Genesis 11:1–9 but also in passages elsewhere in the Hebrew Bible that seemed to echo similar concepts as the Tower of Babel. For instance, Zephaniah 3:9 has been interpreted as a prophetic vision casting a future reversal of the Tower of Babel in which all people speak the same language. If this is a future solution, then multilingualism at Babel must have been the problem. Based on comparative evidence from studying the Tower of Babel narrative, Vitringa argued not only that the States' Translation did not accurately represent the idioms in Genesis 11:1–9 but this translation also failed to make sense of Zephaniah 3:9, even if the States' Translation was the best available.[54] Vitringa's views on how the Tower of Babel and Zephaniah 3:9 should be reinterpreted were the subject of the Classis of Zevenwouden in 1684, the year after Vitringa's publication.[55] While Vitringa's orthodoxy was affirmed by the synod of Friesland, the controversy that Vitringa's reinterpretations caused prompted him to apologize in a later work, published 1712.[56] Like Spinoza, Vitringa's biblical philology had political consequences, and his reinterpretation of the Tower of Babel was at the center of the controversy. Unlike Spinoza, Vitringa remained an orthodox figure in his religious community, but only by recanting (without counterevidence) his earlier assertions.

---

helpfully cautions against some of Telfer's claims regarding Vitringa's methodologies in simplistic "pre-critical" and "post-critical" lenses, though Williamson is appreciative overall of Telfer's work ("Review: *Wrestling with Isaiah: The Exegetical Methodology of Campegius Vitringa (1659–1722)*," *JTS* 69 [2018]: 225–228).

53 Touber, *Spinoza and Biblical Philology in the Dutch Republic, 1660–1710*, 214. Vitringa was not the first to propose the idea that the unity and dispersal was a matter of discord, but not languages. See the exchange between bishop Ward and Thomas Hobbes in *Memoirs of Literature: Containing a Large Account of Many Valuable Books, Letters and Dissertations upon Several Subjects, Miscellaneous Observations, etc., Vol. III* (London: R. Knaplock, 1722), 240.

54 Touber, *Spinoza and Biblical Philology in the Dutch Republic, 1660–1710*, 214.

55 Touber, *Spinoza and Biblical Philology in the Dutch Republic, 1660–1710*, 214–215.

56 As Touber states, Vitringa "apologetically ascribed the controversial remarks in the first edition to the ardour of his young age when confronting the topic. In this new edition he duly excised his critique of the mistranslations of the States' Translation." Touber, *Spinoza and Biblical Philology in the Dutch Republic, 1660–1710*, 215.

THE TOWER OF BABEL AND THE POLITICAL
PROBLEM OF LANGUAGES

Other issues come to the fore. It is not enough to say what Genesis 11 in its historical and literary context is not about but rather what it actually means. The word "language" in Genesis 11:1–9 is a mistranslation, and the word here functions as a metaphor for political action and not grammatical structures, phonological features, and other linguistic categories that give rise to distinct language groups. In fact, the understanding of Genesis 11 as a story about language is due only to the processes (perhaps even accidents) of the editing of the Torah from originally distinct stories. If set in a different literary context, perhaps in the historical context of ancient Near Eastern rhetoric and a literary context of Hebrew that preceded the compiled Torah, Genesis 11:1–9 takes on a completely distinct meaning. Even in light of the biblical narrative in Genesis 10–11, and the influence that its Western, canonical shape has had in culture, good reason exists to understand the Tower of Babel episode as a story about something other than language. If that is the case, then the implications could be far-reaching.

These scenarios may appear too counterfactual or counterintuitive to entertain. Some conceptions about the moral of the Tower of Babel have been resolute and ubiquitous, partly because the traditional interpretation of Genesis 11:1–9 functions as an explanatory cause for societal ills and partly because it serves as a warning against diversity and multilingualism. Yet questioning the traditional interpretation is not simply a matter of exegesis. One of the more practical results of questioning the dominant meaning of the Tower of Babel narrative has to do with the role of language ideology and politics in the modern era, issues reified in the age-old connection between language and state.[57] If the image of the "Tower of Babel" brought to mind a different interpretation than diversity as a result of divine

---

57   "There was throughout later medieval and early modern Europe a detectable shift towards regarding linguistic uniformity as a necessary precondition for a strong and unified state. Language, from being one of the identifiers and prerogatives of each and every people, was being turned into an instrument of state power and uniformity. An early articulation of the new orthodoxy comes, interestingly enough, from late fourteenth-century Ireland, where language had already become a touchstone of loyalty and Englishness. 'Experience teaches us,' so it was observed, that 'diversity of tongues' caused 'wars and diverse tribulations'" (R. R. Davies, "The Peoples of Britain and Ireland 1100–1400: IV. Language and Historical Mythology," *Transactions of the Royal Historical Society* 7 [1997]: 14).

judgment, it could be the case that conceptions of purity as it relates to language, and whether or not multilingualism is desirable, would be different. In the prevailing interpretation, the state of linguistic diversity is the result of divine judgment. Linguistic purity, or even a universal language, is often deemed as a virtuous enterprise.[58] This effort could then find its religious motivation in an attempt to undo the curse of Babel. If the point of Genesis 11:1–9 is not about language, if the use of language in this passage is a metaphor or idiom for something else, and if the pre-edited state of Genesis 11:1–9 is not of the same literary piece as significant portions of Genesis 10, then it raises the possibility that current conceptions of the desirability of linguistic purity that draw from a (mis-)reading of the narrative of the Tower of Babel lose their political and religious legitimacy. At least, such arguments would lose their connection to a dominant text often employed in their hermeneutical goals.

Yet, as already seen in the writings of Kircher, the conceptualization of the Tower of Babel as a story about multilingualism and multiculturalism resulting from divine disfavor, judgment, and curse is deeply embedded in the reception of Genesis 11:1–9. Augustine of Hippo (died 430 CE) offered a series of reflections concerning the relationship between multilingualism, incomprehensibility, and alienation. For Augustine, the confirmation that such incomprehensibility was part of a fallen world appeared in his own search for truth and God. His search for philosophy and the confusion and alienation that it produced signaled an effect from a deeper cause, namely further separation from the divine. The initial step was the fall and expulsion from Eden.[59] The divine judgment of multiple languages after Babel reified

---

58 See, generally, Eco, *The Search for the Perfect Language*.

59 For Josephus and the author of *Jubilees*, the fall was a sort of Babel for the animal world, which had, before Genesis 3, been able to communicate with humans. After the fall, however, such communication ceased and the power to speak in language intelligible to humans was lost forever. See Fyler for these sources, as well as the medieval inheritance of this idea ("Language Barriers," *Studies in Philology* 112 [2015]: 450–452). For Greek thinkers, the primordial golden age in the days of Kronos was marked by the ability of gods and humans to communicate with animals and nature. This state was lost somehow in the past as later Greek thinkers reflected on the limited if not nonexistent capacities of animals and humans to communicate with one another. See Gera, *Ancient Greek Ideas on Speech, Language, and Civilization* (New York: Oxford University Press, 2003), 14–15. These Greek thinkers argued that, since animals could talk in this primordial period, it would have been unethical to eat them and, as a result, a sort of vegetarianism prevailed. Indeed, the fact that

such alienation, resulting in the state of the world as a "region of dissimili-
tude" and "land of unlikeness."[60] Augustine provides a description of this
condition post-Babel: "For when men cannot communicate their thoughts
to each other, simply because of difference of language, all the similarity of
their common human nature is of no avail to unite them in fellowship. So
true is this that a man would be more cheerful with his dog for company
than with a foreigner." True and lasting agreement between humans is not
possible after Babel, resulting in alienation.[61] During the same period in
which Augustine penned these thoughts, the mosaic in the fifth-century CE
synagogue at Huqoq in Israel illustrated this very interpretation, highlighting
the alienation and strife resulting from the events at Babel. The labor appears
arduous, almost like the work in Egypt that resulted in the Exodus, and the
workers are often depicted in conflict with one another.

The legacy of the connection between Babel, sin, and divine curse apparent
in Augustine's *Confessions* finds political expression in the *City of God*. As in
the example above of Birs Nimrud, Nimrod, the warrior and archetypal enemy
of God, was the king under whose commands and powers the Tower of Babel
was built, thereby combining the genealogy and geography of Genesis 10:8–12
with the episode in Genesis 11:1–9. In *City of God* 16:4, Augustine claims that
the tongue of the tyrant was the organ of the body that gave rise to rebellion
against God; therefore, it was speech that was punished, starting with Nimrod, whose orders were impossible to understand and follow.[62] According to
Augustine, Nimrod was an active agent in attempting to transgress proper

---

animals consume each other beyond this golden age was thought to be a distinction
between animals and humans and mark the belief that animals did not have laws or
customs, at least in the sense that human society had them. See Gera, *Ancient Greek
Ideas on Speech, Language, and Civilization*, 10. For issues on diet in the Primeval
period in the biblical narratives, see Boyd, "The Flood and the Problem of Being an
Omnivore," *JSOT* 43 (2019): 163–178.

60 Fyler, "Language Barriers," 417.

61 As Fyler states, "For Augustine, Babel punishes human pride by such human alienation, 'incompatible languages [*voces dissonas*] to match their incompatible minds.'"
Fyler, "Language Barriers," 418.

62 "Since a ruler's power of domination is wielded by his tongue, it was in that organ
that his pride was condemned to punishment. And the consequence was that he
who refused to understand God's bidding so as to obey it, was himself not understood when he gave orders to men." See also the connection between pride, arrogance (and arrogant speech), and politics in Ben Sira 10, which Augustine cites in
City of God book 14, chapter 13 in connection to the pride that preceded Adam's sin
and divine judgment in the Garden of Eden.

divine authority.[63] Not only does the connection between Nimrod and Babel in Genesis 10:8–12 function as the link to posit that Nimrod was the king behind building the city in Genesis 11:1–9 but even the proverb that attested to Nimrod's skill as a hunter displayed a fundamental disposition of antagonism toward God. The phrase is "like Nimrod, a mighty hunter before the LORD." In Greek, the Hebrew preposition *lpny* (meaning "before") was translated as *enantion kuriou*. Augustine observed that the Greek preposition could mean, in addition to "before," something more adversative, as in "contrary" or "in opposition."[64] This preposition described a basic stance of rebellion against God. That such a proverb would encode this antagonism made Nimrod as a character and the most infamous act attributed to him (the construction of the Tower of Babel) highly significant and symbolically rich.[65]

The way in which the symbol of Nimrod functioned allowed him to serve as a stand-in for human pride, sin, and condemnation generally. Later in time, Dante describes hell as full of foreign languages ("diverse lingue").[66] The logic

---

63 Kathleen Glenister Roberts, *Alterity and Narrative: Stories and the Negotiation of Western Identities*, Negotiating Identity (Albany: State University of New York Press, 2007), 82.

64 "Quod non intellegentes nonnulli ambiguo Graeco falsi sunt, ut non interpretarentur contra Dominum, sed ante Dominum; ἐναντίον quippe et contra et ante significat." Augustine's appeal to the Greek is significant since he likely knew very little, if any, of the language. According to Peter Brown, this fact makes Augustine one of the few philosophers of Late Antiquity who did not know Greek, or at least did not know it well, being "virtually ignorant" of the language (*Augustine of Hippo: A Biography*, 2nd ed. [Berkeley: University of California Press, 2000], 24). As Roberts and Haynes remark, Augustine's use of this preposition is a major moment in the fictional biography of Nimrod in the history of interpretation in Christianity (though allusions to Nimrod as a giant also existed in the writings of Tertullian in the second century CE) (Roberts, *Alterity and Narrative*, 82). For the influence of Augustine's interpretation of Nimrod (and the possible influence of Philo on Augustine), see Haynes, *Noah's Curse*, 46–48. Philo stated that " . . . those things that are here [on earth] are against those things which are there [in heaven]. For this reason it is not ineptly said [that Nimrod was] 'a giant *before* God' which clearly [means] *in opposition to* the Deity" (Haynes, 239). For the reception of these interpretations of Nimrod from antiquity to nineteenth-century Europe, and then from Europe to nineteenth- to twenty-first-century American debates on slavery and race, see Haynes, *Noah's Curse*, 41–61, 105–121.

65 Hendel argues that Nimrod's name not only makes a subversive reference to the Mesopotamian god Ninurta but also "links a call for insurrection with the name of Nimrod," which would be spelled נִמְרֹד in Hebrew, meaning "we will rebel" ("Genesis 1–11 and Its Mesopotamian Problem," 30–31).

66 Fyler, "Language Barriers," 420.

extends the situation of Babel and condemnation of Nimrod to humanity in general, though in Dante's description the diversity of languages is a constant: the sin of Babel and Nimrod is, in microcosm (or perhaps in typological significance), like the sin of all humanity, though in each case the sign of this remains the multiplicity of language. As Dante approaches hell, he hears foreign languages and strange accents.[67] Much like original sin in Augustine's thought, the curse of Babel is inherited to all people. Much like original sin, Babel, and the resulting multilingualism, is a curse to be overcome.[68]

Following this logic, the presence of many languages is a sign not simply of divine displeasure but of the ultimate curse, even becoming a symbol of condemnation in Hades. When a particular language shows signs of borrowing words or phrases from another language, the issue is not simply one of linguistics or exploring how, why, and to what effect that language contact occurs. Rather, the issue is theological, moral, and ethical, and at the root of such language contact is evidence of the curse of Babel and signs of the loss of linguistic perfection.[69] These issues are also mapped onto statehood, and concerns about the viability of the nation, reflected through language, often appear. Even Hebrew, the original language and *lingua sancta*, reflected this state of affairs. For example, the ninth-century CE Christian Isho'dad of Merv claimed that such processes of politics and conquest were key for understanding the history of languages like Hebrew and Syriac.[70] Debates regarding

---

67 Fyler, "Language Barriers," 420.
68 For many ancient and medieval thinkers, "the continuing, unending change in human language is itself evidence of fallen imperfection" (Fyler, "Language Barriers," 422).
69 Fyler, "Language Barriers," 422.
70 He observes that:

> It is after all not surprising that Hebrew is a composite of (several) languages, since we may ascertain that even Syriac has been altered and corrupted with the changing of times and the duration of generations. [...] In fact, the Syriac language was especially corrupted in Babylon, because of the kings that carried each other (there) as captives, for the stranger and the immigrant never have a pure and polished language.

> Moss, "The Language of Paradise: Hebrew or Syriac? Linguistic Speculations and Linguistic Realities in Antiquity," in *Paradise in Antiquity: Jewish and Christian Views*, ed. Markus Bockmuehl and Guy G. Strousma (New York: Cambridge University Press, 2010), 133–134. Bar Koni states, in words similar to those of Isho'dad:

> Just as we find with Syriac, which, with the changing of times and the duration of generations, became agitated and corrupted by foreign usages and little by little departed from where it had resided and settled down in other places. Thus

the original language and its significance for understanding the pre-Babel world appear in many texts from antiquity until modern time. In antiquity, recovering Hebrew in this scheme may have been an important factor for the Qumran community and their religious identity since they believed they were living in the end times. In these debates, however, Hebrew was not always the identified language of creation. As such, one could argue that reversing the curse of Genesis 11:1–9 could involve a language other than Hebrew. Further, if the divine plan of salvation was inherited to another, subsequent religion by replacement or supersessionism (from Judaism to Christianity), then the political and linguistic means for reversing the curse of Babel could be found in a situation completely unanticipated in (or, at least, secretly embedded in) biblical rhetoric. In this manner, politicians have applied the situation of Babel and its cure to the founding of America and political ideologies therein, often, though not always, through a Christian lens.

The application of reversing the curse of the fall from Genesis 3 and Babel in Genesis 11 to Christianity finds multiple points of affirmation in the New Testament, though many are from Paul, a Pharisee and someone who considered himself to be Jewish throughout his life. In Paul's logic in Romans 5 and 1 Corinthians 15, the death introduced to the world in Adam's transgression was reversed in the death and resurrection of Jesus of Nazareth. Indeed, all creation was and still exists in futility, even after this resurrection, awaiting a full removal of divine curse. In Romans 8:20–21 Paul compares a futility in which the world was subjected to a promised reversal of this situation.[71]

---

if one compares the tongue of the Babylonians with genuine Syriac, it has not one percent of Syriac in it. And although it remained in Babylon, its genuineness is found in Emesa, in Apamea and in their environs. And it happens that also the rest of the languages became corrupted in this manner, especially from the proximity with other, neighboring languages.

For the Syriac text of bar Koni, see Theodore bar Konai, *Liber Scholiorum (Seert Version)*, ed. Edidit Addai Scher, CSCO. Scriptores Syri series 2 volume 65 (Lovanii: E. Peeters, 1960), 113. For a French translation and manuscript notes, see Théodore Bar Koni, *Liber Scholiorum (Seert Version)*, trans. Robert Hespel and René Draguet, CSCO. Scriptores Syri 187 (Lovanii: E. Peeters, 1981), 127.

71 In ancient and medieval interpretation, this futility applied not only to Genesis 3:17–19, the passage that lies behind Paul's reference but also to the Tower of Babel episode, in which the workers on the city and tower, after the confusion of languages, did not understand one another. The futility resulted in abandonment of the enterprise of constructing the Tower. In some interpretations, such as Dante's, the languages divided along the lines of the manner of work being done, such that each specialist had its own language. See Fyler, "Language Barriers," 419. For Paul's use

Paul contrasts the futility to which creation was subjected with a future freedom in glory, calling to mind an ultimate, eschatological overthrow of the curse of the fall. Second Temple Jewish literature identified, in some sense, the removal of wickedness in the world, as represented in the Christian concept of a "fall," with the reversal of the curse of Babel through the call of Abram. In some manner, Christian interpretation of the reversal of the curse of futility, at least regarding comprehensibility across tongues, occurred in Pentecost in Acts 2. Despite the mutual intelligibility of languages that came with the initial appearance of the Holy Spirit in the New Testament, multiple languages and miscommunication persisted, meaning that the episode in Acts 2 did not entirely do away with the persistent problem of Babel.[72] With the persistence of the problem, solutions for overcoming the curse continued as well.

The seventeenth-century effort to explore and overcome the curse of Babel exemplified in the work of Athanasius Kircher found a political movement in the eighteenth-century colonial and revolutionary America. As seen in the eighteenth century, the Tower of Babel was an important phrase, calling to mind the significance of politically and linguistically unified statehood in the face of British opposition. In this rhetoric the ghosts of Babel show the beginning signs of haunting dreams of nascent nationalism, and the specters reappear throughout American history and well into the twenty-first century whenever ideas of what American statehood should be are challenged, particularly in the areas of immigration policy and language. Already in the *Federalist Papers*, John Jay claimed that "providence has been pleased to give this one connected country, to the united people; a people descended from the same ancestors, speaking the same language, professing the same religion."[73] In this manner the sameness of language was indicative of a unified purpose that augured for the success of the new nation. America would not be Babel in hubris, but the world before Babel, as a way to roll back the curse.[74]

---

of Genesis 3:17–19, see C. E. B. Cranfield, *The Epistle to the Romans: Volume 1*, ICC (New York: T&T Clark, 2001), 413.

72 See, for example, 2 Peter 3:15–16, in which the author discusses the difficulty of understanding and interpreting Paul.

73 As quoted in Shell, "Babel in America," 103.

74 The use of the Tower of Babel, concepts like "providence," and the Bible in America's founding highlights how vital parts of the Bible were for this early period. See James P. Byrd, *Sacred Scripture, Sacred War: The Bible and the American Revolution* (New York: Oxford University Press, 2013). At the same time, general religious devotion from 1775 to 1815, according to Howard Mumford Jones and Thomas Ricks, "had less influence in American life than it did in any later such forty-year period" (*First*

In the face of Jay's defense for linguistic uniformity, dividedness and multi-lingualism were realities and facts, if not also at times political obstacles. Here, too, the Tower of Babel functioned as a useful point of comparison. In terms of political divisiveness, Benjamin Franklin, noting the delegates' hesitation to sign the constitution even on the last day of the Constitutional Convention, said, "I think it will astonish our enemies, who are waiting with confidence to hear that our councils are confounded like those of the Builders of Babel; and that our States are on the point of separation, only to meet hereafter for the purpose of cutting one another's throats."[75] He also appealed to Babel as a foil to his hopes for divine favor in America's founding.[76] Other thinkers ascribed multilingualism as a root cause of this divisiveness. According to Thomas Paine, "if there is a country in the world where concord, according to common calculation, would be least expected, it is America. Made up, as it is, of people . . . speaking different languages."[77] Yet multilingualism, and with it the specter of division that would be fatal to the new nation, was an entrenched part of the early American experience. If any society in history merited the label "polyglot," it was colonial America, and what requires more explanation is not how a mythical "English" was ever a cornerstone of American culture and identity but rather how a society that remained multilingual well into the nineteenth century became so unilingual and politically committed to endorsing such an identity.[78] When accounting for African languages spoken

---

Principles: What America's Founders Learned from the Greeks and Romans and How That Shaped Our Country [New York: Harper, 2020], 55). Ricks points out that in 1775 there were 1,500 Americans for every minister, whereas in 1845 there were 500 Americans for every minister (*First Principles*, 277).

75 John R. Vile, *The Constitutional Convention of 1787: A Comprehensive Encyclopedia of America's Founding*, rev. 2nd ed. (Clark, NJ: Talbot Publishing, 2016), 280.

76 He states:

> I have lived, Sir, a long time, and the longer I live, the more convincing proofs I see of this truth—*that God governs in the affairs of men*. And if a sparrow cannot fall to the ground without his notice, is it possible that an empire can rise without his aid? We have been assured, Sir, in the sacred writings, that 'except the Lord build the House they labour in vain that build it.' I firmly believe this; and I also believe that without his concurring aid we shall succeed in this political building no better than the Builders of Babel.

Vile, *The Constitutional Conventions of 1787*, 593.

77 Shell, "Babel in America," 106.

78 "Anglophone Americans' various fictive idealizations of an independent American language buttressed the spectacular development in the United States of a distinctly monoglottal and linguistic amnesic national literature and culture. For neither in

by one-fifth of the population, for indigenous and Amerindian languages, and for the fact that non-English-speaking Europeans constituted twenty-five percent of the population, the linguistic statistics from 1750 to 1850 reveal a largely multilingual society in America.[79]

Yet the tension between the expressed ideal of unity, especially represented in language, and the multilingual reality in America has fueled political debates as long as America has been a concept. The emergence of an American literature in English masks the complex history in which English was not always considered a preferred national language, particularly in the eighteenth century, given the war with England, whose language (naturally) was also English.[80] As quoted above, Paine saw great risk in the polyglossia of America, which, as he saw it, jeopardized political concord. Which language would become "official," however, was far from certain, and English, the language of American adversaries, was not always the leading candidate.

Many other languages vied for status in American culture and politics, as well as the idea of creating a distinct language, even a distinct form of English (or, a non-British form of American English). Perhaps more than any other, the history of German in America illustrates the complexities of this situation, and the manner in which language and politics have become inseparable. Particularly in Pennsylvania, German had a large purchase on the landscape of languages. In 1732 Benjamin Franklin began to publish *Philadelphische Zeitung*, the first German newspaper printed in America. It failed, and from the 1750s onward, Franklin displayed a more negative attitude toward multilingualism in America, becoming at times xenophobic. It is difficult to know for certain, but the failure of this paper may have had a big influence on perceptions of language in the following history of Pennsylvania and beyond in America.[81]

Yet German would persist as a rival to English for decades after. A congressional committee suggested that "it will be necessary that the laws be translated, and printed in the German language." Benjamin Rush, the foremost physician in America and medical expert for the Lewis and Clark expedition, wanted a German-language college to be established in the newly founded nation. Sentiments changed, particularly as isolationist politics became

---

literature nor in American politics generally did the question of official language assert itself successfully," Shell, "Babel in America," 119.

79   Shell, "Babel in America," 105.
80   Shell, "Babel in America," 107–108, 113–115.
81   Shell, "Babel in America," 109.

popular in the era of the First World War. A 1916 law made it illegal to teach foreign languages in schools.[82] In the following year, Theodore Roosevelt stated that "we must . . . have but one language. That must be the language of the Declaration of Independence. The greatness of this nation depends on the swift assimilation of the aliens she welcomes to her shores."[83]

The significance of this moment for subsequent language policy in American history cannot be overestimated. The political fears of fragmentation, multilingualism, and political decay took a front and center position.[84] Though writing four years prior to Roosevelt's statement, Daniel Gurden Stevens gave voice to the same cultural and historical assessment in 1913 in an article concerning the Tower of Babel. In the midst of analyzing Genesis 11:1–9 in light of the ancient Near Eastern discoveries of previous decades, Stevens made an aside that, while not immediately relevant to his literary and historical analysis, seems to be his real point regarding America and Babel. He wrote positively about unilingualism and its use for a united nation. Stevens's vision for immigrants was total assimilation culturally and linguistically to America, so as to "melt" their own adherence to language and custom out of them. In this manner, he hoped that America would avoid the past mistakes of European nations.[85] For Stevens, where Europe failed, America succeeded.

---

82 See also Paul J. Ramsey, "The War against German-American Culture: The Removal of German-Language Instruction from the Indianapolis Schools, 1917–1919," *Indiana Magazine of History* 98 (2002): 285–303.

83 Shell, "Babel in America," 111.

84 As Shell states, "President Roosevelt's wartime ideology—that the United States has to have only one language just as it has one flag and that this language must be English—has remained the effective unofficial view of America's political officers ever since." Shell, "Babel in America," 111.

85 The quote is:

> A language has connected with it the spirit, the genius, of a people, their very mind and heart. When you have persons speaking the same language, you have evidence of the existence of some great essentials of unity. Until we get on the platform of understanding, through our use in common of some means of communication, we are aliens one to another. The immigrants we call foreigners are very much foreigners to us till by their use of our own speech they have made it evidence that they have grasped and taken into themselves the idea and spirit of Americanism. We have been able to melt the heterogeneous foreign elements into the common substance of our people, because we have succeeded so far in breaking up the little Hungaries and Russias and Italies through education of the masses in our language and in our national mind, manners, customs, and views. So the United States of America has thus far maintained itself, and shows today an astonishing homogeneity; while the

Where Babylon failed, America succeeded, and that success represents, in some manner, a reversal of the curse of multilingualism.[86]

Far from being an historical curiosity of the eighteenth, nineteenth, and early twentieth centuries, the connection between a perception of multilingualism and a threat to national identity and security, as well as the use of the Tower of Babel as the operative political metaphor invoked to warn of the presence of divine curse, has functioned to incite fears in American political discourse to the present. Pat Buchanan's appeal to Babel in a discussion regarding immigration legislation adduces this passage from the Bible to wed a lack of acculturation, viewed through the politics of language, to divine curse and national downfall. In both his presidential campaign and in stumping for Donald Trump's presidency in 2016, Buchanan made these arguments again. Even more recently, media outlets and blogs have used the Tower of Babel as a political metaphor for action against the DACA, or "Dreamers" legislation, and for making English the official and sanctioned language of the United States.[87] The political legacy of the Tower of Babel, understood as a story about divine curse and multilingualism, has had real legislative implications for many people living in America.[88]

While the history of multilingualism in America is complicated, and rhetoric does not always match reality, the foregoing discussion reveals the manner in which the Tower of Babel has been a powerful force in political discourse. National fears of decline from a mythic blessed past stoke the desire for explanation, laid at the feet of immigration and polyglossia. This situation, perceived as a divine curse in the likeness of Babel, then motivates

---

United States of Europe, several times attempted, as Emil Reich points out, has never been an accomplished fact, and the process of national differentiation has rather grown more intense of late.

Daniel Gurden Stevens, "The Tower of Babel: History in Picture," *The Biblical World* 41 (1913): 188–189. The periodical *The Biblical World* was published by University of Chicago Press. The name of the journal changed to *The Journal of Religions* in 1920, still in publication.

86 See also Michael Silverstein, "Monoglot 'Standard' in America: Standardization and Metaphors of Linguistic Hegemony," in *The Matrix of Language: Contemporary Linguistic Anthropology*, ed. D. Brenneis and R. H. S. Macaulay (Oxford: Westview, 1996), 284–305.

87 See chapter 6 of this book for further analysis.

88 Erin Runions, *The Babylon Complex: Theopolitical Fantasies of War, Sex, and Sovereignty* (New York: Fordham University Press, 2014). I return to her insightful analysis of the function of Genesis 11:1–9 in the conclusion of this book.

an attempt to reverse the curse through language ideology, or creating an official language. Signs of too much multiculturalism, too little acculturation, or too much language mixture in this view suggest that America is failing to reverse the curse and becoming Babel, thereby evincing God's displeasure.

BABEL REIMAGINED, OR, HOW TO BUILD A BETTER BABEL

Babel is, therefore, important to understand. It has provided the conceptual framework for political neuroses and the politics of identity. Understood as a curse and punishment, the post-Babel situation is to be overcome with platforms of "purism." The idea is that one language and pure speech, if that was the original condition, was not in itself a bad thing and lost only because of political hubris. For some, achieving the pre-Babel situation is, in essence, to overcome the curse. Yet, at the same time, the story has proven to be elastic in interpretation. The Tower of Babel has been used to show the dangers of diversity and, at the same time, to justify diversity.[89]

Offering a new interpretation of a story as ubiquitous as the Tower of Babel necessarily involves multiple considerations, observations, methods, and lots of data. Historically, when set in the context of Assyrian rhetoric, much of the phrasing in Genesis 11:1–9 has the same flexibility. At times in Assyria, to have "one mouth" is a good thing; at times, to have "one mouth" is a bad thing. When that phrasing, and the rhetorical strategy it embeds, is understood in light of first millennium imperial discourse, a better interpretation of Genesis 11 appears. When that interpretation is understood comparatively and then contextualized within the Tower of Babel's literary context, it provides a critical lens through which to understand, if not deconstruct, the ways in which the Tower of Babel has been used and abused in political history. Certainly,

---

89 Erin Runions, "Empire's Allure: Babylon and the Exception to Law in Two Conservative Discourses," *JAAR* 77 (2009): 680–711. See also Brent Strawn and the illegitimacy of unification and the divine approval of diversity, https://global.oup .com/obso/focus/focus_on_towerbabel/. Note how Strawn highlights the manner in which Genesis 10, which tells of the spread of languages, and Genesis 11, the Tower of Babel, were not redacted in chronological order since Genesis 11 would seem to be the origins story that explains the spread in Genesis 10. Though I argue that a source-critical approach reveals that the spread of languages in Genesis 10 is not related to Genesis 11, making each narrative coherent in the context of its own source, the revised understanding of Genesis 11 argued here makes sense even of the redacted Pentateuch. For more, see chapter 4 of this book.

other cultures produced myths explaining the presence of the multiplicity of languages. Other texts in the Bible, especially in the prophets, imagine a future in which "one lip" unites all peoples, which ancient and modern interpreters have understood in some loose manner as a reversal of Genesis 11. Brilliant interpretations in both Judaism and Christianity envision a reversal of the curse of the mixture of languages as part of an eschatological scheme in which God and humanity become reconciled.[90] Setting aside other cultural myths, the reception of biblical texts in ancient Judaism and Christianity, and lesser-known prophetic rhetoric about "one lip" for the moment, one cannot but wonder if our understanding of language, and the relationship between language, politics, and identity, would be different if our interpretation of the dominant etiology for the advent of multilingualism found in Genesis 11:1–9 were different.

It is a complicated, albeit short, story, with an equally complex legacy, made possibly more intriguing if not more intelligible if Genesis 11:1–9 is not about language at all. The story of the Tower of Babel is, rather, about political unification and fragmentation against proper authority. It is not a statement about language ideology. It could be the case that such a statement in Genesis 11:1–9 reflects anti-colonial sentiments. These conclusions about Genesis 11 arise from setting the narrative in the context of the ancient Near East. To set a part of the Bible in the context of eighth-century BCE Assyrian rhetoric is to enter into the practical realities of empire and the theoretical categories of postcolonial study.[91] These sentiments were not incorporated

---

90 Many of these interpretations are examined more in a subsequent chapter of this book.

91 Uehlinger, *Weltreich und "eine Rede,"* 516–542; David M. Carr, *The Formation of the Hebrew Bible: A New Reconstruction* (New York: Oxford University Press, 2011), 245 and 317; Carr, *Holy Resilience: The Bible's Traumatic Origins* (New Haven: Yale University Press, 2014), 24–66; Hendel, "Genesis 1–11 and Its Mesopotamian Problem," 23–31; William Morrow, "Resistance and Hybridity in Late Bronze Age Canaan," *RB* 115 (2008): 321–339. As such, this project supports Uehlinger and others in identifying in Genesis 11 an anti-colonial sentiment, though the mechanisms analyzed in this book through which that rhetoric is constructed differs greatly from Uehlinger and others. Note, for example, the unique manner in which J takes an interest in Mesopotamia explicitly even if other sources, such as D, also clearly show signs of contact with Assyria. It is the only Pentateuchal source to name Babylon (Genesis 10:10 and 11:9), but it also names Assyria on a number of occasions (Genesis 2:14; 10:11; 10:22; Numbers 24:22–24). See, however, arguments that the passage in Numbers 24 also reflects a post-Persian, Hellenistic era expansion in the wake of Alexander's conquests in Konrad Schmid, "How to Identify a Persian Period Text in

through the reversal of colonial rhetoric nor by challenging it directly but, instead, by using colonial rhetoric in the same literary placement and rhetorical effect with a different authority at the helm.[92] If this background evidence is brought to bear, then the Tower of Babel cannot be the basis for language ideology of purism.

This argument is easier to grasp when multiple perspectives and analyses appear in detail, first with historical backgrounds to Genesis 11:1–9, in the multilingualism of the ancient Near East and in Assyrian imperial rhetoric; then, with an analysis of the Tower of Babel as a self-contained story and with an examination of Genesis 11:1–9 in its source-critical context; and, finally, with an assessment of the relationship between Genesis 11:1–9 and Genesis 12:1–3 in reception history. Each method contains critical arguments of historical, philological, linguistic, and literary observations, all to support the thesis that the Tower of Babel is not a story about language. Once this evidence has been laid out, the necessity of a critical study on how this story has been told in the modern context and its influence on American civil policy will be clearer.[93]

Historical background for interpreting Genesis 11 and for understanding the role of multilingualism in the ancient Near East entails understanding more of how multilingualism was understood at the time when the Tower of Babel was written.[94] The Neo-Assyrian empire in the first millennium BCE created an extent of rule that had never existed prior, giving rise to issues of governance and ideological ways to express these challenges through rhetoric in a variety of texts. These texts contain idioms that many scholars have also attached to language ideology and have argued is also reflected in Genesis 11. However, language is not actually in view in the particular inscriptions

---

the Pentateuch," in *On Dating Biblical Texts to the Persian Period: Discerning Criteria and Establishing Epochs*, ed. Richard J. Bautch and Mark Lackowski, FAT 2.101 (Tübingen: Mohr Siebeck, 2019), 103. Otherwise, the only mention of Assyria in the Pentateuch is in P in Genesis 25:18.

92 For a similar manner in which the authority from a prestigious source can be assumed instead of subverted in the reception history of the text, see Nathan Mastjnak, "Prestige, Authority, and Jeremiah's Bible," *JR* 98 (2018): 542–558.

93 The core engagements with the text in the following chapters, then, are bookended by the practical effects of biblical interpretation and biblical idioms as well as the manner in which they shape and call to mind social fears.

94 To do so, I will juxtapose the Akkadian-Sumerian situation of the second millennium BCE with the Akkadian-Aramaic situation in the first millennium BCE.

that have been adduced to examine Neo-Assyrian royal policy and that have been used as comparative data for Genesis 11. These inscriptions should be part of a comparative examination of Genesis 11, though for different reasons than have been offered previously. As such, a survey of multilingualism in the ancient Near East generally provides a background understanding of whether or not languages functioned as part of imperial ideology (and, if they did, to what degree and which social domains were involved). Crucially, the significance of city-building as a political and religious activity during this time in Assyria also becomes an important comparative datum for understanding the Tower of Babel.

An examination of Genesis 11:1–9 on its own supports the historical analyses, particularly by investigating the terms and phrases in the passage itself and where similar phrases appear elsewhere. When set in the context of other uses in Hebrew, key terms, on their own and in constellation with other words, reveal that a closer philological study of Genesis 11:1–9 confirms the conclusions derived from the study of the passage in its historical context, namely that phrasings in the Tower of Babel lend themselves to a different interpretation than the traditional one. Key aspects of how perspective, point of view, and focus operate in the passage serve as vital methodological frameworks for understanding how the philological conclusions regarding idioms in the Tower of Babel story are reinforced through variant phrasings when the narrator and God both assess the situation in Genesis 11:1 and 11:6.

But the issue of the origin of the traditional understanding of the Tower of Babel as a story about languages remains. A source-critical examination dislocates the association between Genesis 11 and key parts of Genesis 10, a dislocation that also reveals two distinct strands, only one of which clearly pertains to the multiplication of languages. The other, to which Genesis 11:1–9 belongs, uses an idiom that, removed from historical comparison, has been understood to refer to language. Yet when positioned back in historical context, particularly in the Neo-Assyrian context, these idioms show clear application to issues of authority and the creation of unity. The point of the narrative strand to which Genesis 11:1–9 belongs (called the J source) is that unification is something that proper authority offers. It is not something that a king can do, but only the divine. When edited together, however, the two different sources that comprise Genesis 10–11 create the possible, though not inevitable, interpretation that the Tower of Babel is about language. Thus, literary features exist in the Primeval History, or Genesis 1–11, that justify dividing the text into distinct sources, and each source functions with its own plot claims such that it becomes clearer that Genesis 11:1–9 is not about language. By making this initial observation, however, it also becomes possible to offer an explanation as to why the traditional interpretation arose as a product of the compiled Torah.

One of the enduring issues in the study of Genesis is the manner in which the Primeval History of Genesis 1–11 relates to the call of Abram in Genesis 12:1–3 and the subsequent narratives of his family. Relevant readings of Genesis 11:1–9 in reception history make the connection to the call of Abram as, in some sense, a reversal of Babel (or the solution to the problem of Babel). These interpretations in the history of the reception of the Bible provide the basis for examining anew, in light of history, philology, and literary studies, the relationship between Babel and the call of Abram. It becomes possible to demonstrate how the historical and literary approaches to the Tower of Babel specifically and the Primeval History generally relate to the call of Abram in Genesis 12:1–3, and relate to features elsewhere in Genesis and Exodus.[95]

In the process, it also becomes possible to build a better Babel, or at least a better interpretation of the passage, and to make contributions methodologically to biblical studies.[96] Much more than method, it becomes possible to make a contribution to the role of the critical study of the Bible in providing checks on the uses and abuses of biblical texts in the public sphere. Whether viewed in its canonical context or through historical-critical methods, when it is demonstrated that the story in Genesis 11:1–9 is not about language,

---

95 In doing so, I provide a fresh take on what Gary Anderson has called "the surprise of election" by putting a new interpretation on the relationship between Babel and Abram into conversation with the techniques that ancient interpreters used to explore the connection between these stories. Anderson, *Christian Doctrine and the Old Testament: Theology in the Service of Biblical Exegesis* (Grand Rapids, MI: Baker Academic, 2017), 78.

96 The approach to the sources of the Torah in this book generally follows the Neo-Documentarian hypothesis for the development of the first five books of the Hebrew Bible. The methods and justification for this approach have been discussed in detail, and I will not repeat that information here. Nonetheless, Neo-Documentarianism has been said to be nonhistorical, focusing too much on finding a literary solution to a literary problem to the exclusion of testing the theory in light of historical evidence. Joseph Lam, "Review of *The Composition of the Pentateuch: Renewing the Documentary Hypothesis*," *JNES* 72 (2013): 308–309; Carr, *The Formation of the Hebrew Bible*, 115. While this book does not deal with all of the facets of this critique, the comparative approach combined with a Neo-Documentary approach to the Primeval History addresses this assertion.

then it also means that the passage cannot be used as a political metaphor for constructing a language ideology. The history of the Bible and the ways in which the interpretation of it has promoted both oppression and freedom has been written many times over. Even if removing the concept of languages from divine curse in the exegesis of the Tower of Babel episode involves the careful study of only nine verses and their historical and literary contexts, the reverberations of this reanalysis of Genesis 11:1–9 could be felt much wider than the academy.

CHAPTER 2

Locating Babel

Mesopotamian Background and the
Making of Political Authority

"As to what was first pronounced by the voice of the first speaker, that will readily be apparent to anyone in their right mind, and I have no doubt that it was the name of God or El, in the form either of a question or of an answer. It is manifestly absurd, and an offence against reason, to think that anything should have been named by a human being before God, when he had been made human by Him and for Him. For if, since the disaster that befell the human race, the speech of every one of us has begun with 'woe!', it is reasonable that he who existed before should have begun with a cry of joy; and, since there is no joy outside God, but all joy is in God and since God Himself is joy itself, it follows that the first man to speak should first and before all have said 'God'."[1]

INTRODUCTION

According to Dante in *De vulgari eloquentia*, language began in one of two modes: as a question or an answer to the divine presence. Adam's first word was "God," or "El," as either an interrogative or a statement of fact. From Dante's perspective, any other possible first act of talking would be absurd: God was the only entity capable of speech and deserving of a response

---

1   Dante, *De vulgari eloquentia*, I.iv.

preceding humankind.[2] As such, God was the ultimate being and point of reference, the source of "all joy." Humanity's first utterance, then, had only two ways of coming into being, as either questioning or accepting the one reality that existed before Adam. The earliest thing that could be expressed was, of necessity, a manner of speech that acknowledged the fundamental aspect of this relation, an utterance in response to divine presence in the form of a question or an answer with respect to authority. As such, all language, having such a genesis, is political, either in service to or rebellion against divinity and authority.

No less than in the divine sphere, the imposition of political authority to new extents in the human realm also spurs innovative ways of conceiving how language relates to power and governance. This was especially the case with the Neo-Assyrian empire (roughly the tenth century BCE to the late seventh century BCE). The territory it encompassed and administered was unprecedented, as was the pace with which it conquered new regions. The empire developed political savvy in the variety of ways that it designated the entities it controlled, whether as directly incorporated into the Assyrian empire or as subjects to the empire who were, nonetheless, allowed to retain some aspect of autonomy (though as vassals to the Assyrian king).[3]

Military might and the threat of deportation formed avenues through which Assyria projected its power and ensured loyalty to the empire.[4] No less persuasive, however, were other, more subtle means of promoting Assyrian interests and promoting obedience to Assyrian policies. Through a combination of borrowing rhetoric from the earlier, Middle Assyrian kings, of

---

2 According to the creation story beginning in Genesis 2:4b, ascribed to non-P or J, the only living creature preceding the creation of humankind was God, whereas in Genesis 1, belonging to P, other creatures, such as animals, were made before humans. Note also that God speaks to those animals before he speaks to humans in Genesis 1.

3 For the structure of Neo-Assyrian governance and the role of the king (focusing on Sargon), see Josette Elayi, *Sargon II, King of Assyria*, Archaeology and Biblical Studies 22 (Atlanta: SBL Press, 2017), 25–44. For the archaeological evidence, see Bleda Düring, *The Imperialisation of Assyria: An Archaeological Approach* (New York: Cambridge University Press, 2020). For essays on various locations in the Assyrian-controlled regions, including territories that came under Assyrian rule and were governed by Assyria proper, see Eckart Frahm, ed., *A Companion to Assyria*, Blackwell Companions to the Ancient World (Hoboken, NJ: John Wiley & Sons, 2017).

4 For the classic study on such deportations, see B. Oded, *Mass Deportations and Deportees in the Neo-Assyrian Empire* (Wiesbaden: L. Reichert, 1979), revised and expanded as גלות ישראל ויהודה באשור ובבל (Ḥefah: Pardes, 2010).

innovating on this rhetoric, and of creating new idioms, the Neo-Assyrian kings deployed royal ideology in service to the crown in a variety of guises. This achievement created continuity with the past (Middle Assyria) even as Neo-Assyrian rulers confronted unprecedented situations requiring innovations and experiments in governance.[5]

The Tower of Babel's origin story, its birth, begins in the context of the Neo-Assyrian empire as a reflection of this process of developing rhetoric as it pertains to authority. A response to this Neo-Assyrian claim for dominance exists in Genesis 11:1–9.[6] Much as, according to Dante, Adam's first word was formed in response to sovereignty, so the background of the phrasing in Genesis 11:1–9 is in Neo-Assyrian claims to imperial control. A historical sketch of the advent of Neo-Assyrian presence in the southern Levant demonstrates how political idioms were constructed and deployed during this time in a manner that would have been meaningful to the authors and audience of many biblical texts. The political possibilities and problems inherent in such an expanding empire generally as well as in the particular expansion to the region where biblical texts were composed reveal the necessity as well as power that such rhetoric could have.[7]

---

5   See especially the discussion of certain terms and royal epithets from Middle Assyrian kings to Sennacherib in Beate Pongratz-Leisten, *Religion and Ideology in Assyria*, SANER 6 (Boston: De Gruyter, 2015), 174–181. Mario Liverani and Peter Machinist were early pioneers in researching and writing about the ideological backing of the Neo-Assyrian empire. See Machinist, "Assyrians on Assyria in the First Millennium B.C.," in *Anfange politischen Denkens in der Antike*, ed. K. Raaflaub, Schriften des Historischen Kollegs Kolloquien 24 (Munich, 1993), 77–104. For Liverani, see most recently *Assyria: The Imperial Mission*, MC 21 (Winona Lake, IN: Eisenbrauns, 2017); Liverani, *Historiography, Ideology and Politics in the Ancient Near East and Israel*, ed. Niels Peter Lemche and Emanuel Pfoh, Changing Perspectives 5 (New York: Routledge, 2021).

6   In this sense, and as Frahm has argued (though on different grounds than the argument in this book), the Tower of Babel functions as a "countertext" ("Countertexts, Commentaries, and Adaptations: Politically Motivated Responses to the Babylonian Epic of Creation in Mesopotamia, the Biblical World, and Elsewhere," *Orient* 45 [2010]: 3–33).

7   Here it should be noted that I begin the historical backgrounds of the Tower of Babel with politics, and not with general comments on multilingualism, neither its mythic origins nor its political implications, in the ancient world. While it was certainly the case that multilingualism and the origins of diverse languages were a topic of thought and reflection in many ancient societies, I argue that such is not the concern in Genesis 11:1–9. In a myth known as Nudimmud/Enmerkar and the Lord of Aratta, scholars had previously identified a short, though much discussed, passage

The function of political idioms in Neo-Assyrian inscriptions are, therefore, relevant to understanding terminology in Genesis 11:1–9. These idioms refer to words and mouths, hearing and obedience to (or defiance against) authorities. The focus on studying the Tower of Babel in light of ancient Mesopotamian culture has often been archaeological or architectural, honing in on city and building (specifically, ziggurat) constructions.[8] A shift to

---

as an analogue to the Tower of Babel, claiming that Enki had in the past separated all languages. Other scholars have claimed that Enki will, like the "holy tongue" reversing Babel discussed more in chapter 5, in the future unite all languages. In contrast, Crisostomo argues that Enki united all languages to facilitate a contest of riddles between the two cities. Uruk, a city of Sumerian speakers, is the winner in this tale. This linguistic unification involved presumably Sumerian as well, displaying, according to Crisostomo, the superiority of Sumerian in metalinguistic discourse. In contrast to previous scholarship, the tale serves neither as an etiology of multilingualism in ancient Mesopotamia, nor as an anticipated future situation, and so is not a "Babylonian Babel." The story underscores a synchronic use for Sumerian within the narrative, establishing its supremacy, but not in a way analogous to the Tower of Babel episode. See Crisostomo, "'Recount for Me the Spell of Nudimmud' . . . yet again," *JAOS* (forthcoming). Claus Westermann observed that there was no parallel among the neighbors of Israel for stories regarding the confusion of tongues, but cited this Sumerian text as a notable exception, even going so far as to use this Sumerian myth to argue that an original story of the confusion of tongues could have existed in Israel without a Tower myth given the Sumerian evidence that also lacked such detail (*Genesis 1–11: A Commentary*, trans. John J. Scullion, CC [Minneapolis: Augsburg Publishing House, 1984], 539). If Crisostomo is correct, however, there is no parallel text from Mesopotamia to the traditional interpretation in Genesis 11:1–9 as the beginnings of multiple languages. Indeed, as the story of Enmerkar and the Lord of Aratta does not contain an etiology for multilingualism, so also I argue throughout this book that, similarly, the Tower of Babel is also not a mythic origin story for multilingualism. Because my interpretation of the Tower of Babel in its historical background leads me to seek other comparative data to make better sense of the biblical passage, I discuss multilingualism in the ancient world but not as a primary mythic background. The philological reasons for interpreting the Tower of Babel in nonlinguistic terms appear more in chapter 3 of this book.

8 These comparisons exist for good reasons, not least of which involves the long pedigree of reception history placing the narrative in Babylon and correlating the tower with ziggurats in southern Mesopotamia. The idea that exiles from Judah saw ziggurats as incomplete towers, and hence derived a story to explain this appearance, is common in scholarship. Irving Finkel has recently argued that the term *migdal* in Hebrew refers to a rectangular-type construction with straight sides, and the story of the Tower of Babel was composed to explain why the ziggurat in Mesopotamia looks like an incomplete structure (*The Ark before Noah: Decoding the Story of the Flood*, 238–39). Yet, as argued even more recently, David Vanderhooft and Matthieu Richelle have demonstrated that the Tower of Babel is described grammatically as a completed construction in Genesis 11:5, meaning that the city was the

comparison with the rhetoric of empire that might be reflected in Genesis 11:1–9 is helpful, and uncovers important facets of how the Tower of Babel is best understood within the Assyrian milieu.[9]

Of particular note is an inscription from Sargon II, during the time when the Tower of Babel would have been written, that seems to promote language ideology as part of Assyrian governance. The rhetoric within this inscription

---

only structure left incomplete. See Vanderhooft, "Babylon as Cosmopolis in Israelite Texts and Achaemenid Architecture," *HeBAI* 9 (2020): 45–48; Richelle, "Was the Tower of Babel Really Left Unfinished? Genesis 11:5 in Light of Hebrew Syntax, the Septuagint, and Jewish Reception," *Semitica* 63 (2021): 125–139. For more on this argument, see chapter 3. In other words, the story may have been composed for other reasons than explaining why the tower/ziggurat looked the way it did if Genesis 11:5 was meant to convey that it was a completed structure.

As a general methodological stance, comparison is what yields, in many ways, meaning itself. For representative statements of how comparison achieves this result, see J. Z. Smith, *Drudgery Divine: On the Comparison of Early Christianities and the Religions of Late Antiquity* (Chicago: University of Chicago Press, 1994); "In Comparison a Magic Dwells," in *Imagining Religion: From Babylon to Jonestown* (Chicago: University of Chicago Press, 1982), 23–33; Bruce Lincoln and Cristiano Grottenelli, "Theses on Comparison," in *Gods and Demons, Priests and Scholars: Critical Explorations in the History of Religions* (Chicago: University of Chicago Press, 2012), 121–130; Lincoln, *Apples and Oranges: Experiments in, on, and with Comparison* (Chicago: University of Chicago Press, 2018); Margaret M. Mitchell, "On Comparison, and Calling the Question," in *The New Testament in Comparison: Validity, Method and Purpose in Comparing Traditions*, ed. J. M. G. Barclay and B. G. Wright (New York: T&T Clark, 2020), 95–110. Naturally, some have criticized Smith's basic approach, but it remains the touchstone for academic research in the history of religions. For such criticisms, see Kimberly C. Patton and Benjamin C. Ray, eds., *A Magic Still Dwells: Comparative Religion in the Postmodern Age* (Berkeley: University of California Press, 2000). Indeed, as I hope to show, and as Uehlinger already demonstrated, a new meaning of the Tower of Babel also entails new avenues of comparison and generates new comparative data. The comparative data, in turn, provide further framing for the examination of Genesis 11:1–9 itself in chapter 3. Meaning, in this manner, and the comparative endeavor exist hand in hand, particularly in historically situated texts like the Bible. Naturally, the choice of what to compare to the Bible is an active one on my part but also a defensible and testable one, as I hope to demonstrate.

9 This shift opens up more lines of comparison than Uehlinger examined so well in his 1990 volume, and the presentation in this chapter both expands upon his analysis of rhetorical phrasing from Assyria as well as emphasizes aspects of key terms that Uehlinger did not explore as fully as possible. See, also, Andrew D. Giorgetti, "Building a Parody: Genesis 11:1–9, Ancient Near Eastern Building Accounts, and Production-Oriented Intertextuality," PhD Diss., Fuller Theological Seminary, 2017.

seems to be related to the phrasing in Genesis 11:1–9.[10] Yet language ideology was not part of Assyrian policy and is therefore not reflected in this
inscription. Despite this, the inscription nevertheless serves as an informative
comparative datum for understanding Genesis 11:1–9.[11] This specific example,
explored more below, highlights the rhetorical uses of a particular phrase in
Akkadian, a phrase that, properly understood, can illuminate the meaning
and function of idioms in the biblical text.

HISTORY AND MEANING, THE ANCIENT "THEM" AND MODERN "US"

As such, a justification for locating the story of the Tower of Babel during
the Neo-Assyrian expanse into the southern Levant can be convincingly
made, despite the connection to Babel/Babylon in the biblical text. Ratio-
nales exist for reading the political innovations in the mid- to late-eighth
century BCE as the motivation for the composition of the story in Genesis 11:1–9. One might argue that locating the biblical story in this time
period is speculative, and perhaps rehashes the origins fallacy (that what
it meant then should dictate what it means now). These considerations are
particularly important with such a ubiquitous story as the Tower of Babel,
one that broadly (in the traditional interpretation of Genesis 11:1–9) has
analogues in other cultures in which stories regarding the origins and
spread of distinct languages appear.[12] Yet as the history of the study of
the ancient Near East indicates, the authors of the Bible had particular

---

10 Mario Fales, "New Light on Assyro-Aramaic Interference: The Assur Ostracon," in
     *Camsemud 2007: Proceedings of the 13th Italian Meeting of Afro-Asiatic Linguistics:
     Held in Udine, May 21st-24th, 2007*, ed. Frederick Mario Fales and Giulia Francesca
     Grassi, HANE/M 10 (Padova: S.A.R.G.O.N., 2010), 189 n. 3.
11 This is so even if the reasons offered for the comparison in previous discussions were
     incorrect.
12 Arno Borst, *Der Turmbau von Babel: Geschichte der Meinungen über Ursprung und
     Vielfalt der Sprachen und Völker*, 6 vols. (Stuttgart: A. Hiersemann, 1957–1963). See
     R. Van Rooy for engagement with Borst on a number of Greek Christian thinkers
     and the reception of the Tower of Babel and perspectives on the origins of language
     in "'Πόθεν οὖν ἡ τοσαύτη διαφωνία;' Greek Patristic Authors Discussing Linguistic
     Origin, Diversity, Change and Kinship," *Beiträge zur Geschichte der Sprachwissen-
     schaft* 23 (2013): 21–54.

historical and social locations, and their stories and literatures are often reflective of these contexts.

A distinction between two concepts is helpful here: meaning versus significance.[13] Making historical claims about the Bible and the sense of a word or passage in the time and space when it was written involves meaning. In other words, the meaning of a text, even any ambiguity as part of its compositional origins, is a product of the grammar, conventions, and concerns of its historical environment, none of which changes over time, even if the significance that later readers apply to the text does. Having some sense of historical location of texts such as the Tower of Babel aids to clarify such meaning.[14] In the process, we will find that a narrative that centers around "Babel," or "Babylon," might even have justification for positing a better location for its composition, a location in a different place and time other than the Neo-Babylonian empire, despite the major role that "Babel" plays as a pun in the passage and despite the ever-present role for Babylon in subsequent biblical history and interpretation.

Naturally, it is disputable how much meaning and significance can be separated entirely from one another. One might argue that our conception of the meaning of a passage is necessarily framed by its reception, and the significance that interpreters have placed on it. Yet given the constantly refined, if still very imperfect, picture of the world in which the biblical texts were written, exploring Genesis 11:1–9 in the Neo-Assyrian context yields new insights into the meaning of the passage. In fact, a better sense of meaning can also create an improved sense on how the passage should

---

13 E. D. Hirsch, *Validity in Interpretation* (New Haven, CT: Yale University Press, 1967); "Meaning and Significance Reinterpreted," *Critical Inquiry* 11 (1984): 202–225; "Past Intentions and Present Meanings," *Essays in Criticism* 33 (1984): 79–98. For the application of Hirsch's distinction, as well as a helpful discussion of it in light of other approaches to interpretation (such as Gadamer), see John Barton, *The Nature of Biblical Criticism* (Louisville, KY: Westminster John Knox Press, 2007), 86–87.

14 See Hendel, "Historical Context," in *The Book of Genesis: Composition, Reception, and Interpretation*, ed. C. A. Evans, J. N. Lohr, and D. L. Peterson, VTSup 152 (Boston: Brill, 2012), 51–81. See also Hendel's use of Durkheim's statement that "every mythology 'is a morality and a cosmology, even as it is a history'" ("Sex, Honor, and Civilization in Genesis 1–11," in *With the Loyal You Show Yourself Loyal: Essays on Relationships in the Hebrew Bible in Honor of Saul M. Olyan*, ed. Tracy M. Lemos, Jordan D. Rosenblum, Karen B. Stern, and Debra S. Ballantine [Atlanta: SBL, 2021], 129–147, quote at 129). Hendel displays such attention to historical context in "Genesis 1–11 and Its Mesopotamian Problem," 23–36.

and should not function in the public sphere.[15] In other words, both the meaning derived from a passage in historical-critical scholarship and the significance of that same passage in religious and larger cultural and political discourse can challenge, converse with, and maybe even complement one another. In any case, if reading Genesis 11:1–9 in the context of specifically late-eighth- and early-seventh-century BCE Neo-Assyrian imperial rhetoric provides a better sense of the passage in its historical context and sheds new light on the biblical passage as it exists, then such a reading potentially shapes the way in which we investigate the presence of perennial questions about the story. It helps us to understand how these questions have been examined over the millennia. Finding surer footing on "what it meant" in the historical context of its production can, therefore, provide new ways of understanding issues of how Jewish and Christian (and, less so, Muslim) readers have interpreted the Tower of Babel to apply to their own time, including in modernity.[16]

It is difficult to date specifically when the Tower of Babel was written within the Neo-Assyrian period given larger historical and political developments in the ancient Near East. It is also difficult to determine which Mesopotamian king is targeted in its rhetoric (if a particular king is the focus at all), though sometime in the late eighth and early seventh centuries BCE is the most

---

15 See more in chapters 5 and 6.

16 In other words, I hope to avoid the "origins" fallacy of language in interpreting this passage. Any understanding of language as historically conditioned—having a historic environment in which utterances and writing are produced with a specific grammar for communication at a specific moment in history—also recognizes that the definitions and senses of words can change over time. For example, contrary to modern definitions, the English word "awful" used to refer to something that filled someone with awe, in a positive sense. For an anthology like the Bible, the historical context of production, for historical claims about the meaning of a passage, is significant since, as argued in Hirsch and Barton, meaning does not change over time. The grammar during the historical contexts of production is vital for determining meaning. The problem is when the origins fallacy couples with an etymological fallacy. When later readers interpret what a passage "meant," but by recourse to how those readers are familiar with language and translation without an awareness of the dynamics of language change over time, it creates problems for understanding a passage of the Bible. At the same time, simply because a passage "meant" something historically is not always determinative for later readers, since the only means for accessing the passage is the translation and tradition of interpretation that they have. Such is not the case with the Tower of Babel. My thanks to Jeffrey Stackert for thinking through this issue with me.

plausible timeframe.[17] Other parts of the Hebrew Bible show such dynamic, and intense, interaction with Assyrian ideology (such as Isaiah 1–39) that determining which passages may have been composed in specific decades of Assyrian engagements is possible.[18] Within the stock language of empire, one can also discern that different Assyrian kings used distinct rhetorical imagery and strategies, or highlighted aspects of Assyrian rhetoric to varying extents. To the degree that biblical literature meaningfully conforms to the use of these distinct tropes in specific periods, it is a constructive enterprise to explore how a given biblical passage makes sense historically in the light of certain Assyrian rhetoric. This sort of historical contextualization, then, provides the necessary backgrounding against which a new reading of the Tower of Babel emerges.

HISTORY AND POLITICS AS THE BACKGROUND FOR BIBLICAL LITERATURE

The year 744 BCE might not seem to most people as particularly momentous. It does not carry with it the same weight as other major world events in the popular imagination. Even for people with extensive knowledge of the Hebrew Bible, well-versed in the major moments of ancient Israel that accompany the study of the history lying behind and described in the biblical texts, 744 BCE does not register the same historical consequence as dates such as 701 BCE (Sennacherib's attack against Jerusalem) and 586 BCE (the Babylonian destruction of Jerusalem), among others.

Yet it was in this year that Tiglath-Pileser III came to the throne and began a programmatic expansion of Assyrian power and governance into Levantine

---

17 For the dating of other earlier legal and epic biblical sources to this general time period, see David Wright, *Inventing God's Law: How the Covenant Code of the Bible Reused and Revised the Laws of Hammurabi* (New York: Oxford University Press, 2009); "The Covenant Code Appendix (Exod 23:20–33), Neo-Assyrian Sources, and Implications for Pentateuchal Study," in *Formation of the Pentateuch: Bridging the Academic Cultures of Europe, Israel, and North America*, ed. Jan C. Gertz, Bernard M. Levinson, Dalit Rom-Shiloni, and Konrad Schmid, FAT 111 (Tübigen: Mohr Siebeck, 2016), 47–86; Samuel L. Boyd, "Exodus 21:35 and the Composition and Date of the Covenant Code," *WO* 48 (2018): 9–23.

18 Shawn Zelig Aster, *Reflections of Empire in Isaiah 1–39: Responses to Assyrian Ideology*, ANEM 19 (Atlanta: SBL Press, 2017).

territories, such as Israel and Judah.[19] These southern Levantine states had previously encountered Assyrian power, as evidenced in the Black Obelisk, in which Jehu, king of Israel, bows in obeisance to Shalmanesar III in the ninth century BCE. The Assyrian rulers in the decades after Shalmanesar were not able to sustain influence and project power in the western territories. With the ascension of Tiglath-Pileser III to the throne, however, the Assyrian empire inaugurated a new, systematic effort to project control in this region.[20]

In order to understand how the biblical authors generally might have been exposed to this ideology, and might reflect or subvert it in their writings, a brief discussion of key features of the rise, successes, and challenges posed by Neo-Assyrian rule for examining the connection between historical events in the late eighth and early seventh centuries BCE and the Tower of Babel narrative is helpful. How Neo-Assyrian kings constructed the rhetoric of governance highlights developments and innovations that explain important parts of Genesis 11:1–9. As such, understanding the advent of imperial ideology provides historical and theoretical backgrounds for describing how the Tower of Babel can fruitfully be interpreted in the Assyrian period.

The rise of the Neo-Assyrian empire from the ashes of the Middle Assyrian empire centuries prior to Tiglath-Pileser III necessitated new ways to craft a rhetoric of power. The so-called "Great Powers Club" of the Late Bronze Age created a political map in which a small number of large players dominated local populations.[21] As the Assyrians rebuilt and consolidated

---

19   For this coronation and the resulting policy of conquest of western territories from the perspective of Assyria, see Aster, *Reflections of Empire in Isaiah 1–39*, 1–7. See also Frahm, "The Neo-Assyrian Period (ca. 1000–609 BCE)," in *A Companion to Assyria*, ed. Eckart Frahm, Blackwell Companions to the Ancient World (Hoboken, NJ: John Wiley & Sons, 2017), 176–183; Ariel M. Bagg, "Assyria and the West: Syria and the Levant," in *A Companion to Assyria*, ed. Eckart Frahm, Blackwell Companions to the Ancient World (Hoboken, NJ: John Wiley & Sons, 2017), 268–274.

20   Pongratz-Leisten refers to Tiglath-Pileser III's efforts as the fourth, and last, phase of expansion of the Neo-Assyrian empire, which concluded with the "annexation of Egypt and Elam under Esarhaddon (680–669 BCE) and Ashurbanipal (668–631/27?)" (*Religion and Ideology in Assyria*, 174).

21   Amanda Podany, *Brotherhood of Kings: How International Relations Shaped the Ancient Near East* (New York: Oxford University Press, 2010); Marc van de Mieroop, *A History of the Ancient Near East, ca. 3000–323 BC*, 3rd ed., Blackwell History of the Ancient World (Malden, MA: Wiley Blackwell, 2015), 137–158. See also Amélie Kuhrt, *The Ancient Near East, c. 3000–330 BC: Volume I*, Routledge History of the Ancient World (New York: Routledge, 1997), 185–379; Kuhrt, *The Ancient Near East, c. 3000–330 BC: Volume II*, Routledge History of the Ancient World (New

their own imperial reach, they would encounter small states in a variety of locations, particularly in the southern Levant. These states were themselves the product of the formation of identity in the wake of the collapse of the Late Bronze Age palace economy and the faltering of large-scale imperial reach in the region.[22]

Governing this territory, either by conquest or other means, required new ways of communicating Assyrian ideology. Such ideology served to display how governed populations related to the central authority. In some cases, architectural features of Assyrian palaces display Assyrian kings' indebtedness to royal buildings in regions to the west, such as in Neo-Hittite territories and in the Levant, a fact that appears in inscriptions from Tiglath-Pileser III, Sargon, and Sennacherib.[23] In these sources, the kings describe their palaces as either a building in accordance with the "house of pillars," or *bīt ḫilāni*, pattern or, explicitly stated, as an "image of the palace of the land of Hatti." These emulations underscore the indebtedness of Assyrian kings to influences in Anatolia and the west.[24] At the same time, other palatial innovations were designed to reinforce the subject nature of conquered territories from these very regions. At the palace in Khorsabad/Dūr-Šarrukīn, Sargon had more reliefs constructed than typically existed in Assyrian palaces, many with depictions of subjugated peoples, led by their crown prince, all paying homage to the Assyrian king.[25] The effect was to remind subjugated peoples that they were subordinate to the king, and to increase the presence of the king himself, through his representation in the relief art throughout the palace. In this fashion, the king cast an image of himself as omnipresent. The impression was that Sargon ruled over an increasingly diverse and large empire, but

---

York: Routledge, 1997), 385–457 and, for the issue of the Assyrian expansion into the newly formed Levantine states that emerged after the collapse of the Late Bronze Age palace system, see 458–472.

22   Lawrence E. Stager, "Forging an Identity: The Emergence of Ancient Israel," in *The Oxford History of the Biblical World*, ed. Michael D. Coogan (New York: Oxford University Press, 2001), 90–131. For a general overview of this period, see Eric H. Cline, *1177 B.C.: The Year Civilization Collapsed* (Princeton, NJ: Princeton University Press, 2014).

23   Pongratz-Leisten, *Religion and Ideology in Assyria*, 52.

24   Pongratz-Leisten, *Religion and Ideology in Assyria*, 52.

25   For the turmoil of the early years of Sargon's reign and the possibility that western provinces were rebelling or considering rebellion (thereby making such ideology and presentation of the king necessary), see M. Cogan, "Restoring the Empire: Sargon's Campaign to the West in 720/719 BCE," *IEJ* 2 (2017): 151–167.

projected an image of royal capability to rise to the occasion and effectively organize and govern his expansive and varied domain.[26]

The materiality of this ideology was also backed by rhetoric, writing, and performance.[27] The exact goals of this engagement with peripheral territories, especially those in the southern Levant, remains unclear. Perhaps Assyria wanted to, in effect, "Assyrianize" its territories, or perhaps its goals were more pragmatic and less ambitious.[28] In either case, it is clear that Assyria desired, and to some extent achieved, a stability in many parts of its borders and along the fringes of the empire. Just as the phrase "Romanization" has been used to adapt the concept from Rome to one possible aim of Assyria ("Assyrianization"), so also, in any scenario of Assyrian intentions, the result has been compared to the *Pax Romana*, but labeled the *Pax Assyriaca*.[29]

This "peace" was realized on the foundation of other innovations, particularly those of Tiglath-Pileser III. Neo-Assyrians, through a number of strategies, reconceived of space within the empire through a multitude of innovations, all designed for the purpose of bringing together disparate parts of their territories and crafting them into a single, if also "imagined,"

---

26 See Kertai's discussion of the king, the crown prince, courtiers, and subject peoples bearing tribute within the palace reliefs and reliefs in the throne-room courtyard at Dūr-Šarrukīn (*The Late Assyrian Royal Palaces* [New York: Oxford University Press, 2015], 102–104).

27 On the issue of performance and influence of Assyrian ideology in the creation of biblical texts, particularly Deuteronomy, see Laura Quick, *Deuteronomy 28 and the Aramaic Curse Tradition*, Oxford Theology and Religion Monographs (Oxford: Oxford University Press, 2018); Melissa Ramos, *Ritual in Deuteronomy: The Performance of Doom*, Ancient World (London: Routledge, 2021).

28 See, for example, Ariel M. Bagg, "Palestine under Assyrian Role: A New Look at the Assyrian Imperial Policy in the West," *JAOS* 133 (2013): 119–144; Avraham Faust, "Settlement, Economy, and Demography under Assyrian Rule in the West: The Territories of the Former Kingdom of Israel as a Test Case," *JAOS* 135 (2015): 765–789. See also the various essays in Shawn Zelig Aster and Avaham Faust, ed., *The Southern Levant under Assyrian Domination* (University Park, PA: Eisenbrauns, 2018); Craig W. Tyson and Virginia R. Hermann, *Imperial Peripheries in the Neo-Assyrian Period* (Louisville: University Press of Colorado, 2018).

29 See, for example, F. M. Fales, "On *Pax Assyriaca* in the Eighth–Seventh Centuries BCE and Its Implications," in *Isaiah's Vision of Peace in Biblical and Modern International Relations: Swords into Plowshares*, ed. Raymond Cohen and Raymond Westbrook, Culture and Religion in International Relations (New York: Palgrave Macmillan, 2008), 17–35.

community.[30] The strategies involved infrastructure, such as the promotion of better water systems to enhance farming and food for the empire and the creation of roadways, which itself laid the framework for vast, efficient communication across space centuries after the Neo-Assyrian empire fell.[31] Not only were state rituals at the center enhanced but such rituals turned the king into the chief priest of Assur during the ceremonies.[32] Representatives from peripheral territories would have witnessed such ceremonies during their diplomatic visits, as was the case with Manasseh king of Judah who, according to Assyrian records, visited Assur.[33] When such provincial citizens returned home, they encountered other innovations of the Neo-Assyrians to cultivate a sense of imperial community. Capitals in the peripheries were renovated with an Assyrian style at times, and some such provincial centers

---

30 Pongratz-Leisten, *Religion and Ideology in Assyria*, 19. On the relationship between diversity and Neo-Assyrian imperial ambitions, see Jessie DeGrado, "King of the Four Quarters: Diversity as a Rhetorical Strategy of the Neo-Assyrian Empire," *Iraq* 81 (2019): 107–125.

31 Karl Moore and David Lewis, "Entrepreneurs of the Aegean," in *The Origins of Globalization*, Routledge International Studies in Business History (New York: Routledge, 2009), 137. See, especially, the legacy of Near Eastern roads on Rome in Grant Parker, "Environmental Perspectives on Ancient Communication," in *Mercury's Wings: Exploring Modes of Communication in the Ancient World*, ed. F. S. Naiden and Richard J. A. Talbert (New York: Oxford University Press, 2017), 13.

32 See the title of the Assyrian king, *šangû Aššur*, "priest of Assur," and Sargon II in Elayi, *Sargon II, King of Assyria*, 21. See the discussion of iconography presenting the Assyrian king as a priest of Assur in Mattias Karlsson, *Relations of Power in Early Neo-Assyrian State Ideology*, SANER 10 (Boston: De Gruyter, 2016), 87. See also Karlsson for the relationship in the office of the king between being high priest of Assur and the expanse of the Assyrian empire (*Relations of Power in Early Neo-Assyrian State Ideology*, 103, 109–110).

33 On such audiences with Assyrian royalty and exposure to Assyrian ideology, see Aster, "Transmission of Neo-Assyrian Claims of Empire to Judah in the Late Eighth Century BCE," *HUCA* 78 (2007): 1–44. For the primary source texts from Assyria during the reign of Esarhaddon that focus on Manasseh's visits and relationship to Assyria (from the Assyrian perspective, which "complement the biblical reports on Manasseh's reign" in 2 Kings 21:1–18), see Mordechai Cogan, *The Raging Torrent: Historical Inscriptions from Assyria and Babylon Relating to Ancient Israel*, 2nd ed. (Jerusalem: Carta Handbook, 2015), 151, 158, 161, 166, 181, and 182. See also Cogan for the possibility that Manasseh had an *adê* from Assyria in Jerusalem (*Bound for Exile: Israelites and Judeans under Imperial Yoke, Documents from Assyria and Babylonia* [Jerusalem: Carta Handbook, 2013], 55). Hans Ulrich Steymans has argued for a similar thesis given the 2009 discovery of an exemplar of VTE discovered at Tayinat ("Deuteronomy 28 and Tell Tayinat," *Verbum et Ecclesia* 32 [2013]: 1–13).

were on occasion given Assyrian toponyms.[34] Other features of Assyrian governance were designed to ensure the sense of enduring, and persistent, imperial existence. For example, the regular contributions such provinces were expected to make to the temple of Assur and the establishment of stelae at the entryways of subjugated cities reinforced the ever-present watchfulness of the Assyrian king, who himself was backed by the authority of the gods.[35] Finally, Tiglath-Pileser III restricted the earlier-existing provincial system, in effect demoting all the vassals of the Assyrian empire during his reign to provinces.[36] While Judah came into the orbit of Assyria after Tiglath-Pileser's time and remained a vassal, such a development in Assyrian governance produced at least two major changes that created a ripple effect perhaps evidenced in biblical literature itself, such as the Tower of Babel.

For instance, this restructuring massively increased Assyria's imperial territory.[37] Such a vast territory, incorporated fairly quickly, provided the empire with much-needed resources at its more direct disposal and oversight than would be the case were these areas to remain semi-autonomous vassals.[38] This act lengthened the shadow of the empire dramatically and in ways that assured Assyrian interests and presence in the southern Levantine territories, such as Judah. Yet this change also had the effect of creating internal instability, since such rapid growth also resulted in the increased power of high-ranking Assyrian bureaucracy. The power of Assyrian elites had prompted Tukulti-Ninurta already in the Middle Assyrian empire to create a new capital, and similar capital-building would occur for similar reasons in the reigns of other Assyrian kings, such as Sargon II.[39] These high-ranking bureaucrats had more

---

34 Liverani, *Assyria*, 234–238. See especially Pongratz-Leisten, "Toponyme als Ausdruck assyrischen Herrschaftsanspruchs," in *Ana šadî Labnāni lū allik: Beiträge zu altorientalischen und mittelmeerischen Kulturen, Festschrift für Wolfgang Röllig*, ed. Beate Pongratz-Leisten, Hartmut Kühne, and Paolo Xella, AOAT 247 (Neukirchen-Vluyn: Neukirchener Verlag, 1997), 325–343.

35 Pongratz-Leisten, *Religion and Ideology in Assyria*, 19.

36 Pongratz-Leisten, *Religion and Ideology in Assyria*, 19.

37 Pongratz-Leisten, *Religion and Ideology in Assyria*, 327.

38 For a state of the question and balanced assessment of the complexities of Assyrian extraction and economic stance toward its governed territories, including the potential of economic growth and development, see K. Lawson Younger, "The Assyrian Economic Impact on the Southern Levant in the Light of Recent Study," *IEJ* 65 (2015): 179–204.

39 For a discussion, see Boyd, "Place as Real and Imagined in Exile: Jerusalem at the Center of Ezekiel," in *Next Year in Jerusalem: Exile and Return in Jewish History*, ed.

power and wealth than ever before, making them an effective challenge to royal authority when their wishes and visions for Assyria did not align with those of the king.

Additionally, this change created new genres and new literary conventions within those genres. Massive intellectual effort was exerted to find ways to address these bureaucratic elites, to make them feel part of the imperial mission with the king at the helm, and to keep them subordinated to the royal authorities.[40] This was achieved, in part, through an innovation in royal inscriptions, which at times are presented as letters to the gods, or *Götterbriefen*. Kings on occasion would construct their inscriptions as a sort of divine communication, as attested in documents already from Shalmaneser IV's time (who reigned from 783–773 BCE).[41] This framing, often "to" (or, in Akkadian, *ana*) plus a series of divine names beginning with Assur, was not thought to transmit information or actual communication between the king and the divine realm. Instead, such an epistolary form was a rhetorical means to connect the divine realm of cosmic authority to the king, providing royal actions with divine approval.[42] Yet in the text describing Sargon's Eighth Campaign, the king also addresses, and solicits the approval of, the people of Assur. It is possible to contextualize this development within the realm of how the king and his scholars crafted subtle pieces of rhetoric to incorporate, if not also subdue, the interests of the bureaucratic elite in the Assyrian mission, led by Sargon himself.[43] On a pragmatic level, such changes in literary form could simply be seen as a way to deal with a newly empowered upper class that could challenge the king. On an ideological level, however, examples such as this display how political strategy, empire, royalty, and divinity were related, particularly in the late-eighth century BCE.[44] This cultural discourse of addressing a people and body politic clearly entered into

---

Leonard J. Greenspoon, Studies in Jewish Civilization (West Lafayette, IN: Purdue University Press, 2019), 3–4.

40 Pongratz-Leisten, *Religion and Ideology in Assyria*, 327.

41 Pongratz-Leisten, *Religion and Ideology in Assyria*, 327.

42 Pongratz-Leisten, *Religion and Ideology in Assyria*, 327.

43 Pongratz-Leisten, *Religion and Ideology in Assyria*, 327.

44 As Pongratz-Leisten states, "in their function as shapers of the Assyrian *Weltanschauung* and as managers of communication between the gods and the king, scholars had to create a cultural discourse that reflected Assyrian political achievements and harmonized them with the cosmic order so as to foster the illusion of absolute royal control." Pongratz-Leisten, *Religion and Ideology in Assyria*, 327.

biblical literature at about the same time, if not framing the origins of such literature altogether, an observation with obvious implications for discourse, such as in Genesis 11:1–9.[45]

Yet stability and peace were difficult to achieve, and even more difficult to maintain, in both the imperial center and on the peripheries. The threat of revolt was constant, whether by fully incorporated provinces or by semi-independent vassals, and required not only military might but also other ideological and rhetorical strategies to convince would-be rebels that any alliance against the king was treason and against the will of Assur.[46] This rhetoric was not created *de novo*, and the Neo-Assyrians leveraged phrasing from the Middle Assyrian kings.[47] The reappearance of these distinctly Assyrian tropes projected on to the Neo-Assyrian rulers created a sense of continuity with the past. Nonetheless, Neo-Assyrian kings innovated in two key ways. They could use phrasing and terminology from previous empires, particularly from Middle Assyrian rulers. This deployment of older idioms gave the Neo-Assyrian kings an aura of aforementioned continuity with the past.[48] Yet even in using older phrasing, Neo-Assyrian kings could employ them with more or less frequency and play with different shades of meanings.[49]

At the same time, and importantly, the Neo-Assyrian kings and their scribes could coin new phrases altogether.[50] Such innovations were necessary: the Neo-Assyrian empire encountered unprecedented situations in their constantly expanding empire, requiring new ways to think about authority

---

45 Sanders, *The Invention of Hebrew*.

46 See the discussion of the king as the agent of Assur, Assyrians as the population that accepts this obedience, and obedience as a concept expressed both abstractly ("respecting/fearing the word of Aššur and Marduk") and concretely in terms of "supplying taxes, tribute, and service; and foreswearing revolt and foreign alliances" in Machinist, "Assyrians on Assyria in the First Millennium B.C.," 102–103.

47 Machinist, "Assyrians on Assyria in the First Millennium B.C.," 91–92.

48 Machinist, "Assyrians on Assyria in the First Millennium B.C.," 91–92. Such continuity also appeared in physical form in the use of seals, as on the Tayinat exemplar of the Vassal Treaty of Esarhaddon, which contained three distinct seals from the Old, Middle, and Neo-Assyrian empires. For a discussion of these seals and their function in the context of VTE, see Lester, "The Material Transmission of Tradition in Deuteronomy," PhD Diss., Yale University, 2020, 116. Lester's dissertation is forthcoming in the VTSup series.

49 Machinist, "Assyrians on Assyria in the First Millennium B.C.," 92.

50 Machinist, "Assyrians on Assyria in the First Millennium B.C.," 92.

and governance.[51] One such particularly effective mechanism for governance was the Assyrian *adê*, variously translated as a "treaty," "loyalty oath," "work assignment/duty," or even "covenant." The word and institution associated with it were previously thought to originate in Aramaic and West Semitic cultures but have recently been identified as native, Assyrian terminology.[52] The influence in the west, however, is undeniable, particularly after the discovery in 2009 of an exemplar of the Vassel Treaty of Esarhaddon, abbreviated VTE, in the western periphery, though other treaty texts as with Baal of Tyre demonstrate the extent of reach of Assyrian governance implemented through this political instrument.[53]

The fact that Assyrian ideology could find its way into biblical literature, and the fact that changing political circumstances led to changing modes of communicating imperial rhetoric, appears in First Isaiah, or Isaiah 1–39. The variety of entanglements between Assyrian imperial reach, on the one hand, and the reaction to those imperial claims in Isaiah 1–39, on the other, reflect both a consistent pressure on the southern Levant in light of Assyrian expansion as well as dynamic reactions to it.[54] This time period of composition in Isaiah 1–39, from the late-eighth century BCE to the early-seventh century BCE, not only matches roughly the period in which the Tower of Babel was composed but also involves a period of time of successively strong Assyrian

---

51   See, for example, the manner in which the complex of Assyrian rituals could be performed and innovated given new territorial horizons. The rituals functioned as a means for understanding empire, space, and sacred topography in which "elements of mythology, ancestor worship, and theological visions of divinity" merged (Pongratz-Leisten, *Religion and Ideology in Assyria*, 392).

52   For the *adê* as Assyrian and not Aramaic in origin, see the discussion in Lauinger, "The Neo-Assyrian *adê*: Treaty, Oath, or Something Else?," *ZABR* 19 (2013): 100, 115; Radner "Assyrische *ţuppi adê* als Vorbild fur Deuteronomium 28,20–44?," in *Die deuteronomistischen Geschichtswerke: Redaktions- und religionsgeschichtliche Perspektiven zur"Deuteronomismus"-Diskussion in Tora und Vorderen Propheten*, ed. Markus Witte et al., BZAW 365 (New York: De Gruyter, 2006), 357; Radner, "Neo-Assyrian Treaties as a Source for the Historian: Bonds of Friendship, the Vigilant Subject, and the Vengeful King's Treaty," in *Writing Neo-Assyrian History: Sources, Problems, and Approaches*, ed. G. B. Lanfranchi, R. Mattila, and R. Rollinger, SAAS 29 (Helsinki: The Neo-Assyrian Text Corpus Project, 2019), 312; Boyd, *Language Contact, Colonial Administration, and the Construction of Identity in Ancient Israel: Constructing the Context for Contact*, HSM 66 (Boston: Brill, 2021), 145–155.

53   The literature on the *adê* is vast and will not be mentioned in detail here. For the 2009 discovery at Tayinat, see Lauinger, "Esarhaddon's Succession Treaty at Tell Tayinat: Text and Commentary," *JCS* 64 (2012): 87–123.

54   Aster, *Reflections of Empire in Isaiah 1–39*, 7–8.

kings, the so-called "Sargonids."[55] These kings not only expanded the territory of the empire westward but also dealt with rebellions and difficult-to-govern territories. To meet the changing realities of such governance, Assyrian kings employed a number of strategies, idioms, images, and rhetoric to convince such territories to remain subject (as either directly controlled territory or a vassal state) to Assyrian governance.

For the purposes of understanding better the Tower of Babel narrative in the Hebrew Bible, two things are notable. Other compositions composed during approximately the same time as the Tower of Babel was composed display similar responses to Assyrian ideology as exists also in Genesis 11:1–9. Additionally, and importantly, these responses were not singular. In other words, they do not pivot evenly between the poles of borrowing or rejection but display a number of responses, perhaps initiated by both changes in imperial communication as well as changes among the reactions of different groups in the governed.

Perhaps even more relevant for the political and historical background of the Tower of Babel episode, the underlying trajectory of Assyrian rhetoric was one of increasing stature of the king, one in which divine authority and the human realm merged in the person of the ruler. While the theme that the Assyrian king partakes in the divine knowledge of the gods occurs in the second millennium, it was greatly emphasized and promoted in the first millennium, especially in the inscriptions of the Sargonid kings. Mapping onto themes from the Standard Babylonian version of the Epic of Gilgamesh, Sargon II projected an image of himself as this archetypal strong king. Indeed, passages from Sargon's Eighth Campaign allude to Gilgamesh, framing the deeds of the Assyrian king as a sort of mythic hero.[56] Sargon also cast himself

---

55   The Sargonids are the kings following Sargon II, namely Sennacherib, Esarhaddon, and Ashurbanipal. See Elayi, *Sargon II, King of Assyria*, 3. Ashurbanipal, in his *Coronation Hymn*, appeals to Šamaš, the sun god and deity associated with justice, a divine entity that oversees all things. Ashurbanipal did so to convey his absolute authority. Connected to this association is an innovation that occurred in the time of Sargon II and the Sargonids: the concept of the king as judge. This concept was present in Old Assyrian ideology, but absent in the intervening period until the late-eighth and seventh centuries BCE. Pongratz-Leisten, *Religion and Ideology in Assyria*, 216. The emphasis on this idea of king as the ultimate judge is perhaps another datum relevant for plotting the critiques of Assyrian ideology, overstepping of royal powers, and broaching divine prerogative in the Tower of Babel, explored more below and in chapters 3 and 4 of this book.

56   For a more extensive study on the manner in which passages from the Gilgamesh Epic were incorporated into Sargon's Eighth Campaign as an ideological strategy to

as a sort of primordial sage like Adapa, and he drew parallels between his building activity at Dūr-Šarrukīn and the creative acts of Marduk, the high god of the Babylonian pantheon.[57] In some sense, these rhetorical moves not only make the king bigger and greater but mythic and encroaching on the divine. It is precisely this sort of infringement on the divine that is on display in Genesis 11:1–9, and one reason offered in Mesopotamian texts for the fact that Sargon's body was never recovered in war (since he transgressed divine prerogative in city-building).

When set in this background, the possibility that the Tower of Babel episode and the literary context in which it was written came into formation in the eighth century BCE or shortly thereafter becomes more intriguing.[58] To be certain, dating biblical texts by recourse to how themes in those passages match historical events is a fraught enterprise. Yet when a constellation of

---

buttress the expansion of the borders of Assyria in the model of mythological heroes, see Johannes Bach, "Royal Literary Identity Under the Sargonids and the Epic of Gilgameš," *WO* 50 (2020): 318–338.

57 See Pauline Albenda for the innovations involved in the construction of this capital ("Dur-Sharrukin, the Royal city of Sargon II, King of Assyria," *BCSMS* 38 [2003]: 5–13).

58 One of the difficulties that has been raised concerning the placement of Genesis 11:1–9 in the Assyrian period and making comparisons with Sargon's capital building campaign is the issue of access: how would a Judean audience, responsible for the composition and editing of much of the Bible, be aware of such a construction so early, when it was the northern kingdom that was exiled in the Assyrian period and not the southern kingdom? While the relationship between the north and the south is a large and complicated topic, and while there is no necessary correlation that the experiences of the north would be known to or relevant for the south, it is notable at least that Israelite deportees generally had gained some access to the upper echelons of Assyrian society in Sargon's time, and, more specifically, that Sargon used deportees from the northern kingdom to construct Dūr-Šarrukīn. Sargon mentions that he used deported peoples from Samaria from the north in his construction of Dūr-Šarrukīn, providing one possible, though by no means certain, avenue whereby the city building campaign, and all the ideological issues involved, would have become known to authors of the biblical text. A fragmentary letter exists to the king, which states: "concerning what the king, my lord, wrote to me: 'Provide all the Samarians in your hands with work in Khorsabad,' I subsequently sent word to the sheikhs, saying: 'Collect your carpenters and potters; let them come and direct the deportees who are in Khorsabad.'" For this fragment, and for the use of deportees to construct Dūr-Šarrukīn, see Elayi, *Sargon II, King of Assyria*, 204. For more on Israelite and Judean deportees in various settlements and record of their activities in Mesopotamia, see Bustenay Oded, "The Settlements of the Israelite and the Judean Exiles in Mesopotamia in the 8th–6th Centuries BCE," in *Studies in Historical Geography and Biblical Historiography: Presented to Zechariah Kallai*, ed. Gershon Galil and Moshe Weinfeld, VTSup 81 (Boston: Brill, 2000), 91–103.

evidences emerge, giving rise to consilience, one can find that the most satisfying explanation for the odd locutions in Genesis 11:1–9, the theme of city-building (which is more dominant than the tower in the passage, the latter of which was completed according to the grammar in Genesis 11:5) and the unease about encroaching on the divine territory makes sense in the Neo-Assyrian empire in a way that other dating options do not. This observation is not meant to demonstrate or prove this dating to the exclusion of considerations for what significance Genesis 11:1–9 held in the context of subsequent historical periods. Indeed, rereading and supplementing the passage also are vital for historical analysis of the Tower of Babel narrative given the changing imperial regimes into the Neo-Babylonian and Persian periods. Rather, the manner in which the Neo-Assyrian kings, particularly the Sargonids (and especially Sargon II), expanded their territory westward toward the southern Levant and communicated their royal ideologies with sophisticated rhetoric bent on elevating royal power to previously unheard of heights certainly made inroads into Judah and Jerusalem. This development is clear in First Isaiah and the Tower of Babel. It is necessary, then, to explain how a story about "Babel" could actually refer to Assyria, and how an examination of specific examples of Assyrian rhetoric can explain the peculiar phrasing in Genesis 11:1–9. Against the relief of this historical background, other considerations about the phrasing of the Tower of Babel passage itself and key observations about the Hebrew therein gain more traction.

FINDING BABEL IN ASSYRIA:
Dūr-Šarrukīn, Babylon, and the Tale of Two Cities

A variety of evidences, then, connect the rhetoric of the Neo-Assyrian empire to the concerns expressed in Genesis 11:1–9. Neo-Assyrian kings, in constructing their peculiar idioms of empire, used a constellation of phraseology involving "one speech," "city and citadel," "name-making," and "one people" in a manner that corresponds to motifs in the Tower of Babel episode. One could argue that this correspondence was not mere coincidence. Rather, these shared themes appear both in Neo-Assyrian inscriptions and Genesis 11:1–9, but not in other known literary sources. The assemblage of themes in Neo-Assyrian sources and Genesis 11:1–9 means that a plausible, if not convincing, historical situation for the composition of the latter was in the Neo-Assyrian context.[59]

Other clues in the biblical text further support this thesis. For example, the way in which Nimrod in Genesis 10:8–12 is described as a mighty hunter resembles uniquely Assyrian motifs.[60] Since both Genesis 10:8–12 and Genesis 11:1–9 belong to the same source, called J, one could argue that each has broadly the same historical horizon for their composition. Given the Assyrian interest in western, Levantine territories—perhaps most famously indicated in Sennacherib's invasion of Judah in 701 BCE, and in the presence of an Assyrian garrison at Ramat Raḥel—Nimrod's name itself, meaning "let us rebel," is significant.[61]

The figure of Nimrod has been a pivotal one in the exegetical imagination concerning the Tower of Babel. Though not mentioned in Genesis 11:1–9, in the passage's narrative context, J, he functions as the first mighty giant (or *gibbor* in Hebrew) on earth in Genesis 10:8, whose appearance calls to mind illicit divine-human relations that produced giants in Genesis 6:1–4 and whose presence heralds chaos before a disaster. Much like the episode in Genesis 6:1–4, in which similar characters—also giants— appear before the flood, Nimrod's presence raises interpretive puzzles: if he was the first giant, and giants were part of the pre-flood landscape, perhaps Nimrod somehow survived the flood. It could be the case that his presence in Genesis 10:8–12 augurs disaster, much as the story of such giants and their origins did so in Genesis 6:1–4.[62] To the degree that the episode in Genesis 10:8–12 is connected narratively to Genesis 11:1–9, both passages provide some basis for seeing the events therein related to southern Mesopotamia, closer to Babylon. Nimrod is said to be a founder of Babel (Genesis 10:10), an obvious connection to the story in Genesis 11:1–9.[63] Another toponym that locates these passages

---

59   Uehlinger, *Weltreich und "Eine Rede,"* 516–519.

60   W. Lambert, "Assyrien und Israel," in *Theologische Realenzyklopädie 4*, ed. Gerhard Krause and Gerhard Müller (Berlin: De Gruyter, 1979), 272; A. van der Kooij, "The City of Babel and Assyrian Imperialism: Genesis 11:1–9 Interpreted in the Light of Mesopotamian Sources," in *Congress Volume Leiden 2004*, ed. André Lemaire, VT-Sup 109 (Leiden: Brill, 2006), 12.

61   Hendel, "Gen 1–11 and Its Mesopotamian Problem," 30–31.

62   Doak, *The Last of the Rephaim*, 53–70.

63   As explored in chapter 5, an interpretive tradition exists in some areas of Syriac Christianity in which this notice of Nimrod's building activities actually transforms his character into one of virtue. According to Ephraim the Syrian, while Nimrod may have built Babel in the land of Shinar, one reading of Genesis 10:11 is that

in southern Mesopotamia is Shinar, likely a term from Akkadian *Šanḫarra*, referring to southern Mesopotamia as well.[64]

The issue arises regarding how to explain why the story is about Babel, or Babylon, if Genesis 11:1–9 was composed in an Assyrian context, and how to illuminate why the narrator provides the further context for the events in the "plain of the land of Shinar." The connection could simply be a natural extension of telling the story of Nimrod. Though the latter character is Assyrian in his actions as a hunter, the tradition in the Bible lists Babel as the first city he founded. Given this priority, and given the prestige of Babylon and its ziggurat generally, one might claim that the episode of the city and tower was set in Babylon even though the biblical tale was composed in the Assyrian period. In fact, it has been posited that the city that Nimrod built in Genesis 10:12, Resen, may be a reference, however faint, to Sargon's short-lived capital Dūr-Šarrukīn.[65] Further, a particular literary shift in the

---

Nimrod is the subject of the verb "to go out," not Assur. This verse may, then, describe Nimrod's act of fleeing the events in Babel, understood as an attempt to distance himself from the transgressions on the divine that occurred in the city.

64   Toorn and P. W. van der Horst, "Nimrod Before and After the Bible," 2–4; Levin, "Nimrod the Mighty, King of Kish, King of Sumer and Akkad," *VT* 52 (2002): 350–366; Day, "The Tower and City of Babel Story," 171. See Berlejung, who has a discussion of Shinar in "Living in the Land of Shinar: Reflections on Exile in Genesis 11:1–9?," in *The Fall of Jerusalem and the Rise of Torah*, ed. Peter Dubovský, Dominik Markl, and Jean-Pierre Sonnet, FAT 107 (Tübigen: Mohr Siebeck, 2016), 89–111. She advocates for a Persian period for the composition of Genesis 11:1–9 given that during this period, Babylon and its ziggurat Etemenanki lay in ruins. Moreover, she argues that Genesis 11:1–9 functions as an addition, a bridge of sorts, connecting the Primeval and patriarchal stories. See further below and in the next chapter for arguments that (1) the grammar of the Hebrew in Genesis 11:5 describes a completed tower, and the city is what is left unfinished, and (2) arguments against the idea that Genesis 11:1–9 is redactional or editorial but rather key and vital for non-P's or J's story line. Berlejung's general approach to the narrative as one not about diversity of human language but rather as about human action and intent, however, is generally correct, insightful, and persuasive. See more in chapter 3 about Berlejung's assessment of שפה, which is consistent with the thesis of this book. For more on how Shinar came to refer to the entire region of Babylonia, or southern Mesopotamia, see Beaulieu, "What's in a Name? Babylon and Its Designations throughout History," *BCSMS* 17 (2019): 34.

65   Carr argues that Resen as a place name here stands as a critique of Neo-Assyrian capital building. The author of Genesis 10:8–12 could not have mentioned Dūr-Šarrukīn as a city in primeval times since Dūr-Šarrukīn was connected to Sargon II specifically in the eighth century BCE. Instead, the biblical author makes reference to Resen, a place perhaps near Dūr-Šarrukīn, and lists these primeval sites—Babylon,

presentation of Nimrod occurs, from a positive and revered hunter in the mold of Sargon of Akkad (with virtuous characteristcs) to an insertion of a negative and critical tone depicting the king as a megalomaniac, infringing on the divine, not unlike the reputation that Sargon II had in some ancient sources.[66] In light of this shift, it lends further weight to the idea of both northern Mesopotamian (namely, Assyrian) and southern Mesopotamian (namely, Babylonian) influence on the biblical text, providing license for the comparative study of Genesis 11:1–9 in an Assyrian context, even if the story is located in Babel and Shinar.

Further evidence can be seen in the analysis of the Tower of Babel as a text from the Assyrian times, though concerned with Babylon. If one posits that the narrative depicts an unfinished tower, then Genesis 11:1–9 may portray, in its material description, the state of the ziggurat in Babylon during the late eighth and perhaps early seventh centuries BCE.[67] This historical depiction

---

Uruk, Akkad, and Resen—as predating Assyrian kings and constructed by far greater figures from the past. In this fashion, the author of Genesis 11 puts Assyrian kings in historical perspective, and in their place. On the location of Resen, see Hurowitz, "In Search of Resen (Genesis 10:12): Dūr-Šarrukīn?," in *Birkat Shalom: Studies in the Bible, Ancient Near Eastern Literature, and Post-Biblical Judaism Presented to Shalom M. Paul on the Occasion of His Seventieth Birthday*, ed. Chaim Cohen et al. (Winona Lake, IN: Eisenbrauns, 2008), 511–524. Carr, *Genesis 1–11*, IECOT (Stuttgart: Kohlhammer, 2021), 298.

66 Knohl places this shift in the reign of Sargon II, building on the works of Uehlinger and van de Mieroop. Knohl, "Nimrod, Son of Cush, King of Mesopotamia, and the Dates of P and J," in *Birkat Shalom: Studies in the Bible, Ancient Near Eastern Literature, and Post-Biblical Judaism Presented to Shalom M. Paul on the Occasion of His Seventieth Birthday*, ed. Chaim Cohen et al. (Winona Lake, IN: Eisenbrauns, 2008), 45–52.

67 For general arguments for the Neo-Assyrian context for the production of Nimrod and Tower of Babel stories, see Carr, *The Formation of Genesis 1–11: Biblical and Other Precursors* (New York: Oxford University Press, 2020), 238–242. For the incomplete nature of the ziggurat in the time of Esarhaddon and Assurbanipal, until the reign of Nabopolassar, see George, "The Tower of Babel," 79–80. As George points out, discussions have assumed that Esarhaddon and Assurbanipal used mudbricks, *libittu*, as part of their building. If that were true, it would bring the description of the tower closer to the biblical account, which describes לבנים, a cognate to the Akkadian term. The Assyrian kings, however, use a different term in their inscriptions: *agurru*, "baked brick." The ziggurat in Babylon likely had a mudbrick core, which Assyrian kings layered with baked brick, and later finished with mudbrick by Babylonian kings. The Assyrian phrase is still not far from the biblical text, which describes both לבנים and the fire-burning process of baking (נשׂרפה לשׂרפה). As argued in this chapter and in the next, any understanding of the tower misses,

exists in two possible ways. As is well known, the northern Assyrian kings variously destroyed and rebuilt Babylon, with the result that this southern Mesopotamian city eventually had a design and layout that matched northern conventions.[68] It was during the Neo-Assyrian period that the ziggurat in Babylon began to be rebuilt with fired bricks (as in Genesis 11:3), providing one possible anchor for setting the story, if the interpretation centers more on the tower, in the Assyrian period generally.[69] Additionally, the construction of the ziggurat took place in starts and stops over the course of many decades, which could be reflected itself in the narrative of Genesis 11:1–9 if one understands the tower, alongside the city, to be unfinished.[70] Yet grammatically, this scenario is not as helpful for dating the story. According to the grammar of the Hebrew, the tower was actually depicted as completed, in which case the focus of the story and the only building project left incomplete is the city.[71] One might, in this interpretation, have even more license for setting the passage in an Assyrian context: the act of building a city was considered to be a divine prerogative. Traditions existed in which Sargon was thought to have violated that divine authority, explaining why his body was not recovered in battle.[72] Yet such a line of thought would also match nicely with the main issue in the biblical passage (and throughout the source to which the passage belongs). Tragedy happens when humans transgress the boundary of divine authority. So with Dūr-Šarrukīn, so with Babel.

In this fashion, Neo-Assyrian kings not only developed rhetoric, imagery, and literary and artistic motifs to provide justification to expand and to organize the empire but, in doing so, they also met with resistance. For example, texts from Sargon II's time indicate a dissatisfaction with the king's building campaign, specifically the Weidner Chronicle from Babylon. Several

---

to some degree, the actual rhetoric of the passage since the grammar of the Hebrew describes a completed tower, and since the focus of the divine wrath seems to be directed against the city. See the note below for Vanderhooft's and Richelle's articles on the completed tower and in chapter 3 for this thesis.

68   Paul-Alain Beaulieu, "Nebuchadnezzar's Babylon as World Capital," *Journal for the Canadian Society of Mesopotamian Studies* 3 (2008): 10.

69   See the note above.

70   See George for a more complete history of the phases of construction of the ziggurat ("Tower of Babel," 75–95).

71   Vanderhooft, "Babylon as Cosmopolis in Israelite Texts and Achaemenid Architecture," 43–50; Richelle, "Was the Tower of Babel Really Left Unfinished?," 125–139. Chapter 3 contains a much more extensive discussion as to why this is the case.

72   See further below.

key elements of criticism correspond to themes in Genesis 11:1–9. Assyrian kings had long taken credit for the construction of buildings, but did not ever claim credit for the founding of cities *per se*.[73] The act of selecting the site for a new capital was the prerogative of the divine realm. In contrast, Sargon claimed credit for the identification of the location of his capital Dūr-Šarrukīn, comparing himself to the sage Adapa in the process, in addition to the construction of the capital buildings (part of a massive building campaign generally). Even the dimensions of the city contained proportions that called to mind his name, ensuring that the mathematical computation of the height and extent of the walls around the capital encoded and enshrined, in numerological fashion, his place in history.[74] The founding of the city had cosmological significance as well, and Sargon inscribed the language of creation from the *Enūma Eliš* in his description of his new capital.[75] Sargon, then, not only created a parallel between himself and Adapa but between himself and the creative acts of Marduk.

This building act and the rhetoric that accompanied it were met with criticism.[76] The Babylonian Weidner Chronicle was likely written in the Neo-Assyrian period, possibly to criticize Sargon II's building campaign.[77] Additionally, Assyrian cities and Babylon drew comparisons during this same period, at times resulting in an interchange between cities like Nineveh

---

73 Marc Van de Mieroop, "Literature and Political Discourse in Ancient Mesopotamia: Sargon of Assyria and Sargon of Agade," in *Munuscula Mesopotamica: Festschrift für Johannes Renger*, ed. Barbara Böck, Eva Cancik-Kirschbaum, and Thomas Richter, AOAT 267 (Munster: Ugarit-Verlag, 1999), 335–338.

74 Van de Mieroop, "Literature and Political Discourse in Ancient Mesopotamia," 335–336, on Sargon's statement regarding the measurements: "16,280 cubits, the numeral of my name, I established as the measure of its wall and I set its foundation on a solid bedrock." See also Beate Pongratz-Leisten's excellent analysis of Sargon's building campaign within the rhetoric of the construction of capitals in the Neo-Assyrian empire (*Religion and Ideology in Assyria*, 181–191).

75 Pongratz-Leisten, *Religion and Ideology in Assyria*, 189.

76 As Beate Pongraz-Leisten argues, "founding a new city was considered a primordial act of creation by the gods; when performed by a king, it was regarded as an act of hubris." Pongratz-Leisten, *Religion and Ideology in Assyria*, 191.

77 Van de Mieroop, "Literature and Political Discourse in Ancient Mesopotamia," 338–339. Jennifer Finn has recently argued that the dirt removal mentioned in the Weidner Chronicle as part of royal, palatial construction refers not to Sargon's building but rather to Sennacherib's destruction of Babylon (*Much Ado About Marduk: Questioning Discourses of Royalty in First Millennium Mesopotamian Literature*, SANER 16 [Boston: De Gruyter, 2017], 130–138).

and Babylon in a variety of literary texts from this time, perhaps due to their similar sizes.[78] This interchange, if Genesis 11:1–9 represents a critique of Assyrian imperialism, could explain how the Tower of Babel episode in the Hebrew Bible could have been written during the Neo-Assyrian empire and used Babylon instead of an Assyrian city. Indeed, later classical and biblical authors at times also interchanged the Assyrian capital Nineveh with Babylon.[79]

Given the distinctive themes in both Sargon II's inscriptions and the Tower of Babel, the criticisms seen in the Weidner Chronicle attacking Sargon's hubris for taking the divine right of founding a city has obvious correlations to the Tower of Babel episode. Just as the builders of the tower met with divine wrath, so also Sargon II's untimely death was interpreted as an act of divine retribution in another source, called the *Sin of Sargon* text.[80] Therefore, a variety of features of, and developments in, Neo-Assyrian politics and history, particularly during and after Sargon II's reign, may be reflected in Genesis 11:1–9.[81]

The interpretative act of finding a plausible historical circumstance for a biblical narrative and then dating the narrative to that historical time, however, is often a risky enterprise.[82] Nonetheless, additional evidence exists that Genesis 11:1–9 may come from the Neo-Assyrian period. When the book of Deuteronomy retells narrative material from Exodus through Numbers, it does so in correspondence to the strands or sources that scholars have

---

78 Finn, *Much Ado about Marduk*, 135 n. 340.

79 For more historical background on the manner in which later classical and biblical authors confused Babylon and Nineveh, see S. Dalley, "Nineveh, Babylon and the Hanging Gardens: Cuneiform and Classical Sources Reconciled," *Iraq* 56 (1994): 45–58; Dalley, "Babylon as a Name for Other Cities Including Nineveh," in *Proceedings of the 51st Rencontre Assyriologique Internationale 2005*, ed. R. D. Biggs, J. Myers, and M. T. Roth, SAOC 62 (Chicago: Oriental Institute, 2008), 25–34.

80 Sargon's death may have also been the occasion for scribal alteration of the Gilgamesh Epic. See Eckart Frahm, "Nabû-Zuqup-Kēnu, das Gilgameš-Epos, und der Tod Sargons II," *JCS* 51 (1999): 73–90.

81 Carr, *Genesis 1–11*, 298. For general thoughts on multilingualism in the ancient world, connecting Sargon II's rhetoric with the Tower of Babel (though still seeing the latter as an etiology for multilinguaulism), see Marco Santini, "Languages, Peoples, and Power: Some Near Eastern Perspectives," *Chatreššar* 4 (2021): 5–39.

82 Sommer, "Dating Pentateuchal Texts and the Dangers of Pseudo-Historicism," in *The Pentateuch: International Perspectives on Current Research*, ed. Thomas B. Dozeman, Konrad Schmid, and Baruch J. Schwartz, FAT 78 (Tübingen: Mohr Siebeck, 2011), 85–108.

identified as either J or E—in other words, in texts that show composite authorship and the combination of literary sources in Exodus through Numbers, Deuteronomy (or, the portions identified as the D source) repeats only one or another source, but never the compiled narrative. Given the likelihood that Deuteronomy, or at least some portion of it, dates to the seventh century BCE due to correlations with the Vassal Treaty of Esarhaddon and the political concerns in D, then the literary material used in Deuteronomy would also likely derive from the Neo-Assyrian period.[83] Caution is in order, as none of the material (and certainly not the Tower of Babel narrative) from Genesis appears in D; nonetheless, D's use of material from Exodus to Numbers places at least part of the latter in the Neo-Assyrian timeframe. If those reused literary materials in D were part of continuous sources, then J, which contains the Tower of Babel narrative, would be within Neo-Assyrian chronology.[84]

Though conjectural, one might also suppose that, in light of the Assyrian shadow cast over Judah, tales of resistance against the northern Mesopotamian empire might use a different entity as a focus of narratives of imperial critique.[85] Making Babylon the focus, particularly given Assyria's so-called "Babylon problem," might allow Judeans to craft a criticism of Assyrian hegemony without raising suspicions.[86] In any event, it is clear that a solid foundation exists for countering some of the critiques against setting the Tower of Babel in the Neo-Assyrian period.[87]

---

83 On D, see Stackert, *Deuteronomy and the Pentateuch*, AYBRL (New Haven, CT: Yale University Press, 2022), 134–158.

84 See August Dillmann, *Die Bücher Numeri, Deuteronomium, und Joshua*, Kurzgefasstes exegetisches Handbuch zum Alten Testament 13 (Leipzig: S. Hirzel, 1886), 609–611, 679; Joel S. Baden, "Deuteronomic Evidence for the Documentary Theory," in *The Pentateuch: International Perspectives on Current Research*, ed. Thomas B. Dozeman, Konrad Schmid, and Baruch J. Schwartz, FAT 78 (Tübingen: Mohr Siebeck, 2011), 327–344.

85 Another example of cloaked critiques of Sargon may appear in Isaiah 14. An unnamed ruler, but ascribed to be the king of Babylon, is said to have been haughty with aspirations to reach the heavens, yet will die away from his grave (Isaiah 14:19). The similarities with Sargon, who died in battle and whose body was not recovered, are manifest.

86 See J. A. Brinkman, "Sennacherib's Babylon Problem: An Interpretation," *JCS* 25 (1973): 89–95; Machinist, "The Assyrians and Their Babylonian Problem: Some Reflections," *Jahrbuch des Wissenschaftskolleg zu Berlin* (1984–85), 353–364.

87 For example, Gertz argues against Uehlinger's thesis that parts of Genesis 11:1–9 originate in Sargon II's time. Gertz claims that the presence of Babel and Shinar in Genesis 11:1–9 means that one can read the text as originating in the Neo-Assyrian

Good rationale exists, then, for reading the Tower of Babel episode in light of events in the history of the Neo-Assyrian empire. Such a choice might seem counterintuitive, yet the focus on the city in Genesis 11:1–9, which is mentioned three times whereas the tower is mentioned only twice, makes good sense in light of occurrences in Neo-Assyrian history that seem peculiar to that period.[88] It was during that same time that the empire crafted rhetoric to meet new challenges in light of its rapid expansion. Yet further investigation into the specific acts of creating idioms for political purposes in Neo-Assyrian inscriptions reveals even more facets of correspondence to the Tower of Babel. An examination of a particular phrase that has been compared to the odd locution in Genesis 11:1 and 11:6 highlights how the

---

era only through replacing these explicit toponyms with "extra-textual references," a scenario that Gertz does not think is plausible. Gertz, *Das erste Buch Mose (Genesis): Die Urgeschichte Gen 1–11*, Das Alte Testament Deutsch, Neues Göttinger Bibelwerk 1 (Göttingen: Vandenhoeck & Ruprecht, 2018), 333–334. Yet given the historical fact that Babylon was used for a variety of locations as a sort of "stand-in" term to describe their prestige means that Uehlinger's proposal is not as far-fetched as Gertz makes it seem, though it also renders unnecessary some of the diachronic aspects of Uehlinger's argument (namely, that Babel was inserted at a later period). Gertz also argues that no allusion to military might or Assyrian world domination functions as a background to the biblical text. Yet read in light of prerogatives of city building and the limits of human, specifically royal, authority for such construction projects, these themes of domination come into view more clearly when the Tower of Babel passage is set in the context of Sargon's building campaigns. Indeed, a connection appears even more so if one also relates the figure of Nimrod in Genesis 10:8–12 to Genesis 11:1–9 (see more below and in subsequent chapters). In this manner, bringing previously undiscussed aspects of Assyrian royal and imperial ideology to the examination of this passage, or highlighting observations that have previously been proposed but doing so in new light, can address criticisms against the thesis that the Tower of Babel was composed during the Neo-Assyrian period generally, if not in the wake of Sargon II specifically.

88 Richelle helpfully articulates how understanding the tower as completed reframes the "problem" of Babel and the implications of this thesis:

> In addition, it now seems less pertinent, in order to date the text, to look for a period in the history of the tower when its construction was interrupted. The most natural reading of the text would rather lead us to look for a time when a more general problem in the city, related to building work, happened. It is not easy to see what this could correspond to in the history of Babylon, and perhaps it would be wiser to accept the simple fact that the text speaks only in very general terms.

Richelle, "Was the Tower of Babel Really Left Unfinished?," 138. As argued in this chapter, the Neo-Assyrian background of city building in the late eighth and early seventh centuries BCE provides just such an appropriate background for this new understanding of the Tower of Babel story.

biblical idioms function in much the same way as the Assyrian phrasing does. Each historical consideration, in isolation and on its own terms, does not prove the Assyrian provenance of the Tower of Babel story. Together as a collection of evidences, however, they provide a meaningful context in which to make sense of biblical passage, both in terms of the idiosyncratic wording therein and in terms of its place in its literary source material.

MATTERS OF THE MOUTH:
Political Idioms and the Projection of Authority

Rapid expansion of imperial borders entailed new challenges of governance. These challenges, in turn, necessitated the aforementioned innovations in the manner in which the empire communicated its mission and ambitions. Idioms, rhetoric, and projection of imperial ideology into literary texts provided the means through which such obstacles were addressed. The Neo-Assyrian empire deployed the power of metaphor through certain phrasings, and, in doing so, made labels like "Assyrian" into wide nets in which it cast a political category and identity over a variety of governed peoples. By doing so, the empire was also able to project a sense of obedience due to the king and the imperial mission over vast and diverse populations.[89] Key changes in phrasing in royal inscriptions display the manner in which ideology and rhetoric conveyed, in literary terms, how the Assyrian center related to its territories.

In some fashion, this use of phrasings and metaphors to evoke how the king related to his subjects in royal inscriptions is nothing new. Already in the Old Babylonian period, kings used royal epithets that employed such metaphors of governance. For example, both Hammurabi and Samsuiluna called themselves "the king who puts the four quarters at peace."[90] More

---

89 Indeed, Pongratz-Leisten has argued that the "literarization of the empire" involved leveraging certain metaphors for the sake of projecting power and meeting new obstacles. Pongratz-Leisten, *Religion and Ideology in Assyria*, 174–181. As she states, "political developments deeply affected the metaphorical language used in the discourse of royal ideology." Citing the work of Machinist and adding her own analysis of data, Pongratz-Leisten demonstrates the manner in which Assyria incorporated conquered territories, using terms and phrases in a manner that demonstrates that "Assyrian" is less an ethnic label and more of a political category. This category identified those people and territories "that manifest the required obedience" to the Assyrian empire.

90 See Douglas Frayne, *Old Babylonian Period (2003–1595 B.C.)*, RIME 4 (Toronto: University of Toronto Press, 1990), Ha inscriptions 4 and 9; Si inscription 8. See also the Laws Hammurabi, law 10.

woodenly, one could translate the phrase as "the king who makes people listen," though perhaps the translation "the king who makes Sumer and Akkad be of one mind" most adequately renders the idea.[91] The concept is not about literal "hearing" or "listening," as the root employed in Akkadian (*šemû*) might imply, but rather about obedience and unification.

Yet such metaphors of the ears as instruments of obedience, as well as the mouth, particularly in the context of the rise of Aramaic in Assyria beginning in the eighth-century BCE, could at times be interpreted to refer specifically to language. One of the foremost pieces of evidence along these lines has been Sargon II's Dūr-Šarrukīn cylinder inscription, in which he mentions the role of administrators and overseers in an attempt to consolidate his empire and allegedly to "impose one mouth" (*pâ ištēn šuškunu*) on rebellious groups. This last phrase has similarities to the wording in Genesis 11:1 and 11:6.[92] Though ultimately not an idiom that conveys language or an imperial goal to promote or impose a particular dialect, understanding the rhetoric of this phrase in its context sheds important light on the meaning and function of similar idioms in the Tower of Babel. The passage that has been particularly important in this comparison is the following, with key phrases translated in italics:[93]

Subjects of the four regions, *foreign people, of nonharmonious speech*,[94] dwellers of mountains and lands, as many as the light of the gods, lord

---

91 CAD Š s.v. *šemû* s. 8.

92 As noted in a number of studies, such as Fales, "New Light on Assyro-Aramaic Interference: The Assur Ostracon," 189 n 3.

93 The Akkadian is:

> *ba'ulāt arba'i lišānu aḫītu atmê lā mitḫurti āšibūtē šadê u māti mala irte'û nūr ilāni bēl gimri ša ina zikir Aššur bēlija ina mētel šibirrija ašlula pâ ištēn ušaškinma ušarmâ qerebšu mārī māt Aššur mudûte ini kalama ana šûḫuz ṣibitte palāḫ ili u šarri aklī šāpirī uma'iršunūti*

> For a score, see Andreas Fuchs, *Die Inschriften Sargons II. aus Khorsabad* (Göttingen: Cuvillier Verlag, 1994), 43–44, lines 72–74.

94 Liverani translates the phrase *atmê lā mitḫuri* as "untranslatable speech." He then argues that Assyrians accepted linguistic diversity on the periphery of the empire: "Alien and incomprehensible languages linger still more prominently along the outer limits of empire, resisting the work of interpreters because there was little practical need to understand them—whatever their value as curiosities" (*Assyria*, 231). Again, Liverani states that "we have already seen that language—the main instrument of homogenization—was unable to transform all of the provincial inhabitants into Assyrians" (*Assyria*, 238). This phrase in Liverani's analysis, then, points to the acceptance of linguistic diversity in the empire, diversity that was not conceived of

of all, guides, whom, by the order of Assur my lord, with the power of my scepter, I plundered. *I made them act in concert*, and I settled them in its (Dūr-Šarrukīn's) midst. Natives of Assyria, masters of every craft, I dispatched them as *overseers and officials* to teach correct behavior, namely fear of god and king.[95]

Aspects of the inscription appear to superficially support a reading of Assyrian policy as involving the implementation and imposition of a specific language for creating a sense of imperial unity. The rhetoric of "to impose one mouth," a wooden translation of the phrase "I made them act in concert," in the inscription could indicate this very sociolinguistic situation of Aramaic in the Assyrian empire, in which the central authorities employed a standardized language in order to foster and promote a cohesive identity. This imperial promotion and training in language ideology perhaps involved sending administrative scribes, identified in other inscriptions as Arameans, to educate rebellious populations.[96]

---

as a problem to be solved through linguistic unification. Despite the increasingly pervasive use of Aramaic in the Neo-Babylonian period and the official promotion of Aramaic as a chancellery language in the Achaemenid period, under these two empires (and in Babylon even in Neo-Assyrian times), statements regarding multilingualism as a celebrated feature of imperial reach appear. For Babylonian evidence, see Liverani, *Assyria*, 239.

95 Note the translation in CAD Ṣ s.v. ṣibittu s. 5: "I sent overseers and supervisors to teach them (i.e., the natives to be Assyrianized) correct behavior (and) to serve the gods and the king." In the translation above, I understand *palāḫ ili u šarri*, "fear of god and king," to be appositional (or, perhaps epexegetical) to *ṣibitte*, or "correct behavior." In doing so, I emphasize the solution to the problem conveyed in the rhetoric of the passage: the opposite of rebellion and political fragmentation is correct behavior, the latter involving the Assyrian ideology of fear of god and king. Thus, these are not enumerated issues as part of the tasks of the overseers and officials; rather, the appositional statement expresses the manner in which the overseers and officials spread Assyrian ideology and obedience in phrases that overlap and involve one another, reinforcing what the antidote to political fragmentation looks like to Assyrian imperialism.

96 Schniedewind cites the phrase [LÚ]A.BA *armaja ana muḫ[ḫi . . . iš]apparuma*, "the scribe writing Aramaic" (*A Social History of Hebrew*, [New Haven, CT: Yale University Press, 2013], 85). Schniedewind and Laurie Pearce note that the noun *sepīru* for "scribe" does not appear in Assyrian texts from the Neo-Assyrian period, occurring first in Babylon in the reign of Esarhaddon and becoming frequent in texts only in the Neo-Babylonian period. This title for this functionary in the Neo-Assyrian period was spelled only logographically as [LÚ]A.BA (Schniedewind, 218 n. 44; L. E. Pearce, "Sepīru and [LÚ]A.BA: Scribes of the Late First Millennium," in *Languages*

In fact, during this same period in the eighth century BCE if not earlier, Aramaic began to appear as an administrative language in the Neo-Assyrian empire. One interpretation is that this administrative use of the language reinforces the idea that a particular language ideology or strategy in Neo-Assyrian policy existed to incorporate and to govern Western Semitic peoples through the promotion of Aramaic as a *lingua franca*. Understanding why language ideology could be apparent in Sargon's Dūr-Šarrukīn cylinder inscription, then, offers a glimpse into the historical processes reconstructed in this bilingual situation, even if this theory ultimately is not convincing. Moreover, analyzing the rhetoric behind much-discussed phrasing in this inscription unlocks key areas of comparison with Genesis 11:1–9.[97]

---

and Cultures in Contact: At the Crossroads of Civilization in the Syro-Mesopotamian Realm, ed. K. Van Lerberghe and G. Voet, OLA 96 [Leuven: Peeters, 1999], 356). Yet the Neo-Assyrian Sargon inscription under discussion uses the term *šāpiru*, which does not correspond phonologically or etymologically with *sepīru*. See more on this issue below.

On the one hand, Schniedewind argues correctly that the phrase "impose one mouth" does not refer to the speaking of one language specifically. On the other hand, he concludes his discussion of the Dūr-Šarrukīn inscription with a statement regarding the role of Aramaic and linguistic ideology embedded therein: "In the final analysis, a cylinder inscription such as Dûr-Sharrukîn certainly reflects pure ideology, and its concern for language should make us aware of how critical language issues were to the forging of the empire." Schniedewind, *Social History of Hebrew*, 86. See also more recently Schniedewind, "Scribal Education in Ancient Israel and Judah into the Persian Period," in *Second Temple Jewish Paideia in Context*, ed. Jason M. Zurawski and Gabriele Boccaccini, BZNW 228 (Berlin: De Gruyter, 2017), 21.

97   Aramaic's importance for language ideology and language contact in the Neo-Assyrian empire appears in a rightly influential article by Schniedewind ("Aramaic, the Death of Written Hebrew, and Language Shift in the Persian Period," in *Margins of Writing, Origins of Cultures,* ed. Seth L. Sanders, OIS 2 [Chicago: Oriental Institute of the University of Chicago, 2006], 138). See also Schniedewind's *How the Bible Became a Book* (New York: Cambridge University Press, 2004), 65. The influential nature of Schniedewind's article and argument can also be seen in the work of William Morrow, discussing the cylinder inscription: "the reference is probably to encouragement of the use of Aramaic in the Neo-Assyrian empire; cf. William Schniedewind, 'Aramaic, the Death of Written Hebrew, and Language Shift in the Persian Period'" (Morrow, "'To Set the Name' in the Deuteronomic Centralization Formula: A Case of Cultural Hybridity," *JSS* 55 [2010]: 377 n. 54); and see, more recently, the influence of Schniedewind's analysis on the excellent work by Laura Quick, *Deuteronomy 28 and the Aramaic Curse Tradition*, 64.

Yet Schniedewind's arguments that Aramaic in the Neo-Assyrian period can be termed "imperial," and was standardized, is not convincing. See Gzella on the lack of imperial language ideology and policy in Assyria and the Persian period as

A closer examination of the inscription, however, de-emphasizes further the importance of language in it. Such a shift in interpretation of this inscription also has a constructive purpose of reframing the phrasing therein as part of a process of building a foundation for comparative study with Genesis 11:1 and 11:6. The overall context of the inscription has little or nothing to do with linguistic realities or imperial implementation of linguistic unification. Rather, the rhetoric of this passage of the inscription begins with diverse people groups who are described as speaking different languages, and who are made to speak with "one mouth." The phrase "strange tongues" (*lišānu aḫītu*) in the inscription is not about foreign languages (if it concerns language at all) so much as it is about secrecy, the type of talk that can undermine an empire.[98] While language is the operative metaphor, it is questionable at this point whether or not the phrase *lišānu aḫītu* still qualifies as language ideology *per se*, in which a specific language or set of languages are set in contrast. In fact, the resolution of the conflict has nothing to do with languages or linguistic identity: the gods, because of the king's religious fidelity, then allow the king to expand his empire and rule securely for the rest of his days (*ana dāriš*). The problem addressed in this inscription, then, is not one of a diversity of languages but rather a fractured political reality with competing agendas and strife due to the diversity of people groups and interests, synecdochally described through "strange tongues."[99] These groups are then made to agree with one another and live peacefully. It is this political process (not a linguistic agenda) that is set forth in this inscription.

Nonetheless, three aspects of this passage could be understood to lend credence to an expression of language ideology therein: the previously mentioned

---

the era of the standardization of Aramaic in "Aramaic Sources," in *A Companion to the Achaemenid Persian Empire*, ed. Bruno Jacobs and Robert Rollinger, 2 vols., Blackwell Companions to the Ancient World (Hoboken, NJ: Wiley Blackwell, 2021), 118. Note that Liverani claims that the only evidence of the imposition of a language in Assyrian imperial ideology is in the renaming of toponyms of conquered territory, many of which were given Akkadian names (Liverani, *Assyria*, 234–238).

98   Schniedewind, *Social History of Hebrew*, 85.

99   That Assyrian inscriptions and reliefs depict an interest in, and ability to reproduce, the diversity of their empire has been argued recently in Eva Braun-Holzinger, "Darstellungen der Suḫäer und Weiterer Nachbarn der Assyrer im 9. JH. 1. Teil," *Iraq* 80 (2018): 35–62; DeGrado, "King of the Four Quarters"; DeGrado, "Syrian Fashion, Assyrian Style: Clothing Syro-Anatolia in Ninth-Century BCE Assyrian Art," *American Journal of Archaeology* 125 (2021): 479–504.

strange/seditious languages, the phrase "one mouth," and terms that have been interpreted to refer to scribes.[100] These three points merit careful reassessment in evaluating the political rhetoric of the Dūr-Šarrukīn cylinder inscription.[101] Once the rhetoric of the cylinder inscription is better understood, the relevance of this comparative datum for identifying the problem described in the narrative in Genesis 11:1–9 and its solution, described in Genesis 12:1–3, will become clear.

"STRANGE TONGUES" AND ACTUAL LANGUAGES?

The phrase in Sargon's cylinder inscription *lišānu aḫītu*, "strange tongues," as already suggested, does not point to actual language, or at least does not necessarily do so. For example, in texts from Mari the word is used for a secret source.[102] In Neo-Assyrian, this meaning refers to the actions of a king, who retreats in secrecy and private.[103] When applied to language, however, the meaning refers to the source of what is spoken and not the language *per se* (and, chronologically, this meaning seems confined to second

---

100   David Carr helpfully enumerates the issues involved in this passage (*The Formation of the Hebrew Bible*, 305 n. 4).

101   The following discussion agrees largely with Machinist's observations about the Dūr-Šarrukīn inscription, namely that it does not pertain to language ideology and refers, instead, to the contrast between "disorder" and "disobedience," on the one hand, and "order" and "obedience" imposed by Assyrian rule, on the other ("Assyrians on Assyria in the First Millennium B.C.," 96). I provide textual citations to show how this rhetoric was constructed. Note, for example, that Machinist states (in reference to the differences between cylinder, bull, and display inscriptions) that the "variants in the other inscriptions are unimportant" (Machinist, "Assyrians on Assyria in the First Millennium B.C.,"95). Such a statement was true for Machinist's study; however, I hope to show that whether the king imposes "one mouth" (the cylinder inscription) or the rebel alliances impose "one mouth" (the display inscription) makes a big difference in understanding Assyrian rhetoric and how it might be reflected in Genesis 11:1–9.

102   Charles-F. Jean, *Lettres Diverses*, ARM 2 (Paris: Imprimerie Nationale 1950), texts 26:7, 26:10, 40:4, and 40:16.

103   Robert Francis Harper, *Assyrian and Babylonian Letters Belonging to the Kouyunjik Collections of the British Museum*, 14 vols. (Chicago: University of Chicago Press, 1892–1914), volume 6, text 646 rev., lines 1–3; for the text and translation, see Giovani B. Lanfranchi and Simo Parpola, *The Correspondence of Sargon II, Part II: Letters from the Northern and Northeastern Provinces*, SAA 5 (Helsinki: Helsinki University Press, 1990), text 90, rev., lines 1–3.

millennium texts from Mari). The same distinction holds true for the meaning "falsehood."[104] The idea is that someone will change the content of the inscription from its original wording to something else. Only through the contextual application of having something foreign, or outside, compete with the original intent of the inscription does the *lišānu* become *aḫītu* in the sense of false. Here again, different languages are not in view but rather the notion of "falsehood" refers to content of what is written or said.[105]

Where *aḫītu* modifies *lišānu* directly as an adjective, the emphasis is on foreignness, but not necessarily falsehood or potential subversion. Moreover, where this construction appears, the referent to *lišānu* is not a language literally but rather to a foreign person. For example, one text predicts that "foreign people will rule Amurru."[106] The reference of events in the text is not to language change, but to political change. An astrological text also includes this phrasing to designate foreign people.[107] The phrase *lišānu aḫītu*

---

104 E. A. W. Budge and L. W. King, *The Annals of the Kings of Assyria: The Cuneiform Texts with Translations, Transliterations, etc., from the Original Documents in the British Museum, Volume 1* (London: Trustees of the British Museum, 1902), 250. The translation in the CAD provides a better rendering as *aḫītu*, to the best of my knowledge, never means "foreign language" on its own, though *lišānu* certainly does. See the statement in Ashurbanipal's royal inscription: *lišānī* (EME.MEŠ) *ṣīt šamši* (dUTU-*ši*) *ereb šamši ša Aššur* (AN.ŠÁR) *umallû qātū 'a bēl lišānišu* (EME-*šú*) *ul ibšima lišānšu nakratma lā išemmû atmûšu*, "(Among all) the languages (from) sunrise (to) sunset, which (the god) Aššur had placed at my disposal, there was not a master of his language. His language was different and his speech could not be understood." For text and translation, see Jamie Novotny and Joshua Jeffers, *The Royal Inscriptions of Ashurbanipal (668–631 BC), Aššur-etel-ilāni (630–627 BC), and Sîn-šarra-iškun (626–612 BC), Kings of Assyria, Part 1*, RINAP 5/1 (University Park, PA: Eisenbrauns, 2018), 41. In this inscription from Ashurbanipal, it is clear that *lišānu* refers to a foreign language and *atmû* to the words of that language. The issue above is whether or not these lexemes in Sargon's inscription should be translated similarly.

105 The semantics of *aḫītu* and "outside" also appear in Standard Babylonian religious texts from Hama. The referent is not a foreign language but harmful speech. See J. Laessøe, "A Prayer to Ea, Shamash, and Marduk, from Hama," *Iraq* 18 (1956): 62.

106 R. C. Thompson, *The Reports of the Magicians and Astrologers of Nineveh and Babylon in the British Museum: The Original Texts, Printed in Cuneiform Characters*, Luzac's Semitic Text and Translation Series 6–7, 2 vols. (London: Luzac, 1900), text 62, line 3; text 76, line 3; text 77, line 3; text 78, line 3; text 79, line 3; text 80, line 3. See, more recently, Herman Hunger, *Astrological Reports to Assyrian Kings*, SAA 8 (Helsinki: Helsinki University Press, 1992), text 472, line 3.

107 F. Thureau-Dangin, *Tablettes d'Uruk à l'usage des prêtres du Temple d'Anu au temps des Séleucides*, Musée du Louvre, Département des antiquités orientales, Textes cunéiformes, 6 (Paris: P. Geuthner, 1922), plate 17, line 33.

parallels in many ways the expression "foreign language," or *lišānu nakirtu*, a language that, by virtue of its outsider status, can be grouped with other descriptors creating a negative meaning; however, this meaning ultimately points to people and not the specific languages they use.[108]

The metaphorical use of *lišānu aḫītu* in Sargon's cylinder inscription creates a literary connection to the phrase *atmê lā mitḫurti* in Akkadian, woodenly "words that conflict." It could be argued that the mention of "words" then clarifies that *lišānu aḫītu* refers to actual language. Yet the phrase *lā mitḫurti* is informative. On its own, *mitḫurtu* often means "conflict, contrast." Used with *lišānu*, the word could possibly communicate the presence of different languages, as in one interpretation of Enmerkar and the Lord of Aratta, understood as the mythological story concerning communication and the origins of writing.[109] Yet it can also refer to contrasting opinions, and, in some contexts, to overcoming opposing forces, much as is the case in Sargon's cylinder inscription.[110] If the resolution in Sargon's inscription at the end of the conflict was an imposition of unison through a singular ideology of fear

---

108   See, for example, the phrase from the reign of Adad-Nīrārī I: *u lu aššum errēti šinātima nakara aḫâ ayāba lemna lišāna nakirta lu mamma šanâ uma'aruma ušaḫḫazu*, "or if on account of these curses he instructs or instigates a hostile stranger, an evil enemy, a speaker of a foreign language, or anyone else." (E. Ebeling, B. Meissner, and E. F. Weidner, *Die Inschriften der Altassyrischen Könige*, AOBib 1 [Leipzig: Quelle & Meyer, 1926], text 64, line 45).

109   See the discussion in the note at the beginning of this chapter about this story. Even here, however, the reference to one language (eme 1-am$_3$) is best understood not as literal language but rather as a consolidation of political opposition, strife, and contest. The immediately following description, which also leads to the proclamation of a day when all will speak one language, includes a list of those who will have unified speech: a-da en a-ad nun a-da lugal-la. The word a-da refers to a contest or debate, and Vanstiphout translates the phrase as "the debates between lords, princes, and kings" (Herman Vanstiphout, *Epics of Sumerian Kings: The Matter of Aratta*, WAW 20 [Atlanta: SBL Press, 2003], 65). He connects a-da to Sumerian adaman duga, "the term for formal school disputations" (Vanstiphout, *Epics of Sumerian Kings*, 94). The contrast between debate (a-da) and one language (eme 1-am$_3$) as the resolution to the contest in an epic in which riddles play a central role suggests that the problem that Enki overcomes is not multiplicity of languages *per se* but rather political competition. See also C. Jay Crisostimo, "'Recount for Him the Spell of Nudimmud' . . . yet again: Reassessing the Babylonian Babel."

110   See CAD M/2 s.v. *mitḫurtu* s. The word *mitḫurtu* can mean both "conflict, contrast" (CAD M/2, mng. 1) and "correspondence" (CAD M/2, mng. 2), such that *mitḫurtu* in the first sense can also mean the same as *lā mitḫurtu*, the same lexeme negated. It may be the case that the meaning in the cylinder inscription should come, instead, from the word *mitḫartu*, meaning "square" and indicating correspondence. For this

of god and king, then, with the end in mind, the metaphorical application of "language" and "word" in the beginning can be better understood. It is not a literal statement of language ideology but rather a statement of the problem of political fragmentation leading to rebellion, a problem that is overcome with imperial consolidation and organization.[111] As a result, the translation of "nonharmonious speech" is appropriate for *atmê lā mitḫurti*.

The two issues of new subjects coming into imperial reach and the need for organization and projection of royal power find a correlation in the reliefs at Sargon's royal palace in Dūr-Šarrukīn. Late Assyrian royal palaces generally underwent a variety of innovations in architecture to accommodate the needs of a rapidly expanding empire. The challenges inherent in expansion were addressed in propagandistic ways by creating royal palaces in which the image and presence of the Assyrian king were increasingly present in reliefs even as these reliefs depict a correspondingly increasing diversity of governed people groups.[112] The courtyards to Sargon's palaces displayed more monuments, decorated with more figurative reliefs. The effect was to be able to represent more subjects, and in this manner, the courtyard reliefs worked in connection with the rooms and reliefs within the palace to draw attention to the king and his ability to organize, govern, and accommodate a growing number of subject people groups. Writing and relief also work together to communicate the underlying problem addressed in the cylinder inscription, namely the effective administration of the Assyrian Empire, and the role of the king in instituting such governance over a diverse polity.

---

issue of the proper reading and Akkadian root for the semantics of "corresponding," see CAD M/2 p. 138.

111   "Conquering territory—and even conquering the whole world—is incumbent upon the king, but it is not enough. After conquest, it remains necessary to organize the territory in the cosmic sense, which is the ultimate aim" (Liverani, *Assyria*, 165).

112   In analyzing the architectural features of Sargon's Dūr-Šarrukīn royal palace, Kertai claims that, in comparison with previous royal building projects such as at Kalḫu,

> ... The reliefs in Sargon's palace emphasize other, partially new, subjects. . . . the most striking change is a proliferation of rooms decorated with files of people, normally headed by the crown prince, approaching the king. . . . In Sargon's palace they were omnipresent. Their use expanded the presence of the king within the palace . . .

David Kertai, *The Architecture of Late Assyrian Royal Palaces* (New York: Oxford University Press, 2015), 102–103.

OVERCOMING POLITICAL FRAGMENTATION:
pâ ištēn šuškunu

When set within the larger history of the phrase, the parallel uses of *pâ ištēn šuškunu*, "to impose one mouth," reveal a political, not a linguistic, connotation behind this idiom.[113] The phrase is best defined as an expression meaning "to make act in unison."[114] Attestations begin in the reign of Tukulti-Ninurta I in the Middle Assyrian period.[115] The following description in an inscription from Tukulti-Ninurta of these nations bringing tribute to the king is particularly significant: there is no sense of linguistic importance in the phrase; rather, the idiom describes a political reality. Another inscription from the Middle Assyrian period from Tiglath-Pileser I indicates the same situation.[116]

The first occurrence of the phrase in Neo-Assyrian times appears in the inscriptions of Adad-Nirari II, a late-tenth-century king,[117] and other references appear in writings from Ashurnasirpal II, Tiglath-Pileser III, and Sargon, thereby evincing a wide distribution of the phrase throughout this era. The Middle Assyrian attestations are much too early to be a statement of linguistic unification of the empire through the imposition of Aramaic. Both the earlier and later appearances of the idiom (including the Sargon inscription) appear in similar literary contexts: rebels of some sort from various factions and kingdoms within the empire rise up in accord with one another (having "one mouth") or are pacified (or

---

113 For some of these attestations, see also Liverani, *Assyria*, 162–163. As made clear below, the nonlinguistic nature of this idiom will have relevance for translating the locutions in Genesis 11:1 and 11:6.

114 CAD Š/1 s.v. *šakānu* v. 5a *pû* d) *pâ ištēn*.

115 E.g., *pâ ištēn lu ultaškinšunu*, "I made (the conquered lands) act in concert." Ernst Weidner, *Die Inschriften Tukulti-Ninurtas I. und seiner Nachfolger*, repr., AfOB 12 (Osnabrück: Biblio Verlag, 1970), 28. See also A. Kirk Grayson, *Assyrian Rulers of the Third and Second Millennia* bc *(To 1115 BC)*, RIMA 1 (Toronto: University of Toronto Press, 1987), text 1, line 83. Grayson translates similarly: "I brought under one command (the following lands)."

116 Budge and King, *Annals of the Kings of Assyria*, 83. The phrase is *pâ ištēn ušeškinšunūti*, which Grayson translates as "I subdued them to one authority" (*Assyrian Rulers of the Early First Millennium BC I (1114–859 bc)*, RIMA 2 [Toronto: University of Toronto Press, 1991], text 1, column 6, line 46).

117 Otto Schroeder, *Keilschrifttexte aus Assur Historischen Inhalts: Zweites Heft*, WV-DOG 37 (Leipzig: J. C. Hinrichs, 1922), 56.

conquered), resulting in peace and unification of the empire, all parties therefore having "one mouth."

A parallel construction exists using *ēdu*, "individual, solitary, single," instead of *ištēn*. The different phrasings are synonymous and used in similar literary contexts with similar meaning. For example, an Old Babylonian extispicy text states "the whole of the land will be of one mind" (more literally, "as for the whole of the land, its mouth will be made one/single").[118] Another example of the phrase from a later period in the Neo-Assyrian era also occurs in Sargon's display inscription (*die Große Prunkinschrift*): "Ia᾽u-bi᾽di (an evil Hittite) caused the cities of Arpadda, Simirra, Damascus, and Samaria to rebel against me, and he made them act unanimously."[119] This attestation from Sargon in which a rebel leader imposes "one mouth" is important for understanding the phrase as a literary trope, particularly when reading the Genesis 11:1–9 passage, as will become clear.

An inscription from Assurbanipal, Prism A, also has particular relevance for interpreting the rhetoric of Genesis 11:1–9.[120] The significance is twofold,

---

118 Albrecht Götze, *Old Babylonian Omen Texts*, YOS 10 (New Haven: Yale University Press, 1947), text 31, column i, lines 28–30.

119 Hugo Winckler, *Die Keilschrifttexte Sargons: Nach der Papierabklatschen und originalen*, 2 vols. (Leipzig: E. Pfeiffer, 1889); Fuchs, *Die Inschriften Sargons II. aus Khorsabad*, 200–201. See the recently published fragments from Sargon's stele at Tell Tayinat, in which the fragment A 27863 contains very similar phrasing as the Khorsabad Annals, particularly the display inscription cited above. The fragment is as follows: [. . .] [x] [. . . *gi-mir māti*(KUR)-*šu rapašti*(DAGAL-*ti*)] [*ina* ᵁᴿᵁ*q*]*ar-qa-ri* [*ù*]-[*paḫ-ḫi-ir-ma*] [*it*]-*ti-ia* ᵁᴿᵁ*a*[*r-pad-da* ᵁᴿᵁ*ṣi-mir-ra*] [ᵁᴿᵁ*di-maš-qa* ᵁᴿᵁ*s*]*a-me-ri-i-n*[*a uš-bal-kit-ma*], "He [gathered all of his vast land at Q]arqar, [he incited] A[rpad, Ṣimirra, Damascus, (and) S]amaria [to rebel ag]ainst me." The fragment also mentions the overthrow of Yau-bi᾽di, the same person as Ia᾽u-bi᾽di in the display inscription cited above. For the fragment at Tell Tayinat, see Jacob Lauinger and Stephen Batiuk, "A Stele of Sargon II at Tell Tayinat," *ZA* 105 (2015): 63–64. The text is too broken to reconstruct whether or not the "one mouth" phrase is applied to forces opposing Assyrian rule, but given the similar phrasing elsewhere between the Tell Tayinat fragment and the Khorsabad Annals, it is reasonable to suppose that the use of the imposition of "one mouth" to describe enemy activity had wider currency than simply the display inscription from Khorsabad. For more on Ia᾽u-bi᾽di and the Yahwistic element in his name, see Eckart Frahm, "A Sculpted Slab with an Inscription of Sargon II Mentioning the Rebellion of Yau-bi᾽di of Hamath," *AoF* 40 (2013): 42–54.

120 For the text of Assurbanipal's Prism A, see Jamie Novotny and Joshua Jeffers in RINAP, http://oracc.museum.upenn.edu/rinap/rinap5/pager. For a critical edition of Prism A (as well as Prism F, which is "ein wesentlich kürzerer Vorläufer zu Prisma A"), see Rykle Borger, *Beiträge zum Inschriftenwerk Assurbanipals: die Prismenklassen A, B, C = K, D,*

both involving the placement and use of the "one mouth" idiom and also pertaining to the source of rebellion against Assyrian authority. Regarding the first issue, in two places Assurbanipal mentions that forces unite against his rule, both rebellions led by Šamaš-šuma-ukīn, Assurbanipal's brother and rival for power. In column iii, lines 105–6, Assurbanipal states that Šamaš-šuma-ukīn "made all of them [the rebel forces] become hostile towards me."[121] Assurbanipal then employs the idiom of mouth, but by context and parallel usage, the phrase *ittišu iškunū pîšunu* means "they united with him" (woodenly, "they placed their mouths with him").

The second occurrence of the idiom in Assurbanipal's Prism A involves the use of "one mouth," though with a different verb than appears in Sargon's display inscription. In column iv, line 97, Assurbanipal presents a list of rebel forces that challenged Assyrian rule ("in order to decide on their own to become hostile against me").[122] The result is the destruction of this unified front. The result is also imperial consolidation through the imposition of the yoke of Assur and, much like Sargon's cylinder inscription, the sending of Assyrian officials to oversee the rebellious areas. Although Assurbanipal states that the forces became hostile on their own accord, he also identifies a cause behind their opposition, namely the machinations of Šamaš-šuma-ukīn. According to Assurbanipal in line 99, these were forces "that Šamaš-šuma-ukīn got as help and unified."[123] A wooden rendering of the last clause is that "Šamaš-šuma-ukīn turned (them) into one mouth," but the context clearly identifies the action as one of consolidation against Assyrian power and interests.[124]

E, F, G, H, J und T sowie andere Inschriften (Wiesbaden: Harrassowitz Verlag, 1996), 1–85 (quote at p. 7). For an analysis of the features of Prism A as well as the claim that Assurbanipal himself might have crafted the image of the king and empire therein, see M. Cogan, "The Author of Ashurbanipal Prism A (Rassam): An Inquiry into His Plan and Purpose, with a Note on His Persona," *Orient* 49 (2014): 69–83.

121   Borger, *Beiträge zum Inschriftenwerk Assurbanipals*, 40.

122   For the following citations of column iv, see Borger, *Beiträge zum Inschriftenwerk Assurbanipals*, 45.

123   For text-critical issues in this manuscript, see Martin Worthington, *Principles of Akkadian Textual Criticism*, SANER 1 (Berlin: De Gruyter, 2012), 143–144.

124   Uehlinger noted the importance of the rhetoric when the king was not the subject of the phrase *pâ ištēn šakānu*:

> Wo die Formel *pâ ištēn šakānu* nicht den assyrischen König zum Subjekt hat, stellt sie eine Variante der Wendung *pâ/î itti* PN *šakānu* 'sich mit PN verabreden, verbünden, verschwören' dar. Letztere begegnet in assyrischen Texten mehrfach im Zusammenhang mit Verschwörungen gegen den assyrischen König. Dass

In addition to the metaphorical use of "mouth" to designate rebellion against proper authority (from the Assyrian perspective), the use of this idiom has significance in light of the person said to be behind such uprisings. In both cases Assurbanipal lays opposition to Assyrian power at the feet of his brother, Šamaš-šuma-ukīn, whom Esarhaddon installed as king of Babylon. Babylon had proven difficult for Assyria to govern, resulting in Sennacherib's destruction of the city, as well as its ziggurat Etemenanki, in 689 BCE. Rebuilding began under the following Assyrian king, Esarhaddon, and continued with Assurbanipal. As a means for controlling the Babylonian population, Esarhaddon installed his son, Šamaš-šuma-ukīn, on the throne as king of the city in 669 BCE, though with obvious connections to the Assyrian empire. Šamaš-šuma-ukīn would later, in 652 BCE, foment a revolt against his younger brother, Assurbanipal, who was designated crown prince of Assyria.[125] Esarhaddon's succession plan, with Assurbanipal on the throne in Assyria and Šamaš-šuma-ukīn in Babylonia, was solidified in the famous Vassal Treaty of Esarhaddon, or VTE (variously labeled EST for Esarhaddon Succession Treaty). Both the fact that this rebellion against a previously instituted imperial structure took place in Babylon as well as the fact that Assurbanipal describes the manner in which Šamaš-šuma-ukīn unifies the fragmented rebel alliances into a cohesive front through the metaphor of mouth have obvious implications for understanding Genesis 11:1–9. These observations give further weight to the late eighth and early-to-mid seventh centuries BCE as the backdrop to the composition of the biblical story, making the operative political idioms in the Assyrian context all the more vital for examination of Genesis 11:1 and 11:6.

---

jemand "seinen Mund (unter Umgehung des Grosskönigs) mit NN gesetz" habe, bezeichnet den Tatbestand der Konspiration. (Where the formula *pâ ištēn šakānu* does not have the Assyrian king as the subject, it represents a variant of the phrase *pâ/î itti* PN *šakānu* "to arrange, ally, conspire with someone." The latter occurs several times in Assyrian texts in connection with conspiracies against the Assyrian king. The fact that someone "has set his mouth (bypassing the great king) with someone else" describes the facts of the conspiracy.)

Uehlinger, *Weltreich und "Eine Rede,"* 440. He then cited the case of Assurbanipal and Šamaš-šum-ukīn. Crucially, however, Uehlinger does not connect this observation to the rhetoric of Genesis 11:1–9.

125 For more on Šamaš-šuma-ukīn's civil war, see Paul-Alain Beaulieu, *A History of Babylon, 2200 BC–AD 75* (Chichester, UK: John Wiley & Sons, 2018), 211–216; van de Mieroop, *A History of the Ancient Near East*, 273–274; Kuhrt, *The Ancient Near East: c. 3000–330 BC, Volume 2*, 586–589.

Another example of an idiom referring to the "mouth," one that had a relatively long life in Akkadian dialects, including Neo-Assyrian inscriptions, and one whose rhetorical utility is helpful for interpreting the biblical passage, is the phrase *pî ṭābu*. The precise translation of this idiom depends on context. A brief examination of *pî ṭābu* displays the manner in which such metaphors of the mouth could operate in different ways, whether referring to approved sources of authority or against such sources. When speaking of divinity or royalty—in other words when describing approved, sanctioned sources of authority—the phrase *pî ṭābu* designates "sweet" or "kind" talk. This employment of the idiom refers to words often spoken in praise or as honorific with respect to deities or kings.[126] Yet the reverse also occurs with the same phrase, in which it is applied to treachery when malevolent forces use "honeyed words" or "sweet talk."[127] The point in this example is to display the treachery of such talk, and its ability to usurp through deception the proper authority or course of action. Much as the meaning of "to impose one mouth" was context dependent (it was good when the king did it, but bad when the enemies to the crown did it), other idioms of the mouth function in a similar fashion.[128] This example, then, makes the observations about the rhetorical placement of "imposing" or "turning" into "one mouth" above in Assyrian sources more certain, an argument that will also pay dividends for understanding the enigmatic phrasing in Genesis 11:1 and 11:6.[129]

---

126 CAD P s.v. *pûm* s. A 5a. The phrase can also have, with reference to divinity, meaning as opposites in omen texts, where *pû ṭābu* signifies a positive omen and *pû lemnu* the opposite (an ominous portent). See CAD P s.v. *pûm* s. A 14e.

127 CAD Ṭ s.v. *ṭābu* s. o 3´.

128 The general study of wordplays, figurative language, and the flexibility of literary constructions in the ancient Near East has had a robust history of analysis. See M. Mindlin, M. J. Geller, and J. E. Wansbrough, eds., *Figurative Language in the Ancient Near East* (London: University of London, School of Oriental and African Studies, 1987). See also Scott Noegel, ed., *Puns and Pundits: Wordplay in the Hebrew Bible and Ancient Near Eastern Literature* (Bethesda, MD: CDL Press, 2000); and Scott Noegel, *Wordplay in Ancient Near Eastern Texts*, ANEM 26 (Atlanta: SBL Press, 2021).

129 Indeed, the value of seeing how these idioms of the "mouth" as political metaphors operate appears in Gertz's critiques of Uehlinger's proposal to read Genesis 11:1–9 (or a portion thereof) in light of Neo-Assyrian politics. Gertz argues that the fact that the king, in Sargon's Cylinder Inscription, "imposes one mouth" makes the Assyrian idiom at odds with the biblical expression in Genesis 11:1 and 11:6, where the people (and not a king or God) have "one lip," a condition, according to Gertz, that is simply unproblematic and a precondition for the actual problems in the narrative of city and tower building. Gertz states that "Sodann zwingt in der

SCRIBES OR ADMINISTRATORS?

The function of the *šāpiru* in the cylinder inscription has proven difficult to define. The word is from the well-attested Akkadian verb *šapāru*, meaning "to send." The meaning of the verb extends to the authority to enact what is sent, and can therefore mean "to order, give orders, command, administer, control, govern, rule," and even "write," all well-attested uses for the verb in a variety of dialects and time periods of Akkadian.[130] As such, the noun *šāpiru* refers primarily to a "governor," "overseer," or "commander," and the term typically designates this function as an office.[131] The authority invested in this manner then broadened the meaning of the *šāpiru* to include a person who sends messages or acts in an official capacity in government business delivering information and overseeing a territory in an authoritative capacity. In Sargon's cylinder inscription, such agents of imperial organization and control, along with another representative of the crown called an *aklu*, are sent to the rebellious areas in order "to teach correct conduct, namely fear

---

neuassyrischen Weltherrschaftsrhetorik der Konig den Volkern „einen Mund" (*pu ištēn*) auf, wahrend *s̀āpā 'aḫāt* in Gen 11,1 die unhinterfragte (urgeschichtliche) und bis zum Bau von Stadt und Turm unproblematische Voraussetzung der Erzahlung ist" ("Then, in the Neo-Assyrian rhetoric of world domination, the king forces 'one mouth' on the people, while *s̀āpā 'aḫāt* in Genesis 11:1 is the unquestioned (prehistoric) and unproblematic prerequisite of the narrative up to the building of the city and the tower") (*Das erste Buch Mose: Genesis*, 334). Gertz seems to make a distinction between "one speech," on the one hand, which he claims is not problematic, and human ambition, on the other, which is infinite and is problematic. As argued above, however, such a distinction misses the rhetorical importance of this phrasing in Genesis 11:1 and 11:6 if one reads the Assyrian phrasing in the background of "one mouth." One feature of the Tower of Babel story (having "one speech") is a non-neutral disposition toward authority, highlighting a sort of stance that then results in such unbridled and unsanctioned ambition. Yet as shown above, the trope in Assyrian inscriptions was actually more dynamic than Gertz supposes, and does appear at times in rhetorically similar places as in Genesis 11:1 and 11:6, namely the opponents of authority, in allying themselves with one another, have "one mouth" against the king. In this sense, the phrase in Hebrew is not an unproblematic precondition but rather reflections of a stance or disposition against authority, out of which other actions (fighting against the king or building a city and tower without divine approval) occur. A similar flexibility exists with other political idioms, such as the phrase *pî ṭābu*, demonstrating how these metaphors functioned in imperial rhetoric. This observation then blunts, if not obviates, Gertz's critiques of Uehlinger in an often otherwise helpful discussions of Genesis 11:1–9.

130   For the glosses, see CAD Š/1 s.v. *šapāru* v.

131   See CAD Š/1 s.v. *šāpiru* s.

of god and king." In this manner, the Assyrian king conquers his enemies, an act that accords with the Assyrian imperial mission.[132] The use of *šāpiru* and *aklu* in this context is consistent with other fringe groups whom Sargon describes as existing outside of Assyrian control and organization, such as Arab populations "who do not know overseer or commander."[133] The Assyrian king's concern is not with their language but rather with their political status relative to the sphere of Assyrian influence.

What sort of organizational activities were included in the "teaching" of Sargon's administrators as mentioned in the Dūr-Šarrukīn cylinder inscription is unclear beyond the content of "fear of god and king." Yet the word *šāpiru* in this context has implications for language ideology in the spread of Assyrian propaganda, and has been translated as "scribe."[134] Despite the secondary meaning of the verb *šapāru* as "to write," this particular semantic sense of the verb never extends to the noun *šāpiru*, and this title never means "scribe" or "one who writes" in currently attested uses.[135] This semantic problem concerning the translation of a *šāpiru* is an important one and has gone unnoticed in scholarly treatments of the cylinder inscription.[136] Yet even beyond the semantic issue mentioned above, the translation value of *šāpiru* as "scribe" is not persuasive on multiple grounds,

---

132 In the words of Liverani, such conquest "is not enough. After conquest, it remains necessary to organize the territory in the cosmic sense, which is the ultimate aim." Liverani, *Assyria*, 165.

133 A. G. Lie, *The Inscriptions of Sargon II* (Paris: P. Geuthner, 1929), 22:121. For an analysis of this phrasing and what it meant in the rhetoric of Assyrian inscriptions to be "non-Assyrian," see Machinist, "Assyrians on Assyria in the First Millennium B.C.," 85.

134 For example, Luckenbill translates the *aklu* as "scribes" and the *šāpiru* as a "sheriff or superintendent." As Schniedewind argues, *aklu* never means "scribe" but rather is an "overseer." Schniedewind, *Social History of Hebrew*, 218 n. 40. To correct Luckenbill's translation, Schniedewind appeals to D. G. Lyon's original publication of the cylinder inscription, where Lyons translates *šāpiru* as "Schriftgelehrte," or "scribe." For the edition discussed in the note, see David G. Lyon, *Keilschrifttexte Sargons, Königs von Assyrien (722–705 v Chr.): Nach den Originalen* (Leipzig: J. C. Hinrichs, 1883). For the semantic differences between the *aklu* and *šāpiru*, see the notes at the end of the lexical entry for *šāpiru* following the final definition CAD Š/1 p. 458.

135 This definition is not found in CAD Š/1 s.v. *šāpiru*.

136 For example, Carr views this functionary as spreading Assyrian education and language ideology to the peripheries and, therefore, as an important arm of Assyrian propaganda who could influence local scribal traditions on the periphery of the empire, such as those located in Israel and Judah. "Moreover, it seems that the 'overseers' and 'administrators' are envisioned as playing some kind of role vis-à-vis this

most notably because it confuses this root with another, a *sepīru*.[137] Each is derived from well-attested verbs in East Semitic (*šapāru*) and West Semitic (*spr*), the latter eventually being loaned into Neo-Babyloian as *sepēru*.[138] The two occupations whose titles were derived from these verbal roots, the *šapiru* and the *sepīru*, had no necessary overlap in function or content of

---

'one' [linguistic] 'mouth,' even if one does not translate the terms as 'scribes'" (Carr, *Formation of the Hebrew Bible*, 305 n. 4).

137   As Schniedewind observes, Lyon translates *šapiru* as "Schriftgelehrte" based on the correspondence between *šapiru* and the Aramaic term for scribe, *sāprā* ', as in Ezra 4:8. For this discussion, see Schniedewind, *Social History of Hebrew*, 218 n. 40. The correspondence cannot be one of historical relatedness, however, as the sibilants derive from distinct proto-Semitic roots. A proto-Semitic voiceless fricative [s] should appear as /š/ in both Akkadian and Aramaic, whereas a proto-Semitic voiceless affricate ['s] would appear in both Akkadian and Aramaic as /s/. See the table of sibilants in Paul V. Mankowski, *Akkadian Loanwords in Biblical Hebrew*, HSS 47 (Winona Lake, IN: Eisenbrauns, 2000), 156. For the reconstruction of proto-Semitic sibilants, see the following works by Alice Faber: "Phonetic Reconstruction," *Glossa* 15 (1981): 233–262; "Semitic Sibilants in an Afro-Asiatic Context," *JSS* 29 (1984): 189–224; and "Akkadian Evidence for Proto-Semitic Affricates," *JCS* 37 (1985): 101–107. While Wolfram von Soden connects *šapārum* and Aramaic *spr* as related roots, his lexicon was completed the year that Faber's work on sibilants in Semitic began to appear, and von Soden, as a result, does not take her analysis into account. See von Soden, *Akkadisches Handwörterbuch*, vol. 3 (Wiesbaden: Harrassowitz, 1965–1981), 1170. Indeed, according to Faber's reconstruction, *spr* in Hebrew and Aramaic (written with a *samekh*) corresponds to S₃, originally the sound /ts/, whereas the sibilant in *šapārum* derives from S₁, an original /s/ sound, which appears in Naram-Sin's Bassetki Statue. See line 22 with the form URU^KI-*lí-su*, normalized *ālīsu* for "his city," where the last sign indicates the third person masculine suffix, normally–*šu*. For the text of the Bassetki Statue, see A. H. al-Fouadi and T. A. Madhloom, "Bassetki Statue with an Old Akkadian Royal Inscription of Naram-Sin of Agade," *Sumer* 32 (1976): 63–77. A distinction in dialect occurs between Neo-Assyrian and Babylonian, where Proto-Semitc ['s] appears as /s/ in Babylonian, as /š/ in Neo-Assyrian, and as a *samekh* in Aramaic and Hebrew; a Proto-Semitic [š] appears as /š/ in Babylonian, /s/ in Assyrian, and a *shin* in Aramaic and Hebrew (Stephen Kaufman, *Akkadian Influences on Aramaic*, 140–142; Mankowski, *Akkadian Loanwords in Biblical Hebrew*, 156). The appearance of /š/ in *šapiru* in the cylinder inscription is not a result of dialect interference, however, as the sibilant is simply part of the historical root of the word and not a function of phonetic realization in the Neo-Assyrian dialect. If the latter was the case, *šapiru* would be spelled with an /s/ in the cylinder inscription, but no such spelling occurs in the passage under examination. The problem addressed above of historical relatedness remains, since these words (*šapiru* and *sepīru*/ספרא) derive from distinct roots.

138   CAD S s.v. *sepēru*. As Pearce notes, the precise etymology of a *sepīru* has been debated, though the lexeme's derivation from the verbal root loaned from Aramaic into Akkadian *sepēru* has not ("*Sepīru* and ^LÚA.BA," 355).

work.[139] In fact, many other attestations exist in which the *aklu* and *šāpiru* are mentioned together, and in none of these examples is scribal activity a part of their joint efforts.[140]

In sum, none of the three elements in the cylinder inscription typically identified as pertaining to language actually have any language referent at all. Two of the phrases involve metaphors or idioms of "tongues" and "mouth," but the application and rhetorical use of the metaphors make clear that language is not in view. The particular phrase *pâ ištēn šuškunu* has gained currency as a datum for language ideology, and its meaning and usages have implications for somewhat parallel idioms in the Tower of Babel story. For the Akkadian text, as will be clear also in the biblical story, it is questionable whether or not language ideology is apparent anywhere in this passage from the Dūr-Šarrukīn cylinder inscription. Instead, political consolidation either against the king (if the enemies impose "one mouth" on one another against Assyria) or in light of royal imperial consolidation (if the king imposes "one mouth") lies behind the rhetoric of the phrase *pâ ištēn šuškunu*.

CONCLUSION

Every story has a context in which it makes sense, whether such a context is the historical surroundings of its production or the larger literary environments in which it appears.[141] Situating the Tower of Babel narrative within a plausible historical context in the Neo-Assyrian period allows for attending to the features of the narrative and its discourse better than

---

139 As Pearce observes, the main function of the *sepīru* was to serve as a witness to economic transactions. Within this domain, "it is primarily in the Neo-Babylonian period that we find attestations of *sepīrus* engaged in activities related to their (apparently bilingual) literacy skills" ("*Sepīru* and ᴸᵁA.BA," 357). Even if Sargon's Dūr-Šarrukīn cylinder inscription included mention of a ᴸᵁA.BA, which it does not, this attestation would still be too early to reconstruct much of the bilingual activity for these scribes. For more on the function of the *sepīru*, and for an argument that the lexeme should be vocalized as *sēpiru*, see Yigal Bloch, *Alphabet Scribes in the Land of Cuneiform: Sēpiru Professionals in Mesopotamia in the Neo-Babylonian and Achaemenid Periods*, Gorgias Studies in the Ancient Near East 11 (Piscataway: Gorgias Press, 2018).

140 CAD A/1 s.v. *aklu* A s. a) 1'-3'; CAD Š/1 s.v. *šāpiru* s. 1.–3.

141 I return to the latter issue in chapter 4.

other historical explanations. Vital in this regard are the explorations of the ideology of city-building in the ancient world as well as political discourse shared in both Assyrian ideology and in Genesis 11:1–9. When enemies of the Assyrian king "impose one mouth," it constitutes treason and challenges the authority of the king.[142] It signifies unified intent to usurp the prerogatives of proper authority (from the perspective of the Assyrian king). So also when the inhabitants of the plain of Shinar have "one lip" and mobilize with unified intent to build a tower and city, a resolution appears in which divine authority reinstitutes order in the call of Abram in Genesis 12:1–3.[143]

A study of the historical context of the Tower of Babel has, therefore, highlighted issues of authority and governance. The narrative makes the most sense interpreted in light of Neo-Assyrian idioms, and, as a result, one can fruitfully read the passage in this historical context. This historical claim appears more clearly through situating the political activities, such as city-building and imperial rhetoric regarding governance, in the context of the eighth and seventh centuries BCE. Such an analysis provides new comparative data with the Tower of Babel, as the latter focuses more on the city than on the tower, despite its popular title. All of these considerations then set the composition of the Tower of Babel in the long eighth and seventh centuries BCE, during which, as evidenced on a variety of grounds, the Bible began to be written. The political and ideological map of imperial ambition explains, then, why the Assyrian background of this story is such a productive backdrop for interpreting its features.

Like any well-written text, Genesis 11:1–9 has had a momentous history of interpretation and reinterpretation after its composition. It became even more obviously connected with Babylon given the pun on Babel in the sixth

---

142   See Uehlinger, who notes this twofold use of "one mouth" in Akkadian inscriptions (as either in the interests of, or against the interests of, the Assyrian king) (*Weltreich und "Eine Rede,"* 436). See Uehlinger generally for a much more extensive discussion of terms in Akkadian for "tongue," "language," and "mouth." In this chapter, I have provided a more literarily contextual analysis with respect to how this rhetoric was constructed, and how it relates to current discussions regarding Assyrian rhetoric in inscriptions. I have also provided additional evidence and considerations for supporting Uehlinger's earlier insightful claim that the terminology in Genesis 11:1 and 11:6 should be read in light of this imperial rhetoric, even as I depart from Uehlinger in other respects, particularly in the diachronic development of this passage within the Primeval History.

143   I explore the evidence for these conclusions more in chapters 3 and 4.

century BCE and took on more explicit relevance for exiles from Judah in southern Mesopotamia. Yet placing the narrative earlier in the Neo-Assyrian empire, and examining it in light of imperial rhetoric at this time, provides clarity on many of the otherwise obscure phrasings and aspects of this passage. Such historical background highlights the facets of the biblical text that are better understood as communicating issues of authority and defiance against it, and not idioms that point toward an etiology for multilingualism. With the exile to Babylon in 586 BCE and the compilation of the Pentateuch, new readings become possible: the city recedes in the shadow of the tower, or ziggurat, even more literally and concretely situated in Babylon. Moreover, the combination of literary strands in the editing of the Pentateuch allowed, even encouraged, a different meaning behind the obscure idioms in Genesis 11:1–9, laying the framework for the passage to be interpreted as an origin story for multilingualism.

CHAPTER 3

Words Have Consequences

Phrasing and Perspective in Genesis 11:1–9

"When *I* use a word," Humpty Dumpty said, in rather a scornful tone, "it means just what I choose it to mean—neither more nor less." "The question is," said Alice, "whether you *can* make words mean so many different things." "The question is," said Humpty Dumpty, "which is to be master—that's all."[1]

"A tower can be made with only two bricks or two words."[2]

---

1 Lewis Carroll, *Alice in Wonderland and Through the Looking Glass* (Hertfordshire: Wordsworth Classics, 1993), 205–206. See particularly Humpty Dumpty's assessment of the flexibility of adjectives compared to verbs, the latter of which are more rigid; therefore, it is more difficult to make verbs mean whatever the reader might want them to mean. This assessment is especially true of the wording in Genesis 11:1 and 11:6, involving various inflections of the cardinal number "one" (אחד). Waltke and O'Connor note that this number "is the most adjectival of the cardinals," perhaps giving rise to the polysemy and extra work that interpreters have made the word do in Genesis 11:1 and 11:6 (*An Introduction to Biblical Hebrew Syntax* [Winona Lake, IN: Eisenbrauns, 1990], 15.2.1.a). As Humpty Dumpty might claim, he would pay this word extra for all the work it has done in the history of interpretation. So he states "When I make a word do a lot of work like that . . . I always pay it extra."

2 Eric Reymond, "Similitudes of Nimrod," in *Nimrodia* (New Texture, 2018), 23. See further Reymond's ability to capture the constructive possibility of words and the building of the tower:

We have made this world, the engineers like to say, from our own conceptions. We have drawn from our own minds all the materials employed

The tower is made of only nine:

INTRODUCTION

In the long history of interpreting the Bible, exploring the phrasing of the scriptural text for meaning was more than a simple matter of limning the precise nature of Hebrew grammar in any given passage in its moment in history. Rather, the ambiguity of many parts of the Bible created the need for interpretation. Such ambiguity in the text from the perspective of later readers could be understood to rest on a number of facets. The age in which the texts were written could be far removed from the time of the interpreters, which resulted in the possibility that the phrasing of the verses was no longer clear in the later idiom of exegetes. Additionally, the belief that a divine voice was speaking to later generations through the Bible became a platform to investigate ambiguous phrasings for deeper layers of significance.[3]

Given how scribes could often play with language when producing such texts in history, it could also be argued that ambiguity is inherent in the composition of some parts of the Bible.[4] In this manner, ambiguity is understood to function

---

noun, pronoun, verb, adverb, participle, conjunction, preposition, and interjection. Words are strong as baked bricks.

Reymond, *Nimrodia*, 13.

3   As indicated in verses like Numbers 12:8, divine speech can be legitimate revelation, though not spoken clearly and involving mysteries and riddles, even as a figure like Moses stands as an exception, to whom God spoke plainly. For these and other presuppositions of premodern biblical exegetes, see James Kugel, *Traditions of the Bible*, 3–22. See especially the four assumptions in ancient biblical interpretation, including that the Bible was a "cryptic" document, in pages 14–19.

4   For a volume of how scribes can "play" when producing texts, some of the contributions in which also address the construction of ambiguity in the process, see Alex de Voogt and Irving Finkel, ed., *The Idea of Writing: Play and Complexity* (Boston: Brill, 2010). See Heath Dewrell for how ambiguity functions in the composition of prophetic texts ("Textualization and the Transformation of Biblical Prophecy," in *Scribes and Scribalism*, ed. Mark Leuchter, The Hebrew Bible in Social Perspective [New York: T&T Clark, 2021], 95–106). Scott B. Noegel has recently explored wordplay in ancient sources, focusing parts of his discussion on ambiguity as an intentional strategy in this regard (*"Wordplay" in Ancient Near Eastern Texts*, especially 302–303). Research on both scribes in their historical contexts and on the reception history of the Bible has been extremely productive in the past few decades, and an extensive overview of this literature will not be reproduced here.

Literary studies in the Hebrew Bible have also explored the manner in which authors composed passages and episodes with ambiguity as part of their artistry. Robert Alter, for example, discusses "deliberate" and "purposeful" ambiguity, as well as "indeterminacy," as part of the repertoire of the composition of biblical texts (*The Art of Biblical Narrative*, 2nd rev. and updated ed. [New York: Basic Books, 2011], xv,

as part of the intentional scaffolding of passages, intrinsic in the literature and not simply imposed by the circumstances and beliefs of later interpreters.[5] Perhaps as much as any part of the Bible, the locutions that appear within the Tower of Babel episode, which are often unparalleled, rare, or peculiar within the corpus of Classical Hebrew found in the Bible and contemporaneous inscriptions, have been seen to operate as ambiguous elements of the story. It could be a clever way to craft a tale about the confusion of languages by framing the problem of the episode as voiced by the narrator in Genesis 11:1 and by God in 11:6 through intentionally difficult and obscure phrasing. As a result, the idioms in these verses were often a locus of interpretation and reinterpretation in antiquity, splintering and multiplying meaning much as the traditional understanding of the passage contends that the episode describes the multiplying of languages.[6] The terms employed in the story, however, are sensible enough such that some meaning seems inherent, and derivable, through further examination. The tension between meaning in the text and interpretation derived from potentially ambiguous phrasing, then, calls to mind the famous episode of Humpty Dumpty from Lewis Carroll's *Through the Looking-Glass*:

19, 30). See Meir Sternberg and Yair Zakovitch, respectively, in *The Poetics of Biblical Narrative: Ideological Literature and the Drama of Reading*, ISBL (Bloomington: Indiana University Press, 1985), 186–229; "'God Said One Word, I Heard Two': Ambiguous Expressions in Biblical Literature," in *"I Will Utter Riddles from Ancient Times": Riddles and Dream-Riddles in Biblical Narrative* (Tel Aviv: Am Oved, 2005), 98–100.

5   Parts of the Christian Bible make this claim about itself. For example, 2 Peter 3:15–16 underscores that the writings of Paul are difficult to understand.

6   On the seemingly repetitive nature of phrasing in Genesis 11:1 and 11:6, and how such perceived repetition yielded multiple interpretations, see Kugel, *Traditions of the Bible*, 237. For a survey of how the phrasing in Genesis 11:1–9 invited many divergent understandings of the passage, see Phillip Michael Sherman, *Babel's Tower Translated: Genesis 11 and Ancient Jewish Interpretation*, BibInt 117 (Boston: Brill, 2013). See Yuliya Minets for the varying interpretations in early Christianity that arose from this obscure terminology in the biblical passage, giving rise to a number of understandings, the two most dominant being that there was cognitive confusion (though not necessarily an actual confusion of languages) at Babel or that there was linguistic diversity that arose from God's punishment in Genesis 11:1–9. Minets, *The Slow Fall of Babel: Languages and Identities in Late Antique Christianity* (New York: Cambridge University Press, 2022), 99–109. Naturally, many early Christians viewed Pentecost in Acts 2 as a sort of answer to the problem of Babel. It should be noted, however, that the understanding of what Acts 2 claimed occurred was varied in the early church. Minets argues that the writings of Eusebius represent a turning point. After his writings, the predominant interpretation of the passage in Christianity was that the linguistic diversity that was the result of the Tower of Babel was overcome in the event recorded in Acts 2 (*The Slow Fall of Babel*, 185–188).

"which is to be master," in the words of Humpty Dumpty, refers to whether meaning resides in the words themselves or in Humpty Dumpty's own ability to play with them. This vignette highlights the tension between the significance imposed by interpreters and the senses that the words themselves can bear.

HISTORY AND MEANING, INTERPRETATION
AND THE SENSE OF WORDS:
Relating Backgrounds to Foregrounds

From a historical perspective, comparative evidence exists in Assyrian inscriptions for the locutions found in Genesis 11:1 and 11:6, phrasings that are notoriously ambiguous within the small corpus of the Hebrew Bible but that find some clarity in light of Assyrian imperial practice and rhetoric. As such, Assyrian ideology generally is relevant for understanding the historical context for the production and interpretation of Genesis 11:1–9 as a whole.[7] But this conclusion is made manifest only by reframing a key piece of evidence: Sargon's cylinder inscription does not have a language policy embedded in its rhetoric, particularly the phrase "to impose one mouth," despite the increasingly bilingual Akkadian-Aramaic situation in Mesopotamia at this time. Viewing the rhetoric of Sargon's cylinder inscription as part of political consolidation, activity that can be conducted in the service of Assyrian royal interests or against it (if rebel factions have "one mouth"), means that similar, somewhat cognate phrasing in Genesis 11:1 and 11:6 could also indicate a story about something other than language, despite the reception history of this passage. These verses are vital for understanding what the Tower of Babel means as a piece of literature. A number of lines of evidence suggest that the Tower of Babel, at least in its earliest forms, does not describe a mythological origin of multilingualism. Instead, like the Assyrian rhetoric, the idioms in this passage are phrasings that evoke how an entity relates to authority, whether in service to it or—as in Genesis 11:1–9—against it.

Even the reception history of the story contains elements of correspondence with the political rhetoric behind Sargon's inscription.[8] For example,

---

7 For more on the recognition in recent scholarship of the Assyrian background as the time period for the production of the Tower of Babel text, see Carr, *The Formation of Genesis 1–11*, 239–242.

8 See especially the retelling in Pseudo-Philo, also called *Biblical Antiquities* or *Liber Antiquitatum Biblicarum*, and in Josephus, explored more in chapter 5, both of which entail aspects of politics in the retelling of the narrative.

along similar lines as the rebel factions that had "one mouth" against Sargon, many interpreters of Genesis 11:1–9 identify in the story the attempt to invade heaven and wage a battle against God as a motivation for the actions in the narrative.[9] The phrasing in Genesis 11:1 ("The whole world had the same plan [literally, one lip] and the same customs [literally, few words]") called for two interpretations. On the one hand, the first part of the verse (*safah akhat* in Hebrew, "one lip") was thought, as has been dominant in interpretive history, to refer to the speech of a single language.[10] It is this phrase that has invited comparison to *pâ ištēn*, "one mouth," in Sargon's cylinder inscription. The idea behind this phrasing in Genesis 11:1 for Philo of Alexandria (died 50 CE) and other ancient interpreters included the meaning "to act in unison" as was the case for the Akkadian in Sargon's Dūr-Šarrukīn cylinder inscription.[11] This interpretation nonetheless existed alongside the understanding

---

9   James Kugel, *Traditions of the Bible*, 228–229. For more on this trajectory in the history of interpretation of the passage, particularly in Pseudo-Philo, see chapter 5. Later interpreters could even marshal evidence from the materiality of the tower to demonstrate the nefarious intent of the builders with respect to God's desires and plans. According to Genesis 11:3, they constructed the tower from bricks (לבנים) and mortar (חמר). Such seemingly passing details have excited the minds of modern exegetes, who have attempted to coordinate these building materials with features of the ziggurat in Babylon at various times of its construction. See chapter 2 for some proposals. For ancient interpreters, these materials called to mind an equally notorious structure: the building projects of Pharaoh. Though modern source critics see Exodus 1:14, to which the phrasing of materiality for Pharaoh's building projects belong, as part of the P source (whereas the Tower of Babel is part of J), ancient exegetes saw these seemingly minor details in both stories as significant and interrelated. If such features of construction in Exodus 1:14 evoked unfair labor and oppression, then the same materials used in the Tower of Babel must communicate something similar. More, the only pairing of these materials in the Hebrew Bible appears in these two episodes, making the link even stronger in the mind of ancient interpreters. Just as Pharaoh imposed oppressive measures against Israel to build his edifices from tar and brick, so also Nimrod, the evil ruler in the history of interpretation who oversaw the construction of the Tower of Babel, must have equally been harsh and tyrannical in his building of the tower. See chapter 5 for some observations on the reception of this episode in Islamic history that makes the parallel between Pharaoh and the Tower of Babel as well.

10   For the difficulties of the phrasing in this verse, see Sherman, *Babel's Tower Translated*, 22–26. See the volume throughout for the manner in which Genesis 11:1–9 has been interpreted in light of Abraham's call in Genesis 12. For more on the relationship between these passages in light of the thesis of this book, see especially chapters 4 and 5.

11   Philo, *On the Confusion of Tongues*, 15. See the citation in Kugel, *Traditions of the Bible*, 237. For a more extensive discussion of Philo and the Tower of Babel, see Uehlinger, *Weltreich und "eine Rede": Eine neue Deutung der sogenannten*

of the clause as referring to language. In Philo's view the latter understanding of the diversity of languages was itself an outgrowth of their acting in unison against the divine, which resulted in confusion and dispersal.[12] For Philo, both understandings of this phrase served each other since the advent of multilingualism was a response to an illegitimate act of unification, and such acting in unison was possible for Philo only because all people spoke the same language.[13]

To sustain the argument that the Tower of Babel is not a story about the spread of languages but that the idioms in Genesis 11:1–9 that have

---

Turmbauerzählung (Gen 11, 1–9), 153–72. Philo is also ambiguous on the nature of the tower: Was it completed or not? See a discussion in Richelle, "Was the Tower of Babel Really Left Unfinished?," 135; Sherman, *Babel's Tower Translated*, 266–268. That many ancient readers were keenly aware of the critical issues addressed in this book is a theme throughout these chapters. Note, for example, Richelle's listing of Josephus and Rabbi Hiyya ben Abba in the *Midrash Tanhuma* as other sources that acknowledge that the tower was finished ("Was the Tower of Babel Really Left Unfinished?," 135–137). Also in rabbinic literature, in the Jerusalem Talmud Rabbi Eleazar calculated that at least seventy languages existed prior to the Tower of Babel narrative based on counting the nations in Genesis 10, which are also said to have their own languages (לשׁון) in 10:5, 20, and 31. If multiple languages exist prior to Genesis 11:1–9, then the Tower of Babel cannot be an etiology for multilingualism. See below for this reference. Yet, other ancient interpreters will engage this issue, an issue created by chronological complexities between Genesis 10 and 11, and, as I argue in this chapter and chapter 4, resolved by observing the distinction between the use of lexemes in Genesis 10 (לשׁון) and 11 (שׂפה), and by observing the source-critical division between P (to which these passages in Genesis 10 belong) and J (to which the Tower of Babel narrative belongs).

See also Isaiah 9:8–10 in the LXX, where the allusion to the story of the Tower of Babel is apparent, though without any trace of the story as the advent of multilingualism. See the treatments in Jean Koenig, *L'Herméneutique analogique du Judaïsme antique*, VTSup 33 (Leiden: Brill, 1982); and Arie van der Kooij, *Die Alten Textzeugen des Jesajabuches: Ein Beitrag zur Textgeschichte des Alten Testaments*, OBO 35 (Göttingen: Vandenhoeck & Ruprecht, 1981).

12 See generally Philo, *On the Confusion of Tongues*. Other ancient interpreters found in the text indications that intent and planning were the key sentiments and problems presented in the passage and that caused divine judgment. See Wisdom of Solomon 10:5. Other sources, such as *Jubilees* 10:22 and Targum Pseudo-Jonathan to Genesis 11:1, make both the confusion of languages and confusion of planning key parts of the problem in the narrative. See Kugel for these texts (*Traditions of the Bible*, 237).

13 It was nonetheless the case that Philo's interpretation of Genesis 11:1 and the idioms therein highlighted unity of action, utilizing the concept of a "symphony," but one gone wrong, producing discord and not harmony. See Sherman, *Babel's Tower Translated*, 236–244.

traditionally been translated as "one language" are actually terms from the eigthth and seventh centuries BCE referring to political actions of governance (or rebelling against proper authority) entails at least two processes. As an initial consideration, a reassessment of the narrative in Genesis 11:1–9 on its own terms needs to be offered. This step involves the examination of the phrasings in the biblical account, showing how terminology in it leads to a different understanding of the narrative than the traditional interpretation that the passage functions as an etiology for multilingualism.[14] The second step involves putting the story back together again, offering a more satisfactory account for the individual words and how they relate to the meaning of the unit as a whole. In perhaps an odd twist, these same observations can also explain the processes through which Genesis 11:1–9 could be interpreted as a story about language.[15]

Further implications exist in the process of arguing that the Tower of Babel as a story is about something other than language. The story is, instead, better interpreted as a political statement regarding the authority to unify or fragment governed entities. In one sense, tackling such a deeply entrenched interpretation of such an influential passage and offering a new one involves also interrogating some of our deepest presuppositions regarding how reading a narrative happens, and how we make meaning from stories. The dominant and unwavering sense that the story is "about" the origin of multilingualism remains in academic and popular presentations. Challenging this millennia-old interpretation necessarily requires the investigation of our assumptions of how stories are written and read.[16] As a result, it is helpful, if not necessary,

---

14 This step risks making the story like the frog in a quote attributed variously to Mark Twain or E. B. White. The quote is that "explaining a joke is like dissecting a frog: no one is interested and the frog dies of it." The ubiquity and assuredness with which readers have accepted the explanation that Genesis 11:1–9 is a story about language could mean that a reassessment in which this explanation dies, or is at least challenged, may not excite most readers. Yet I will argue in chapter 6 that the payoffs are worth the risk.

15 For more, see chapter 4.

16 For example, Uehlinger's analysis has been critiqued along a number of lines. See Hendel's remarks that Uehlinger's proposal entails an idiosyncratic, if also convoluted, theory of the development of the story over time, in a number of phases and layers. I offer a simpler thesis regarding the history of the story, understanding it as a unified composition; however, I also locate this composition within the Neo-Documentary Hypothesis, a framework for understanding the compilation of the Pentateuch that has, on other grounds, been widely discussed and productively utilized in a number of works. In other words, my reading of Genesis 11:1–9 will

to provide a very short discussion regarding how narratives are constructed and work.[17] Understanding how narrative works is crucial as well for a reassessment of Genesis 11:1–9 since the shifting narrative perspective and frame between key statements in Genesis 11:1 and 11:6 help to unlock otherwise enigmatic phrasing in the biblical text.

In addition to such methodological reflection, a "nuts-and-bolts" examination of the individual phraseological constituents that comprise the Tower of Babel story is also a necessary step. The goal is not simply semantic or philological explorations, though those are worthy ends in themselves and, done rigorously, can provide much more exacting interpretations and meanings of texts.[18] Rather, a thorough investigation of the more obscure as well as familiar terms, idioms, and expressions in Genesis 11:1–9 can shed light on important narratological features of the story. The phraseology that has been most vexing, and yet most fundamental for constructing the interpretation that Genesis 11:1–9 is a story about the spread of languages, appears in Genesis 11:1. When a careful search for parallel phrasing elsewhere is combined with the manner in which the divine perspective in Genesis 11:6 both repeats and alters the original estimation in Genesis 11:1, a different understanding, and one consonant with the political rhetoric from Assyria, emerges.[19] Such observations serve as a prelude to source-critical analyses, in which the reinterpreted (and retranslated) story of Genesis 11:1–9 can be better situated in the context of the critical theories regarding the Primeval History in Genesis 1–11, as well as the manner in which these chapters connect to the call of Abram in Genesis 12:1–3.[20]

---

contextualize my understanding of the passage within a recognized approach to the compilation of the Pentateuch and will, as a result, not be subject to the same criticism as Hendel offered against Uehlinger's study. See Hendel, "Review: Weltreich und 'eine Rede': Eine neue Deutung der sogenannten Turmbauerzählung (Gen. 11,1–9) by Christoph Uehlinger," *CBQ* 55 (1993): 785–787.

17 Fronting my methodological discussion in this manner makes clear how the following sections of this chapter relate to a larger theory of how to examine, interpret, and reinterpret the narrative.

18 In addition, such examinations can also frame more and less likely interpretations of a text.

19 As such, I will focus on key phrases, unlocking more closely what each word means in the context of the passage based on usage elsewhere in the Hebrew Bible. I will offer a philological analysis of the Tower of Babel as a self-contained story, and then put that reading into comparative conversation with the Assyrian backgrounds studied in chapter 2.

20 See chapter 4 for more.

It remains necessary, however, to offer a positive explanation regarding how the narrative as a whole in Genesis 11:1–9 functions. In other words, it is not enough to argue against the interpretation that the Tower of Babel contains an etiology of multilingualism; rather, it is necessary to demonstrate how the reconsideration of phrasing and terminology builds to a cohesive interpretation of the story in its entirety, and one better than other interpretations. A new interpretation should constitute a coherent story in which all the parts serve to drive forward the major issue in the narrative, namely who has the authority to unify or fragment political entities.[21]

In this fashion, historical backgrounds of political idioms and anxieties in Assyria and philological foregrounds of words in the passage itself should be brought together. The goal is not to offer discrete methodological examinations of Genesis 11:1–9 but to demonstrate how each consideration (historical, philological, source-critical, and reception history) depends on the others. All of these combine to show how Genesis 11:1–9 is not about language, how it became possible to see it as about language, and what a new interpretation of the story means for its use in modern society.

In one sense, then, an investigation of phrasing and terminology in Genesis 11:1–9 functions as the foundation for understanding what the story of the Tower of Babel is about. The idea that the Tower of Babel could be a story that does not include in it an etiology for the spread of languages is contrary to the overwhelmingly dominant interpretation in academic, religious, and popular conceptions. Indeed, Campegius Vitringa, one of the most revered philologists in the seventeenth century CE, writing when initial (though foundational) work in biblical criticism began, recanted his thesis that the Tower of Babel was not a story about languages thirty years after he first published this argument.[22] This episode demonstrates that a philological basis has been claimed already that Genesis 11:1–9 is about something other than multilingualism, but also that such a thesis encountered significant resistance. The claim, then, that Genesis 11:1–9 is a story containing political idioms that have no reference to languages requires careful consideration of the manner in which phrasing and narrative work together, namely the building blocks of plot. The focus on the terms and phraseology as a means for reconceiving

---

21 As will become clear in chapter 4, this question provides a coherent framework in which to read the narrative strand to which the Tower of Babel story belongs, namely J.

22 See chapter 1 for further discussion on Vitringa.

Genesis 11:1–9 not only clarifies the Tower of Babel as a self-contained story but also as part of a larger narrative. Viewing the passage through both of these lenses allows for a methodologically sound reassessment of the story in a variety of contexts, both pre- and post-compilation of the Pentateuch.

ON WORDS AND THEIR MEANINGS:
How to Build and Read a Narrative

Prior to examining the details and wording of Genesis 11:1–9 on their own terms, it is worth spending time on methodological aspects of narrative. The value of these considerations is not that they solve every question that the passage has posed, nor are these theoretical orientations a replacement for linguistic and philological analysis. Beginning with theoretical and methodological approaches to narrative, however, achieves a number of objectives. Certain topics have become the focus of study in research on how narratives are constructed and operate.[23] Such analysis brings to the fore common elements of the construction of narrative, but also the idea that such elements may not be self-evident. Levels of discourse, aspects of narration, and the pivoting of perspectives are important for a better understanding of enigmatic phrasing in Genesis 11:1–9, and for clarifying how such phrasing relates to the larger meaning of the passage. Yet such aspects of the story have not been fully appreciated in scholarship, and leveraging a discussion of narratology, or the study of how narratives are constructed, allows for new lenses through which to examine the passage.[24] Additionally, attuning oneself to the

---

23 A number of works in the field of narratology isolate aspects of story for such critical discussion. See, for example, Seymour Chatman's classic presentation of the various features of narrative in *Story and Discourse: Narrative Structure in Fiction and Film* (Ithaca, NY: Cornell University Press, 1978). Vital for the analysis below is Gérard Genette's conception of "focalizing," particularly the key shift in point of view between the narrator, who frames the situation as an omniscient narrator in Sternberg's wording, and the divine perspective. Indeed, God acts as a character within the narrative and his assessments of the situation at Shinar provide a sort of internal focalization to use Genette's term. See Genette, *Narrative Discourse*, trans. Jane E. Lewin (Oxford: Blackwell, 1980); *Narrative Discourse Revisited*, trans. Jane E. Lewin (Ithaca, NY: Cornell University Press, 1988). See more below, engaging with Manfred Jahn's use of focalization as well.

24 See particularly the use of narratology in Liane Feldman in reframing the relationship between law and narrative in P (*The Story of Sacrifice: Ritual and Narrative in*

complexities of how a narrative can be constructed, particularly the Tower of Babel, provides a balanced perspective for arguing what a narrative means without claiming that the meaning offered is exhaustive or cannot change in varying historical and literary contexts. This is exactly what happens in the compilation of the Pentateuch when it becomes possible to read the Tower of Babel as about language.

Narratology is the study of how stories are structured.[25] However, narratology can (and should) also demonstrate how narratives influence and motivate readers.[26] The Tower of Babel, particularly in the age of the nation-state and nationalism, has spawned all sorts of political discourse, and thus an examination of the narrative should also invite political criticism. The Tower of Babel has a particular historical context of production and stands at a particular junction in a larger story, both of which influence the meaning of the passage to some degree. Narratology, however, tackles the issue of narrative from a different, though by no means mutually exclusive, perspective. Narratology asks not just the history behind the words in a story, who authored them and who speaks them as the narrative unfolds, though such considerations are still central; it addresses what kind of literary world is being created in a narrative, how the parts of an episode relate to one another in all their complexities, and how that world addresses, makes claims on, and changes its audience in the act of reading.[27] In a sense, the "obviousness" of what a narrative means, even well-known and familiar ones, is suspended, if not undermined. Otherwise,

---

the Priestly Source, FAT 141 [Tübingen: Mohr Siebeck, 2020]). Jacqueline Vayntrub has also critically engaged narrated spaces and aspects of narrative in reference to the משל in a broader project that reframes scholarly dichotomies between poetry and prose, as well as orality and writing in biblical literature (Beyond Orality: Biblical Poetry on Its Own Terms, The Ancient World [New York: Routledge, 2019]).

25 In a manner of speaking, my phrasing here is intentional: "structure" is a key feature of the discipline, arising as it did out of structuralism. For a definition and history of the concept, for critiques of the structuralist legacy in narratology, and for the recognition of the social function of narrative (as in Kristeva and Ricoeur), see Paul Perron, Narratology and Text: Subjectivity and Identity in New France and Québécois Literature, Toronto Studies in Semiotics and Communication (Toronto: University of Toronto Press, 2003), 3–17. Despite the legacy of structuralism, as Mieke Bal demonstrates, one does not need to be a structuralist to appreciate the facets of story brought to light through narratological theory (Narratology: Introduction to the Theory of Narrative, 4th ed. [Toronto: University of Toronto Press, 2017], x–xi).

26 Mieke Bal has argued, as a result, that "aesthetic and political criticism" belong together in this field (Narratology, vii).

27 Bal, Narratology, xxi.

approaching narratives from such a perspective in which the meaning is so easily grasped can occlude a fuller, richer examination of a story and how it affects its readers.[28] The relevance of such an approach for unpacking the meaning of the Tower of Babel, one of the more famous episodes from the Bible, is obvious.

Among the many passages from the Bible that have received critical and literary analysis, the Tower of Babel is perhaps one of the most studied and famously discussed. It has been argued that literary features of the passage suggested that it originated from the combination of two independent stories: one about a city, and one about a tower.[29] This thesis rests at least partially on the fact that the narrative claims that the city was left unfinished, but is silent about the tower (Genesis 11:8). Others claimed, in contrast, that a number of features of the passage indicated its literary unity, not least of which were a chiasmus and a phonological play on the consonants *l-b-n*, the various combinations and associations of which can yield the words "brick," "Babel" (for *b* and *l*), and "let us confuse."[30] Yet the literary features that these scholars found in the text all fall in either one or the other of the reconstructed stories (either the city or the tower), or the feature is found in both.[31] In other words, their literary explorations did not undermine the two-story hypothesis.[32]

---

28   Bal, *On Story-Telling: Essays in Narratology*, ed. David Jobling, Foundations and Literary Facets (Sonoma, CA: Polebridge Press, 1991), 146. This statement applies especially to such a well-known text from the Hebrew Bible as the Tower of Babel.

29   Gunkel, *Genesis*, 3rd ed., trans. Mark E. Biddle (Macon, GA: Mercer University Press, 1997), 94–102.

30   For this observation, see Cassuto, *A Commentary on the Book of Genesis*, trans. Israel Abrahams (Jerusalem: Magnes, 1992), 232–233. For Kikawada's works arguing for the unity of Genesis 11:1–9, see "The Shape of Genesis 11:1–9," in *Rhetorical Criticism: Essays in Honor of James Muilenburg*, ed. Jared J. Jackson and Martin Kessler, PTMS 1 (Pittsburg: Pickwick, 1974), 18–32. Indeed, Kikawada also argued for the unity of all of the Primeval History in a coauthored article with Eric W. Heese, "Jonah and Genesis 1–11," *Annual of the Japanese Biblical Institute* 10 (1984): 3–19. For Fokkelmann, see *Narrative Art in Genesis: Specimens of Stylistic and Structural Analysis*, 2nd ed. (Sheffield: JSOT Press, 1991), 11–45.

31   As Baden argues, only in the case that the literary feature in its entirety is found in none of the separated stories and sources can the claim be made to have discovered artistry and unity. See Baden, "The Tower of Babel," 209–224.

32   Indeed, citing von Rad, who noted that J could use earlier traditions though such use does not provide a foundation for composition history within J, Baden concludes that the Tower of Babel is, indeed, a literary unity, though not for the reasons that Cassuto, Kikawada, and Fokkelman proposed. Baden, "The Tower of Babel," 218; von Rad, *Genesis*, OTL (Philadelphia: Westminster, 1972), 148.

The nature of Genesis 11 invites literary analysis of the highest order, and, as such, has been subject to such deep methodological reflection. Yet from those scholars who have argued for the literary unity of these verses, a number of features went unexplored. Perhaps this is due to the underlying goals of many of these studies, namely to stake a claim as to the extent of artistic and compositional coherence of a passage. Features in service of this conception of artistry were highlighted, but others have yet to occasion sustained reflection regarding how they contribute, under scrutiny, to yield the meaning of the passage. As a result, it could also be added that many of these literary approaches, whatever the motivation—religious or academic—that lead to the correct conclusion that the text is a unity, did not investigate the elements of narrative that then give rise to meaning in the fashion that narratology as a discipline encourages.[33]

FOCUS AND PERSPECTIVE:
Who Thinks What and Why?

For example, the persistently obscure phrasing that itself has occasioned endless commentary in Genesis 11:1 is a fundamental feature of framing what the story itself is about. It is vital, then, to ask questions about who the speaker is and how the speaker's point of view functions in the story. The comparative evidence brought forth from elsewhere in the Hebrew Bible and cognate literature to explain the obscure phrasing *safah akhat udevarim akhadim*, or "same plan (literally, one lip) and the same custom," in Genesis 11:1 certainly helps. What has been less utilized in exploring the meaning of these terms is a narratological approach.

To answer the question above from a narratological framework, the person speaking is the narrator.[34] Strictly speaking, the narrator and author, in the

---

33   For more in the unity of the passage, and for an overview of previous proposals beginning with the theory of a "double myth" in G. L. Bauer's 1802 work, see Westermann, *Genesis 1–11*, 536–537.

34   See the concept of "external focalization" of the narrator, instead of the "zero" focalization of the author, who stands above and out of the story world, and "internal" focalization of perspective portrayed by actors in the narrative themselves (Monika Fludernik, *An Introduction to Narratology* [New York: Routledge, 2009], 36–39). For Jahn, "zero focalization" does not exist and should no longer be used as, in the world of the story, there is no access to the author itself, only the perspective of the narrator

sense of the actual, physical person or persons who produced the text, are not the same. An example of such a distinction appears in Mark Twain's *Adventures of Huckleberry Finn*. The narrator of the story is Huck Finn himself, who may or may not share the views and perspectives of the author, Mark Twain.[35] Similarly, the narrator frames what occurs in the story, ceding this perspective to one of the characters when that character speaks. Nonetheless, the key element of the narrative is the narrator. The narrator is the one who conveys, or narrates, the story, and the story is then communicated through a medium via the narrator's control.[36] Turning back to the biblical text, the narrator in Genesis 11:1 provides the evaluation of the situation on earth, that it was characterized as *safah akhat udevarim akhadim*.[37] While this phrase occurs nowhere else in the Hebrew Bible, and while many avenues of comparative evidences have been marshalled to arrive at an adequate translation, it is obviously important to investigate its meaning, since it provides

---

or characters (*Narratology 2.3: A Guide to the Theory of Narrative*, online publication, http://www.uni-koeln.de/~ame02/pppn.pdf, 35).

35 For this and other examples of "implied author" and the distinction between author and narrator, see Suzanne Keen, *Narrative Form*, 2nd ed., rev. and exp. (New York: Palgrave Macmillan, 2015), 36.

36 So Ball states that the narrator "converts" the story "into signs." She argues further that

> An agent who relates, who utters the signs, produces these signs. This agent cannot be identified with the writer, painter, composer, or filmmaker. Rather, the writer withdraws and calls upon a fictitious spokesman, the *narrator*. But the narrator does not relate continually. Whenever direct speech occurs in the text, it is as if the narrator temporarily yields this function to one of the actors. When describing the text layer, the key question is *who* is doing the narrating.

Italics original. Ball, *Narratology*, 8.

37 The narrator in this source more broadly often provides evaluations of the situations and characters therein. See, for example, the comments on the serpent in Genesis 3:1. The narrator also presents the divine perspective at times, as in Genesis 6:5–8 (see more below). The perspective of the narrator and God is not necessarily always the same in this source. For example, in Genesis 18 the narrator recedes and Abraham "steps in the breach" (to use Yochanan Muffs's term), and the two characters in the episode, God and Abraham, hash out details of what will or will not happen to the wicked and righteous in Sodom and Gomorrah. The particular views of the narrator are not known in this situation, though it is clear that the narrator knows God's private thoughts and allows Abraham to win the debate. See Muffs, "Who Will Stand in the Breach? A Study of Prophetic Intercession," in *Love and Joy: Law, Language, and Religion in Ancient Israel* (New York: Jewish Theological Seminary of America, 1992), 9–48.

an assessment of the problems entailed in the Tower of Babel story. From a theoretical perspective, the fact that the narrator speaks these words already introduces another important aspect of narratology, namely, focalization.[38] It may not seem to be a significant observation, or even pertinent. Much of biblical narrative has been described as operating through the lens of a third-person omniscient narrator.[39] Yet the narrator itself has a perspective, which may or may not be aligned with characters in the narrative, including God's.[40]

It can hardly be emphasized enough that the phrasing in Genesis 11:1 lies at the heart of much of what the story is thought to be about and mean. The lack of repetition elsewhere of this phrasing might give rise to doubts that any firm meaning can be established or might be thought to confirm that the biblical text contains an intentionally ambiguous wording in a story believed to tell of the origins of multilingualism. Yet a similar, though not exact, phrasing as found in Genesis 11:1 does appear elsewhere in Genesis 11:6.

Two observations require comment before the significance of this parallel occurrence is examined in more detail. It is not a given that the narrator and divine actor agree on the perspective of the situation in the plains of Shinar. Just as a distinction exists between the narrator and author, so also the narrator, often labeled a "third-person-omniscient narrator," and the actors in a passage can diverge in their respective motivations, intentions, and assessments of the situation described. In the intervening verses between Genesis 11:1 and 11:6, the people have constructed their tower and begun work on the city at large. Events have occurred and the situation may have changed such

---

38 So Bal states that "narrator and focalization together determine the *narrative situation*" (italics original; *Narratology*, 12). Similarly, Benjamin Harshav states that narration and point of view are essential "regulating principles," fundamental elements of literature and story that "tell us 'in what sense' to take the senses of the words" (*Explorations in Poetics* [Stanford: Stanford University Press, 2007], 82).

39 For a disagreement of this assessment, however, see David M. Gunn and Danna Nolan Fewell, *Narrative in the Hebrew Bible* (London: Oxford University Press, 1993), 53–56.

40 Bal's claim is that "narration implies focalization," entailing the "notion that language shapes vision and world view." Bal, *Narratology*, 12. See her more extensive analysis of focalization as "the relation between the vision and what is seen, perceived" in *Narratology*, 132–153. The interplay between the narrator in Genesis 11:1 and the divine voice in Genesis 11:6 falls into this category.

For Jahn, such an example of multiple perspectives presented in a narrative, including that of the narrator, is an example of "variable focalization" (*Narratology 2.3*, 31). The task of the reader/interpreter is to explore how such points of view relate, since they may or may not be aligned.

that the perspective of the narrator in Genesis 11:1 and the divine actor in 11:6 might not be identical. It could be the case, for example, that the narrator describes the precondition of united action in Genesis 11:1 in the phrase "same plan and the same custom," *safah akhat udevarim akhadim*, but that the situation has changed, possibly escalated, in light of the construction of the tower and the beginnings of the construction of the city by Genesis 11:6.[41] In this case, perhaps the phrasing in Genesis 11:6 "they are one people and have the same plan," or *am akhad vesafah akhat lekullam* in Hebrew, frames a more intense and critical situation that merits divine action than the one in Genesis 11:1.

DO THE NARRATOR AND GOD HAVE THE SAME PERSPECTIVE IN GENESIS 11:1 AND 11:6?

More of the terminological and semantic exploration concerning a specific word "lip," *safah*, and its possible meanings will be important to consider in detail. For now, the focus is on the framing of the assessment in Genesis 11:6 to investigate how it relates to the narrator's voice in Genesis 11:1, all to demonstrate how perspective, point of view, and variations in phrasing support an interpretation of the narrative devoid of language. For example, one of the greatest distinctions between the narrator's statement in Genesis 11:1 and God's statement in 11:6 is the order and the replacement of one of the twofold phrases with another. In Genesis 11:1, the assessment is that the earth is united, having the "same plan" ("one lip," *safah akhat*) and the "same custom," or *devarim akhadim*, literally "few words." In 11:6 God claims that the

---

41   See, for example, Yairah Amit, who identifies Genesis 11:1 as an "exposition," or the beginning of a story that is initially "static." For Amit, this verse provides information that then leads, at the end of the exposition, to a dynamic situation in which change, drama, and plot move the story along. The exposition continues into Genesis 11:2, which describes how the people settle and dwell in the plain of Shinar. Nothing would happen unless an event compels things to change. Amit identifies Genesis 11:3 as the moment when the story changes and moves, when the people begin to bake bricks for construction projects. See Amit, *Reading Biblical Narratives: Literary Criticism and the Hebrew Bible* (Minneapolis: Fortress Press, 2001), 33–34. She provides a five-fold narrative structure to Genesis 11:1–9, also called a "pediment structure," which consists of (1) the exposition, (2) a complication, (3) change in the narratives, (4) unraveling of events, and (5) an ending. Amit, *Reading Biblical Narratives*, 47–48.

people are "one people," *am akhad*, and then, shifting the order of elements, have the "same plan" (*safah akhat*). Such variation might appear insignificant, though triangulating these terms reveals a political and nonlinguistic evaluation of the scene.[42] For this discussion of framing, it is worth observing that the assertion in Genesis 11:6 begins with "look," or *hen* in Hebrew, a word (often called a "particle") absent in Genesis 11:1. Genesis 11:6 is as follows:

> The LORD said, "Look (*hen*), they are one people and have the same plan! This is the beginning of what they will do. And now, nothing they propose will be withheld from them!

The identification of the particular function of the word *hen* could influence how one relates this verse to Genesis 11:1. Two options are available: it is either a presentative particle (a short form of the longer *hinneh*, a common—though difficult to translate—word in Biblical Hebrew often rendered as "look") or a conditional particle (translated as "if").[43]

---

42 See below for more.

43 Waltke and O'Connor use this term "presentative particle," which introduces "presentative exclamations" (*An Introduction to Biblical Hebrew Syntax*, §40.2.1). While T. O. Lambdin termed this particle a "predicator of existence," along the same lines as יֵשׁ, a number of factors have led scholars to see a different, or at least more nuanced, use of the particle as its most basic function (*Introduction to Biblical Hebrew* [New York: Scribner, 1971], §135). See Waltke and O'Connor for more.

 Note the parallel use of הֵן in Genesis 3:22. Indeed, the syntax of Genesis 3:22 and 11:6 is striking: in each verse, the divine responds with an initial הֵן followed by a וְעַתָּה clause that conveys something that is a further implication, and a further transgression, of the divine-human boundary. In Genesis 3, humans have eaten from the tree of knowledge of good and evil, becoming like the gods (so the הֵן clause Genesis 3:22a), but they cannot have the tree of life and become immortal (a response inaugurated by the וְעַתָּה). So also in Genesis 11:6, God assesses the situation and sees that the people have completed their tower (on parallel to the tree of knowledge of good and evil, an assessment beginning with הֵן), but they cannot build a city, which, on parallel to the tree of life, would cross the divine-human boundary, a consideration that begins with וְעַתָּה. Given that in Genesis 3:22 the הֵן functions as a presentative particle, the same, given the parallel construction, is likely the case in Genesis 11:6, though it is worth considering the possibility that it is a conditional particle. It is noteworthy that the only occurrences of הֵן as the short form of the presentative particle (the long form being הִנֵּה) plus a clause with וְעַתָּה in this sort of syntax occurs in Genesis 3:22 and 11:6 and nowhere else. Both passages derive from the J source, the significance of which is unpacked more in chapter 4. See that chapter for a more extensive discussion. That the short form of the presentative particle in this syntactic layout is distinctive in J might be significant given

If the particle *hen* is understood as a presentative particle, then it represents the presentation of a situation or scene from the perspective of one of the characters.[44] The particle often changes the perspective or point of view in biblical narrative, in this case offering the divine viewpoint on the situation.[45] Such a perspective is not necessarily the same as the narrator's in Genesis 11:1 given the events that have taken place in the narrative: between the narrator's assessment in Genesis 11:1, beginning with the Hebrew phrase *wayehi*, "and it was (the case that)," which expresses background information to the following narrative, and the divine voice in Genesis 11:6 the people have constructed a tower and have begun building a city.[46] One could argue that only in light of this action could they be called *am akhad*, or "one people."[47] It would nonetheless be an assessment in line with the notice in Genesis 11:1,

---

that distinctive orthography appears in J also in the form of "his tent," אהלה. For a fuller discussion, see Baden, "'His Tent': Pitched at the Intersection of Orthography and Source Criticism," in *"Like ʾIlu Are You Wise": Studies in Northwest Semitic Languages and Literatures in Honor of Dennis G. Pardee*, ed. Humphrey Hardy, Joseph Lam, and Eric Reymond (Chicago: Oriental Institute Press, 2022), 283–290. See also below where other narrative techniques from J appear in both the flood narrative and in the Tower of Babel.

44 See Adele Berlin's observations regarding point of view in biblical narrative, particularly the use of הנה in changing point of view at a variety of levels of discourse both within the narrator's perspective and within the dialogue of the characters themselves (*Poetics and Interpretation of Biblical Narrative* [Winona Lake, IN: Eisenbrauns, 1994], especially 66–68 for uses of הנה).

45 Berlin, *Poetics and Interpretation of Biblical Narrative*, 66–68.

46 Sherman states that the building has resulted in the people being one political entity, as though the situation changed, or became official, with the building activity: "Prior to the Yahweh's speech, the people have been characterized as possessing 'the same language and few words.' They have been referred to as 'the entire world.' For Yahweh, however, this group represents a political collective. They are 'one people, with one language for all of them.' Something new has come into existence with this phrase. There is a shift from linguistic unity to national unity; or, rather, the two are equated" (*Babel's Tower Translated*, 36). A more dynamic assessment of the situation between the narrator in Genesis 11:1 and the divine perspective in Genesis 11:6 appears in his remarks than I argue here (in which I claim that both the narrator and God share the same perspective), though his interpretation of the political aspects of the phrasing in Genesis 11:6 is correct.

47 Note the volume that plays on this phrasing, connecting the wording of Genesis 11:6 and the relationship between nation and language: Shlomo Karmi, עם אחד ושפה אחת: תחיית הלשון העברית בראייה בין תחומית, קורות ומקורות (Tel Aviv: Ministry of Defense, 1997). The distinction between the main title and subtitle is instructive: evoking the story of Babel and its political aspects means borrowing the biblical wording שפה in the main title, yet the subtitle, referring to language, uses לשון.

even if as an escalation of the same evaluation. Indeed, it seems as though the divine, upon descending in Genesis 11:5, has realized that the situation is as the narrator claimed in Genesis 11:1.

If the particle *hen* is understood instead as a conditional particle establishing a protasis (the "if" part of the conditional clause), then it more clearly describes the precondition in light of which the activity of the people represents an affront to the divine. The verse could be translated as "then the LORD said, 'if, as one people and having the same mind, this is how they have begun to act, then anything that they intend to do will not be withheld from them.'" Many aspects of this translation require further comment and defense, but for the purposes of this discussion, the focus is on the conditional and how it relates to the divine perspective. In this interpretation, the divine voice grants the condition that such united action on the part of the people in Genesis 11:1 presents a problematic disposition as far as God is concerned, and evidence of the problematic nature of this disposition then appears in the activity of the people in constructing a tower. In other words, God agrees with the assessment of Genesis 11:1, and, in so doing, points to the tower (as a completed construction) as evidence for the veracity of this description.

In both cases, whether *hen* as a presentative or conditional particle, the divine perspective aligns with the narrator's assessment in Genesis 11:1. This alignment occurs either as a realization after the descent that occurs in 11:5, or as a precondition that grants the background information in Genesis 11:1 as the disposition that gives rise to the divine affront of the completed tower and, especially, the potential of building a city. As such, the phrasing in Genesis 11:1 and 11:6 are synonymous statements. The narrator cedes its perspective when an actor, such as God in Genesis 11:6, speaks; however, in this case the two evaluations of the conditions on earth agree with one another. If so, then the variations in terminology can be triangulated as part of discerning what the otherwise obscure locutions denote, particularly *safah akhat* and *devarim akhadim*. The phrase *devarim akhadim* in Genesis 11:1 is replaced by *am akhad* in Genesis 11:6, but if these are roughly synonymous (and therefore the divine can use the latter instead of the former, but maintain the same perspective as the narrator), then they could be understood as parallel constructions.[48] Elsewhere, the use of *akhadim* conveys oneness,

---

48 Though Westermann does not explore the implications and pursue the analysis as I do above, his statement about the relationship between 11:1 and 11:6 is apt: "God's

in the sense of a "few" or, as in Ezekiel 37:17, becoming one. In this sense, *devarim akhadim* evokes the idea that the people are few of words, or agreeing with one another.

Alternatively, but also in line with this interpretation, the word *davar* (plural *devarim*) often refers to custom or law.[49] Particularly relevant is the use of "one voice," or *qol akhad*, for unanimity, and *devarim* referring to the content of law in the ratification of the ceremony in Exodus 24:3. In the context of Exodus 18:16–19, *davar* refers to a legal dispute. In this fashion, the phrase in Genesis 11:1 could mean "few disputes," where *akhadim* functions like the phrase "few days," *yamim akhadim*, in Genesis 27:44; 29:20; and Daniel 11:20. Conversely, if *davar* has the more general legal sense of a custom or law, as in Deuteronomy 15:2 and 17:8 (and elsewhere), then the phrase *devarim akhadim* in Genesis 11:1 could mean "the same custom/law." In either case, the focus is on unified existence and concerted action. This understanding of Genesis 11:1, *safah akhat udevarim akhadim*, "same plan and same custom," makes sense of the parallel use of *safah akhat* in Genesis 11:6, where the phrase is paired instead with *am akhad*, "one people." The wording *devarim akhadim* is, then, somewhat synonymous with "one people," and the problem in Genesis 11:1, according to the narrator, is equivalent to the problem according to the divine perspective in Genesis 11:6.[50]

Further discussion of *safah*, "lip," particularly in relation to *davar*, "custom," and *am*, "people," will solidify the idea that the phrasing in Genesis 11:6a concerns united action against divine authority, and that all the elements in these clauses build to this idea and not a statement about linguistic unity. Additional support that these words and the divine perspective pertain

---

reflection is not a direct reaction to the people's work that he has come down to look at. It begins rather with a summation of the situation and repeats almost word for word the sentence of the exposé, v. 1" (*Genesis 1–11*, 551). I argue that the divine response is a summation of sorts, and the repetitions are important; however, the variations in phrasing are also vital for understanding how the narrator's assessment and divine wording relate to one another and then communicate what the story is about.

49   See, for example, Exodus 18:16–19, 22–23, 26; 22:8; Leviticus 8:5 and 26.

50   Wenham is led astray here by preconceived notions that עַם refers to "people" in a "racial" sense (itself a very problematic assessment given modern studies on race and culture), whereas גּוֹי refers to "people" in the sense of a political nation, a distinction he borrows from the *Theological Dictionary of the Old Testament*; however, as argued in this chapter, this does not hold, at least for עַם. See Wenham, *Genesis 1–15*, WBC 1 (Waco, TX: Word Books, 1987), 240.

to authority can be found in Genesis 11:6b. In the second half of this verse, God states, "and now, nothing they propose to do will be held from (or will be impossible for) them!" The only other verse with the verb *baṣar*, meaning "to be impossible," and a word derived from the root behind the translation "propose," *z-m-m*, which denotes intention, is Job 42:2.

> I know that you can do all things, and that nothing you intend (*mezim-mah*) is impossible (*yibbaṣer*) for you.

In the context of Job, this passage is significant.[51] Job 42:2 exists at a position in the book that reveals something of divine essence. The denouement of God confronting Job is Job's epiphany about God's nature. As such, one might see in the phrasing of this verse a fixed doxology of sorts, describing the power of God particularly as it concerns the realm of humans. The phrasing of this passage evokes the omnipotence of God and the relatively limited nature of humankind.[52]

Returning to Genesis 11:6, the construction of city and tower represents divine aspirations from the perspective of God. Even more, the idioms and phrasings in this verse point to one, not two, problems. The first half of the

---

51 As Westermann argues, "God has put Job in his place; and Job now acknowledges God for what he really is." Westermann, *Genesis 1–11*, 551.

52 This omnipotence, then, is what God is afraid the people will desire or even have. Such anxieties about the human and divine boundaries are a theme throughout the Primeval History in Genesis 1–11, particularly in the literary units that have been identified as J. See chapter 4 for more. Greenstein understands the discourse in Job 42:2 and its relation to Genesis 11:1–9 differently. Given his translation and analysis of Job 42:6 as parody against the divine (and in sympathy for humans and the human condition), by extension other verses such as 42:2 reflect disdain toward God. Greenstein also makes the connection to the Tower of Babel literarily, but not as seeing the phrasing as a witness toward an independent tradition as Westermann does. Rather, Job is "alluding" to the Tower of Babel, using God's negative appraisal of human ambition against God, who actually has such power and might. As such, Job is mocking God since, "if God is all about power and not morality and justice, Job will not condone it through acceptance" (Greenstein, *Job: A New Translation* [New Haven, CT: Yale University Press, 2019], xxi). As Wenham observes, the verb "to plot," זמם, has a positive meaning when applied to God (Jeremiah 4:28; 51:12) in the sense that such plotting is God's rightful prerogative. When applied to people, however, the meaning is often more negative in tone (Deuteronomy 19:19; Psalm 31:14; 37:12). See Wenham, *Genesis 1–15*, 240–241. Similarly, other words like גאוה, when applied to God, are positive ("majesty," as in Deuteronomy 33:26 and Psalm 68:35, though it also occurs with this meaning for Israel in Deuteronomy 33:29). Elsewhere, when applied to people, the word means "arrogance."

verse does not describe linguistic unity but rather all the rhetoric in the verse is consistent in describing a situation of united action (11:6a) leading to an attempt to usurp divine privilege. The entirety of the verse reveals the problem from the divine perspective: with united intent, humans will not be complacent and will challenge God's place.[53]

The narrator frames stories, but yields, in direct discourse, to actors in the story, as in Genesis 11:6. The question, however, is what the divine actor in Genesis 11:6 actually sees, and whether this perspective provides any focus regarding what the story is about. The grammar of 11:5 clarifies what God perceives and explains how the story ends, thereby underscoring what the story might have meant on its own terms as an independent narrative. The syntax of 11:5 in particular functions in two ways: first, the relative clause "*that* the children of mankind had built," *asher banu benei ha-adam*, has as its referent the tower, and not the compound tower and city; second, the syntax of the relative pronoun plus the verb in a suffix conjugation ("had built," *banu*) refers to a completed action, antecedent to the main line of the narrative.[54] In other words, the tower, and only the tower, was built as a completed action prior to God's descent. These observations are vital for unpacking the meaning of the narrative, and are, therefore, worthy of sustained consideration.

Exegetes have long observed this issue, but the full import of the syntax of Genesis 11:5 has not been brought to bear on the meaning of Genesis 11:1–9 as a whole until recently. While interpreting this verse correctly as a completed action, other scholars have opted to allow contextual factors to determine how Genesis 11:5 is translated and understood. For example, the medieval rabbi David Kimḥi observed that a completed action seemed to be described in the clause in Genesis 11:5, but imported the words of 11:6, "to begin," *hakhillam*, into Genesis 11:5.[55] As a result, and despite the explicit reference to incomplete building in Genesis 11:8 as pertaining to the city, Kimḥi translates Genesis 11:5 as "began to build." The result is an understanding of Genesis 11:5 and 11:1–9 based on a divine assessment in 11:6 of the overall activity of humankind, and in contradiction to the plain sense of 11:8 in which it is only the city that

---

53   The analysis of chapter 2 of this book supports this understanding, particularly the focus on the building of the city.

54   Vanderhooft, "Babylon as Cosmopolis in Israelite Texts and Achaemenid Architecture," 45–48; Richelle, "Was the Tower of Babel Really Left Unfinished?," 125–139.

55   Vanderhooft, "Babylon as Cosmopolis in Israelite Texts and Achaemenid Architecture," 45–48; Richelle, "Was the Tower of Babel Really Left Unfinished?," 125–139.

is left incomplete. Yet everywhere else, such syntax of the relative followed by the suffix conjugation narrates a completed action that is itself anterior to the main line. In other words, the antecedent to the relative clause was completed ("had built" as a finished act) prior to God descending.[56]

---

56 As VanderKam and Vanderhooft note, *Jubilees* is harmonistic in its retelling of the account, adding that the people stopped building the city and tower in *Jubilees* 10:24, whereas Genesis 11:8 makes mention only of the cessation of the construction of the city. Yet Vanderhooft observes that the phrasing in *Jubilees* 10:19 ("let us ascend through it to heaven") may imply a completed action of construction of the tower in the retelling in *Jubilees*.

Other evidence points to tension in *Jubilees* between harmonizing what happens to the tower and city (so the statement that the people ceased construction on both in *Jubilees* 10:24) and also, perhaps, recognizing that the biblical text might describe the completed state of the tower prior to divine judgment in Genesis 11:5. In *Jubilees* 10:20, the Ethiopic grammar marks the beginning of the construction of the building project in the past with a perfective plus imperfective construction, highlighting the non-completed, though narrated as a past act, nature of the building. The aspect switches, however, in *Jubilees* 10:21, that the people have built it, solely using the perfective aspect. This all occurs prior to the divine descent in *Jubilees* 10:22.

It is clear that the suffix on the perfective verb in Ethiopic refers to the tower alone due to context. Though the same verbal and suffixal forms appear in 10:19, employing the so-called *waldu la-negus* construction in which the verb and suffix "they built it" governs both city and tower quite explicitly, this phrasing is perhaps part of the same harmonization strategy as in *Jubilees* 10:23–24. In these verses, God and the angelic accompaniment descend to see the city and tower which "humankind had built," so that humans will, in *Jubilees* 10:24, be dispersed and will cease building both of them. Yet the actual description of their initial building activity and the completion of construction in *Jubilees* 10:20–21, in which the particularly curious combination of imperfective and perfect aspect occurs, refers only to the building of the tower, perhaps especially anticipated in the note, borrowed from the biblical text, in *Jubilees* 10:19 that the tower's height will ascend to heaven. So, in *Jubilees* 10:20–21, the focus is on construction materials and dimensions that relate to the tower alone. For the difficulties grammatically in these verses, see VanderKam, who eliminates the issues of the Ethiopic through appeal to the Catena of Nicephorus, particularly in VanderKam's commentary. The Catena may preserve a more original reading, but the Ethiopic text as it stands could offer additional insight into the struggle to understand the Tower: according to the standard and long-held interpretation from antiquity, the Tower should have been incomplete, yet the grammar of the biblical text indicates otherwise. Note especially the wording in the Ethiopic that the bricks used to build the tower are "complete bricks." See VanderKam, *The Book of Jubilees*, CSCO 511 (Leuven: Peeters, 1989), 61–62; *Jubilees 1–21*, Hermeneia (Minneapolis: Fortress, 2018), 414. For more on the grammatical aspects of Ethiopic mentioned above, see, most recently (alongside the older grammars of August Dillmann and

The issue remains regarding the antecedent to the relative clause in Genesis 11:5 and how to identify what the "that" refers to. In isolation, the syntax in Genesis 11:5 permits both the tower and the city. The Masoretic pointing, a medieval liturgical marker in the preservation of the biblical text (with an *atnakh* after *migdal*, or "tower"), seems to favor the idea that both the city and tower are the antecedents ("the city and tower which they had built"), in which case both, since the city is clearly left unfinished in verse 8, are in the process of being built, but are not completed as such.[57] Yet, the syntax of the suffixal form *banu* is actually a pluperfect, "had built," which means that the antecedent to the relative clause is a completed task. Since the city is explicitly said to be left unfinished in Genesis 11:8, contextually and grammatically the tower was complete in its construction, while the city was not.

More details can be offered in this syntactical consideration. If a relative clause plus suffix conjugation (*qatal*) always describes a completed act "anterior to the main narrative line," for Genesis 11:5 the antecedent to the relative clause was completed prior to God's descent to observe it. Though the relative could, in theory, apply to the city and the tower, in Genesis 11:4 there is license to see them as distinct. In this verse, the phrase "with its top to the heavens" modifies only one noun, the tower, and, as such, the relative in Genesis 11:5 could also be seen to modify only one noun. The masculine singular near demonstrative in Genesis 11:6, "this," *zeh*, most naturally indicates the nearest masculine singular antecedent, the tower, and not the city, which is a feminine noun.[58] Nor does the pronoun likely refer to the totality of the actions of the people, though some possibility exists for this option in isolation of other factors.[59] When the syntax and narrative of Genesis 11:4–6 are examined alongside the notice that only the city was left incomplete in 11:8, then the relative pronoun in Genesis 11:5 most clearly refers to the tower.

T. O. Lambdin), Josef Tropper and Rebecca Hasselbach-Andee, *Classical Ethiopic: A Grammar of Gəʿəz*, LANE 10 (University Park, PA: Eisenbrauns, 2021).

57   Richelle, "Was the Tower of Babel Really Left Unfinished?," 129–130.

58   Vanderhooft, "Babylon as Cosmopolis in Israelite Texts and Achaemenid Architecture," 48; Richelle, "Was the Tower of Babel Really Left Unfinished?," 133.

59   Abstract referents such as this, to a grouping of actions, are historically feminine in grammatical form and function cross-Semitically. See Edward Lipiński, *Semitic Languages: Outline of a Comparative Grammar*, OLA 80 (Leuven: Peeters, 1997), 236. See also Waltke and O'Connor, *Introduction to Biblical Hebrew Syntax*, §6.3.2f. One might expect a feminine demonstrative, though as Waltke and O'Connor demonstrate, זה, as the masculine near demonstrative pronoun, can function as a "vague" referent for any preceding activity (*Introduction to Biblical Hebrew Syntax*, §17.4.3b).

The suffix verb form following the relative, describing a completed event prior to the main narrative line, conveys a finished tower, which in Genesis 11:6 stands as an example that God provides of only the first of many things that the people will now accomplish.

In one sense, the arguments about Genesis 11:5 pertain to the grammar and meaning of the narrative of Genesis 11:1–9 on its own, since they entail the syntax of some clauses in the story and how they relate to other aspects of the passage and its plot claims. Yet the observation that the tower was finished, as required by the syntax of Genesis 11:5 and as ancient interpreters seem to have recognized in some fashion, also provides a framework through which to examine the significance of the historical context for the production of Genesis 11:1–9 and their implications for understanding the Tower of Babel story. The focus, like ancient reflection on Dūr-Šarrukīn, is on the incomplete city.[60]

This thesis, then, also makes the arguments about the political idioms of authority and governance in Neo-Assyria more concrete, which are not linguistic in nature, though they use terms involving the lexeme "mouth," but are relevant for unpacking the otherwise difficult and obscure clauses in Genesis 11:1 and 11:6. These phrasings in Hebrew have also been mistakenly understood to refer to language, though they were political and nonlinguistic in nature in the historical context of production of the passage. A reanalysis of the importance of the city in Genesis 11:1–9 supports the comparative data

---

60   As Richelle remarks,

> Thus, the main focus is not on the tower but on the city, which confirms what some exegetes have already noted. The tower is briefly mentioned as a striking illustration of the projects that the Babylonians could continue achieving if Yhwh did not intervene; it is most likely the tower that the latter alludes to when he says: "this is only the beginning of their doing" (v. 6). In addition, it now seems less pertinent, in order to date the text, to look for a period in the history of the tower when its construction was interrupted. The most natural reading of the text would rather lead us to look for a time when a more general problem in the city, related to building work, happened. It is not easy to see what this could correspond to in the history of Babylon, and perhaps it would be wiser to accept the simple fact that the text speaks only in very general terms.

Richelle, "Was the Tower of Babel Really Left Unfinished?," 138. It should be noted that Vanderhooft does not draw this conclusion, but instead advances the idea that Babylon functions as a background to the story. He argues well and thoughtfully concerning this background, though the examination in this book diverges from his assessments.

about city-building from Mesopotamia as meaningful for an analysis of the biblical narrative.[61] Likewise, the political idioms from the same Neo-Assyrian period are also vital for interpreting Genesis 11:1 and 11:6.

SEEKING THE SENSE OF AMBIGUITY AND GIVING LIP:
How Does "lip"/safah Function in Similar Contexts Elsewhere?

To give a more precise sense of Genesis 11:1, it is helpful to return to the first phrase to confront the reader of the Tower of Babel narrative: "now all the earth had the same plan (literally, was one lip)." The translation "one lip" woodenly renders the Hebrew, which normally is translated as "one language." Most lexica list "language" as a translation possibility for *safah* in Hebrew, which otherwise means "lip" or a host of other idiomatic uses.[62] Yet there are

---

61   Though unconvinced about the analysis in the Sargon cylinder inscription, as well as unconvinced about the reading of the Tower of Babel also without language, Fales makes a striking observation about the connection between the rhetoric in Sargon's inscription and the formation of Dūr-Šarrukīn. As Fales notes, the Akkadian *pâ ištēn ušaškin-ma* links the idea of imposing unity with the next clause, in which Sargon causes diverse inhabitants to dwell in his city. The idiom of unification is intricately related to the action of building the city in a manner with notable similarities, as argued in this chapter and chapter 2 of this book, with the idioms in Genesis 11:1 and 11:6 and the focus on the city as the problem as uncovered more in the syntactic reading of Genesis 11:5 as offered by Vanderhooft and Richelle. For Fales' insightful comments, see "Su un passo di Sargon e la "Torre di Babele," in *"Suadìti?" Scritti di amici e colleghi in memoria di Francesco Aspesi*, eds. Vermondo Brugnatelli and Leonardo Magini, Studi Camito-Semitici 9 (Milano: Centro Studi Camiti-Semitici, 2022), 160.

Fales remains unconvinced about the reading of Sargon II as having no language involved given the increasingly bilingual Mesopotamian heartland. Yet simply because Mesopotamia was increasingly bilingual, and simply because Assyria did utilize Aramaic as an administrative language for some occasions, does not necessitate that such is the referent behind Sargon's rhetoric. The long history of the idioms involved stand on their own and do not require unspoken and unacknowledged historical realities to interpret them, as important as the growing presence of Aramaic certainly was. For more, see Boyd, *Language Contact, Colonial Administration, and the Construction of Identity in Ancient Israel.*

62   For more on the semantics of שׂפה, particularly from a diachronic perspective, see Yael Landman, "On Lips and Tongues in Ancient Hebrew," *VT* 66 (2016): 66–77. See also Boyd for a slightly different take, though one that builds on Landman's insightful research ("Sargon's Dūr-Šarrukīn Cylinder Inscription and Language Ideology," 102–105).

few other verses and passages that share the purported meaning "language," and ultimately even these cases do not use the term on its own to denote this gloss without other identifiable markers. It is necessary, therefore, to explore *safah* on its own, as well as what it might mean for the world to have "one lip."

Indeed, examining the semantics of *safah* is important for a variety of reasons. While most occurrences of the lexeme are easy enough to translate as "lip" or a commonly accepted idiom, this word never means "language" when used on its own, as found in Genesis 11:1–9. It can mean language, but only in certain contexts in which it appears alongside other key terms that carry this meaning and transfer it to *safah* by context. These contexts, however, do not appear in Genesis 11:1–9. Because the word in the Tower of Babel episode never means "language" in other, similar phrasings elsewhere in Biblical Hebrew, the interpretation and translation of the lexeme in Genesis 11:1–9 should be changed. The examination of other features and phraseology in this passage confirms this conclusion.

The only other occurrence of "one lip" in the Hebrew Bible is in Genesis 11:6. In this verse, as already demonstrated, the situation that the narrator described in Genesis 11:1 is presented from the divine perspective, in which God perceives the threat as "one lip" as in Genesis 11:1, but in Genesis 11:6, this phrase is preceded by and conjoined with "one people," *am akhad* (and not *devarim akhadim*). This change in terminology is significant and helps to clarify why God was not pleased with the situation. When referring to speech, "lip" primarily denotes the content of what is said, such as oaths, curses, truth, and lies (Leviticus 5:4; Numbers 30:12; Proverbs 12:22). The only time that *safah* refers to language when not conjoined with *lashon*, "tongue," and governed by the adjective "unintelligible," *imqey* in Hebrew, is Isaiah 19:18.[63]

---

63   Adele Berlin and Marc Brettler identify the Egyptian language behind the phrasing in Psalm 81:6: שָׂמוֹ בְּצֵאתוֹ עַל־אֶרֶץ מִצְרָיִם שְׂפַת לֹא־יָדַעְתִּי אֶשְׁמָע: עֵדוּת בִּיהוֹסֵף, "He made it a decree in Joseph when he went out over the land of Egypt. I heard a language I had not known" ("Psalms," in *The Jewish Study Bible*, ed. Adele Berlin and Marc Zvi Brettler, 2nd ed. [New York, 2014], 1316). They connect this verse with Psalm 114:1: בֵּית יַעֲקֹב מֵעַם לֹעֵז: בְּצֵאת יִשְׂרָאֵל מִמִּצְרָיִם, "When Israel went out from Egypt, the house of Jacob from a people speaking a strange language." Yet the lexemes involved in the two verses differ (שָׂפָה versus לֹעֵז), and it is not clear whether the phrase in Psalm 81:6 refers backward to Egypt (speaking a language not known) or forward toward the next set of verses. The speaker changes in Psalm 81:7 to God. The phrase immediately preceding this change of speaker (שְׂפַת לֹא־יָדַעְתִּי) could refer not to the difficulty of understanding a foreign language, but to the difficulty of understanding the divine speech that follows. Thus, Psalm 81:6 is, at best, an ambiguous reference

In that day, there will be five cities in the land of Egypt speaking the "lip" (from *safah*) of Canaan, and swear allegiance to the LORD of host. One of these cities will be called City of Destruction.

Even here, however, the argument could be made that the denotation of *safah* still refers to the content of what is spoken generally, and only through connotation, being governed by "speaking" (*medabberot* in Hebrew), and contrasting two entities that clearly speak different languages, does *safah*/"lip" take on the sense of language per se.

In all other uses of the noun, the only times in which "lip" refers to language are when it is both governed by the adjective "unintelligible" and conjoined with "tongue," *lashon*, the latter clearly, on its own in other verses, meaning "tongue" in the sense of "language."[64] In Genesis 11:1, 6, and 7, *safah*, "lip," is not governed by "unintelligible" or by a verb of speaking, nor does "tongue" appear anywhere in Genesis 11:1–9. The noun "tongue," *lashon*, appears in the Priestly Table of Nations in Genesis 10, and it is reading Genesis 10 and Genesis 11 together that reinforces the traditional interpretation that the latter chapter is about language. In this manner, the traditional interpretation of Genesis 11:1–9 is perhaps an accident of the compilation of the Pentateuch, as Genesis 11:1–9 does not belong to the Priestly source, whereas Genesis 10:5, 20, and 31, which all mention "language" as a translation of *lashon*, are all clearly P.[65]

Further, as in Genesis 11:6, in all cases where only "people," *am*, and "lip," *safah*, appear without *lashon*, the clear emphasis is on what a national entity speaks in terms of fidelity toward authority, not in terms of grammar or language (Isaiah 6:5; 29:13). Other examples of *am* with *safah* and *lashon* clearly refer to foreign language (Isaiah 28:11; 33:19; Ezekiel 3:5–6; 36:3), but *safah* or

---

to language but more likely does not refer to language at all. Like Psalm 81:6 as well as Exodus 6:12, 30, and Numbers 30:9–13, the comprehension and persuasive power (or lack thereof) of what is spoken is the issue in the confusion in Genesis 11:7, as with the Assyrian phrase *atmê lā miṭhurti*. These verses, like all verses containing שמע and שפה without לשון and עמקי, pertain to content of what is spoken, but not the language of speech.

64 Contra John Day, who states that "language" as a definition of שפה is a meaning "well attested elsewhere in the Old Testament (cf. Isa. 19:18; 33:19; Ezek. 3.5, 6)" (*From Creation to Babel: Studies in Genesis 1–11*, Library of Hebrew Bible/Old Testament Studies 592 [New York, 2013], 175). In all these verses except for Isaiah 19:18, שפה is modified by עמקי and is conjoined with לשון.

65 See, for example, Westermann, *Genesis 1–11*, 499.

"lip" has this connotation only with the conjoining of "tongue," *lashon*, which is not present in Genesis 11:1–9. Of special note is Zephaniah 3:9:

> For at that time I will turn to the peoples a pure speech (or, pure lip, *safah berurah*), so that all of them may call on the name of the LORD, to serve him with one accord.

Here, in contrast to the Primeval History of Genesis 1–11, is a prophetic envisioning of a future situation in which all peoples are divinely turned to a "pure lip" for the purpose of acting in accord in service to Yahweh. The focus is on unity of action, much like the description in the Assyrian inscriptions in chapter 2 and in Genesis 11:1–9, and not on language. In Job 33:3, while not an exact syntactic parallel to Zephaniah 3:9, "my lips" (*sefatai*) and "pure" (*barur*) appear together to evoke sincerity of speech. For Zephaniah 3:9, the purpose behind the people having a pure "lip" is for unified, concerted action ("to serve him with one accord"). Similarly, in Genesis 11:1–9, much like in Neo-Assyrian rhetoric, the idea behind the terminology of "one mouth" is concerted political action and not language ideology and mythology.[66]

Further comparative evidence, or the lack thereof, with respect to "lip" highlights the issues with how this word is normally translated. Examining the role of the lexemes *lashon* and *safah* for how each develops its own semantic domain underscores a distinction vital for understanding the Tower of Babel. In related Semitic languages, *lashon* can, and often does, refer to "tongue" in the sense of "language." In no other related language does the cognate root for "lip," *safah*, develop the sense of "language." It has been suggested that Hebrew is unique in this regard in light of how the word putatively functions in the Tower of Babel.[67] Yet there is just as much, if not more, reason to posit that Hebrew is not unique in this regard in light of the evidence above. Given a variety of lines of comparative and internal

---

66 For more details about the cultic speech and lack of connection to the Tower of Babel in this verse, see (including the bibliography cited therein) Boyd, "Sargon's Dūr-Šarrukīn Cylinder Inscription and Language Ideology," 103–104. See especially Zephaniah 3:13, in which the remnant will not have deceitful speech (literally, "tongue"), which clarifies what a "pure lip" might mean in 3:9. Note also the combination here of "lip" in 3:9 and "tongue" in 3:13, but in a way that refers to the content of what is said and its ethical nature but not in reference to distinct linguistic systems.

67 Daniel I. Block, "The Role of Language in Ancient Israelite Perceptions of National Identity," *JBL* 103 (1984): 323.

considerations, "lip"/*safah* in Genesis 11:1–9 is best translated as something other than "language."

The comparative data from Assyria supports the analysis offered so far for this exploration of Genesis 11:1–9 on its own terms. Underlying the biblical account could be an anti-Assyrian polemic, such that the meaning of the passage in its historical context is fundamentally engaged with anti-imperial sentiments.[68] Specifically, the story may have existed as a polemic against Assyrian imperial policy of consolidation and capital building, specifically Sargon's capital Dūr-Šarrukīn. The claim is not necessarily one of historical connection between the Tower of Babel narrative and the Dūr-Šarrukīn cylinder inscription specifically but rather the resulting interpretation of Genesis 11:1–9 in light of the analysis of Sargon's inscription, building campaigns, and Neo-Assyrian imperial ideology generally.[69]

---

68   Christoph Uehlinger, *Weltreich und "eine Rede"*; Carr, *The Formation of the Hebrew Bible*, 313. The first half of Uehlinger's book contains an extensive presentation of the reception history of the narrative in order to explain how the passage has been misunderstood over time and in order to make way for a new, more historically sensitive interpretation.

Part of this argument involves identifying, in Uehlinger's analysis, four stages of redaction, including the addition of the Babel-Babylon connection as a subsequent layer of the story. Other scholars have also proposed complex redactional histories for Genesis 11:1–9. See Reinhard G. Kratz, who proposes that Genesis 11:2–5, 6a, and 8a belong to a base J layer, whereas 11:1, 6b, and 8b-9 belong to a mix of supplements added to J and a redactor who added materials based on P. Kratz, *The Composition of the Narrative Books of the Old Testament* (London: T&T Clark, 2005), 259. As argued in many other studies (see below), scholars view Genesis 11:1–9 as a unified composition. See Westermann's balanced assessments (*Genesis 1–11*, 536–37). For Kratz's recent statements on the study of the composition of the Pentateuch, see "The Analysis of the Pentateuch: An Attempt to Overcome Barriers in Thinking," *ZAW* 128 (2016): 529–561.

For somewhat critical reviews of Uehlinger, see Hendel, "Review: Weltreich und "eine Rede": Eine neue Deutung der sogenannten Turmbauerzählung (Gen. 11,1–9) by Christoph Uehlinger," 785–787; Michael H. Floyd, "Review: Weltreich und "eine Rede": Eine neue Deutung der sogenannten Turmbauerzählung (Gen. 11,1–9) by Christoph Uehlinger," *JBL* 111 (1992): 321–323; and Pardee, "Review: Weltreich und "eine Rede": Eine neue Deutung der sogenannten Turmbauerzählung (Gen. 11,1–9) by Christoph Uehlinger," *JNES* 53 (1994): 220–221. Pardee's criticism of comparing as parallels the Akkadian *pâ ištēn* and the Hebrew שפת אחת when, if this connection is intended in Genesis 11:1, Biblical Hebrew already has פה אחד, a much closer cognate phrasing for "to agree, to act in concert," is worth noting. See below for this issue.

69   For the history of Babylon in the Neo-Assyrian period, see Brinkman, *Prelude to Empire: Babylonian Society and Politics, 747–626 B.C.*, Occasional Publications of

Yet the use of "one mouth" may not be a simple inversion of Assyrian rhetoric for anti-colonial purposes. The centrality of city and the rhetoric of "one mouth" that Sargon imposes upon enemy forces in the cylinder inscription is reversed in Genesis 11:1–9, where the people have "one lip" and arrogantly build a city. It has been proposed that the futility of the enterprise in the narrative is a critique of Sargon's capital building campaigns. Nonetheless, the rhetoric of the enemies as having "one mouth" appears also in Sargon's display inscription, as well as in Assurbanipal's Prism A.[70] In this manner, the appearance of "one lip" in Genesis 11:1 reflects, instead of reverses, Assyrian usage of the trope. If this phrase does not refer to language but rather political consolidation, then, instead of reversing the Dūr-Šarrukīn cylinder inscription, Genesis 11:1–9 is consistent with the other use of the phrase in Sargon's time. In both Sargon's display inscription and in Genesis 11:1, the situation described is one of concerted action against the proper authority. In this manner, Genesis 11:1 can be said to be anti-colonial, but by using an existing trope in the same literary placement (describing the enemies of authority as having "one lip") to ascribe to Yahweh, and not to the Mesopotamian king, the power to organize and to govern the earthly sphere. The nature of this problem of authority in Genesis 11:1–9 is manifest not simply in the tower but ultimately the building of the city with it. Further, the syntax of Genesis 11:5 portrays a completed tower, and even some ancient sources like the *Midrash Tanhuma* suggest that God allowed humans to finish it.[71] This observation puts the focus squarely on the city, which was left unfinished, and connects the comparative evidence from Assyria on city-building with an analysis of what the passage is, and is not, about (based on the grammar of the Hebrew itself). The scattering involved, then, entails not the confounding of languages since "lip," *safah*, on its own never takes this meaning; rather, the confusion involves the destruction of unified plans that could result in a challenge to authority.[72]

---

the Babylonian Fund 7 (Philadelphia, PA: Babylonian Fund, University Museum, 1984). For Esarhaddon's reconstruction of Babylon, see Paul-Alain Beaulieu, "Nebuchadnezzar's Babylon as World Capital," 10. For a critique of Uehlinger's removal of Babylon from the original core of Genesis 11:1–9 and for Genesis 11:1–9 as a countertext to the *Enūma Eliš*, see Eckart Frahm, "Counter-texts, Commentaries, and Adaptations: Politically Motivated Responses to the Babylonian Epic of Creation in Mesopotamia, the Biblical World, and Elsewhere," 3–33.

70 For more, see chapter 2.

71 Richelle, "Was the Tower of Babel Really Left Unfinished?," 137.

72 A number of passages envision a unified sort of "collective mind," as in Deuteronomy 5:29 and Jeremiah 31:31–34. Though using פה and not שׂפה, Jeremiah 23:16,

ON THE TIP OF "LIPS" AND "TONGUES":
Semantics and the Chronology of Genesis 10 and 11

This survey of linguistic, literary, and historical information regarding the uses of "lip" in a number of biblical passages, with and (more relevantly for the Tower of Babel) without *lashon/* "tongue" as a conjoined term, begins to resolve a major issue with respect to how Genesis 11:1–9 relates to the preceding chapter, often called the Table of Nations. The observation that *lashon* and *safah*, on their own and not conjoined with one another (as they appear in Genesis 10 and 11 respectively), do not mean the same thing offers a framework for resolving some of the critical issues in how these chapters relate to one another. Other factors, such as plot and the literary sources to which these narratives belong, will corroborate the conclusions reached here and further, though not entirely, resolve the story worlds to which these chapters belong.

From a semantic perspective, then, Genesis 10:5, 20, and 31, which employ *lashon*, describe something different than Genesis 11:1–9, which contains *safah* alone. If "tongue," *lashon*, is able to bear the semantic load of "language" on its own, then Genesis 10 portrays a development in early world history of the progression of linguistic differentiation in three verses, and in a chapter that precedes the Tower of Babel. That the literary material in Genesis 11:1–9 follows the narrations of linguistic divergences in Genesis 10 does not necessitate that the former is a sort of "case-in-point" of how multilingualism came to exist. Indeed, the figure of Nimrod stands tall in Genesis 10:8–12, a passage in which he is said to have built a number of famous Mesopotamian cities.[73]

Psalm 19:15, and Ecclesiastes 5:1 employ "mouth" as parallel to intentions of the heart (לֵב). My thanks to Jeffrey Stackert to drawing my attention to these verses. The point here is that the content of what is spoken and the intent or condition of the heart appears in a number of places in the Bible along the lines argued here, even if those places employ פֶּה and not שָׂפָה. See below for possible reasons that Genesis 11:1 and 11:6 utilize שָׂפָה instead of פֶּה to convey the same idea.

73 For recent treatments of the individual of Nimrod in Genesis 10:8–12 as well as the placement of this passage prior to the Tower of Babel story (and arguments that the non-P material in Genesis 10:8–12 originally was after the Tower of Babel but was moved in the editing of the Pentateuch by influence of the Priestly order of genealogy in Genesis 10:6), see Carr, *The Formation of Genesis 1–11*, 189–193; John Day, "The Table of Nations in Genesis 10," in *From Creation to Abraham: Further Studies in Genesis 1–11*, LHB/OTS 726 (New York: T&T Clark, 2022), 163–187; Day, "In Search of Nimrod: Problems in the Interpretation of Genesis 10:8–12," in *From Creation to Abraham: Further Studies in Genesis 1–11*, LHB/OTS 726 (New York: T&T Clark, 2022), 188–206. The classic treatment of the historical backgrounds of the

The fact that the passage ascribes the construction of Babel to Nimrod creates the possibility of reading both the episode in 11:1–9 as an instance of such activity and the identification of Nimrod as the architect of the project. The previous genealogy in Genesis 10:2–5, which includes the note of language diversification in 10:5, entails the spread of a family line (Japheth) from a separate one as recounted in 10:6–20, which belongs to the sons of Ham and includes the verses about Nimrod. As such, the identification of the diverging of languages occurs as a distinct act from Nimrod and his building activities, along an entirely distinct clade of Noah's descendants; therefore, a reference from the Jerusalem Talmud understandably has seventy languages already spoken prior to the Tower of Babel (taking, then, the cumulative references in 10:5, 20, and 31 as license to correlate language and nation, since there are roughly seventy-two nations).[74]

Nimrod story and its reception history remains van der Toorn and van der Horst, "Nimrod Before and After the Bible." Note that the reading of Nimrod as the subject of Genesis 10:11 ("and he [Nimrod] went to Assyria") is grammatically defensible and, according to Day, more likely ("In Search of Nimrod," 202–203). Yet it has also produced two divergent pictures of Nimrod in the history of interpretation: either this notice conveys the continued expansion of his kingdom, which, given his nature as a cruel despot in the history of interpretation, was not a good development; or, along the lines of later interpretation about Enoch, Nimrod became the model of repentance. This latter understanding appears in the works of Ephrem the Syrian, who views Nimrod as fleeing the events of Babel toward Assyria after concluding that such works were evil and against the divine. Ephrem, therefore, had a similarly constructive interpretation of the phrase in Genesis 10:9 that Nimrod was a "mighty hunter before the LORD" (*St. Ephrem the Syrian: Selected Prose Words*, ed. Kathleen Mcvey, trans. Edward G. Mathews, Jr. and Joseph P. Amar, Fathers of the Church 91 [Washington, D.C.: Catholic University of America Press, 1994], 146–147; Mary Katherine Y. H. Hom, " . . . A Mighty Hunter before YHWH": Genesis 10:9 and the Moral-Theological Evaluation of Nimrod," *VT* 60 [2010]: 64). On positive traces of Nimrod in Armenian Christian sources, see Stephen H. Rapp, Jr., "The Georgian Nimrod," in *The Armenian Apocalyptic Tradition: A Comparative Perspective. Essays Presented in Honor of Professor Robert W. Thomson on the Occasion of His Eightieth Birthday*, Studia in Veteris Testamenti Pseudepigrapha 25 (Boston: Brill, 2014), 188–216.

74 *y. Meg.* 1:9. The debate is attributed to two rabbis taking two different positions across different generations of rabbinic thought (in typical Talmudic fashion). One is Eleazar, a disciple of Akiva in the second century CE and one of the Tannaim, and the other is Johanan, an Amoraim of the third century CE. One rabbi argues that seventy languages were already spoken by the time the notice in Genesis 11:1 has been given in biblical chronology and other argues that the biblical verse means that היו מדברין בלשון יחידו שלעולם בלשון הקודש, "they were speaking in the language of the unique/elect of the world, the holy language," namely Hebrew. This passage has been

Uncoupling *lashon*, "tongue," from *safah*, "lip," and therefore laying the groundwork for seeing parts of Genesis 10 as telling a distinct story than Genesis 11:1–9, provides semantic license to see further distinct literary material in the Table of Nations unit as doing something different than the Tower of Babel.[75] The meanings of the words involved, upon closer inspection, reveal that "lip," as in the Tower of Babel narrative, refers to something other than languages given the distribution and uses of meaning attested elsewhere. When *safah* is understood better in light of other aspects of Biblical Hebrew, in the context of Genesis 11:1–9, the lexeme evokes the concept of the content of what is spoken in a similar sense as Sargon's phrase *pâ ištēn šuškunu*.

This argument could encounter a difficulty that needs to be explained.[76] Biblical Hebrew has a phrase already, *peh akhad*, which matches both the Assyrian idiom more precisely in the words employed, literally "one mouth," and also means to act in unison, in the sense of "(to speak) with one accord."[77] If the phrasing in Genesis 11:1 and 11:6 were attempts to evoke the same meaning as found in Assyrian imperial rhetoric, perhaps by intentional mirroring, then why not make such allusions clearer and more transparent through the use of already existing terminology in Hebrew like "one mouth"?

It is possible that when the author or authors of Genesis 11:1–9 composed the narrative of the Tower of Babel, they had at their disposal a number of ways to express unified action already, excluding the possibility that the locutions in Genesis 11:1 and 11:6 could mean "with one accord."[78] In addition to *peh akhad*, both Genesis 48:22 and Zephaniah 3:9 contain the phrase "one shoulder," *shekhem akhad*, meaning roughly "(to act) in unison," or "with

---

cited in a number of works dealing with how languages were perceived in antiquity. See the citations of Rubin and Fraade in Minets, *The Slow Fall of Babel*, 103 n. 6.

75   The narrative implications for this observation appear in more detail in chapter 4 in the context of diachronic theories of the development of the Primeval History.

76   For this observation about פה אחד, see Dennis Pardee, "Review: Weltreich und "eine Rede": Eine neue Deutung der sogenannten Turmbauerzählung (Gen. 11,1–9) by Christoph Uehlinger," 220–221; H. Seebaß, *Genesis 1. Urgeschichte (1,1–11,26)* (Neukirchen-Vluyn: Neukirchener, 1996), 281.

77   Joshua 9:2; 1 Kings 22:13 (and the parallel passage in 2 Chronicles 18:12).

78   This scenario is itself dependent on the possibility that these parallel phrasings existed prior to the composition of the Tower of Babel story.

one accord."[79] A number of possibilities existed in Biblical Hebrew for the idea of acting in unison, such that Genesis 11:1–9 could contain this idea without necessitating the use of the terminology that more closely matched the Assyrian phrasing. Indeed, the selection of an alternate locution that did not match the lexemes of the Akkadian could have been important for political reasons. A variety of elements in the Primeval History (all belonging to J) reveal engagements with larger, cultural facets from Mesopotamia, likely from a time when Assyrians were setting their gaze on the southern Levant as a strategic land position.[80] Such Assyrian interest manifested itself militarily in Sennacherib's incursion in 701 BCE, which, though not resulting in the destruction of Jerusalem, drastically altered the religious and political landscape for Judah.[81] This changed landscape included the installation of a military garrison a few kilometers to the south of Jerusalem at Ramat Rahel. It may have been advantageous to avoid the terms that looked too close to those of the imperial overlords so as not to arouse suspicion when crafting Genesis 11:1–9.[82]

---

79   See the discussion in Ahuva Ho on why Zephaniah 3:9 might employ שׁכם אחד instead of לב אחד or פה אחד, perhaps as an oblique reference to Jeremiah 32:39–40 (*The Targum of Zephaniah: Manuscripts and Commentary*, Studies in the Aramaic Interpretation of Scripture 7 [Boston: Brill, 2009], 357).

80   Hendel, "Genesis 1–11 and Its Mesopotamian Problem." For a linguistic and historical perspective on the Hebrew of non-P/J in the Primeval History, see Hendel, "How Old Is the Hebrew Bible? A Response to Konrad Schmid," *ZAW* 133 (2021): 361–370.

81   For the archaeology of unification after 701 BCE and the dramatic population increase of the Jerusalem, see Ephraim Stern, *Archaeology of the Bible, Volume II*, ABRL (New York: Doubleday, 2001), 131; Lisabeth S. Fried, "The High Places (Bāmôt) and the Reforms of Hezekiah and Josiah: An Archaeological Investigation," JAOS 122 (2002): 461. Whatever rhetoric of cultic unification might appear in Deuteronomy, which itself has been argued to result in 701 BCE and the destruction of local shrines, the reality, as seen in the new discoveries at Tel Motza, may have been much more complicated. Indeed, the temples at Elephantine and Leontopolis into the Persian and Hellenistic periods may indicate that deuteronomic rhetoric and reality may be two different things, even if the rhetoric of centralization became the dominant narrative in popular and scholarly imagination. The scholarship on Deuteronomy 12 and Israelite religion, from Wellhausen in the nineteenth century to Bernard Levinson and Simeon Chavel in the late twentieth and twenty-first century, is voluminous and will not be rehearsed here.

82   Note also similar issues later in time, as in rhetoric regarding Zerubbabel, which may have aroused Persian imperial anxieties. See Grabbe for a discussion of political aspirations, the possibility of rebellion, the rhetoric of Haggai and Zechariah, and the fate of Zerubbabel (*A History of the Jews and Judaism in the Second Temple*

There are other documented cases in which biblical authors mirror the use of imperial phrasing, but without employing borrowed terms or using terms in Biblical Hebrew that more closely resemble the locutions of the overlords. First Isaiah reflects a variety of reactions to Assyrian imperial interests in Judah, from elite entanglements that are more welcoming to more clearly delineated rejection of these claims, and everything in between.[83] Such diversity of reactions displays changing historical realities from the last third of the eighth century BCE to the early seventh century BCE, but also underscores the point about phrasing in Genesis 11:1–9. In Isaiah 10 the prophet engages Assyrian ideology generally and some of the rhetoric from Sargon's time (such as terminology from his Eighth Campaign) specifically.[84] Such engagements involve mapping Hebrew terms and syntax onto Akkadian phrasings, yet without directly borrowing Akkadian words and blending such constructions with phrasing already available in Hebrew.[85] The idea, then, that the otherwise difficult terms in Genesis 11:1 and 11:6 are not employed on the basis of already existing idioms in Hebrew that would more closely, and more obviously, nod to Assyrian claims has precedent and makes sense. Allusion and ideology can be subtle, and, when ideologically significant, can result in unique phraseology, even when more familiar idioms might be available. Later in time, other evidence exists that engagements with imperial systems can be cloaked, as in the hidden coding in Jeremiah 25 and a cryptic reference to Babel.[86]

On a variety of grounds, then, the terminology in Genesis 11:1 and 11:6 is distinct in meaning from Genesis 10 and can be understood as reflecting the semantics of Assyrian phrasing, even as other locutions were available in

---

Period, Vol. 1: Yehud, A History of the Persian Province of Judah, LSTS 47 [New York: T&T Clark, 2004], 283).

83 Aster, *Reflections of Empire in Isaiah 1–39*, 6. This reference gives a brief overview of such diverse responses, from elites to other sectors of society, and much of Aster's volume gives examples of such varied reactions.

84 Aster, *Reflections of Empires in Isaiah 1–39*, 190–206.

85 See, for example, Aster's claim that Isaiah 10:5–15 contains an "implicit," though "clear," critique of Assyrian ideology, particularly Sargon's pride expressed in his Eighth Campaign (*Reflections of Empire in Isaiah 1–39*, 205). This assessment, "implicit but clear," expresses well the balancing act that critique of empire could entail, as argued above.

86 For more on this phenomenon in Jeremiah, see S. B. Noegel, "Atbash in Jeremiah and Its Literary Significance: Part 1," *JBQ* 24 (1996): 82–89; M. Leuchter, "Jeremiah's 70-Year Prophecy and the *Atbash* Codes," *Biblica* 85 (2004): 503–522.

Biblical Hebrew to communicate the same idea. Yet the overlapping chronology and ideas in both chapters encouraged later readers after the compilation of the Pentateuch to interpret these chapters as part of the same period of history, which also meant reading "tongue"/*lashon* with "lip"/*safah* together. Keeping the lexemes distinct, however, respects their different semantic domains. As a result, it also allows us to understand Genesis 11:1–9 better and to interpret more accurately its relationship to Genesis 10.

ON TRANSLATING GENESIS 11:1–9

To translate Genesis 11:1–9, one must consider a number of factors, particularly for such a narrative that embeds the broader cultural and historical environment of the production of the Bible in its plot and for a passage that contains such peculiar and potentially ambiguous phrasings. Though the story has attached itself in the popular imagination and in art history as focusing on an incomplete tower come to ruins, a closer look at the grammar and semantics of the passage can shed light on such a well-known episode from the Bible. Our assumptions—what we think it is about—can hide features of the Hebrew text, which, when more fully explored, reveal new aspects of oft-read and repeated narratives.[87] Even ancient interpreters show in their writings how they, too, struggled with components of the story, at times indicating that they understood the tower to have been completed. There also have been some precursors to the theory that the story does not concern itself with language at all, a proposition borne out by placing the locutions of the narrative in their possible historical settings and in light of phrasing elsewhere in the Hebrew Bible.

It remains necessary to explore not just parallels of the individual terms and idioms but also matters of narrative and plot, evaluating how the story of the Tower of Babel, argued to be about politics and authority and not about language, relates to other passages in the Hebrew Bible.[88] It is worth observing

---

87   See the discussion earlier in this chapter regarding Bal's observation that predetermining what a story means can occlude some more important facets of literary and narratological analysis.

88   In other words, can Genesis 11:1–9 be put meaningfully into conversation with other narratives as part of a larger plot, and, if so, which ones are most meaningful? I will explore in chapter 4 the literary strand to which Genesis 11:1–9 belongs and ask

for now how matters of a philological study of the biblical text connect to other, historical considerations. The relatedness of these methodological perspectives demonstrates how one facet of analysis cannot be kept at bay from others.[89] In light of the comparative evidence already presented, which can be defended as significant and meaningful for biblical terminology, given the attested Neo-Assyrian interests in the southern Levant when biblical texts were being written, and in light of the data from within the realm of Biblical Hebrew, we are in a better position to offer a translation of Genesis 11:1–9. Both inputs, external information from broader political and cultural pressure and internal considerations within the world of the narrative itself and in the realm of philological data from elsewhere in the Hebrew Bible, help to frame what the story is about. These considerations, then, provide a more rigorous foundation to discuss meaningfully a translation of the story.

All the world was unified (or, had the same plan) and had the same custom. As they migrated from the east, they found a plain in the land

---

how such an approach might indicate what the story is about, what the problems of the narrative might be, and what the solution to the story is.

89 For example, both Vanderhooft and Richelle arrive at their conclusions about the meaning of Genesis 11:5 from grammatical considerations, which they then buttress through demonstrating how later interpreters may have seen, though at times not so clearly, the same aspects of the text. For Vanderhooft, the fact that the tower was completed but the city was left incomplete makes the city no less a locus for consideration in the narrative. Indeed, it belongs to a constellation of other biblical reflections on Babylon as a city in Vanderhooft's view. The tower, while completed, still also has significance, belonging as it does to that prominent urban center known for its ziggurat in antiquity.

Richelle's focus shifts the narrative, and does so in a way that is consistent with the thesis argued in this book that the historical background belongs to a period other than the Neo-Babylonian era. The starting point is the same as Vanderhooft's, namely the observation that the grammar of Genesis 11:5 entails a completed tower. The tower is a "striking illustration" of what people could, and did indeed, achieve. Having been completed, then, Richelle argues that it is not important historically to correlate the narrative with any moment when the ziggurat in Babylon may have been left incomplete. Rather, it would be much more vital for dating the text to identify a time when the city in question may have been abandoned. As seen in chapter 2, just such a historical background exists in the Neo-Assyrian period, a time when "Babylon" functioned as a title for a number of important cities in Mesopotamia and when Dūr-Šarrukīn, which itself had a ziggurat, was left incomplete and abandoned for reasons—according to texts from Mesopotamia produced after Sargon's demise—to do with Sargon II breaching the divide between human and divine realms.

of Shinar and they dwelt there. They said to one another, "Come, let us make bricks, and let us burn them thoroughly." They had brick for stone, and bitumen for mortar. They said, "Come, let us build for ourselves a city and a tower with its top in the heavens, and let us make a name for ourselves lest we be dispersed over the face of all the earth." Yahweh came down to see the city, as well as the tower that the children of humankind had built. Yahweh said, "Look, they are one people and have the same plan! This is the beginning of what they will do. And now, nothing they propose to do will be withheld from them! Come, let us go down that we might confuse there their plan, that no one will heed the plan of his companion." So Yahweh dispersed them from there over all the face of the earth, and they stopped building the city. Therefore, its name was called Babel, because there Yahweh confused the plan of all the earth, and from there Yahweh dispersed them over the face of all the earth.

This translation reflects the conclusions of both historical and philological analyses in a number of ways. First, the difficult idioms translated as "same plan" and "same words" in Genesis 11:1 and "one people" and "same plan" in Genesis 11:6 reflect the same stance against divine authority that enemies of the Assyrian rule had when they "imposed one mouth" on each other. In triangulating the terms "lip"/*safah* (minus "tongue"/*lashon*); "custom/word," *davar*; and "people"/*am* elsewhere, a relevant grouping since the narrator and divine share the same perspective, and thus their phrasings can add up to the same idea, it seems clear that all indications point to issues of authority. The story, in all its wording, can be understood without recourse to a mythological origins story regarding multilingualism. Indeed, the parallel locutions of intent as found in Job 42:2 affirm this conclusion: the divine perspective is concerned with how the people are attempting to transgress divine prerogative. The sum of the wording in the passage portrays this situation and works to create this meaning. Not only is the origin of multilingualism not warranted as part of the translation and interpretation but adding such a feature obscures the rhetoric. God's solution to the problem of Babel is dispersal and confusion, but not of a linguistic sort. Rather, they no longer have a unified plan, and so they cease their building and scatter over the face of the earth.

Moreover, the divine perspective takes the completed tower as evidence of only the beginning of things that people will try to do, and God will not allow the people to complete the city. The completion of the city would, in this understanding, then be an act that would entirely breach the permitted limits for humanity. This thesis has been argued persuasively on the basis of Hebrew grammar. Combined with this internal evidence, the comparative evidence from Assyria, particularly the so-called *Sin of Sargon* and the Weidner Chronicle, again provides helpful corroboration: the act of building a city without divine approval was the ultimate breach of human limitations, and, according to some cuneiform scribes, may have contributed to the untimely and unprecedented death of Sargon II.

All these indications offer a simpler explanation and interpretation of the passage. The thrust pertains to unified action as an affront to the divine realm. Many previous interpretations attempt to relate language to this unified stance of humanity; however, in the thesis offered here, one can understand all of the idioms of the passage better as directed simply toward the issue of how the builders of the tower and city relate to divine authority.

An implication of this interpretation is that the narrator's voice in Genesis 11:1 and the divine voice in Genesis 11:6 are describing the same situation. In this fashion the narrator provides an overall assessment, and the actions of the people and the divine voice all support and affirm this perception. Genesis 11:1 is the condition in which all the events therein occur. As such, it is not the case that the narrative frames an initial situation that then develops as the people act and build but rather the narrator's perspective in the opening verse is the same as God's conclusion in Genesis 11:6. In other words, the narrative has not advanced and the circumstances have not changed between Genesis 11:1 and 11:6. Temporally, a similar use of the narrator occurs in Genesis 2:4b, which describes the general timeframe in which the subsequent events in this creation story occur: the narrative frames the following events, at least through Genesis 2:7, as in the "day" when God made the earth and the heavens.

Further, the flood narrative in Genesis 6:5 prefaces the devastation with a narrator's description of the divine point of view that is the same as in Genesis 8:21: the situation on earth, as far as the condition of humankind is concerned, has not changed between these verses. This is a similar strategy as Genesis 11:1–9: an initial evaluation of humanity frames the following events, not as an assessment that changes, develops, evolves, or is addressed significantly but as an overarching perspective that remains throughout. Naturally, in the flood the narrator attributes this perspective to the divine in Genesis 6:5, whereas the description in Genesis 11:1 is more directly from the perspective of the narrator. Yet in both cases, an evaluation of the human condition appears first in narrative preface of the event and then directly from the divine voice. In Genesis 6:5 and 8:21, the phrasing is largely the same with some slight differences, but it is clear that the slight differences do not alter the fact that the same situation is being described.[90] Similarly, the slight divergences in phrasing in Genesis 11:1 and 11:6 point to the same assessment, the meaning of which is clearer when one explores how the terminology is used elsewhere. The exploration of narration in Genesis 2:4b, 6:5, and 8:21 are all the more relevant for framing how to interpret Genesis 11:1–9 since they belong to the same documentary source, J, in the Primeval History prior to the compilation of the Pentateuch. Many other plot features in Genesis 11:1–9 also match consistent themes in this source, all of which add weight to the analysis offered here.

These aspects of the story become more evident through a philological analysis of Genesis 11:1–9. Yet one might also ask if there is some role for ambiguity in this passage, if the wording in Genesis 11:1 and 11:6 could perform more than one task or be put to work for multiple purposes. Such ambiguity becomes more possible with the compilation of the Pentateuch, in which chronological issues are created in Genesis 10 and 11 when multiple sources are combined. This process creates the framework in which Genesis 11:1–9 could be read as a story about language in addition to being about human affront to divine authority. At the same time, this process of compilation also potentially obscures how the call of Abram in Genesis 12:1–3 functions as the solution to the issue of Babel: when the possibility of language as a feature of the Tower of Babel is introduced when J and P are combined, it creates an aspect of the narrative in Genesis 11:1–9 that does not seem to be addressed in Genesis 12:1–3. The reading of the story without language demonstrates that all the issues in the Tower of Babel story find their resolution in the call of Abram in J (and, in turn, this observation explains features of this call that have long vexed interpreters). Understood, then, in light of philological analysis and the comparative analysis from Assyria, a source-critical examination

---

90   The assessment is כל יצר מחשבות לבו רק רע כל היום in Genesis 6:5 ("every intent/incli-
nation of the thoughts of his [humankind's] heart was only evil all the time"), and
כי יצר לב האדם רע מנעריו in Genesis 8:21 ("for the intent/inclinations of the heart of
humankind is evil from his youth"). Note how יצר, as something made or shaped—
in this case as an action with respect to the divine realm—relates to issues of intent
and inclination, much as discussed in Genesis 11:1–9 above.

will further corroborate that, from the perspective of plot, there is no evidence that Genesis 11:1–9 in its earliest phases functioned as an etiology for multilingualism. While ambiguity may be a feature of many texts in the Bible in their compositional structure and while the compiled Pentateuch creates the possibility for reading locutions in Genesis 11:1 and 11:6 in more than one manner, philological considerations provide some clarity to otherwise difficult and obscure phrasing.

The payoff for this insight appears when new features of the story come to the fore, ones that combine with other grammatical examinations to show how elements of the narrative that have been underappreciated or unnoticed take on new life. The result is not only a better translation but also an increased understanding of what the narrative is communicating, and how the parts combine to portray a unified story. To the degree that Genesis 11:1–9 is a passage within a literary context with its own plot claims and trajectory of events, a better grasp on the component parts of the pericope also aids in understanding how this unit functions within the larger story world to which it belongs. It is to this consideration of literary strata in the Primeval History and the role of the Tower of Babel in its own source that we will now turn.

CHAPTER 4

Babel's Narrative Context

*Genesis 11:1–9 in J's Primeval History,
the Redaction of the Pentateuch, and How
Babel Became a Story about Language*

"If the creation narrative introduces the Bible's metaphysics, the story of the Garden of Eden its theology, and the tales of Cain and Abel and the flood its ethics, then the story of the Tower of Babel serves to present the Bible's politics. It is here that the biblical text sets forth its ideas of nationhood, ethnicity, and heterogeneity, notions that were revolutionary for their time and went on to play a central role in the political thought of generations to come."[1]

INTRODUCTION

All stories have a context that gives them definition, shape, and meaning. Even in an analysis of the Tower of Babel on its own terms, the examination of phrasings and words therein necessarily involved recourse to other parts

---

1 Daniel Gordis, "The Tower of Babel and the Birth of Nationhood," *Azure* (2010): 19–20. See Sherman, *Babel's Tower Translated*, 36 n. 58, for this quote and an excellent analysis of the political observations of the divine in assessing the situation in Genesis 11:6. It should be noted, however, that Gordis's conclusions—that the Tower of Babel offers an ancient example of the idea of nation-states defined by language, land, and culture along analogous lines as found in modernity—differs significantly from the conclusions offered here.

of the Bible. The meaning of words and narratives is never self-contained, and an exploration of definition and denotation involves constructing contexts for analysis.[2] The question is how to identify and interpret the narrative context of the Tower of Babel within the Pentateuch. Though the issue may seem simple, the scholarly proposals for reconstructing the literary history of this passage have revealed an underlying complexity to this critical topic. Nonetheless, such reconstructions also highlight the importance of the role of the story in Genesis 11:1–9, not only for the Primeval History (or Genesis 1–11) in the book of Genesis but also for much of the rest of the Pentateuch, or the first five books of the Bible traditionally attributed to the authorship of Moses.

Already the presentation of philological data in the previous chapter gave rise to the type of literary questions that are resolved when diachronic approaches, seeking to uncover the various sources of the Pentateuch immediately prior to its editing, are applied to the Primeval History. These approaches are, then, also essential for uncovering how one strand of the Primeval History, the J source, transitions to the call of Abram and then advances the story into the narratives of the patriarchs and matriarchs.[3] Understood in light of the comparative study in the Assyrian context and the philological

---

2   See Brent Strawn's helpful comments in this regard, though dealing with the comparative method, in "Comparative Approaches: History, Theory, and the Image of God," in *Method Matters: Essays on the Interpretation of the Hebrew Bible in Honor of David L. Peterson*, ed. Joel M. LeMon and Kent Harold Richards, RBS 56 (Atlanta: Society of Biblical Literature, 2009), 117–142, esp. 121.

3   While entering into a full survey of the state of the question regarding non-P generally, and especially in the Primeval History, is a large issue and one that would distract from the point of this chapter, it should be acknowledged that many scholars in the past few decades, particularly since Rolff Rendtorff's groundbreaking work, have questioned whether non-Priestly material in the Tetrateuch could be considered unitary literary strands. See Rendtorff, *The Problem of the Process of Transmission in the Pentateuch*, trans. John J. Scullion, JSOTSup 89 (Sheffield: Sheffield Academic, 1977). Though some in German and continental European circles still might appeal to a Yawhist, what is meant is quite distinct from J in traditional source-critical thought. For an overview, see Jan C. Gertz, Konrad Schmid, and Markus Witte, ed., *Abschied vom Jahwisten: Die Komposition des Hexateuch in der jüngsten Diskussion*, BZAW 315 (Berlin: Walter de Gruyter, 2002). Note, however, David Carr's recent works, arguing that though P and non-P in the Primeval History each have their own diachronic developments, each, including non-P, can be thought of as a literary whole in this section of Genesis. See Carr, *The Formation of Genesis 1–11* and *Genesis 1–11*. In other words, non-P for Carr, overlapping with the J of traditional source criticism, is a literary strand in the Primeval History. See further in this chapter for a

analysis of the words in Genesis 11:1–9 itself, all of the problems of the narrative in the Tower of Babel find their resolution in the call of Abram when language is removed as a feature of Genesis 11:1–9, a conclusion affirmed in the diachronic analysis of the literary material.

THE CHALLENGE OF FINDING BABEL'S NARRATIVE CONTEXT

Indeed, as a singular episode of hubris, scholars have identified how various chapters in the Hebrew Bible function as an antidote to Babel. Such discussions reveal how Babel is thought to relate to other biblical texts in some fashion, as is the case for Genesis 11:1–9 and Genesis 12:1–3. Yet to the degree that these studies have not attended to the diachronic factors of the composition of the Pentateuch, they have not yielded satisfactory results. For example, in a literary reading of Genesis 28, one scholar claims that this story of Jacob and his vision of a ladder "with its head to the heavens" is the Israelite answer to the negative portrayal of Babel and the Babelites in Genesis 11:1–9.[4] The phrasing of the heights of the ladder and tower are not the only areas of correspondence identified in the story. At least five other literary traits occur in this theory that link these stories as mirror narratives, one a problem (Genesis 11:1–9) and the other a divinely approved vision of how the human realm can (and should) relate to the heavens (Genesis 28).[5]

---

defense of the use of the Neo-Documentary Hypothesis for envisioning this literary unity, though Carr himself would not ascribe to the hypothesis as such.

4 Zakovitch, *Jacob: Unexpected Patriarch*, Jewish Lives (New Haven, CT: Yale University Press, 2012), 54–57.

5 For example, the story of Jacob is an inversion of the Tower of Babel, since Jacob remains on the ground, whereas the builders of Babel try to scale to the heavens; God descends to see what is happening in the Babel episode whereas he remains exalted and elevated in Genesis 28; the tower builders construct their own mudbrick "as stone," replacing divinely created means for building with their own, whereas Jacob utilizes natural stone for the foundation of his shrine; whereas the Babelites migrate from the east and then construct their tower, Jacob heads to the land of the east (Genesis 29:1) after the episode of the ladder; the tower builders are scattered as punishment, whereas God promises Jacob that he will return to the land of his origin (28:15) and Jacob's descendants will fill the land as a blessing (28:14); and the etymology of the name of Babel is negative, in contrast to the positive etymology of the name Bethel. See Zakovitch, *Jacob*, 56–57.

Yet in a source-critical assessment, these two episodes belong to distinct literary strands, or plots, one J and the other E.[6] The long history and more recent developments in the research on the compilation of the Pentateuch will not be repeated here, and literary readings like the one connecting Genesis 11:1–9 as problem to Genesis 28 as solution are not built upon the same assumptions as source-critical studies. Nonetheless, the analytical claim that one story was intentionally crafted as a response to the other is a historical and literary assessment, and should, therefore, attend to the history and literary development of the Pentateuch itself. Insightful though this reading is, the idea that Jacob's encounter at Bethel is an "inversion" of the story of the Tower of Babel relies on impressionistic details; however, it underscores how readers have been motivated to identify a solution to the problem at Babel. As will become clear, such a solution, in its entirety, occurs in the call of Abram.

This thesis, though, relies on the argument that Genesis 11:1–9 does not function as an etiology for the diversity of language. For those interpreters who see language as an integral part of the story, the call of Abram, lacking this feature, does not resolve all of the problems presented in the Tower of Babel.[7] Abram's election can only be a partial solution, and the issue of

---

6   Baden has argued convincingly that aspects of Genesis 28 and 29, such as the prom- ise in 28:14 and the itinerary in 29:1, all belong in the story and narrative flow of ma- terial ascribed to J (*The Composition of the Pentateuch: Renewing the Documentary Hypothesis*, AYBRL [New Haven, CT: Yale University Press, 2012], 71). The story of Jacob's construction of a pillar in Genesis 28:18 belongs to E, in which "pillars play a recurring role in Jacob's travels" (*The Composition of the Pentateuch*, 236). In other words, the features that Zakovitch identifies as functioning, in whole, to create an antidote to Babel belong originally to two distinct stories in the composition of the Pentateuch. Parts of Zakovitch's argument make literary observations that align with source-critical conclusions; for example, the travel notices in Genesis 28 and 29:1 belong to J, perhaps adding some weight to the connections of directionality be- tween Babel and Genesis 28–29 that Zakovitch makes, even if these connections are part of the plotline of this particular story and not necessary a counterpoint between two narratives. The composition history of Genesis 28 is complex and involves more than one narrative edited together, and, therefore, cannot be said to be written as a whole as a response to Babel. Though one might argue that the editor has created these connections intentionally, such an assertion is difficult to prove, particularly since the connections that Zakovitch offers are relatively nonspecific.

7   See, for example, how Leon Kass identifies the transition between Babel and the call of Abram as "abrupt," and how Kass attempts to understand how one relates to the other, making language in the divine sphere a forgotten detail of Babel that, in a sense, resolves in modern mathematical symbolic language, as also found in physics. Kass, "What's Wrong with Babel?," *The American Scholar* 58 (1989): 41–60.

multilingualism, and how it relates to divine judgment, remains. For these exegetes, a solution to Babel's problem of language might appear in Zephaniah 3:9, a seemingly prophetic vision in which, in some understandings, all people will speak a pure language.[8] The targumic texts, or ancient Aramaic translations of the Bible, see in this prophecy aspects of the revival of the holy language, perhaps Hebrew; however, as already argued, Zephaniah 3:9 does not actually envision a unity of language as a reversal of Babel but rather ethical or cultically pure speech. This example of relating Genesis 11:1–9 to another passage in the Bible as the solution to the seemingly abiding problem of multilingualism demonstrates, much like the discussion of Genesis 28, how interpreters have sought to identify a solution to unresolved issues in the Tower of Babel episode.

These cases are presented here simply to demonstrate how Babel presents a problem: whether hubris (the relationship between Genesis 11:1–9 and Genesis 28) or, in the traditional interpretation of the passage, multilingualism (the relationship between Genesis 11:1–9 and Zephaniah 3:9), some solution must be offered to overcome the wound depicted in the Tower of Babel.[9] The dynamics of this interface created worlds of interpretation in which readers struggled to relate the Tower of Babel to other texts, or to unfulfilled aspects of prophecies, awaiting a time in the future when unified speech will undo the curse of Babel. Such anticipations, in the context of the nation-state, have been at the center of the use of the Bible to underpin political aspirations. If multilingualism is a sign of divine curse, and such a sign is still abiding, then perhaps the nation-state could be used to enact policies to reverse engineer the effects of Babel.

Yet a different translation and analysis of the story, both in its historical background and in light of philological evidence elsewhere in the Hebrew Bible, suggests that all the idioms in Genesis 11:1–9 underscore the issue of how the actors involved on the plain of Shinar relate to, or against, divine authority. As such, this fresh reading also opens up new insights into how the solution to Babel occurs in the call of Abram.[10] A brief overview of the

---

8 Frits Staal, "Oriental Ideas on the Origin of Language," *JAOS* 99 (1979): 6.

9 See more on the apocalyptic analysis of Babel as a "wound" in humanity to which a number of cures have been theorized in Tina Pippin, *Apocalyptic Bodies: The Biblical End of the World in Text and Image* (New York: Routledge, 1999), 43–63.

10 Examples of the way that different proposals for the meaning of a word influence a number of other aspects of discourse appear often in biblical interpretation. See, famously, the debates surrounding the translation of עלמה in Isaiah 7:14 in early

method employed when discussing how the Tower of Babel story connects to other literary material in the Primeval History will be offered, though this discussion is brief as this approach, known as Neo-Documentarianism, has been extensively presented elsewhere.[11] Moreover, the intent is not to

---

Christianity and Judaism. See also the debates about the translation of various aspects of Abram's call in Genesis 12:1–3, particularly the phrase ונברכו בך כל משפחת האדמה in Levenson, *Inheriting Abraham: The Legacy of the Patriarch in Judaism, Christianity, and Islam* (Princeton, NJ: Princeton University Press, 2012), 18–35. See, especially, the philological analysis in Baden, "The Morpho-Syntax of Genesis 12:1–3: Translation and Interpretation," *CBQ* 72 (2010): 223–237.

11 For an analysis in the Neo-Documentarian perspective regarding how the editor of the Pentateuch created the Torah from disparate sources, see Schwartz, "How the Compiler of the Pentateuch Worked: The Composition of Genesis 37," in *The Book of Genesis: Composition, Reception, and Interpretation*, ed. Craig A. Evans, Joel N. Lohr, and David L. Peterson, VTSup 152 (Boston: Brill, 2012), 263–278. For a response to the criticisms against the documentary hypothesis, see Schwartz, "Does Recent Scholarship's Critique of the Documentary Hypothesis Constitute Grounds for Its Rejection?," in *The Pentateuch: International Perspectives on Current Research*, ed. Thomas B. Dozeman, Konrad Schmid, and Baruch Schwartz, FAT 78 (Tübingen: Mohr Siebeck, 2011), 3–16. Other, more programmatic statements about Neo-Documentarianism appear in Baden, *The Composition of the Pentateuch* and Stackert, *A Prophet Like Moses*, 20–22 and *Deuteronomy and the Pentateuch*, 3–8. Recently, Schmid has published an article critiquing Neo-Documentarianism. He identifies the literary focus of Neo-Documentarians as one of the major dividing lines between it and the Continental European approach ("A Neo-Documentarian Manifesto: A Critical Reading," *JBL* 140 [2021]: 468–470). As Schmid notes, however, Neo-Documentarians such as Stackert are fundamentally occupied with historical matters as well. The issue is methodological: can we use historical considerations and reconstructions as interchangeably determinative aspects to derive literary strata, or are the two independent methodological approaches, though each with utmost relevance for the other in terms of creating a comprehensive picture of the development of the Pentateuch in light of the history of Israel and Israelite religion?

When Schmid critiques Stackert, asking if it is not only the case that literary considerations help to uncover the history of the Pentateuch but if historical considerations should also be "relevant for dealing with the literary problem of the Pentateuch," he misses Stackert's main concern in the citation offered from *A Prophet Like Moses* on two grounds. First, though the term "document" may hearken to German *Urkunde*, which evokes not simply literary records but memories and historical facts, such an observation is hardly determinative for how one ought to approach these texts. Important though the genealogies of our categories may be, they cannot be programmatic for how research ought to be conducted henceforth. Stories in the Bible are narratives that can be interpreted to the degree that their dialects employ grammar to communicate meaning. The relationship of grammar to plot, in which one can consider a variety of linguistic features of a text that link vignettes, means that it is properly an independent consideration of the history of

offer an extensive analysis of Genesis 1–11, which has been studied and examined well in other recent publications.[12] Instead, only those features that demonstrate how Genesis 11:1–9 functions within its literary strata will be highlighted for the purposes of demonstrating how a new interpretation of the passage makes better sense of its role in terms of plot within its story world.

Part of making this narrative context clearer involves, as another consideration, how the literary strand to which the Tower of Babel belongs describes a unique plot from the other source commonly identified in the Primeval

---

a text. Historical events, no matter how concrete and real, cannot override how grammar relates to larger claims in a narrative; otherwise, it would be theoretically possible for historical considerations to compete with a narrative constructed from grammatical utterances, making it also possible to arrive at a reconstructed text in which history overrides linguistic factors, resulting in grammatically incoherent literary strata (or, at least, literary strata that could otherwise be grammatically more complete and coherent than their scholarly reconstructions). As Stackert argues, plot and history are vitally relevant for one another, but as independent lines of inquiry that, as a second order, can and at times should be brought into conversation for the reconstruction of the Pentateuch. Naturally, grammar has its own history, and changes over time, meaning that a coherent document likely speaks with a relatively coherent way of communicating over against documents produced at earlier or later times, whose grammar may vary from one another.

Second, Stackert's concerns in *A Prophet Like Moses* involve both a broader methodological intervention in the history of Israelite religion (by use of the independent and primary step of reading the independent strands of the Pentateuch) as well as a more specific concern to engage Wellhausen and his legacy regarding prophecy in the E source. As recognized by Machinist, Wellhausen's commitments to Romantic paradigms of history and how history ought to function were, in some fashion, determinative for his literary reconstruction of much of the Pentateuchal sources. So P is late and ossified religion for Wellhausen, reflecting larger anti-Semitic sentiments. J and E are earlier and supposedly warmer to a prophetic, if also anti-nomistic, spirit (though Stackert demonstrates otherwise for E, which argues for an end to prophecy and an abiding vision for law). See Machinist, "The Road Not Taken: Wellhausen and Assyriology," in *Homeland and Exile: Biblical and Ancient Near Eastern Studies in Honour of Bustenay Oded*, VTSup 130 (Leiden: Brill, 2009), 469–531. Given the widely acknowledged manner in which Wellhausen's historical commitments skewed his literary analysis, Stackert's emphasis that they be properly independent though intricately related concerns is well warranted. For a different methodological framing, in which established literary readings are given priority over "presumed historical and social settings," see Shimon Gesundheit, "Philology and Theory: Exodus 12:21–27 as a Case Study," *VT* 70 (2019): 414–425.

12   See especially Carr's recent publications, *The Formation of Genesis 1–11* and *Genesis 1–11* and Gertz's *Das erste Buch Moses*.

History, namely the P source.[13] This discussion of P in Genesis 1–11 is not intended to deter from the focus on the Tower of Babel in J; rather, it draws in relief the plotlines of J, which entail a distinct narrative thrust from P. By understanding how P diverges and constructs its own world, then, one can get a better perspective on J's unique narrative flow, and how the Tower of Babel functions within this source.

Yet all of this presupposes, in some sense, a continuous narrative that can be reconstructed as a literary unity, traditionally labeled "J." It is exactly this issue of the existence of a coherent non-Priestly strand, or strands beyond the Primeval History (into J and E), that has been debated in the past four to five decades.[14] It is not the goal to address a much larger debate in the field. The issue, rather, is in justifying how to read parts of the Primeval History as a coherent narrative, as what scholars have traditionally categorized as "J."[15] In doing so, it will be easier to see how the Tower of Babel functions as a crescendo of affront to the divine, and how the call of Abram functions as its antidote. Indeed, scholars have long seen a relationship between these two passages, perhaps most famously in the German theologian Gerhard von Rad's assessments.[16] Given the widely shared observation that some sort of

---

13 Bill Arnold has argued that Genesis 1:1–2:3 is an originally independent composition of the later Holiness Code, and that many parts of Genesis 1–11 typically attributed to P are actually the product of redactional activity by the authors of the Holiness Code. See "The Holiness Redaction of the Primeval History," *ZAW* 129 (2017): 483–500. A thorough engagement of Arnold's thesis is beyond the scope of the discussion here, though for another approach for examining H as an author whose sole concern is engagement with P and for finding H material outside of Leviticus 17–27, see, respectively, Stackert, "The Holiness Legislation and Its Pentateuchal Sources: Revision, Supplementation, and Replacement," *The Strata of the Priestly Writings: Contemporary Debate and Future Directions*, ed. Sarah Shectman and Joel S. Baden (Zürich: TVZ, 2009), 187–204; "Compositional Strata in the Priestly Sabbath: Exodus 31:12–17 and 35:1–3," *JHS* 11 (2011): article 15.

14 Since Rolff Rendtorff's 1977 publication on the traditions of the Pentateuch. Rendtorff, *Das überlieferungsgeschichtliche Problem des Pentateuch*, BZAW 147 (Berlin: De Gruyter, 1977). The volume appeared in English as *The Problem of the Process of Transmission in the Pentateuch*.

15 See the collection of essays in J. C. Gertz, Konrad Schmid, and M. Witte, ed., *Abschied vom Jahwisten*; Thomas Christian Römer, et al., ed., *A Farewell to the Yahwist? The Composition of the Pentateuch in Recent European Interpretation*, SBLSymS 34 (Atlanta: SBL Press, 2006).

16 See von Rad's assessments that the Tower of Babel is actually the penultimate episode in the Primeval History, which, in a sense, ends with the call of Abram. In this fashion, he identifies, in very Christian terms, dual themes of sin and rebellion, on

relationship exists between the Tower of Babel and the call of Abram, a new reading of Babel, then, will also reframe the call of Abram.

Finally, leveraging insights into the compilation of the Pentateuch can also show how the Tower of Babel became a story about language with the editing of P and J. It is not enough, especially for such a well-known story as the Tower of Babel, to argue what it was or was not conveying historically. For many readers of the Bible, it is what the final, edited Pentateuch seems to be saying that is paramount for its meaning, not its original literary context, much less, for many lay readers, in its original language. As already discussed, even scholars like Campegius Vitringa, who did not ascribe to diachronic theories of the development of the Pentateuch, would argue that the Hebrew alone and the meaning of "lip"/*safah* could be grounds for seeing in the story a narrative of something other than the origins of multiple languages. Source criticism affirms this thesis; yet, as Neo-Documentarians argue, diachronic theories are not simply about reconstructing hypothetical earlier forms of the Pentateuch but they are, perhaps more importantly, interested in explaining why the Bible looks the way it does. In other words, a firm grasp on a coherent theory of what the Torah looked like the moments before it was edited together can also explain much of the literary features of the text after it was redacted. It is this process of editing that made it possible, through the splicing of distinct literary material in Genesis 10 and 11, to interpret the Tower of Babel as a story about the origins of multilingualism. In this fashion it is also possible to demonstrate how the narrative became the episode *par excellence* of linguistic diversity through divine judgment, though this feature was entirely lacking in its original form. It is this understanding that becomes paramount in the history of interpretation, though still with a thrust toward connecting Genesis 11:1–9 to the call of Abram.

FROM PERICOPE TO NON-P/J:
A Neo-Documentarian Approach to the Primeval History

A number of recent works have demonstrated how the Neo-Documentarian approach can contribute to research on a variety of facets of the Pentateuch,

---

the one hand, and divine grace, on the other, as operative themes throughout this section. See von Rad, *Genesis: A Commentary*, trans. John H. Marks, OTL (Philadelphia: Westminster John Knox, 1972), 143–150.

whether in terms of its history of composition or its final form. Aspects of Israelite "religion" have been clarified, such as the history of prophecy or the diversity of views of the covenant between God, Abra(ha)m, and Israel.[17] Most fundamentally, the approach to the composition of the Pentateuch addresses what it means to read the first five books of the Hebrew Bible as literature, and, when reading the literary material as a coherent composition begins to break down, it seeks models that explain why the text looks the way it does. As such, perennial issues in the study of biblical literature, such as the relationship between law and narrative, have also been clarified.[18]

The extent and history of this manner of research on the biblical text will not be rehearsed here. It is worth, however, contextualizing the problems and possibilities of how Genesis 11:1–9 as a unit relates to literary material elsewhere in the Primeval History and beyond, as it can serve as part of an approach to understand if this passage relates to a larger plot. While the Primeval History in Genesis 1–11 was one of the earliest areas of academic focus for the critical study of the Bible, and while the identification of one of the sources of this section—the Priestly source—is largely agreed upon in critical scholarship, it is by no means uncontroversial with respect to how to relate the non-Priestly material to a larger theory of composition.[19] That more than one story and literary source appears in Genesis 1–11 has been recognized since the early works of Henning Bernard Witter, Jean Astruc, and Johann Gottfried Eichhorn, but how one grouping of texts (non-P parts of the Primeval History) connects to other texts elsewhere in the Hebrew Bible and relates to the P portion of the Primeval History have been active, and contested, areas of research.[20]

The P portion of the Primeval History will be discussed below on its own terms for several reasons, not least of which is to provide a contrast, and thus to clarify how the narrative strand to which the Tower of Babel belongs functions differently. Each story makes different narrative claims and entails a distinct plotline. If this Priestly material can be said to be an area of relative consensus in terms of identifying the clauses and units that give it shape, the same cannot be said of the non-P material. As many have pointed out,

---

17   Stackert, *A Prophet Like Moses*; Baden, *The Promise to the Patriarchs* (New York: Oxford University Press, 2013).

18   Feldman, *The Story of Sacrifice*.

19   See more below on issues and agreements in scholarship on P.

20   Carr, *The Formation of Genesis 1–11*, 7.

problems exist in linking non-P passages together to construct a literary whole. In light of these problems, situating the Tower of Babel in this context is difficult. Such an attempt to find its narrative context is important since it is part of determining, and examining, what the passage means, particularly in light of the historical and philological evidences already explored.

LITERARY PROBLEMS IN NON-P'S PRIMEVAL HISTORY

Since Henning Bernard Witter in 1711, and reaffirmed in the long history of critical scholarship thereafter, the creation story in Genesis 1:1 inaugurates one narrative (later identified with P in the oft-labelled "groundbreaking" scholarship of Hermann Hupfeld).[21] This creation story extends to Genesis 2:4a, at which point a new story begins. The non-P creation account extends from Genesis 2:4b through Genesis 3, yet it is not entirely clear how it relates to the narrative of Cain and Abel in Genesis 4, also ascribed to non-P. A number of issues arise: if, according to Genesis 3 and the beginning of Genesis 4, the only people alive are Adam, Eve, and their two sons (Cain and the soon-to-be-deceased Abel), then it is unclear who the wife of Cain in Genesis 4:17 could possibly be and where she could come from. Even the text of Genesis 4 is notoriously difficult, itself containing odd phrasings and even, in a vital moment, a seeming omission in the manuscript evidence in Genesis 4:8.

Further, the stories of Adam, Cain, and Noah seem to rehash a troubled relationship with the land and agriculture, but in ways that do not obviously relate to one another or connect in a narrative fashion. In contrast to popular imagination, and to the snake, who is not so lucky, God does not "curse" Adam. Instead, the ground is cursed on account of Adam. Adam's former state of living in the garden, which involved work in some degree (Genesis 2:15), ceded to a relation of toil with the ground. The land would produce, but only by human exertion and sweat, and in a state of famine. Cain receives a double measure of divine wrath for murdering his brother, though without any narration that acknowledges Adam's fate in the previous chapter. God curses Cain directly and informs Cain that the land will not easily yield

---

21   Carr, *The Formation of Genesis 1–11*, 7. On the groundbreaking literary method of Hupfeld in identifying features of plot, or historical claim, of J, E, and P in Genesis, see Baden, *J, E, and the Redaction of the Pentateuch*, FAT 68 (Tübingen: Mohr Siebeck, 2009), 13–19; *The Composition of the Pentateuch*, 56, 111–112, 114–115.

produce, as though God had not already told Adam something similar. Relief appears in sight with the advent of Noah, whose name is attached as offering respite from the curse that God has laid on the land. Yet this background to Noah's name raises questions, such as which act of cursing is in view in Noah's birth (the episode with Adam, Cain, or both), and how exactly Noah's life enacts a reprieve of the divinely instituted toil of the land. While Noah is connected to viticulture and wine-making in Genesis 9:18–27, this episode raises more problems, and certainly does not seem to ameliorate a curse. In fact, it results in drunkenness and even more maledictions in Genesis 9:25. Moreover, whatever predictions about Noah as a cure to divine cursing of the land in Genesis 3 and 4 might lie behind his name, the toil of agriculture seems nowhere in view in the event that overwhelmingly the narrative attaches to his life in the flood. It is unclear how this catastrophe relates to Noah's name and the enduring theme of toiling the land for food in famine as a divine curse.

The complexities multiply when trying to discern how the dispersal of humanity in Genesis 10 relates to Genesis 11:1–9, though one could see in the latter an instance of the more global phenomenon described in the former. Even more, it is not immediately evident how the Tower of Babel relates to the literary problems presented in the Garden of Eden, Cain and Abel, and Noah and the flood narratives. If there is a story that unfolds in these chapters, it raises the issue of how one can identify a plot, narrative development, and how each passage creates problems and solutions that allow the literary world to evolve.

To compound the difficulties of the internal evidence contained in gaps and questions about the Primeval History, especially the non-Priestly material as a unified story, the evidence from other cultures in the ancient Near East indicates that flood narratives often end stories that start with creation. For example, both the Atra-Ḥasis epic and the Sumerian flood story begin with the creation of humanity and end with a deluge. As a result, it could be argued that the Primeval History originally ended with Noah's flood and that the Tower of Babel was added later.[22]

---

22 Gertz, "The Formation of the Primeval History," 131–132. Following the work of Witte and Hartmut Gese, Gertz has also recently proposed that the Tower of Babel was added to the Primeval History as part of a more extensive expansion, which he calls a "humility edition." It includes other stories, along with the Tower of Babel, of humans being denied the tree of life and, in Genesis 6:3, denied a life over one hundred and twenty years. See Gertz, "Genesis in Form and Tradition Criticism Today,"

Yet certain details in the Tower of Babel story connect, at least superficially, with the call of Abram in Genesis 12:1–3, particularly the aspect of name-making. Whereas the people in the plain of Shinar intend to make a name for themselves, God promises to increase Abram's name in Genesis 12:2. Finding the framework for understanding how these narratives do or do not relate has therefore been a considerable topic of research.

One approach has been to see non-P's primeval history as a series of stories depicting "crises and decline," the resolution to which is the call of Abram in Genesis 12:1–3. Within this scheme, however, the Tower of Babel stands out. It is unclear, in this view, how its particular narrative details fit with the other examples of crisis and decline, particularly those themes of land and divine curse.[23] As a result, it could be the case that the non-P Primeval History is the result of a series of independent traditions that have accumulated in writing over history, and that the story of the Tower of Babel specifically functions as a secondary bridge of sorts, linking the first chapters of Genesis to the patriarchal and matriarchal narratives in Genesis 12 and following.[24] One finds in these stories, then, evidences of possible redactional links of discrete episodes, and maybe some original core of a story; however, this approach would not ascribe to the non-Priestly portion of the Primeval History any cohesive, overarching plot or story throughout Genesis 1–11, which, given the endings of the Atra-Hasis and Sumerian epics, may have ended in the flood before proceeding to the patriarchs. The Tower of Babel, at best, is a secondary editorial addition.[25]

---

in *The Cambridge Companion to Genesis*, ed. Bill T. Arnold, Cambridge Companions to Religion (New York: Cambridge University Press, 2022), 95.

23 Gertz, "The Formation of the Primeval History," in *The Book of Genesis: Composition, Reception, and Interpretation*, ed. Craig A. Evans, Joel N. Lohr, and David L. Peterson, VTSup 152 (Boston: Brill, 2012), 129, 131.

24 Gertz, "The Formation of the Primeval History," 112. Witte argues that Genesis 11:1–9 functions as an excursus in Genesis 10–11 more broadly, but one that also picks up themes in Genesis 6:1–4, as argued also here, both texts (among others) being the product of a redactor who bridges the Primeval History with the strongly Yahwistic promise in Genesis 12:1–3 (though Genesis 12:1–3 is not the same author as the redactor). Witte, *Die biblische Urgeschichte*, BZAW 265 (Berlin: De Gruyter, 1998), 98, 199. See also Gertz, "Babel im Rücken und das Land vor Augen: Anmerkungen zum Abschluß der Urgeschichte und zum Anfang der Erzählungen von den Erzeltern Israels," in *Die Erzväter in der biblischen Tradition*, ed. Anselm C. Hagedorn and Henrik Pfeiffer, BZAW 400 (Berlin: De Gruyter, 2009), 9–34.

25 Gertz, "The Formation of the Primeval History," 131–132.

Yet there are problems with this hypothesis. From a comparative perspective, it is also the case that epics containing a flood narrative, such as Gilgamesh (which, as has been demonstrated, incorporated its flood episode in Tablet XI from the Atra-Ḥasis epic), end with profound reflections on mortality and the limits of human power and endurance compared to the divine. Indeed, one could argue that Gilgamesh contains the same elements as found in the non-P Primeval History, albeit in a different order. A flood appears in Tablet XI of Gilgamesh, corresponding to Genesis 6–9. Utnapishtim informed Gilgamesh that immortality, the object of Gilgamesh's quest, is reserved for gods and goddesses (and flood survivors); however, Gilgamesh can find a plant with a fruit that keeps anyone who eats it young much longer. Gilgamesh finds the plant, but while he strips naked to take a swim, the snake steals and eats the fruit. This in turn explains why snakes shed their skin, which hearkens Genesis 2–3.[26] Further, the end of Gilgamesh results in the king of Uruk finding his comfort in realizing that his name and memory will last much longer than his life, and thus he will be the closest he can get to immortality if he channels his energy into building the city of Uruk, whose walls will endure, a parallel to the Tower of Babel.

The point here is not that the non-P Primeval history might know Gilgamesh, though, on other grounds, good arguments exist that biblical authors were aware of this epic or some version of it.[27] Rather, it is clear in many ways that biblical authors could creatively adapt their literatures to the conventions and genres of the cultures surrounding them, but without doing so slavishly. There is no need for the non-P Primeval History to have to follow the plot contours of Atra-Ḥasis and Sumerian flood stories, particularly when other sources in the literary milieu, such as Gilgamesh, demonstrate how these themes can be combined in a number of ways. In the case of Gilgamesh, one could equally use this external evidence to argue that the Tower of Babel story fits perfectly well where it does as part of this literary strand given the relationship between mortality/immortality, name-making, and building in both stories.

---

26 See also the loose correspondence between Enkidu as half animal, half human and the manner in which animals are brought to Adam as a companion.

27 For an extensive treatment, see Adam Miglio, *"Peering into the Deep:" Humanism in the Gilgamesh Epic and Primeval History* (New York: Routledge, forthcoming). For another connection between Genesis 2–3 and ancient Near Eastern epics, see Abraham Winitzer, "Etana in Eden: New Light on the Mesopotamian and Biblical Tales in Their Semitic Context," *JAOS* 133 (2013): 441–465.

Further, the "crisis and decline" model identified as linking Genesis 2–3, 4, and 6–9, at least the non-P portions, fits quite well with a new understanding of the Tower of Babel. The idioms typically translated as referring to language in Genesis 11:1 and 11:6 are actually political terms that, when spoken from the mouths of subversive actors as in Genesis 11:1–9, convey the desire to act against authority. A number of factors support this conclusion, but such observations show how a reconsideration of the historical background and meaning of terms within the passage reveal literary themes that provide a means through which the Tower of Babel can be read with other non-P material in the Primeval History. A framework for interpreting Genesis 1–11 that attends both to the reality of compositeness and to the features of the literature that allow for meaningful plot connections to unfold, all buttressed by historically grounded data, should be preferred in explaining how the Tower of Babel fits in its narrative context. In other words, one should come to the biblical text and attempt to read it as a unified document, claim that multiple stories underlie the final form and posit multiple authorship only where necessary, and then form a framework for analysis in which literary solutions can explain the particular literary problems that this literature poses. Anchored with historical context, such an approach yields a readable non-P narrative in the Primeval History, traditionally labelled J.[28]

The advantage of this approach of grouping meaningful literary material for reconstructing the narrative context of the Tower of Babel story is that it takes seriously a necessarily multipronged approach to interpreting the Bible. The links that appear in J's Primeval History are built on the back of historical, comparative, and philological analyses, securing all the more how a renewed understanding of the passage uncovers aspects of the narrative and how it relates to other stories. This is not to claim that J itself does not have

---

28   It has, at times, been assumed that simply because Neo-Documentarians discuss a "J" as a continuous source that such scholars simply represent a return to Wellhausen. See, for example, the claims that Neo-Documentarians want to "revive the Graf-Wellhausen model" in G. Geoffrey Harper, *"I Will Walk Among You": The Rhetorical Function of Allusion to Genesis 1–3 in the Book of Leviticus*, BBRSup 21 (University Park, PA: Eisenbrauns, 2019). Such is not the case, particularly given the insistence in Neo-Documentarianism that, contrary to Wellhausen, J and E can be meaningfully separated. See Baden, *J, E, and the Redaction of the Pentateuch*, 29–30; Stackert, *A Prophet Like Moses*, 17–18. Even non-Neo-Documentarians like David Carr have arrived at the basic solution that non-P in the Primeval History, while having its own history of composition, represents a unified story and narrative. See his arguments in *Genesis 1–11* and *The Formation of Genesis 1–11*.

its own history of composition. The sources that were compiled to make the Pentateuch have a history no less than the final form of the Pentateuch itself. Yet this fact does not obviate the claim that meaningful literary analysis exists in the individual sources as coherent stories immediately prior to the editing to form the Torah as it exists today. This time depth for analysis of the sources, the moments immediately prior to editing, is the object of study that conveys most clearly the manner in which the Tower of Babel has its own literary context.[29] Before exploring the literary world to which the Tower of Babel belongs, it can, by contrast, be useful to examine the other story in the Primeval History. Indeed, P constructs a distinct plot and different narrative claims than non-P material, and J and the Tower of Babel become all the clearer in their narrative purpose in relief.

LANGUAGE, THE PRIESTLY PORTION OF THE PRIMEVAL HISTORY, AND DISPERSAL IN THE NON-BABEL STRAND:
How Language Functions in P in Genesis 1–11 (and Beyond)

If language was originally not a feature of J's Tower of Babel and Primeval History generally, the same cannot be said for P. Despite the fact that a continuous P narrative is one of the hallmarks of scholarly reconstruction, and fairly close to some sense of scholarly consensus, even if disagreements remain, it, too, contains identifiable features of compositeness.[30] Exploring the ways in which it functions as narrative, and how language plays a role in its plot, can shed light on how J's Primeval History is both a composite and also a unified story, and how language does not play a role in the latter's narrative.

The Priestly creation of the cosmos contains a number of significant details that highlight aspects of its story world, which is then continued and developed in succeeding chapters. God divides and separates waters, holding the

---

29 As has been pointed out, the fact that these sources are the result of their own histories of composition could very likely also mean that more than one version of each source could have existed.

30 See Schmid, who claims that "the delimitation of the Priestly document in the Pentateuch as an originally independent source document is one of the most widely acknowledged achievements of biblical criticism" (*The Old Testament: A Literary History*, trans. Linda M. Maloney [Minneapolis: Fortress Press, 2012], 147). While "widely acknowledged," the extent of P and other aspects of its nature remain debated. See Arnold, "The Holiness Redaction of the Primeval History," 484.

cosmic ones in check, which are then unleashed in the flood as an act of the reversal of creation. Even more, themes of creating in the "image" and the phrasings of the act of creation in P's origin story of the world reappear in Genesis 5, in the description of the generations of Adam through Noah. Essential to the plotline of P is the role of diet.[31] Both humans and animals are created to be vegetarians in Genesis 1:29–30. The "violence" that precipitates the flood in Genesis 6:11 appears to be a violation of this principle, particularly given the manner in which God permits humans and animals to eat meat after the flood as a sort of inevitable concession to the appetite of some creatures in creation to consume flesh (Genesis 9:3). Yet the consumption of humans remains off-limits, and, vital for P's story, the act of eating meat cannot include eating the blood of the animal. Nowhere yet do humans know or understand the act or intricacies of sacrifice. They simply cannot fathom such an act since, in the progression of the narrative, there is no Tabernacle, Temple, cult, or priesthood that would allow for such rituals to occur. While the authors and audience of P, however they are understood, no doubt were well aware of sacrifice, the characters in the story wait until the construction of the Tabernacle, the instructions for sacrifice, and the ordination of priests in order to be initiated into these aspects of the Priestly plot. The same could be said of Sabbath. While God ceases the labor of creation (or, Sabbaths) in Genesis 2, Israelites in the story of the narrative do not know what this means until Exodus 31:12–17.[32] Despite the common belief that Genesis 2 explains something of the celebration of the Sabbath day, such an explanation does not actually occur until Exodus 31.

A number of features of God's creation of the world, de-creation in the flood, and re-creation in the covenant with Noah, then, attach themselves to aspects of P's story in the Tabernacle.[33] In the latter God designs and then commands the Israelites to create and commune with the divine in this

---

31 For more on this plot in P, see Stackert and Jeremy Shipper, "Blemishes, Camouflage, and Sanctuary Service," *HeBAI* 2 (2013): 458–478; Boyd, "The Flood and the Problem of Being an Omnivore."

32 Stackert, "How Priestly Sabbaths Work: Innovation in Pentateuchal Priestly Ritual," in *Ritual Innovation in the Hebrew Bible and Ancient Judaism*, ed. Nathan MacDonald, BZAW 468 (Boston: De Gruyter, 2016), 79–111.

33 For a classic articulation of how P's creation account informs much of its subsequent narrative about the flood and creation of the Tabernacle, see Levenson, *Creation and the Persistence of Evil: The Jewish Drama of Divine Omnipotence*, 2nd ed. (Princeton, NJ: Princeton University Press, 1994).

portable abode, as a sort of ordered creation within creation. Humans, created as vegetarians, cannot develop into sacrificial worshipers without the plotline in between. Even the traditional divide between narrative and law as distinct compositions reflects some aspect of reality, yet also finds elements of literary cohesion: Israelites do not learn how to sacrifice until Leviticus 1–7 and 17, and, in support of the narrative context of this legal development, the patriarchs in Genesis do not sacrifice in any of the narratives within P.[34] Such an act, the space for the act, and the regulations that attend it are not revealed yet.

These observations do not eliminate the fact that P, like J, has its own history of composition. In Leviticus 1:1–2, for example, the introduction to the sacrifices seems to begin with a header for meat sacrifices that would cover the burnt offering in Leviticus 1 and the well-being offering in Leviticus 3. The appearance of the grain offering in Leviticus 2, not anticipated in the introduction to sacrifices, has been thought to have been inserted to care for the poor who cannot afford meat offerings.[35] The Priestly Primeval History, no less, contains evidences that it, too, is the result of a history of composition. In the flood narrative in Genesis 6:9, Noah is said to "walk with God," a clause used of Noah and of Enoch in Genesis 5:24 but used for no one else in the Hebrew Bible. Further, in all other ancient Near Eastern flood accounts, the survivor either becomes a god or lives forever, which matches the description of Enoch, though conspicuously in the generation of Noah, God limits the timespan of human life to deny mortals the possibility of such a long duration on the earth.[36]

Parallels exist in ancient Near Eastern literature for such a combination of genealogy, flood, and limitation of human lifespan, notably in the Sumerian King List. Yet the fact that Enoch resembles in many ways the eternal destiny of flood heroes elsewhere makes the scenario that the flood in P could have been an addition more probable. Combined with another datum in the genealogies in P, this theory takes on added weight. At the end of Genesis 5, the formulation of P's genealogy shifts. This shift is a marked contrast to the

---

34   Baden, *The Composition of the Pentateuch*, 66.

35   Schwartz, "Leviticus," in *The Jewish Study Bible*, ed. Adele Berlin and Marc Z. Brettler, 2nd ed. (New York: Oxford University Press, 2014), 196–198. See also Schwartz's observation that the burnt offering for fowls in 1:14–17 is also unanticipated in the heading for Leviticus 1–3, and, like the grain offering, is likely a later addition.

36   For parallels between Noah and Enoch in later literature, see Andrei A. Orlov, *The Enoch-Metatron Tradition*, TSAJ 107 (Tübingen: Mohr Siebeck, 2005), 304–334.

otherwise very constant style of Priestly writing, and is the sort of change that, when introduced, is unlikely to be interrupted unless a literary insertion has been added. The genealogy formula in Genesis 5 until verse 32 in P follows a steady sequence of events: the number of years of life a father lived, then the notice of begetting another generation, the number of years after the begetting of the firstborn child and the accompanying mention of other children as well, and then the sum of all the years of the person's life concluding in the note that he died. The insertion of more information regarding Enoch is a notable exception, though one that can be explained along the lines presented above. Beginning in 5:32, however, the genealogy shifts to a form in which the person's sons are listed together, each branch of descent having their own genealogies. This branching of brothers in the same generation anticipates the P genealogy in Genesis 10, which follows the same formula. The formula is introduced in Genesis 5:32, and anticipates the spread of humanity in Genesis 10; yet, sandwiched in between is the flood account, which is not anticipated in the Priestly genealogy, which itself could be read quite smoothly without the flood from Genesis 5:32 to Genesis 10:1–2.[37] Combined with the observation about Enoch, such details lead to the hypothesis that P's flood account might have been an addition within P, a conclusion that has support both in J's flood account and in manuscript evidence from Mesopotamian flood epics.[38]

It appears to be the case, however, that P's addition of the flood was, in some fashion, essential to its unfolding plot. In other words, despite the possibility that the flood narrative could have been added to P, it serves a vital role in transitioning the state of humanity from vegetarians to meat eaters and, ultimately, to sacrificial worshippers, as the cult in ancient Israel entailed both meat and grain offerings. In this way, Israel, as separate from the rest of humankind, can participate by divinely sanctioned means in a diet that more closely resembles the divine diet, and thus, as like attracts like, God can dwell more closely in Israel's midst when the Tabernacle, where such sacrifices occur, is constructed.[39]

---

37   Westermann, *Genesis 1–11*, 360.

38   See below for more.

39   See the literary analyses of poetic structures of concentric circles, mirroring in some aspect how all things relate to the divine in Leviticus, in Mary Douglas, "Poetic Structure in Leviticus," in *Pomegranates and Golden Bells: Studies in Biblical, Jewish, and Near Eastern Ritual, Law, and Literature in Honor of Jacob Milgrom*, ed. David P. Wright, David Noel Freedman, and Avi Hurvitz (Winona Lake, IN: Eisenbrauns, 1995), 239–256. For further analysis of the food laws in Leviticus 11, see

The presentation of P's spread of humanity after the flood also contains, uniquely, a description of the diversification of languages along the lines of the manner in which each family and nation was constituted with their own language. Such a view of language as attached to the spread and diversification of distinct families and nations is entirely consistent with this particular source. When God creates the world in the Priestly account in Genesis 1:1–2:4a, it is his speech that institutes and brings into being aspects of the cosmos. The related aspect of "naming" occurs in the non-Priestly creation story in Genesis 2:19, yet this is a distinct act with a distinct focus: when Adam names animals, it is an act perhaps of dominion or authority albeit in companionship, but not one of creation-by-speech. In the spread of nations in Genesis 10 in P, speech itself, the phenomenon of a family branch having its own language, is part of what constitutes the condition of creating that nation, of it coming into being. The story of creation in P, then, entails significant narrative links that drive events forward. God orders the cosmos in a manner that collapses in the flood narrative, and the flood itself is due to the violation of God's command to eat only vegetation. This situation proves dynamic, as God concedes that humans can eat meat post-flood, which drives the narrative forward ultimately to humans sacrificing in the Tabernacle. Likewise, God's use of language to speak things of the cosmic order into being is connected literarily to the close relationship between the creation of family lines, nations, and language.[40]

In this fashion, the notices of language in Genesis 10 are not a prequel or macrocosmic view of linguistic diversification in relation to the Tower of Babel in Genesis 11, as perhaps some sort of specific example. These notices of language in Genesis 10 have a literary place in the Priestly world, and specifically within the Priestly world. Language has creative power, both in God's act of forming the cosmos and in the development of nations, in which language functions as a constitutive feature. The formulations of the genealogy that include the notice of languages in Genesis 10:5, 20, and 31 exactly match that of the evolution of P's genealogy in Genesis 5:32. Like other biblical sources, including the narrative to which the Tower of Babel belongs, P's history of

---

Naphtali S. Meshel, "Food for Thought: Systems of Categorization in Leviticus 11," *HTR* 101 (2008): 203–229.

40   For the importance of the formula in Genesis 10:5, 20, and 31 for P, though without the specific connection to the language of speech and creation in Genesis 1, see Westermann, *Genesis 1–11*, 508–510. See also Carr, *The Formation of Genesis 1–11*, 97, 197–199.

composition is complex; however, the narrative additions, including, perhaps, the flood, all exist for the purpose of driving the story world to the Tabernacle and advent of sacrifice, when time slows down.[41] The patriarchal narratives in the story follow exactly these constraints: no patriarch sacrifices because, while P allows people to eat meat in Genesis 9, God has not yet revealed what sacrifice is, where to do it, and how it ought to be done. The same is true for P's view of speech, language, and creative potency.

Narrative details in P's Primeval History, then, serve its distinct plotline, even as this literary strand has its own history of composition. Such details drive the narrative forward along its own trajectory, one that does not include the Tower of Babel in Genesis 11:1–9. In other words, any mention of language in Genesis 10 serves its own purpose in its pre-compilational literary context, exclusive of what occurs Genesis 11:1–9, which does not have a narrative role or function in P, even if the editing of the Pentateuch eventually alters how it is possible to read these literary materials together. Indeed, Genesis 11:1–9 is also a story within its own narrative context, and part of a plot trajectory with its own function and purpose in distinction to what unfolds in P.

A parallel between P and J exists, however: the beginning of both stories in the Primeval History unfolds in ways that set the narrative arc and, in some fashion, leads to a pivotal moment of encountering God on the mountain (called Sinai in both sources). For P, aspects of creation and flood in the Primeval History connect to constructing an ordered space in the Tabernacle and the inauguration of sacrifice that can be performed within its compound. The blueprint for this Tabernacle is the revelation that Moses receives on the mountain (in contrast to other sources, E and D, in which the revelation involves legal material), and it is in that Tabernacle where sacrifice occurs, where God will reveal laws to Moses (Exodus 25:22), and, crucially, where God will dwell with Israel.[42] Such a trajectory requires the flood as the event that transitions humanity from vegetarians to meat eaters. A similar relationship exists in the narrative arc of J between the events of the Primeval

---

41   For a robust and excellent examination of time in P at Mount Sinai, see Liane Feldman, *The Story of Sacrifice*.

42   See Schwartz, "What Really Happened at Sinai?," https://www.thetorah.com /article/what-really-happened-at-mount-sinai; Schwartz, "The Priestly Account of the Theophany and Lawgiving at Sinai," in *Text, Temples, and Traditions: A Tribute to Menahem Haran*, Michael V. Fox, et al., eds. (Winona Lake, IN: Eisenbrauns, 1996), 103–134; Boyd, "Applied Ritual: The Application of Blood and Oil on Bodies in the Pentateuchal Sources," *BibInt* 29 (2021): 120–147.

History and Moses's encounter with God on the mountain. This observation merits investigating the literary context of J in which the Tower of Babel functions as an episode, and it also helps to clarify how J constructs a story world separate from that of P.

NARRATIVE CONTINUITY IN NON-P'S
PRIMEVAL HISTORY, OR A DEFENSE OF J

If reading a continuous story in J is problematic in the Primeval History, then a defense of finding some sense of narrative continuity and plot arc in these stories is required before claiming that the Tower of Babel has a distinct narrative context from P and before stating what the role in that narrative context might be. These problems in J have led to the theory that J's material is supplemental to P, or that some portions of J material, such as the Tower of Babel, were significantly later additions to bridge primeval stories to the patriarchal personas and their lives. Much like the reading of P above, where evidence for literary growth over time—particularly in the flood narrative— exists alongside details that indicate a real narrative world that links all of the Priestly material to the exclusion of others, J's Primeval History appears both to be a composite as well as a crafted literary work. This work contains the features of plot and style that merit analysis of the stories as a narrative arc. Once explored in more detail, the role of the Tower of Babel within this arc will become clearer, as will the implications for reception history into modernity of this well-known passage.

Among many other details that indicate that Genesis 1:1 and Genesis 2:4b both begin distinct, and at times contradictory, creation stories is the temporal clause that inaugurates both (and that is a common feature in other ancient Near Eastern creation myths, as in the Enūma Eliš, which means "when on high"). For Genesis 2:4b, this initial clause prefaces a single idea, or sentence in the equivalent of modern punctuation, which extends until the end of Genesis 2:7. In this story of creation, water is scarce (so God has to cause rain and mist to spring from the ground to get vegetation), in contrast to Genesis 1, in which water is so abundant that it constantly needs to be held back in the act of creation. Man is made "on the day" of creation, though which day that might correspond to is unclear in Genesis 1. Aligning this day with the notice of humankind as created last in Genesis 1 does not work since vegetation (day 3 in Genesis 1) comes after man is created in Genesis 2:5. Adam meets animals in the J story, which appear after Adam in Genesis 2, though they were created prior to humans in Genesis 1, but they do not prove to be a suitable companion in J. That position goes to Eve. Though God tells Adam in Genesis 2 not to eat from the tree of knowledge of good and evil, both he and Eve partake of it. The divine reflects that lest they eat the tree of life and become like the gods, they must be dismissed from the garden (Genesis 3:22–24).[43]

Here, then, is the first literary pattern in the unfolding plot that connects as well to the Tower of Babel. Humans can cross, or at least attempt to cross, the boundary between humanity and divinity.[44] Sargon II, in how he constructed his capital city, was thought to have usurped divine privilege in the act of building in some Mesopotamian texts. The inhabitants of the plain of Shinar attempted to do the same in building a tower and a city, though the parallel with the garden episode is greater than a surface analysis might indicate. Both episodes, the Garden and Eden and the Tower of Babel in J, received the same critical analysis in the pioneering work of Hermann Gunkel, who posited that each story originally consisted of more than one tale that focused on only one element.[45] So, for example, the Garden of Eden was composed of a story involving the tree of knowledge of good and evil, and another of

---

43 Note Kawashima, citing P. D. Miller, who argues that God addresses the divine counsel only twice in Genesis 3:22–24 and 11:1–9, speaking in the first-person plural when humanity encroaches on the divine ("*Homo Faber* in J's Primeval History," *ZAW* 116 [2004]: 495).

44 David J. A. Clines, "The Significance of the 'Sons of God' Episode (Genesis 6:1–4) in the Context of the 'Primeval History' (Genesis 1–11)," *JSOT* 13 (1979): 36. Himmelfarb frames the literary issue well: "The primeval history (Genesis 1–11) represents the beginnings of human history as a series of attempts to cross the boundary between humanity and the divine, always with disastrous results. In the Garden of Eden and at the Tower of Babel, at the beginning and end of the primeval history, it is human beings who presume to usurp divine privileges" (*Ascent to Heaven in Jewish and Christian Apocalypses* [New York: Oxford University Press, 1993], 4). See especially the manner in which "boundary" functions as a translation in the Tower of Babel in Genesis 11:6 in Harold Bloom and David Rosenberg's translation ("it leads up until no boundary exists to what they will touch"). Bloom and Rosenberg, *The Book of J* (New York: Grove Weidenfeld, 1990), 73. Bloom elsewhere identifies this pattern as part of a "sublime irony," in which J explores "unresolved clashes of totally incommensurate realities" (*Ruin the Sacred Truths: Poetry and Belief from the Bible to the Present* [Cambridge, MA: Harvard University Press, 1991], 11). My thanks to Seth Sanders for drawing my attention to these references.

45 See the notes in chapter 3.

the tree of life. This analysis rested on the identification of the function of each tree, with the tree of knowledge of good and evil serving as the focus of divine prohibition in Genesis 2:16–17, whereas the tree of life, introduced in Genesis 2:9, recedes from the narrative until Genesis 3:22–24. In this latter passage, it becomes evident that partaking of the tree of knowledge of good and evil was one step over the divine-human boundary, which threatened God's position relative to mortals. To partake of the tree of life would entirely violate the distinction, and God must, therefore, act to prevent this situation from occurring. For Gunkel, the fact these trees have distinct functions, and the fact that their joint introduction in Genesis 2:9 belies the sole focus on the tree of good and evil as God's prohibition, offered grounds for positing that Genesis 2–3 in J resulted from the combination of two traditions.[46]

In parallel fashion, Gunkel argued that Genesis 11:1–9 was also the sum of two distinct traditions, one from a story about the construction of a tower, and the other from a story about the construction of a city. This theory explained the literary detail that while, like the trees in the garden, both structures are introduced together in Genesis 11:4–5, only the city is mentioned as left incomplete in Genesis 11:8. Gunkel even went as far as attempting to divide Genesis 11:1–9 into its presumably constituent traditions, each highlighting its distinct focus of construction (city or tower).[47]

Yet just as Genesis 11 is a literary unity, as has been demonstrated extensively in studies on the Tower of Babel, so also is Genesis 2:4b to Genesis 3.[48] Other parts of biblical literature convey how the traits that each tree represents are intricately linked in total to how gods were thought to function.

---

46 For Gunkel, Genesis 2:4b through Genesis 3 could be separated into two distinct stories, one about Paradise and expulsion, and the other a sort of creation narrative. The tree of the knowledge of good and evil belongs to the Paradise story and serves as the means through which humanity loses its innocence and is expelled from the Garden (*Genesis*, 27–28). Gunkel, following Stade and Budde, argued that Genesis 3:22 and 3:24 were separate conclusions from the narrative of the Paradise story, since these verses mention the tree of life, which does not appear elsewhere except Genesis 2:9. As such, the tree of life addition in 3:22 and 3:24 was, according to this theory, an addition appended to give further insight into the mortal plight of humans after the expulsion. After this amendment in 3:22 and 3:24, the tree of life was added as a detail in Genesis 2:9. See a discussion of this and other theories in Westermann, *Genesis 1–11*, 272–75. Westermann argues that J included both trees as part of its narrative (whatever else the prehistory of J might entail). See Westermann, *Genesis 1–11*, 212–214.

47 Gunkel, *Genesis*, 94–102.

48 See the notes above for the literary unity of the Tower of Babel.

In Psalm 82, for example, clear statements in the poetry depict the manner in which the divine realm is associated with discernment and judgment, a key feature of "knowing good and evil" in the terminology of Genesis 2 and 3.[49] Those gods who do not execute wisdom and knowledge, manifested in righteous judgments for the orphan and destitute, are condemned to die like mortals. In Genesis 3 the improper use of the knowledge of good and evil through manipulation (not to eat or touch, whereas God simply prohibited consumption) and through direct violation of divine command resulted in mortality, in much the same manner as Psalm 82. A parallel set of characteristics of divinity appears: the proper use of good and evil (or, knowledge and wisdom) and eternal life. Genesis 3, then, explains why humans are somewhat like the gods in knowing good and evil, though, in the improper use and acquisition of such traits (like the divine beings in Psalm 82), humans are not like gods in that they die.[50] In similar fashion, Gilgamesh learns that, excepting the flood hero Ūta-napišti and his wife, humans are mortal and will die.[51]

For the purposes of comparison with the Tower of Babel episode, however, the manner in which both trees work together in the ideology of the story in Genesis 2–3 functions as a meaningful parallel to the manner in which the tower and city, together, point to aspects of divinity. The tower was intended

---

49 See the insights in Kawashima on this aspect of divine and human knowledge ("*Homo Faber* in J's Primeval History," 488–489).

50 The resonances of the Eden episode in Psalm 82, as well as others, are explored in Ziony Zevit, *What Really Happened in the Garden of Eden?* (New Haven, CT: Yale University Press, 2013), 253–254.

51 See the Old Babylonian Gilgamesh Tablet X in Dalley, *Myths from Mesopotamia: Creation, The Flood, Gilgamesh, and Others* (Oxford: Oxford University Press, 2008), 150. It is a theme in both this Old Babylonian version as well as the Standard Babylonian version of Gilgamesh that the gods appoint the time for mortals to die, a relevant observation for Genesis 4. The Standard Babylonian version differs slightly in phrasing, but the idea is the same: when gods created humanity, they decided that humans would die, in contrast to the gods who live forever. Moreover, as for the time of death, "the day of death they [the gods] did not reveal." See Andrew George, *The Babylonian Gilgamesh Epic: Introduction, Critical Edition and Cuneiform Texts, Volume 1* (New York: Oxford University Press, 2003), 699. This fact creates a stark divide between humanity and divinity, though survivors of the flood, such as Ūta-napišti, were granted immortality, but this immortality is a once-granted gift and not something that Gilgamesh can repeat. There were various traditions in ancient Babylonian texts on this belief about immortality and humanity, one of which in the Atra-Ḥasis epic indicated that humans at one point were immortal, but at a conference between Enki and Nintu, the former urged the latter to "assign death to the people." For more, see George, *The Babylonian Gilgamesh Epic*, 507.

to reach to the heavens, and, having been constructed, was an example of the divine-like aspirations of humans in similar fashion to the consumption of the fruit from the tree of knowledge of good and evil.[52] Partaking in the other feature, whether the tree of life or the construction of a city, would entirely transgress the limits destined for humans. Whatever prehistory each passage may have had, Gunkel's insights into both episodes highlight less about oral backgrounds and more about the actual workings of constituent features of each narrative, both emphasizing how humans and divinity relate, and how humans attempt to transgress such boundaries. The way in which both Genesis 2–3 and Genesis 11:1–9 function as unified stories is also what draws them together as part of the same plot of the drama of humans encroaching on the divine.

The first murder in the Cain and Abel story also evokes the theme of encroaching upon the divine.[53] God stated that Adam would die "on that day" when he ate the fruit. The fact that Adam lived until almost a thousand years old proved a puzzle, solved in ancient biblical interpretation, if imperfectly, with the reading of Psalm 90 that a thousand years to humans is a day to God. One might more simply see in God's statement of human death an immediacy of mortality, but it points to some aspect of divine-human relations in which God is the agent who appoints the life span of humans. This aspect of God's oversight of life is most clearly articulated in Genesis 6:3, also belonging to J and also in a passage replete with the problem of the transgression of divine-human boundaries. This verse depicts the divine decision that humans will live one hundred and twenty years and no more. Again, the psalms prove helpful in making concrete and explicit the point of view that operates implicitly in these J narratives. And, again, Psalm 90 in particular unpacks this aspect of human and divine relations. In Psalm 90:3, and, to a lesser degree, in Psalm 90:10, the finitude of human existence and when such existence ceases appear as aspects of God's decision. Like Adam in Genesis 2–3, who came from dust and to dust he returns, the psalmist ascribes to God's power the timing and the fact that humans will die. Seen in this light, Cain's jealousy led to ending a life prematurely, since it was another human, and not

---

52   For the ziggurat at Babylon, its history, and its function, see the bibliography cited in Day, "The Tower and City of Babel Story," 172 n. 15.

53   Note that Cain's line builds cities, and J, as in the Tower of Babel, has been argued to have an anti-urban bias. See more in Theodore Hiebert, *Landscape of the Yahwist: Nature and Religion in Early Israel* (New York: Oxford University Press, 1996).

God, who made this decision. Abel's name means "vanity," or a sort of mist that appears and is gone, signifying an impermanence that underscores the use of "vanity of vanities" in the book of Ecclesiastes (a phrase derived from the same noun as Abel's name). Abel's life is a vanity in its impermanence, in its premature departure without divine approval.[54]

In the context of thought in ancient Israel and in the context of J's narrative in the Primeval History, this act fits the "crime and punishment" scheme that has already been identified as a feature in these texts. It is also, perhaps even more importantly for connecting a coherent story in J's Primeval History, an act that defies the divine-human boundary. In this sense, the passage is not concerned with some anthropological conflict between pastoralists and agriculturalists, though the story of Cain and Abel clearly contains subsurface elements of cultural and mythological significance.[55] Rather, the fratricide and act of murder connects the Cain and Abel story, even with all the difficulties of determining who the unstated wife of Cain could be, with the same concern for divine-human relations as appears in Genesis 2–3 and as will continue, eventually, to the Tower of Babel.

Standing between creation and the Cain and Abel story, on the one hand, and the Tower of Babel, on the other, is the story of Noah and the flood. Here again the underlying concern of the narrative is the unfolding drama of how the human and divine realms relate or do not relate to one another in J. In fact, the cause of the flood is most directly stated in this source as one of divine displeasure in how the sons of gods and humans transgressed the boundary between the heavenly and earthly realms in Genesis 6:1–4. This short vignette inspired countless stories about fallen angels, watchers, and demigods in early Jewish literature, and the four verses became a way to explore demonology, gender, and magic, among other topics. The flood in the P story was caused by improper meat eating, labeled "violence" in Genesis 6:11. Considering the context of the story—the command for humans to be vegetarians in Genesis 1:29–30, the fact that Noah took a pair of animals on the ark and then his food (Genesis 6:20–22, implying that Noah was a vegetarian and so merited

---

54   See here particularly the phrasing Psalm 144:3–4: "O Lord, what is man that you should be mindful of him, the son of man that you should consider him? Man is like breath [the same word as "Abel"]; his days are like passing shadow." See Zevit for this connection to Genesis 4 (*What Really Happened in the Garden of Eden?*, 254).

55   See Alan F. Segal, *Sinning in the Hebrew Bible: How the Worst Stories Speak for Its Truth* (New York: Columbia University Press, 2012), 195.

saving; the animals were not his food and the paired animals convey the same point since, should he consume one, he would annihilate the species), and the concession that people were allowed to eat meat but with divine stipulations of what that consumption could look like—all these factors point to the cause of the Priestly flood. The logic is clear: people were consuming meat, and, perhaps like other flood accounts in the ancient Near East, this created a sensory problem for God. The gods of Mesopotamia were bothered by human noise, so possibly Yahweh was bothered by a sensory experience as well—the smell, or sight even, of meat consumption. Smell appears to be the most likely offense, given that proper sacrifices in P create a "pleasing aroma to Yahweh." This cause is not spelled out overtly in P but rather is the logical conclusion given the narrative trajectory.

The cause of J's flood narrative stands out more explicitly and relates clearly to J's theme of divine-human boundary-crossing. In Genesis 6:5, God, having already limited the lifespan of humans in Genesis 6:3, evaluates the wickedness on earth and vows to destroy all life in Genesis 6:6–7. This wickedness, leading to the deluge, is an assessment of the situation presented in Genesis 6:1–4, in which the sons of the gods took daughters of humans as wives. The Nephilim, often understood to be "fallen" angels of sorts in later interpretation, roam the earth, and the offspring of divine-human relations were giants, *gibborim*, and "men of renown," or "men of the name," *anshei ha-shem*. Both of these features of Genesis 6:4 entail connections to the Tower of Babel and Genesis 11:1–9, though in different ways. Nimrod was also a *gibbor* and was thought to be responsible for the construction of the tower, given his connection to the construction of Babel in Genesis 10:8–12. Since such giants were the product of illicit divine-human relations, which precipitated the flood, Nimrod's affiliation as also a "giant"/*gibbor* in Genesis 10 could only presage disaster, realized in Genesis 11:1–9. Moreover, if one understands him to have an active role in the construction of the tower, Nimrod as a *gibbor* reinforced the literary theme of Genesis 11:1–9 as an example of improper boundary-crossing between the realm of God and the realm of humanity. Finally, the offspring of the sons of gods and daughters of humans in Genesis 6:4 were "men of the name," foreshadowing in some manner the ambition of the inhabitants of the plain of Shinar to start a construction project that would make a name for themselves. This connection, too, underscores the theme of improper boundary-crossing between the heavenly and earthly realms, and, in some manner, also calls to mind the manner in which God, from the divine initiative, will make Abram's name great in Genesis 12:2, an important literary connection in these stories.

The flood, like the Garden of Eden, the story of Cain and Abel, and the Tower of Babel, concerns how the human and divine realms relate and the consequences when those relations go awry. Seen from this perspective, like the Tower of Babel, all the narratives in J's Primeval History point to the problem of divine and human relations, even if they do so in their own ways. Each story likewise has its own prehistory, as is likely the case for P's flood narrative. For example, in J, Noah may have originally been the survivor of a famine that was inaugurated with the curse on the ground in the Adam story, not a flood.[56] The etymology of his name points to this possibility, as the terms not only behind his naming but also in J's notice that God will never curse the ground again on account of humankind in Genesis 8:21 draw attention elsewhere to famine and the possibility of survival in such dire times. Naturally, this divine promise regarding cursing and the land also hearkens back to Adam, but given the specific phrasing that appears elsewhere in the Bible to describe scarcity of food in famine, and given Noah's role in being the first tiller, planting a garden, and producing wine, the connection between Noah and the land makes sense. It could have been the case, then, that Noah's story of finding relief refers originally to the survival of famine, not a flood. The ground was cursed on account of Adam, who had to produce food with strain. Even in the Garden, Adam had to work for food (Genesis 2); however, the conditions for such work, in the act of cursing the ground, would become connected to agricultural toil in famine. Cain directly received a curse, but God also reinforced the toil that would come with agriculture in this malediction. The terms for cursing are distinct: in the stories of Adam and Cain, the root is '-r-r, whereas the verb is q-l-l with respect to the land in Genesis 8:21.[57] Nonetheless, the relationship between these stories, and how Noah

---

56 For more details on the following arguments, see Idan Dershowitz, "Man of the Land: Unearthing the Original Noah," *ZAW* 128 (2016): 357–373.

57 It is notable, though perhaps not significant in itself for literary claims of unity, that J's Primeval History employs both ארר for "to curse" in Genesis 3, 4, and in the etymology for Noah's name in Genesis 5, and קלל in Genesis 8:21 for cursing the land after the flood. The call of Abram in Genesis 12:3, also J, combines these terms: ומקללך אאר, "and whomever curses you, I will curse." The only other passage in which both lexemes appear is Exodus 22:27, in the Covenant Code (or, E), though in this verse קלל is something one does to God, in parallel to the act of cursing ארר, which one can do to a human authority figure. The distinction is perhaps theological, since it may have been difficult to imagine someone "cursing" God in the sense of the root

functions as a tiller with respect to the consistent theme in J of relationship to the land, is still apparent. The addition of the flood narrative in Noah's lifetime provided the ultimate rationale for the end of famine conditions.

It might be objected that such a reading of a pre-flood Noah story in J is speculative, and that Noah's survival of famine conditions and the reversal of such conditions were occasioned by the deluge, which could function in the original frame of the story. Yet the divine response in Genesis 8:21 reflects on the tragedy ("cursing the land") in a manner that elsewhere exclusively refers to famine. Moreover, given the manuscript evidence in Gilgamesh that the flood narrative in Tablet XI was added from Atra-Ḥasis, and given the possibility that P's flood narrative was added later to P's story, the prospect that J, too, added a flood story in the editing of its literary material is not so farfetched. This observation gives rise to another implication, namely that J and P added their flood stories prior to being edited together.[58] In other words, each deluge narrative in J and P is complete on its own, with its own rationale and details that make sense in their own story worlds and not in the other.[59] This hypothesis explains many of the literary features of each source, as well as many of the contradictions of the compiled Pentateuch. Moreover, it also provides an analytical lens through which one can understand how J accumulated prior, possibly independent, stories in the editing of its own narrative. It further anchors the validity of the comments that others have made regarding how the Tower of Babel does not entirely match its narrative surroundings while at the same time demonstrating that such editorial activity of accumulating independent stories can still be conducted in service to creating a coherent story. If evidence exists elsewhere in J's

---

אַרַר, but the idea is parallel. Even here, however, the idea that one can קלל God was problematic for some who preserved the consonantal text, leading to the *tiqqune sopherim* issue in 1 Samuel 3:13. For more on the *tiqqune sopherim*, see E. Tov, *Textual Criticism of the Hebrew Bible*, 3rd ed. (Minneapolis: Fortress Press, 2012), 59–61.

58   For more, see Dershowitz, "Man of the Land: Unearthing the Original Noah," *ZAW* 128 (2016): 357–373.

59   J's literary material, therefore, should not be thought of as a post-Priestly supplement. Some alignments could be present in the flood story between the sources, perhaps in the number of days. P's forty days and J's 150 days may have, in combination, significance in light of Mesopotamian mathematical calculations for total destruction. See Avi Winitzer, "Assyriology and Jewish Studies in Tel Aviv: Ezekiel among the Babylonian *literati*," in *Encounters by the Rivers of Babylon: Scholarly Conversations Between Jews, Iranians and Babylonians in Antiquity*, ed. Uri Gabbay and Shai Secunda, TSAJ 160 (Tübingen: Mohr Siebeck, 2014), 173–174.

Primeval History for such compilational activity within J prior to its editing with P, then it lays the foundation for seeing the same process at work in the Tower of Babel.

Yet not only is J's Primeval History connected through a consistent plot, if also a storyline with evidences that reveal an underlying history of editing from smaller units, but aspects of style and grammar further reinforce the connectedness of these stories across J's material in Genesis 1–11. Certainly lexical repetition, though on its own not as significant, aids in structuring the link of these stories. For example, Adam names both the animals and Eve, the giants are "men of the name," and the builders of the Tower of Babel desire to build a name for themselves. Further, out of the Primeval History in J, God promises to make Abram's name great in Genesis 12:2. This link, however, is not sufficient on its own as a buttress to link the literary stories. Naming features in the Priestly Primeval History as well (see Genesis 5:2–3, for example).

Beyond lexemes, the syntax and word order in J's Primeval History, and how these features create a story, aid in drawing more concrete connections between these narratives. The parallel between the tree of life and tree of the knowledge of good and evil in the Garden of Eden, on the one hand, and the city and tower in Genesis 11:1–9, on the other, is notable beyond the literary and ideological aspects already mentioned. In each case, humans partake of one (the tree of the knowledge of good and evil in the garden and a completed tower in Genesis 11:5–6, though in both instances, expulsion and dispersal prevent humans from enjoying these aspects of the story for long), but are denied the other (the tree of life in Genesis 3:22–24 and the city in Genesis 11:8–9). In both passages, the introduction of the pairs begins with the element that humans are denied (the tree of life and the city). Moreover, when the divine assesses the situation, this point of view is expressed in unique syntax that appears nowhere else in the Hebrew Bible. In Genesis 3:22, God's perspective appears with the presentative particle "look," *hen*.[60] The clause that introduces the divine conclusion on the possibility of another act that could lead to human immortality appears with "and now," *we-atah*, though the negative "lest" (*pen* in Hebrew) immediately indicates that God will not let this situation realize itself. Similarly, when the divine assesses the situation

---

60 The same ambiguity about this particle in Genesis 11 applies also to Genesis 3, though either understanding (as a presentative or conditional particle) supports the analysis above.

in Genesis 11:6, the particle *hen* introduces God's point of view, and *we-atah* leads the clause that includes the further possibility that humanity could achieve unlimited potential. These are the only two verses in the Bible that contain this syntactic layout, demonstrating more concretely how grammar ties the themes of the passages even more closely together.[61]

The same observation could be made between aspects of style and rhetoric in the flood and the Tower of Babel stories, an examination that also contains implications for debates regarding the composition history of the Primeval History. For example, it has been argued that non-P aspects in the flood narrative, particularly in Genesis 6 and 8, are the result of post-Priestly redactions and additions, but are not part of an independent J story.[62] In this theory, it is posited that we could find an original non-Priestly grouping of texts in Genesis 2–4 and 11, that Genesis 4:16 links to Genesis 11:1–2, and that there is no awareness in this material that would point to a flood story, nor is there an awareness of non-P material in Genesis 10. Further, terminology in the non-P flood, as in Genesis 6:5–8 and 8:20–22, according to this thesis, presupposes Priestly ideology. Distinctions such as clean and unclean animals, words such as "create" (*bara*) in Genesis 6:6, and phrases such as "a pleasing odor" all seem to borrow from the world and system of thought conveyed in P. The framing of the flood as well, in this view, points to Genesis 6:5–8 and 8:20–22 as being inspired by Priestly ideology. The flood transforms "divine

---

61   Witte notes the connection in 3:22–24 and 11:6–7 as related divine observations on human hubris, both from the same editorial hand. He does not make the linguistic observations that I provide above, nor does he draw more general connections between these narrative literarily as I do. See Witte, *Die Biblische Urgeschichte*, 189.

62   The recent history of the identification of such post-Priestly additions precedes Schmid, who provides more of a summary of such findings. See Kratz for an argument concerning the post-Priestly supplements in non-P's flood traditions in Genesis 6:5–8 and 8:20–22 (*The Composition of the Narrative Books of the Old Testament*, 256–268). For supposed post-Priestly elements in Genesis 1–11 generally, see the bibliography cited in Carr, "Strong and Weak Cases and Criteria for Establishing the Post-Priestly Character of Hexateuchal Material," in *The Post-Priestly Pentateuch: New Perspectives on its Redactional Development and Theological Profiles*, ed. Federico Giuntoli and Konrad Schmid, FAT 101 (Tübingen: Mohr Siebeck, 2015), 29–30, nn. 22–23. For more recent analyses and proposals of the post-Priestly hypothesis, see Rainer Albertz, "The Recent Discussion of the Formation of the Pentateuch/Hexateuch," *HS* 59 (2018): 65–92; Domenico Lo Sardo, *Post-Priestly Additions and Rewritings in Exodus 35–40*, FAT.2 119 (Tübingen: Mohr Siebeck, 2020). For Schmid's presentation of this issue, see *The Old Testament*, 156–157.

logic," in which God decides not to destroy humanity or the world again, even as humans have not changed.[63]

Though the topic of post-Priestly supplements in the Pentateuch is a large and vast area of research, these arguments for such a phenomenon in Genesis 6–9 are not persuasive, and their lack of persuasiveness points to a unified story in non-P's Primeval History from Genesis 1–11, also called J. To begin with terminology, sources other than P use "create"/*bara* to describe the act of creation, even if in the Primeval History this specific word is isolated to P's creation story.[64] In other words, though P uses the lexeme in contrast to J, which instead employs "to make," *asah*, it cannot be argued that J somehow does not know the verb, as though J is less fluent in Biblical Hebrew. In other passages, such as Exodus 34:10 and Numbers 16:30, non-Priestly authors use the term, indicating that the verb is not the exclusive domain of P. Exodus 34:10, in fact, has been argued on narrative grounds to belong to J, and Numbers 16:30 to belong to E.[65] Good arguments exist in both cases that neither is a post-Priestly supplement but rather each belongs to distinct narrative strands.

When the narrative trajectory of J is taken seriously, other arguments for seeing non-P in the flood as an accumulation of post-Priestly supplements also become less persuasive. For example, the distinction between clean and unclean animals exists in more than one source. In P the distinction appears in Leviticus 11, and in D it appears in Deuteronomy 14. For both sources, this distinction functions as part of divine revelation given to Moses on the mountain (or at the foot of the mountain in the Tabernacle at Sinai in P and on Mount Horeb in D). Yet as has been observed, J has no law collection for such a revelation to be made to Moses on a mountain. The mountain experience in J has a different purpose: not the transmission of divine law but the assurance of divine presence entering the Promised Land in Exodus 33. This goal of the plot has implications for understanding J's Primeval History

---

63   Schmid, *The Old Testament*, 157.

64   Though Carr does not make the specific argument that I do regarding the appearance of ברא elsewhere in other biblical sources, he astutely critiques this point generally regarding the use of vocabulary to identify post-Priestly supplements. Simply because an idea about sacrifice or term is prominent in P does not make the appearance of that idea or term in non-P therefore post-Priestly. See Carr, "Strong and Weak Cases and Criteria for Establishing the Post-Priestly Character of Hexateuchal Material," 25–30.

65   Baden, *The Composition of the Pentateuch*, 78–80, 117.

generally and the Tower of Babel specifically. For the argument here, since J has no legal collection, for this narrative, there are no constraints as to when the clean and unclean distinction of animals could be known in its story.[66] In J, whose narrative also includes the death, utilization, and consumption of animals from the beginning (so leather skins in Genesis 3, burnt offerings of animals in Genesis 4, and sufficient numbers of a single species on the ark for Noah and his family to eat meat), there is no reason that the clean/unclean divide, known also in D, could not function as a meaningful plot detail from the beginning. Likewise, since J has no law of sacrifice, Noah and the other patriarchs freely sacrifice (in contrast to P, whose narrative excludes the possibility of sacrifice until such ritual is revealed in Leviticus 1–7 and 17). As a writer who is fully immersed and fluent in ancient Hebrew, there is no reason that J cannot use the phrase "pleasing odor" as part of its story.[67]

The "post-Priestly supplement" theory incisively identifies the significance of the framing in Genesis 6 and 8, claiming that it shows that the narrative has not progressed from a human perspective, even if divine logic has transformed. The "that" (*ki* in Hebrew) in Genesis 6:5 is causative (because God saw the wickedness, he regretted making humans), whereas the same particle is adversative in Genesis 8:21 (God will not destroy humanity again, even

---

66 See more in Meshel, "Food for Thought," 208–209. Scholars used to posit that Exodus 34 contained the "J Decalogue." It has been shown, however, that this legal material is a later compilation and insertion, composed of laws and phrasings from other, previously existing legal collections in E, D, and P. It does not belong to J since J has no law collection. See, most comprehensively, Shimon Gesundheit, *Three Times a Year: Studies on Festival Legislation in the Pentateuch*, FAT 82 (Tübingen: Mohr Siebeck, 2012).

67 For further implications of reading the Primeval History in J with the lens that J has no legal collection, see Joseph Ryan Kelly, "Does God Command and Punish in the Garden of Eden?," *VT* (2021): 1–22. Kelly, though not addressing the Tower of Babel in J, insightfully teases out the implications of a lack of legal collection in J for how God might be reimagined as offering warning and consequences, but not commands and laws that render obedience or disobedience resulting in punishment. He explores issues of divine-human boundary-crossing, knowledge, and agrarian aspects of Genesis 2–3. Yet the line in J as "instruction giver" as distinct from commands, simply because J has no legal collection, is drawn in Kelly's article too hard and fast. For example, in both Genesis 26:5 and Exodus 15:26, God refers to his "commandments," *mitzvot*. As Baden argues, these verses belong to J, "which typically uses clusters of legal terminology to signify general obedience to the will of Yahweh (since J has no law code to which it might refer)" (*The Composition of the Pentateuch*, 139).

though people remain evil).[68] This contrast indicates how divine rationale assesses the manner in which people have not changed, but God has to change in order to keep the narrative going. This technique of pivoting between the narrator's framing and divine perspective belongs to both the flood story and the Tower of Babel, and is a vital literary tool in each, though in a manner that underscores how these narratives congeal to form a unified story. Humanity does not change in the Tower of Babel story between Genesis 11:1 and 11:6, in much the same manner that humanity does not change from the start to the finish of J's flood story. God's way of dealing with the lack of human change does, indeed, evolve.

In this sense, the narrative, as far as humans are concerned, has not progressed in the flood, in the same way that it did not progress after the expulsion of Eden, the murder of Abel, and, ultimately, the Tower of Babel. God's logic changes, because the human condition has not (or, it has only gotten worse). Babel is a crescendo here, requiring a different approach for how the divine and human relate.[69] The problem in all of these passages in J's Primeval History that drives the plot forward is the persistent attempt to cross the divine-human boundary. In a new reading of the Tower of Babel as part of this source, the story matches the themes and components of non-J Primeval History that have been identified as making Genesis 2–3, 4, and 6–9 a coherent story, and that another scholar claims as making Genesis 2–4 and 11 a literary unit.[70] It is this underlying feature of these stories that will ultimately change divine

---

68 Schmid, *The Old Testament*, 156–157.

69 In this fashion, Kawashima's observation is astute that "The initial plenitude of the garden – the abundance of nature, the absence of death, the presence of Yahweh – gives way to want – natural scarcity, human mortality, divine absence. But J's conception of »human nature« grants mortals god-like creativity and freedom, for better as well as for worse" ("*Homo Faber* in J's Primeval History," 485). See also R. E. Friedman, *The Disappearance of God: A Reverent Investigation of Three Divine Mysteries* (Boston: Little, Brown, 1995), 7–29. Indeed, God walked with Adam in the Garden, yet retreats to the heavens and needs to descend to see the tower and city, an act often interpreted as ironic, if also dismissive, with respect to human ambition to build a tower "with its top in the heavens." Yet this retreat is a symptom of a problem that requires a solution: how is God going to relate to his creation? See Kawashima's further reflection on the "dialectic" between Yahweh and humanity, and how such a dialectic is at the heart of J's vision of what it means to be human, in "Sources and Redaction," in *Reading Genesis: Ten Methods*, ed. Ronald Hendel (New York: Cambridge University Press, 2010), 55–56.

70 See Gertz ("The Formation of the Primeval History," 112) for the former proposal, and Schmid (*The Old Testament*, 156–157) for the latter.

logic in the call of Abram as a solution to the persistent issue presented in J's Primeval History. Before this literary connection can be understood better, it is necessary to examine in more detail how the Tower of Babel functions as a crescendo to the pervasive problems that appear in J's Primeval History. Only then will it become evident how the call of Abram works as a solution that resolves all of the issues of the Tower of Babel, which encapsulates the pervasive problem of how God can relate to humanity. The hinge between problem and solution in the transition between Babel and Abram, perhaps more significantly, is strengthened given the preceding analyses of the historical backgrounds, philological data, and literary context of Genesis 11:1–9. Without language, the way that the Tower of Babel functions as a crescendo of human problems to which the call of Abram, in the changed divine logic, operates as a solution becomes all the more evident.

THE PROBLEM OF HUMANITY IN J
AND BABEL AS A CRESCENDO

In light of this narrative context, the historical background for the production of the passage, and the philological examination of the words of Genesis 11:1–9, the Tower of Babel is not a story that is primarily concerned with a tower but rather with a city that humans cannot build, and which would, if they did, violate divine prerogative. Nor is the story about Babylon; rather, it is set in the Assyrian period, utilizing political idioms of that time period. Finally, the passage is not about language, which instead belongs to the Priestly source. The phrasings in Genesis 11:1–9, on more extensive investigation, have nothing to do with language or multilingualism at all.

If Genesis 11:1–9 is not about a tower, Babylon, or multilingualism, then it remains to argue what the passage actually is communicating. The reorientation of the story in light of the evidence brought to bear has, in essence, shown the problematic nature of the most enduring images that the passage has evoked. Arguing against such dominant and long-held interpretations is no small feat, yet sticking with images of an incomplete tower set in Babylon as the backdrop for a biblical etiology for multilingualism encounters simply too many issues to continue with this understanding of the text.

Yet by taking these elements out of the interpretation of the Tower of Babel, a reanalysis supported by historical, philological, and literary considerations, it becomes clearer how the story functions within its precompilational liter-ary context in J. The themes of J's Primeval History increase in intensity, as humans become more and more brazen about encroaching upon, and (to use the category of ancient interpreters) even "invade," the divine realm. If Adam was presented with a clear directive about what he should not eat from God; if God also confronted Cain and gave Cain the opportunity to act well in Genesis 4:6–7 prior to Abel's murder; if Genesis 6:1–4 presents a scenario of another illegitimate divine-human boundary crossing, though initiated by divine beings; then the Tower of Babel portrays a crescendo. Without any encounter with the divine, humans decide by themselves, on their own initia-tive and without any conversation with God, to construct a tower and a city. God has receded into the background, and humans act without any reference to God, representing a new, if also dire, situation in J's Primeval History.

The entirety of J's Primeval History comes to a head, then, and conveys a growing crisis regarding how God can relate to humans. The answer to this issue arrives, in some fashion, in the call of Abram, in which all of the problems of Babel, if not also the Primeval History in J, find their resolve. The construction projects on the plain of Shinar at Babel represent the last straw, and the "divine logic" changes yet again into an entirely distinct strategy for engaging with humanity.[71]

In both sources of the Primeval History, J and P, events prior to the call of Abram also set in motion narrative progress much later on. For P, humans are created vegetarians, but the situation is not sustainable, leading to the flood and divine concession that people are now allowed to consume meat with a number of restrictions. This is a necessary development to thrust the story toward a pivotal moment on the mountain, in which God reveals to Moses the blueprint for the Tabernacle, constructed later at the foot of the mountain. This structure, in contrast to the Tower of Babel, is a divinely ordained abode in which the divine and human realm can meet, but for the purposes of P, it is where God makes his legal vision known to Moses and where sacrifice occurs. In some fashion, then, the issue of order, arrangement, diet, and how the divine and human relate in P's Primeval History find their solution in the Priestly vision of the Tabernacle, revealed to Moses on Mount Sinai.

---

71 Westermann argues that J's Primeval History is not an escalating series of stories that demonstrate the "crescendo of sin," but, rather, that these stories demonstrate a variety of ways in which "the creature can turn against the creator" through a num-ber of narratives about crimes and punishments (*Genesis 1–11*, 53).

In a similar manner, the themes and issues of J's Primeval History also find a certain resolution in Moses's encounter with God on Mount Sinai. Even prior to this mountain experience, J presents aspects of how Abraham, having been brought into a relationship or covenant with God, can confront the divine, but in a context in which God responds positively (in contrast to Genesis 11:1–9). Human initiative still proves to go awry. For example, in J Abram tells Sarai to pretend that she is his sister and not his wife, which results in plagues for Pharaoh even if Abram himself leaves Egypt richer than he arrived. The foreshadowing of the Exodus is patent, but it belies the immediately preceding divine promise to Abram that he will be a blessing to the nations (though perhaps this signals that Egypt is exempt from such blessings).[72] Clearly, Pharaoh might disagree that Abram would function in this manner on the world stage. Further, Sarai's plan to have Abram conceive a child with Hagar also proves to steer things in the wrong direction. Instead of bringing the couple closer to God's promise of a child, it leads to tension between Sarai and Hagar, with the result that Hagar runs away.

Yet stories in J also show how appointed human relationships can challenge divine intent in a mirror image of the Tower of Babel. If the latter is the precipice of human affront to divine prerogative, after which the call of Abram functions as a solution, then, once called by God and once he has in some fashion proven worthy of the covenant, Abraham (as he is called after P's renaming in Genesis 17) is in a position to confront divine authority in a way that those who built the Tower of Babel were not. Abraham passed the test of hospitality in welcoming three strangers in Genesis 18, offering the best of what he had to feed and comfort them. This story is notable in a number of ways, not least of which in the manner in which it laid the foundation for Abraham to be understood as "hospitable" in the history of interpretation of this text.[73] It also functions as a foil against which the inhabitants of Sodom

---

72   Baden, *The Promise to the Patriarchs*, 114–115.

73   Kugel, *Traditions of the Bible*, 334–336. Note how Lot, a foreigner, met the visitors at the city gate, a place where judicial proceedings often occurred. See, for example, Absalom's activities at the gates in his attempt to usurp David in 2 Samuel 15:2. That representatives from Sodom were not present but Lot was, and in contrast to Abraham's actions in Genesis 18, the inhabitants from Sodom clearly, if also implicitly, fail the hospitality test. For more on the importance of city gates in Mesopotamia and Israel, including judicial functions, see Natalie N. May, "Gates and Their Functions in Mesopotamia and Ancient Israel," in *The Fabric of Cities: Aspects of Urbanism, Urban Topography and Society in Mesopotamia, Greece and Rome*, CHANE 68 (Boston: Brill, 2014), 77–121.

and Gomorrah would be judged in Genesis 19.[74] Passing the hospitality test gives God license to allow Abraham to gain insight into divine logic, which is apparently equally as malleable in the Primeval History as in this encounter with Abraham. Abraham steps "into the breach," and when God reveals his intent to destroy Sodom and Gomorrah, Abraham challenges God's proposed action.[75] Abraham, having passed the test that also gives insight into the contingent nature of the covenant with God, can now approach and confront the divine with the result that, in a manner of prophetic boldness and as an act that accords with the office of a prophet, God changes his mind. Though Abraham is called a prophet explicitly in Genesis 20 in E, J's narrative shows, functionally, how Abraham performs the duties of this office in calling God to justice.[76] In this fashion, Abraham forces the divine to understand the human sphere in a manner that could not be further from the actions of the builders on the plain of Shinar.

In contrast, the inhabitants of Sodom and Gomorrah—calling to mind the inhabitants of the plain of Shinar—boldly propose actions that would, as in the Primeval History, challenge the boundary between humanity and divinity, not unlike Genesis 6:1–4. Continuing the theme of J regarding how the divine and human realms relate, the story of Sodom and Gomorrah in Genesis 19, which also belongs to J, demonstrates the calamity that occurs when the line is blurred without divine sanction. Though the inhabitants of Sodom and Gomorrah label the visitors "men," it is not clear that this word excludes the possibility that they might have also understood how these beings represented the divine realm. Even after Abraham knows that he was speaking to God in Genesis 18, and, therefore, that the two other beings were companions of the divine, the narrator still calls them "men" in Genesis 18:16. The products of the breach of the divine and human realms in Genesis 6:4 were, likewise, called "men (of renown)." In other words, even if the inhabitants of Sodom and Gomorrah call the visitors "men," these inhabitants might be acting with an awareness that they have a connection to the divine, which then locates,

---

74 The contrast could not be greater, and, for this reason, the so-called "sin" of Sodom and Gomorrah was almost exclusively understood to be guilt of inhospitality. For more, see Kugel for ancient interpretations (*Traditions of the Bible*, 329–330, 333–336).

75 See Muffs' classic essay, "Who Will Stand in the Breach?," as cited in the bibliography.

76 In an equally striking juxtaposition of J and E material, Abraham pleads for the lives of strangers in Genesis 18 in J, but is silent and offers no protest when God tells him to kill his own son in E in Genesis 22.

along with inhospitality, the crime committed as another example of human overreach. This observation also, and necessarily, decenters the obsession with imposing the modern gender binary on the actors in the story to find a transgression that maps onto modern concerns of sexuality, politics, and religion. The point of God's displeasure in Genesis 19 simply does not accord with such an interpretation.[77]

Later interpreters, engaging in apocalyptic Jewish literature that also continues the reflection on humanity and divinity, understood the manner in which this episode constitutes an illegitimate breach of the divine line between God and humans. Jude 14–15 in the New Testament cites 1 Enoch 1:9 as an example of God's punishment on the ungodly, a particularly apt citation in this analysis as Enoch himself crossed the divine and human boundary, though with God's blessing. When the author addresses Sodom and Gomorrah earlier in Jude, it is one of the few occurrences of sexual sin ascribed to this episode in the Bible (Jewish or Christian) outside of Jeremiah 23:14 (which itself clearly references adultery and evildoing, but not "unnatural" desire).[78] Yet the nature of sexual transgression maps on to the issue in J: the "just as"

---

77 A different narrative cycle in Judges 17–21 shows a distinct situation, though with literary parallels to the Genesis account, that may demonstrate an episode that possibly, though not necessarily, refers to something along the spectrum of same-sex relations in the human sphere. Coming from a different biblical source and perspective, however, such an account is not necessarily reflective of what Sodom and Gomorrah can or cannot mean. On other, potential diverse perspectives on sexuality in ancient Israel, see Baden, *The Historical David: The Real Life of an Invented Hero* (New York: HarperOne, 2013), 72–74; Susan Ackerman, *When Heroes Love: The Ambiguity of Eros in the Stories of Gilgamesh and David* (New York: Columbia University Press, 2005); Martti Nissinen, *Homoeroticism in the Biblical World* (Minneapolis: Fortress Press, 1998). Jeremiah 23:14 seems to contain another tradition about Sodom and Gomorrah's sexual sins, which were, instead, adultery and the promotion of evildoing, all without repentance.

78 The same argument could be made with respect to 2 Peter 2:6–11. The condemnation of the sensual transgressions in this passage seems to hinge on angelic and celestial sphere and their proper, or bounded, relationship to humanity. The transgression of this boundary, evidenced also in the teaching of false prophets who flagrantly (according to the author) deny the authority of the "Master" or God who "purchased" them, reflects the same issue to establish and promote distinct spheres between heaven and earth and their relative authority. Any unnatural "sensuality" belongs the in context of this rhetoric. This conclusion is supported as well by the fact that preceding the discussion of Sodom and Gomorrah is the notice of the flood and Noah, as in Genesis 6:1–4, in 2 Peter 2:4–5. The nature of sexual transgression in this episode is clearly divine and human, but not on the spectrum of human sexuality per se.

and "likewise" in Jude 7, when the author addresses the nature of Sodom and Gomorrah's sexual sin, draws comparison and likeness to the angels that left their "proper dwelling" in Jude 6. It is the manner in which the human and divine boundary-crossing affronts God's prerogative that the author of Jude claims is at root in the sexual motivation of the inhabitants of Sodom and Gomorrah. This later interpretation, then, highlights how the literary theme present in J's Primeval History, particularly in the Tower of Babel, continues as well in J's narrative into the life of Abraham.

Similarly, the mountain event for J is one that, significantly, involves how (or whether) God will relate to humanity. The major theme for J in the Primeval History that comes to a crescendo in the Tower of Babel, and that develops even in the life of Abraham, whose call answers in some manner how God will deal with humanity, comes to a head on the mountain in Exodus 33, and in a mirror image to the machinations of the builders of the tower and city at Babel. The narrative precursor to Exodus 33 and Moses's encounter with God on the mountain occurs in Exodus 17, in which Israel quarrels with and tests God. The issue, stated clearly in Exodus 17:7, is whether God is to be present with Israel. Here again is J's theme of how the divine and human realms will relate.[79] From Israel's perspective, God appeared to be receding, as also in J's Primeval History in which—by the events on the plain of Shinar—he is nowhere to be found in the initial verses, such that Israel in Exodus 17 believed that they would be left to their own devices. The answer comes in Exodus 33: God, fed up with Israel, intends, indeed, to recede and depart from Israel. Instead, an angel will lead Israel, but God will not be in their midst. For J this crisis leads to the theophany on the mountain. In contrast to E and D, in which God reveals legal material on the mountain (called Horeb in those stories), and in contrast to P, in which God reveals the blueprint for the Tabernacle on the mountain (so Exodus 25:22), for J the major point of God's appearance is to sort out how God will relate to humans, specifically to Israel. In this fashion, the Primeval History in J, like P, sets the themes and agendas that drive the

---

79   In a manner of speaking, the way in which the human and divine relate, and the series of crises that unfold in J, reach their climax in Exodus 17:7. There, the people ask, "Is the LORD among us or not?" In response, God offers a theophany, in which he reveals his intent not to be directly in the midst of Israel, which, itself, inaugurates a back-and-forth between Moses and God. See below. See Baden for the narrative flow of J between Exodus 17 and the Sinai theophany in parts of Exodus 19, 24, and 33–34 (*The Composition of the Pentateuch*, 76–77). My contribution is to connect this arc with the themes in the Primeval History in J.

narrative forward to a pivotal moment of an encounter on a mountain, even if J stands apart from the other sources in the sense that its encounter does not include legislation or instructions. Even as such legislations and instructions are themselves the agenda for constructing how the divine and human realms relate in E, P, and D, the issue of divine encounter and presence with humans in Exodus 33 rings true to J's own concerns.

Much like Abraham, the resolution in Exodus 33 involves a sort of give-and-take of divine and human negotiation in which Moses speaks God's own words back to God to change divine logic even if people do not evince any propensity to alter their behavior.[80] Though using distinct terminology, the challenge that Moses presents to God in Exodus 33:16 calls to mind many of the issues of the Tower of Babel. In the latter passage, all people were united, whereas a clear distinction of Israel has now been made from all people on the earth. If God's presence for the Babelites spelled doom and scattering, for Moses and Israel, it entails a successful entry and consolidation into the Promised Land. In J people have called on the divine name Yahweh since Genesis 4:26, the theme of the "name" occurs in important passages from Adam naming animals in Genesis 2 to the "men of the name" in Genesis 6:4 to people building a "name" for themselves in the Tower of Babel, and God promises to make Abram's name great in Genesis 12:1–3. Yet a new significance is attached to this concept when God reveals an aspect of his name in the theophany in Exodus 33:19 as evidence of his presence with Israel, the implications of which extend to the divine promise to be with Israel as they enter the land in Exodus 34.[81]

Divine presence, and how God and humans relate, is a constant theme in J's Primeval History, and the Tower of Babel episode in Genesis 11:1–9 functions as a thematically appropriate and literarily savvy story to transition this theme into the period of the patriarchs and matriarchs. Like all good stories, the theme evolves and develops. Just as P's Primeval History lays a foundation for the narrative toward an encounter with God on a mountain, so also J's Primeval History establishes themes that continue in this source until the question of divine presence with Israel and how God will relate to humanity through Israel is affirmed once and for all on Mount Sinai.

---

80 For theological reflections on Moses's actions and the concept of divine "impassibility," see Anderson, *Christian Doctrine and the Old Testament*, 23–40.

81 Baden, *Composition of the Pentateuch*, 77–78.

RELATING GENESIS 11:1–9 AND GENESIS 12:1–3

Notable aspects of J's plot and its concerns become more apparent after such an analysis. For example, nowhere in J is language or multilingualism a prominent feature of the plot. In other words, if, as in the traditional interpretation, Genesis 11:1–9 presents a story of the origins of multiple languages as part of its narrative, then one might ask where that theme gets picked up elsewhere within J. That Abram will somehow be a blessing to "nations" is not sufficient; as argued above, the connection between nations and languages appears exclusively in the Priestly Table of Nations, not in J. Naturally, not every part of a story needs to relate to larger narrative trajectories. An episode within a larger narrative can simply relate features of an event that serve more limited scopes.

Even in view of these observations, in light of the historical, philological, and literary facets of the Tower of Babel passage, there is good reason to see the call of Abram and the covenant established with him as a direct response to Babel. Such a claim is not to obscure the complexity of the multiplicity of covenants and the distinctiveness of how each version of the promises between God and Abram functions within its own literary source.[82] In fact, understood within its literary context, the covenant between God and Abram in J in Genesis 12:1–3 functions as a response to the Tower of Babel. Interpreters have long made this connection, evident perhaps enough by the fact that the Tower of Babel appears in Genesis 11 and the call of Abram in the very next chapter. Yet defining exactly how these two episodes relate to one another is another matter. A few observations in light of the argument that the Tower of Babel was not originally a story about languages highlight the manner in which the call of Abram functions as a solution to all of the problems presented in Genesis 11:1–9 specifically and the Primeval History generally.

Perhaps most superficially, there are the verbal linkages. Some have identified these connections as a secondary bridge to the patriarchal stories; yet in light of the ways in which Genesis 11:1–9 serves a larger plot, it could equally be argued that these verbal links are simply part of how the stories are related.[83] For example, the concept of the "name" as a theme throughout

82   See, more fully, Baden, *The Promise to the Patriarchs*.
83   Gertz, "The Formation of the Primeval History," 112, and bibliography in note 16. See also Ska, who views Genesis 9:20–11:26 as a sort of bridge between the Primeval History and the Patriarchal periods, though he identifies the Tower of Babel as

J's Primeval History has a specific function in pivoting between the Tower of Babel and Abram. The builders of Babel sought a "name" for themselves in the sense of fame, yet were denied such a stature by divine wrath (though, perhaps ironically, their reputation survives prominently in the biblical story and cultural imaginations of it, making them infamous). A further irony exists: if all the people were gathered at one spot, how the builders could achieve fame beyond their own, already congregated population is unclear.[84] Yet God promises Abram a "name" in the sense of fame to the now spread and diversified groups of people over the face of the earth. There is an audience that can now act as the recipients of Abram's fame, an audience that will hear of his reputation. This contrasting situation is itself a function of other mirror-image distinctions between the two stories, such as the urban collection of Babelites compared to Abram, whose life is largely nomadic (giving him, perhaps, wider exposure so that even more could know his great name). One could also add the scattering of the Babelites away from the city of their choice, in contrast to the gathering of Abram and his descendants to a land that God will give them. Of course, the builders of Babel want to acquire this name for themselves, without conferring with any other authority, whereas God is the source of Abram's name being made great.

Related is the thematic link of "nations" or "nationhood" between Babel and the call of Abram, both in Abram's initial encounter with God's promise and in the manner in which the promise plays out in Abram's narrative. As has been pointed out, J's focus in the covenant is on the inheritance of the land. Like other Pentateuchal sources (E and P), J's promise has both land and progeny at its core, though with more emphasis on land than the other sources. Such an emphasis makes sense in literary context: after Babel and the scattering of all the people gathered there, humanity is left wandering. God's concern to promise Abram land and rootedness in J functions as an antidote. Even more, J repeatedly demonstrates the manner in which all nations are related to Abram's progeny.[85] While land is the focus, peoplehood and how all the groups of the earth are related to Abram through his progeny appear in a number of places in J. In this fashion, J conveys how Abram is related to all people, even the unified "one people" (*am akhad*) of Genesis 11:6. In

---

important for setting up the call of Abram (*Introduction to Reading the Pentateuch*, trans. Sr. Pascale Dominique [Winona Lake, IN: Eisenbrauns, 2006], 22).

84   For this point, see Baden, *The Promise to the Patriarchs*, 115.

85   Baden, *The Promise to the Patriarchs*, 113–115.

response to human initiative, attempting to forge a unity of purpose, God will make Abram a "great nation," *goy gadol*, but one in the midst of other nations. Despite the reality of the multitude of nations in the wake of Babel, J goes to great lengths to show that Abram, his call, and his descendants are still connected to other people groups in this larger context. In other words, in the Tower of Babel story, the idioms in Genesis 11:1 and 11:6 thought to express language actually express senses of unity and peoplehood. The J source is concerned in its promise to Abram and his life (as well as his descendants) to portray how God relates, through Abram, to all people groups. The idioms in Genesis 11:1–9 underscore the contrast between the two episodes. Understood in this way, this observation highlights the contrast and reveals how Abram is the solution to all the problems posed in the Tower of Babel.

A further implication of the foregoing observations, and perhaps also more significant, is the manner in which Abram is called.[86] Genesis 12:1–3 and the nature of the call of Abram demonstrate in subtle but important ways how God responds to the Tower of Babel and the persistent issues of divine-human relations in the Primeval History. Later interpreters will be intrigued, if also bothered, by the observation that nothing of Abram's youth, or what he was doing in Ur or Haran prior to God's call, is told in the Bible. There is no description in Genesis of his virtue, or any merits that may have resulted in God's decision to call Abram out of his homeland. Passages such as Joshua 24:2–3 draw a contrast between Terah, Abram's father who worshipped many gods, and Abram, who was called to a different way of life. Yet the passage nowhere credits to Abram any pre-existing disposition or insight that would merit such an election.

This arbitrariness, which exercised the exegetical imagination—or perhaps bothered the religious sensibilities—of later interpreters who envisioned Abram smashing idols or arriving at a monotheistic belief through philosophical introspection, is an intentional feature of the text. All of the idioms and phrasings in the Tower of Babel narrative traditionally mistranslated as signs of a unilingual world are actually in service of another idea: people are unified politically against the divine. The terms evoke a stance against divine authority, a theme throughout J's Primeval History. People are not content to stay on their side of the divine-human divide. They will constantly test the relationship from the ground up. Abram's call, seen in this light, exists as an

---

86 Gary Anderson has, in more theological terms, labeled this facet of Abram's call the "surprise of election" (see more below).

ultimate top-down decision. There is nothing Abram did, no background information, no pre-existing condition, to draw God's favor. The silence about his youth is purposeful, and the arbitrariness of his call underscores the point of how his election reverses the Tower of Babel: if there is going to be a relationship between humanity and divinity, it will be on God's terms, and entirely on divine grounds. Yet again, divine logic has changed, but this time to a degree that highlights how the Tower of Babel was the last straw of J's Primeval History. God needs a new plan, a new direction, and a new starting point.

In this reading, all the problems of the Tower of Babel, and J's Primeval History generally, are resolved in the call of Abram. This relationship, however, is clear only to the degree that multilingualism is taken out of the narrative of the Tower of Babel, a thesis that has historical, philological, and literary warrant. Where other interpreters may see this relationship still functioning (Abram's call as a reaction to the Tower of Babel) to the degree that they posit that Genesis 11:1–9 contains the Bible's etiology for multilingualism, God's communication with Abram leaves the feature of multilingualism unresolved. It is worth noting that history, philology, and literary considerations merge to underscore the same meaning of the passage. The call of Abram, then, establishes a top-down, not bottom-up, relationship with humanity. As evident throughout Abram's life in J, there is reciprocity. God tests Abram, not unlike Adam and Eve, and Abram and his descendants are expected to be faithful to keep up the relationship.[87] But the terms are agreed upon and divinely initiated, which provides the greatest possible contrast to Genesis 11:1–9.

HOW BABEL BECAME A STORY ABOUT LANGUAGE:
Combining lashon and safah in the Compilation of the Pentateuch in Genesis 10–11

If this relationship is clearer to the degree that language is removed as part of the Tower of Babel, then it remains necessary to explain how the narrative became about the origin of multilingualism. The combination of the two originally independent sources that comprise the first eleven chapters

---

87 Abram is obedient to a sort of "natural law" according to Baden (*The Promise to the Patriarchs*, 115). There are more specifics (Abram is to go to where God shows him, and to be hospitable), but it's not a "law" in the sense of E, D, or P.

of Genesis as it currently exists transformed the passage. The compiled, final version of the Pentateuch has not always dictated that interpreters find in the story an etiology for multilingualism.[88] It is nonetheless the case that the editing of the Pentateuch entailed the interweaving of literary material that created the possibility, perhaps even encouraged the possibility, that the Tower of Babel was an origin story of multilingualism. The overlapping chronologies of Genesis 10 and 11, in their canonical version, weave together *lashon* (P in Genesis 10) with *safah* (J in Genesis 11). It becomes possible to read Genesis 11:1–9 as an example of how the languages (*lashon*) in Genesis 10, in the Priestly portions, spread. In this fashion, the Tower of Babel functions just as the examples from elsewhere in the Hebrew Bible function, in which *lashon* and *safah* are conjoined, a connection that otherwise would indicate a story about languages.[89]

It could be proposed that the editor crafted this possible interpretation, on literary grounds, on purpose. Here, however, there was no other way that the editor could work. At least in this case, there exists no alternate way that the editor could arrange the material. They may have had an underlying motivation and theology in editing, but one cannot recover it.[90] This is not to argue that the editor was entirely mechanical in the process. Good evidence exists that the episode of Nimrod was moved to its current location in Genesis 10:8–12 because of the pattern of P's genealogy.[91] Even this editorial move, however, keeps the material within the same sphere of events between the flood and the call of Abram.

Indeed, there could be no other position for P and J material in Genesis 10 and 11 from the flood to Abram and the patriarchs and matriarchs, or elsewhere in the Primeval History for that matter. The Tower of Babel, in this editing, cannot go after Abram's call for a variety of reasons, perhaps foremost because of the manner in which the stories relate to one another (Babel as a problem to which the call of Abram is a solution). Neither can the Tower of Babel precede the flood narrative in the editing process, standing as it is in its own source as the last straw of primeval rebellion. Since the flood stories are necessarily combined into one (there cannot be two flood stories in which God destroys everything and then promises not to do it again), the Tower of

---

88 As the work of Vitringa and, more recently, Uehlinger and Berlejung demonstrate.
89 See chapter 3 for details.
90 For more, see Baden, *The Composition of the Pentateuch*, 214–229.
91 See the notes in chapter 3.

Babel has to come afterward. The only place the literary material in Genesis 10 and 11 can exist in the editing process is precisely where they are. Since the P material contains the story of the spread of humanity through language, the similarly edited and chronologically parallel story of human spread in J will, by the process of combination, be influenced by this theme as well.[92] Notably, however, the only explicit mention of human spread in Genesis 10:18 in J occurs without a mention of languages. Yet the verb in Genesis 10:18 (*putz*), originally part of J but surrounded in the compiled Pentateuch by P's material that evokes language as part of this process, is the same for spreading in the Tower of Babel. In this fashion, the final form of the story, with both J and P, evokes the sense of this spread as entailing linguistic differentiation given how Genesis 10:18 is surrounded by P material that makes this claim explicit.[93]

---

92   It could be argued that in J, humanity was not necessarily intended to spread at all or to "be fruitful and multiply" in P's language. Carol Meyers, Joel Baden, and Candida Moss have claimed that the Garden narrative did not entail an original plan for childbearing, and the advent of childbirth arrives in the narrative only after eating the fruit in Genesis 3. See Meyers, *Rediscovering Eve* (New York: Oxford University Press, 2013), 88–93; Baden and Moss, *Reconceiving Infertility: Biblical Perspectives on Procreation and Childlessness* (Princeton, NJ: Princeton University Press, 2015), 85–87.

    Further implications of this observation can be drawn out. Built on comparative and philological analysis, J does not have an etiology for language spread. Perhaps this is so because, unlike P, it tells a story in which population spread and multiplying is somewhat of an unintended consequence and not a natural outflow of a divine command. J conceives of Adam as fine by himself, until he is not. Then animals are introduced, and then, as a companion, Eve. They are fine, until they are not in Genesis 3. So, childbirth enters. Human spread is, therefore, somewhat problematic by definition and a divinely unintended consequence. One could argue that J would be all the more interested in obsessing over the details about how human spread happens, but given J's clear distaste for cities and dense populations, it could also be the case that J does not like to discuss the details of human spread. So, there is no information about Cain's wife; she's just there. Babel, understood in this way, shows the problem: there are too many humans, they were not part of the original plan, and they cross and bother the divine realm, not unlike the sensory problems of overpopulation in other flood accounts in the ancient Near East, such as Atra-Ḥasis. The consequence of judgment, like Cain, is spread and dispersal, perhaps to prevent too many problem-causing people in one place. This could explain why Cain's line is so bad: they spread, but build cities nonetheless.

93   Recent models have suggested that J, in a very different form and function than the original Yahwist of other documentary hypotheses, was an early redactor of sorts. See, for example, Christoph Levin, "The Yahwist: The Earliest Editor in the Pentateuch," *JBL* 126 (2007): 209–230.

One might more strongly call this transformation of the Tower of Babel into a story of multilingualism an accident of the editing of the Bible. But it is a very productive one in terms of interpretive possibilities. It yields an image of language in the Primeval History that has set the agenda for discourse in an astounding number of disciplines in the humanities, social sciences, and even natural sciences. Even if we cannot derive an overriding purpose behind such compilational activity—which may be more a factor of historical distance and scholarly limitations in reconstruction—we can appreciate the process through which Genesis 11:1–9 was transformed into an etiology for multilingualism. More, we can acknowledge, though the passage was not originally written as an origin story for the spread of languages, the power and intrigue that such an interpretation has left in the history of the reception of the Bible. Such influence has crafted religious and political traditions in ways that have greatly shaped the modern world. Yet the analysis of the Tower of Babel's literary context has bearing on the use of the story in society. In J, and at least not explicitly in P, there is no story in which multilingualism is the product of divine wrath and judgment. While the compilation of the Pentateuch might make the reading of Genesis 11:1–9 as an etiology for multilingualism possible, and while the story certainly entails God's disapproval of human activities, laying at the feet of biblical rhetoric multilingualism as a sign of divine curse, as some modern political commentators have claimed, is foreign to the original intent and literary horizon of the passage.[94]

---

94   See more in chapter 6.

CHAPTER 5

Babel's Antidote

The Solution to the Problem of Babel in Interpretive History

"When the nations in their single-minded wickedness were put to confusion, she [wisdom] recognized the righteous man [Abraham] and kept him blameless before God."[1]

INTRODUCTION

Like a pebble thrown into a lake that creates ripples of ever-increasing concentric sizes in its wake, the relatively small story of Babel has created an outsized effect in its wake over time. Only one hundred and twenty-one words in Hebrew, the passage has been an object of reflection in a number of different historical circumstances. Interpreters produce distinct strategies of how to relate this passage, or "translate" it as one scholar has termed it, to their unique social, cultural, and political contexts.[2] Both the thrift of prose and manner in which political concerns are embedded in the narrative attest to the power and vitality of this story, as well as its malleability in interpretation.

---

1 Wisdom of Solomon 10:5. For the relationship of this passage to other traditions, such as Pseudo-Philo's *Liber Antiquitatum Biblicarum*, and the interpretive logic that leads to the possibility that Abram was himself present at Babel, see Peter Enns, "Pseudo-Solomon and His Scripture: Biblical Interpretation in the Wisdom of Solomon," in *A Companion to Biblical Interpretation in Early Judaism*, ed. Matthias Henze (Grand Rapids, MI: Eerdmans, 2012), 401–403.
2 Sherman, *Babel's Tower Translated*.

Once the compilation of the Pentateuch occurred, it became possible to understand Genesis 11:1–9 as an origin myth of multilingualism. Despite this shift in possible interpretation, the foundational relationship between the Tower of Babel as a problem and Abram's call as a solution was still an ever-present feature of how exegetes understood the purpose and thrust of Genesis 11:1–9.[3] Yet the introduction of language as a potential element of the story in the editing of the Torah also created a problem for its relation to the call of Abram: if these narratives are related as a problem (Babel) to a solution (call of Abram), then one must explain how the issues of Genesis 11:1–9 find a resolution in Genesis 12:1–3.[4] If language is a component of the Tower of Babel, perhaps even a vital aspect of the story, then it is necessary to explore how this element of the advent of multilingualism has anything do to with God's relation to Abram.

What follows is an examination of how ancient interpreters understood this puzzle, at times highlighting how this mismatch of the problem to the solution created new, unresolved problems that endured in Babel's legacy.[5] Two strategies appear as a result: ancient interpreters attempted to reconcile the call of Abram to the issue of language (in one case modifying, if in subtle ways, the role of language at Babel); or, if language has no part in the call of Abram, then multilingualism functions as an unresolved problem stemming

---

3   Kugel encapsulates the interpretive possibilities for ancient readers: "God's promise to Abraham comes at the start of Genesis 12. The previous chapter deals with the tower of Babel and God's punishment of the tower builders. If, shortly afterward, the Bible suddenly turns to Abraham and his journey from Chaldea, could it not be hinting at some relationship between the two incidents?" Kugel, *Traditions of the Bible*, 258.

4   For Hiebert, who provides a rich though idiosyncratic interpretation of the Tower of Babel, Genesis 11:1–9 is not about "pride and punishment" but is rather a description of God's act of providing for cultural (including linguistic) diversity in world history. The description of Abram's ancestors and the call of Abram in Genesis 11 and 12 is simply part of setting the multicultural stage in which Abram's call occurs. Hiebert, "The Tower of Babel and the Origins of the World's Cultures," *JBL* 126 (2007): 54. See general criticisms of Hiebert's reading in John T. Strong, "Shattering the Image of God: A Response to Theodore Hiebert's Interpretation of the Story of the Tower of Babel," *JBL* 124 (2008): 625–634; and Andrew LaCocque, "Whatever Happened in the Valley of Shinar? A Response to Theodore Hiebert," *JBL* 128 (2009): 29–41.

5   For an excellent overview of how ancient biblical interpreters examined the Bible and used some parts of Scripture to elucidate others, see James L. Kugel and Rowan A. Greer, *Early Biblical Interpretation*, LEC 3 (Philadelphia: Westminster John Knox, 1986).

from the Tower of Babel. This lack of resolution underscores either the role of language in a community's relationship with God or the role of language in an eschatological age when God deals with the wrongs of the world. The inheritance of the abiding problem of multilingualism into modernity also entailed issues of how the architects of the modern nation-state saw their relation to the biblical story of Babel.[6] Prior to examining this modern land-scape in more detail, it will help to investigate representative samples of how ancient interpreters struggled to relate Genesis 11:1–9 to Genesis 12:1–3, and how this struggle brings to the fore the difficulty of relating language to the call of Abram. This observation itself might also shed light on and give credence to the foregoing arguments that the story of the Tower of Babel was not originally about the advent of multilingualism, though perhaps from a different angle.

THE "WOUND" OF BABEL AND ABRAM AS THE CURE:
Biblical Perspectives and Beyond

In J's account of the Primeval History, we read of continual attempts on the part of the earthly realm to transgress, or—to use the language of some ancient interpreters on the Tower of Babel—to invade the divine realm. Even in the compiled and edited Pentateuch, combining J and P into the broad contours of the text (either Masoretic or Septuagintal) that we have now, the consistent themes of boundary-crossing between the divine and human realms are apparent. Disaster results in each instance, whether in the expulsion of the garden in response to eating the forbidden fruit, in a devastating flood in response to the children of the gods having sexual relations with women, or in a divine judgment when humanity builds a tower and, the greater offense, a city without consulting God.

Genesis 11:1–9 stands as the ultimate event and affront to divinity in the Primeval History of J. Gerhard von Rad came to the same conclusion, argu-ing, though in a rather Christian scheme of soteriology, that Babel was the last moment of the judgment of sin before God's gracious call of Abram in

---

6   See both general comments about the curse of multilingualism, Babel, and the mod-ern nation-state, as well as incisive research in the specific case of Malaysia in Rachel Leow, *Taming Babel: Language in the Making of Malaysia* (New York: Cambridge University Press, 2016).

Genesis 12:1–3, also belonging to J. In other words, for von Rad, Abram's relationship to God was an antidote to Babel, though a Babel that, in von Rad's interpretation, was still about the change in history from monolingualism to multilingualism.[7] The way Abram functions as the solution to the problem posed by Babel, and indeed posed by all of J's issues with humanity in the Primeval History, can best be understood, however, with the Tower of Babel in Genesis 11:1–9 in nonlinguistic terms.

In this manner, all of the problems portrayed in Genesis 11:1–9 find their resolutions in Genesis 12:1–3: in response to the persistent manner in which humans cross the divine-mortal boundary, God chooses an individual seemingly at random. This randomness has sparked the imagination of ancient interpreters in both Judaism and Islam more so than Christianity: what was Abram doing in Ur to deserve such a call? Though Joshua 24:2–3 paints a picture of Abram's ancestors as worshipping other gods, a situation from which Abram was called, there is no indication that Abram himself did anything to merit a new relationship with God. No smashing idols (so the Genesis Rabbah and Islamic traditions), no philosophical spark that led him to the conclusion of monotheism (so Maimonides), no conflict with Nimrod (so rabbinic and Islamic sources), nothing. The biblical text is intentionally, if deafeningly, silent, which highlights the deliberate presentation of this call as a response to the problems of the Primeval History. In what has been called the "surprise of election" of Abram, God provides a mirror-image antidote, reversing the persistent result of the crossing of the divine-human boundary through a unilateral, top-down connection.[8] It is not a relationship that stretches from the ground up, nor is it the result of illicit actions by divine

---

7   See the discussion and citation of von Rad in chapter 4.

8   Blenkinsopp comes close to the conclusions arrived at here regarding the call of Abram and the Tower of Babel as related stories, though he does not draw out the implications further, nor does he make the same arguments about the Tower of Babel per se as made in this book. He states:

> The builders of the tower and city of Babel (11:1–9) confer among themselves and the deity deliberates with himself, but they do not interact; there is no communication. The revelation to Abraham comes, then, as a sudden, unanticipated, and profoundly transformative irruption into the course of events. Nothing we have been told about Abraham has prepared us for it, or provided any explanation why it happened to him, or why it happened at that time or in that place.

Blenkinsopp, *Abraham: The Story of a Life* (Grand Rapids, MI: Eerdmans, 2015), 32–33.

hosts (as in Genesis 6:1–4). Abram has no claim or merit on his own, and no action, disposition, or ethical state precedes divine election.[9] This is not a religious claim entailing some specifically Christian notion of election and grace. Rather, it is a way to highlight how the wounds of Babel are, in the context of J and of the compiled Pentateuch, related meaningfully and as a narrative prelude to the call of Abram as a solution.

The relationship between these two stories is important to highlight for a number of reasons. A new reading of the Tower of Babel, which understands the idioms therein in terms of political rhetoric and not as idioms pertaining to language, makes better sense of how these passages relate to one another. Their proximity in consecutive chapters of the Bible (Genesis 11 and 12) already invites a reading in which they are related somehow. Yet demonstrating the manner in which the call of Abram functions as a solution to the "wounds" of Babel, as Umberto Eco has termed it, can uncover more precisely how the two function together.

The awareness that Babel left wounds open and festering, a conclusion arrived at in the traditional, language-based interpretation of the narrative

---

9   With reference to the "surprise," Anderson states that "we have no better example than the call of Abraham in Gen. 12." He observes, further, that "after the curtain goes down on Gen. 11—and with no proper transition—the reader comes face to face with" God's call of Abraham. This "textual gap" provokes the question:

> Why Abraham? We must ask, as have many interpreters. The history of the Jewish interpretation of these verses is littered with various midrashim as to what Abraham had done to merit this boon. Consider, for example, the book of Jubilees, one of our earliest examples of biblical interpretation (second century BCE). It devotes dozens of verses to filling the textual gap between Gen. 11 and 12. By its account, God revealed the secret of monotheism to Abraham in Mesopotamia. In that land of polytheism and idolatry, the doctrine proved quite controversial. Abraham's courage to affirm God's oneness in the face of physical danger became the occasion for God to reward him with the supreme promise. This interpretive tradition makes for wonderful midrash, but the louder it sounds, the more deafening is the Bible's silence about the same.

See Anderson, *Christian Doctrine and the Old Testament: Theology in the Service of Biblical Exegesis* (Grand Rapids, MI: Baker, 2017), 78–79 (quote at 79). In the reading offered above, the silence is intentional, productive literarily for J, and has specific function relative to Babel as a crescendo of human encroachment on the divine. See also Diana Lipton for this "deafening" "silence," "The Reluctant Brick Maker: Babel and Abram in Pseudo-Philo and Bereshit Rabbah," in *Ve-'Ed Ya'aleh (Gen 2:6): Essays in Biblical and Ancient Near Eastern Studies Presented to Edward L. Greenstein, Volume 2*, ed. Peter Machinist, et al. (Atlanta: SBL Press, 2021), 1065–1066.

and arrived at in the experience of multilingualism and statecraft in modernity, led Dante and others to theorize how to deal with Babel as an abiding problem. In the understanding of the passage without the advent of multilingualism as a plot detail, no abiding problem exists in its original context: within J, Abram answers the problem posed by Babel, and, indeed, posed by all the transgressions of humanity and incursions into the divine realm in the Primeval History. The call of Abram closes this scene of biblical history and inaugurates a new one, but the previous scene is truly closed and resolved.

Even in light of the compilation of the Pentateuch, when it became possible to interpret the Tower of Babel as a story of the advent of multilingualism, it was clear to subsequent interpreters that Babel and Abram existed somehow in relation to one another. But the question was how to relate them if a central problem of Babel, in the compiled text, was multilingualism as a sign of a divine curse. The following explores the strategies employed in interpretive history to find a solution to Babel if Babel was understood as an etiology for multilingualism, yet no traces of the call of Abram appear to remedy this part of Babel in the biblical story. Interpreters use one of two strategies.[10] They can chronologically conflate Babel and Abram, and, as a result, either a) make language part of the call of Abram and so insert Babel into the life of Abram, or b) cast Abram as a bystander to witness against the act of the building of the tower and city in the plains of Shinar and so insert Abram into the narrative of Babel. Alternatively, they may posit that the problem of Babel is only partly addressed in the call of Abram, leaving the aspect of divine curse and language to be resolved at a future time.

---

10   For Uehlinger, who dealt extensively with the history of interpretation of Babel at the start of his book, the history of interpretation was, in a sense, a moving away from the meaning of the words in the text (as noted in Sherman, *Babel's Tower Translated*, 5). See Uehlinger, *Weltreich und Eine Rede*, 3. I place the study of reception history of the text at the end of this book to highlight, instead, how ancient readers were attuned to the issue of language in their understanding of Genesis 11:1–9. This detail of the text led them to explore how it related to Abram's call. The exegetical energy, then, was not a move away from the text, but an attempt to understand it given the interpretive traditions that they had. Uehlinger clearly respects the history of interpretation and spends considerable energy exploring ancient readings of the passage. But I hope that this chapter, standing as it does after historical, philological, and source-critical considerations, demonstrates how the reception history of the passage can be brought into consideration with historical-critical insights. Reception history, in this sense, is not a demonstration of how later readings can be dismissed as "sekundär an den Text herangetragene Interpolationene," though such activity can happen, but rather an attempt to engage passages meaningfully given the texts and traditions available. See Uehlinger, *Weltreich und Ene Rede*, 3.

What these considerations and the sample of interpretations reveal below is that the connection between Babel and Abram was not understood as simply a literary ploy of problem-to-solution. Beyond the Bible, these subsequent traditions took the narrative to describe real events, such that the words on the page also reached beyond the Bible. While skeptical readers of Greek myths might later influence some medieval readers of the biblical narratives in the Geonic period, for most ancient and medieval interpreters, the distinction between text and event was collapsed, even if some thinkers would favor allegorical approaches to many stories.[11] In other words, if Babel inflicted a wound on humanity, and Abram was a cure of sorts, any ailments left unaddressed in Abram's call, such as multilingualism, of necessity resulted in real-world situations of abiding theological significance. The relationship was not academic, or a function of literary poetics, but rather one of practical consequences, with the result that relating Babel and the call of Abram became a locus of much intellectual activity.

It should be noted that such intellectual activity could be quite pluriform in some details. Not every tradition of interpretation of the Tower of Babel would cast the problem of Babel in the same ways. Even traditions that agreed that Genesis 11:1–9 encoded a major transgression against the divine differed in how they interpreted the figures involved. A particular case is the character of Nimrod in Syriac Christianity. Two prominent figures, Ephrem and Ishodad, understood Nimrod not as the founder of Babel and its tower but as the founder of Babel who fled in disgust as others constructed the offence against God. In this manner, Nimrod became the paradigm of a righteous person fleeing wickedness instead of the architect of the ultimate affront to God.[12]

The interpretation itself was grounded in a reading of the biblical text: by combining Genesis 10 and 11. Yet a crucial syntactical relationship between a verb and a place name occurs in Genesis 10:11. The verse is as follows:

From that land, Assur went out (or, he went out to Assur), and he built Nineveh, Rehoboth-Ir, and Calah.

---

11   Gideon Bohak, *Ancient Jewish Magic* (New York: Cambridge University Press, 2011), 36–38.
12   Joel Walker, "The Legacy of Mesopotamia in Late Antique Iraq: The Christian Martyr Shrine at Melqi (Neo-Assyrian Milqia)," *ARAM* 18–19 (2006–2007): 483–508.

Most translations of this verse understand the verb "went out" to have Assur as its subject (so the JPS), though others opt to translate Assur as a destination, in adverbial relationship to the verb ("he went to Assur"). The modern translations that opt for this second option understand that Nimrod, the unstated subject of the verb (assumed because he is explicitly the subject in 10:9 and implicitly so in 10:10), goes north to Assur to expand his empire territorially.[13]

Ephrem and Ishodad both analyzed the relationship between Assur and the verb in the second manner, the toponym as an adverbial destination for Nimrod, the implied actor of the verb. Yet for them, Nimrod's move to the north was not one of territorial ambition but rather flight. Nimrod "went forth from that land to Assur" in the sense that he fled the area of Babylon. His move to the north, to found Assyria, was one of necessity. The issue requiring explanation, then, is why Nimrod had to move. For Ephrem and Ishodad, he witnessed the construction of the Tower of Babel. Sickened by the hubris and defiance against God, Nimrod fled to the north. As such, he represented for many Syriac Christians faithful flight instead of associating with wicked activities.

The example of Ephrem and Ishodad demonstrates how defining the problem of Babel is complicated. The grammar of Genesis 10:8–12 is not entirely straightforward, and reading Genesis 10 and 11 as overlapping chronological events creates its own set of difficulties. If Genesis 10:8–12 presents background to Genesis 11, then a particular reading of the former can shape how an interpreter approaches the latter. Indeed, for Ephrem and Ishodad, understanding Nirmod as a sympathetic character who wanted nothing to do with the events of Genesis 11:1–9 made more sense of the biblical text. The Tower of Babel episode, despite the overwhelming tendency otherwise in interpretive history, nowhere identifies the leader of the rebellion against God within Genesis 11:1–9 itself.

In this manner, Ephrem and Ishodad identified the problem of Babel along similar lines as many interpreters. Hubris and a desire to cross into the realm of God, stemming from concerted action—since everyone spoke the same language—resulted in divine punishment manifest in the advent of multilingualism. Yet the moral of the story, and one solution against the actions of Babel, is to flee. Abram might present another option to counter the events

---

13   For a recent study and argument for Nimrod as the subject of the verb, see Day, "In Search of Nimrod," 202–203.

of Genesis 11:1–9, but he exists along with (and not pitted against) Nimrod as dual exemplars of faithful action. What this Syriac interpretation reveals about the problem of Babel is that the issues involved in interpreting Genesis 10 with Genesis 11 are complicated and manifold such that no interpretation is a simple given; rather, each tradition needs to be examined in order to see how the exegetes construct their arguments.

HOW ANCIENT INTERPRETERS UNDERSTOOD THE RELATIONSHIP BETWEEN GENESIS 10, 11, AND 12

In order to explain how Babel functioned as a problem to which Abram was a solution, ancient interpreters had to explain how Genesis 10, 11, and 12 relate to one another, not simply Genesis 11:1–9 and Genesis 12:1–3. The overlapping chronologies in parts of these chapters, itself a product of the editing of Pentateuchal sources, invited a certain amount of conflation in which later interpreters could collapse the timelines of these chapters. Genesis 10, containing both J and P, told an at times confusing account of the division of the nations and with them of tongues, or languages. Whatever the prehistory of the Nimrod episode in Genesis 10, belonging ultimately to J, the fact that he is said to be responsible for the building of Babel further highlights the city-centered nature of the building project in Genesis 11:1–9, though Nimrod is nowhere mentioned in the latter. Further, the material from P not only made it possible to understand the Tower of Babel as a story of multilingualism but also as part of the same chronological landscape as Genesis 10. For many later interpreters, the puzzle of chronology was simply a matter of the Bible as it was received and, they believed, as it always was. Source-critical conclusions explain how the Bible came to look the way it does in its final form by recourse to isolating distinct, pre-existing narratives, but the reception history of the text had to navigate how these features functioned in the text at hand.[14]

Further, the call of Abram in Genesis 12 places him as coming from Ur of the Chaldees, and the word for Ur connected his place of origin with "fire" ('-w-r in Hebrew), linking Genesis 12 to Genesis 10 and stories in later traditions of fiery conflicts between Nimrod and Abram. Genesis 11, sandwiched

---

14   Naturally, the text at hand could also vary given manuscript differences.

between, must then have been part of the same scene, a case in point of Genesis 10 and, for some interpreters, directly related to the call of Abram. The point here is that for ancient interpreters, the chronological puzzles and tantalizing details between these three chapters indicated to them that they must be related somehow, not simply making the Tower of Babel a specific instance of the more general spread in Genesis 10 but also somehow enveloping Abram. In this fashion, the efforts of ancient sources of interpretation to define how exactly Babel and Abram relate draw upon the features of the text itself, though the puzzle of language became a difficulty without a clear explanation. Taking language out of the equation for interpreting Babel can provide a satisfactory and convincing way to understand how Genesis 11:1–9 and Genesis 12:1–3 function as problem to solution. The sheer energy that exegetes expended on defining how they relate points toward the fact that refining our knowledge of the pivot between Babel and Abram in J and the compiled Pentateuch not only aids in explicating the transition between the Primeval History and much of the rest of the Pentateuch but also underscores how language does not fit easily in this literary transition between Genesis 11:1–9 and 12:1–3.

If such a complicated overlap in chronology created an interpretive puzzle for exegetes to explain, it also provided opportunities to juxtapose Babel more directly as problem to Abram as solution. This is precisely the tactic employed in the book of *Biblical Antiquities*, formerly known as Pseudo-Philo (also called *Liber Antiquitatum Biblicarum*, the passages in which are abbreviated as *L.A.B.* below). The work contains a number of examples of interpretation that hew closely to later rabbinic approaches to the text, though in origins, the work derives from between the first century and second century CE.[15] The retelling of the Tower of Babel involves not only Abram as a virtuous resistor of such construction but also the attempt to cast him into a fiery furnace, calling to mind the consonantal text in Genesis 12 of "Ur," which looks like the root for "to light on fire" (*he'ir*).[16] For the author of the text, a major issue throughout its recasting of biblical material involves the topic of leadership: how, when a community feels pressure to buckle, proper leaders of the community react and respond to God.[17] Though Nimrod is not mentioned specifically in the particular chapters under investigation here (*L.A.B.* VI and VII), the theme

---

15   Sherman, *Babel's Tower Translated*, 123.

16   Enns, "Pseudo-Philo and His Scripture," 403.

17   Sherman, *Babel's Tower Translated*, 126–127.

of resistance to idolatry and survival of a trial by fire in a furnace call to mind later interpretations in which Abram directly confronts Nimrod.

This example in *Biblical Antiquities* displays how the overlapping chronologies and linkages between the three chapters created a distinct possibility not only to pivot between Babel as problem and Abram as solution but to place Abram at the scene of the crime itself.[18] In doing so, the virtue of the patriarch and the corrupt actions of the Babelites are brought into sharp, if also immediate, relief. The themes that bring Genesis 11:1–9 and Genesis 12:1–3 together are heightened in the retelling of Babel in the *Biblical Antiquities*, particularly "naming."[19] The name that people want to make for themselves in the biblical Tower of Babel transforms into a proposal of a very concrete nature, namely, to emblazon the bricks of the tower with their names. All of this contrasts, naturally, with the fame of Abram, achieved by divine deliverance and not divine condemnation.

The role of language and speech in *Biblical Antiquities* highlights the way in which Babel and Abram were thought to function together. Though the division of the earth from a unilingual to a multilingual landscape occurs in *L.A.B.* VI, it does not become a topic of discussion in *L.A.B.* VII until after the scene of Abram at Babel finds its resolve in the previous chapter. *L.A.B.* VI begins with notice of the movement of humanity from the East to Babylon, and the text describes conversations that evoke unity of intent. In this scene, people decide to burn their names on bricks, a play on words that also comes full circle when Abram is thrown into a furnace. Here, his salvation cements his own legacy, but in direct opposition to the Babelites.[20] In the entirety of the scene in which Abram is at Babel, no mention of language appears. In fact, the absence of language in Abram's silence is perhaps the

---

18   Other Christian traditions will have Nimrod as the figure at Babel who takes righteous exception to the building activities. See Arye Zoref, "The Influence of Syriac Bible Commentaries on Judeo Arabic Exegesis as Demonstrated by Several Stories from the Book of Genesis," *SCJR* 11 (2016): 1–18.

19   On this and other exegetical techniques between Babel and Abram in *L.A.B.*, see Kugel and Greer, *Early Biblical Interpretation*, 88. See especially Lipton for Abram's role in Pseudo-Philo ("The Reluctant Brick Maker," 1065–1078 [esp. 1069–1070]).

20   Sherman rightly stresses that the names on bricks in *L.A.B.* VI reference the census of Noah's descendants in the preceding chapter, but one can see how such a reference could function in addition to the manner in which having a "name" is a dominant feature of Babel and Abram's call in Genesis. Sherman further makes an interesting connection to the materiality of inscribing in Deuteronomy 27 and Joshua (*Babel's Tower Translated*, 128–130, 138).

most notable feature of this story. A prince, Joktan, offers twelve righteous people refuge from the evils of Babel.[21] Eleven verbally accept the refuge, but Abram remains silent until bidden to speak. Nowhere in *L.A.B.* VI does the note about language appear, though the denouement of God's judgment also does not occur in this chapter. Still, in the activities of the builders in *L.A.B.* VI and the description of the world during construction, no mention of the unilingual nature of humanity occurs.

A contrast appears in *L.A.B.* VII, and, as noted, these chapters entail two distinct perspectives on the Tower of Babel story. Abram also functions as a foil to Babel, but in *L.A.B.* VII, the foil includes the role of language and confusion as a vital feature of the story, a confusion out of which Abram will be called.[22] In one document, then, a diversity of approaches appear in which Abram's call is placed in the immediate context of the events at Babel as a solution to the problem. It is almost as if *L.A.B.* VI and VII represent the two themes attached to Babel in the traditional interpretation of the story; each dealt with in their own narrative setting with Abram as the righteous foil: hubris through unity of action and expressed through language. Isolated in these ways, the manner in which Abram functions as the antidote to Babel, whether at Babel in *L.A.B.* VI or in God's decree in light of Babel in *L.A.B.* VII, can be explored more fully.[23]

The picture of the Tower of Babel in *L.A.B.* VI functions well in a society in which the question of leadership was paramount. The passage retelling Babel in *L.A.B.* VI highlights the unity of action of the Babelites and also

---

21 It could be the case that these twelve were derived from the biblical syntax in Genesis 11:3, where there is a potential redundancy in "let us make bricks and let us burn (them) hard." Sherman notes that the redundancy could be the origin of the story of the twelve targeted for fire. The making of bricks would be enough, so perhaps the lack of an explicit object on the verb "to burn" could create an implicit reference to action not explicitly stated in the narrative, but filled in an extra biblical account. Sherman, *Babel's Tower Translated*, 134–135.

22 Murphy, *Pseudo-Philo: Rewriting the Bible* (New York: Oxford University Press, 1993), 48–50. Murphy also argues that *L.A.B.* VII "sticks closer to the biblical plot," and "rewrites Gen 11:4–9" (*Pseudo-Philo*, 41).

23 In this fashion, Sherman's observations that *L.A.B.* VI, no less than *L.A.B.* VII, though perhaps in a different manner, engages with the Bible as a quiet dialogue of sorts is helpful, even if *L.A.B.* VII is more explicit in its engagements. For how *L.A.B.* VII clarifies aspects of Genesis 11:1–9, see Howard Jacobson, "Biblical Interpretation in Pseudo-Philo's *Liber Antiquitatum Biblicarum*," in *A Companion to Biblical Interpretation in Early Judaism*, ed. Matthias Henze (Grand Rapids, MI: Eerdmans, 2012), 188.

points toward the actions of Joktan in hatching a plan that ultimately fails. Abram, though leading no one, stands nonetheless as an exceptional character, unwilling to go along and, instead, resolutely remaining unwavering in his trust of divine deliverance.[24] Through these contrasts, the author of *L.A.B.* is able to make Abram a part of the scene at Babel in order to more pointedly demonstrate good versus bad leadership.[25]

This overview of how ancient interpreters could leverage the chronological overlaps and connections between Abram and Babel, if not also from Nimrod in Genesis 10 to Babel in Genesis 11 to Abram's call in Genesis 12, has been both general of necessity as well as inclusive of one particular instance of exegesis. It is general since many more examples of how the Table of Nations were thought to relate to Babel and Abram could be adduced, but all would point to the same issue: Babel is a problem to which Abram is a solution, a configuration that included the figure of Nimrod or some similar character in the mix for many ancient readers of the text. Yet the specific examples of the *Biblical Antiquities* display most vividly how one text actually placed Abram at Babel. It was distinct in doing so for its time. Though some later rabbinic passages will place Abram generally at Babel, and though the Wisdom of Solomon may make an implied claim that Abram was present, only *Biblical Antiquities* makes such a connection so early and so explicit, and makes such a concerted effort to describe Abram's role in this regard.[26] Yet if language in unity of action was part of the problem resulting in multilingualism as a sign of divine curse, how Abram as a solution was thought to operate, particularly when language appears nowhere in his biblical story, remained a detail to explain. In *L.A.B.* VI, where Abram features most prominently in *Biblical Antiquities*'s engagements with the Tower of Babel story, language does not feature at all as part of the description. In contrast, the retelling of Babel in *L.A.B.* VII hews closer to the wording of the biblical text, even if *L.A.B.* VI engages in its own way with the biblical narrative. In this fashion, God mentions Abram as a solution to Babel and as an elect individual called out of the confusion of tongues in *L.A.B.* VII, though the multilingualism abides and is not directly addressed in Abram's election. For *L.A.B.* VI, if language was not a part of the solution with Abram, the narrative of Babel could also be told in which language was absent. Other sources in antiquity,

---

24 Sherman, *Babel's Tower Translated*, 140.
25 Sherman, *Babel's Tower Translated*, 145–146.
26 Sherman, *Babel's Tower Translated*, 27.

such as *Jubilees*, will also posit a parity in the stories, but instead will offer an interpretation in which language functions both in the Tower of Babel and in the call of Abram.

JUBILEES
Babel and the Call of Abram as Related Stories about Language

In the book of *Jubilees*, this struggle to identify how language in the Tower of Babel relates to the call of Abram is manifest in a number of ways. In a sense, the struggle is aided by very real historical factors, which itself displays the attempts to make the passage speak about contemporaneous events of the authors in ways that are analogous to the modern applications of the text. The book of *Jubilees* was edited in the second century BCE around the time of the Maccabean revolt.[27] Most scholars view the book as, in some fashion, representing Hasmonean ideology on a number of fronts, though the precise relationship between the Maccabees and the book remains somewhat elusive.[28] While its particular view of the solar calendar may have facilitated its adoption at Qumran as an authoritative text, the main undercurrent of the document involves a rewritten account of the creation of the world until Exodus 14, in which later legal material was inserted into the earlier story to demonstrate how it was practiced already from the beginning of time.[29] After all, if the law was reflective of the divine nature, then aspects of it, such as purity in childbirth, should have been followed by righteous individuals, such as Abraham, and even Adam and Eve, even from the very start.

---

27 James C. VanderKam, "The Origins and Purposes of the *Book of Jubilees*," in *Studies in the* Book of Jubilees, ed. M. Albani, J. Frey, and A. Lange, TSAJ 65 (Tübingen: Mohr Siebeck, 1997), 4–16.

28 See the discussion in VanderKam, "Recent Scholarship on the *Book of Jubilees*," *CBR* 63 (2008): 407–408. See his argument that *Jubilees* 23 may reflect a "vague" response to the persecutions of Antiochus IV and a date for *Jubilees* in the 150s in *Jubilees 1–21*, 37–38 (and a general overview of theories of dating from 32–38).

29 Liora Ravid, "The *Book of Jubilees* and Its Calendar—A Reexamination," *DSD* 10 (2003): 371–394. See, recently, the comments on the calendar in *Jubilees*, its concept of revelation, and the authority of the text at Qumran in Sidnie White Crawford, *The Text of the Pentateuch* (Boston: De Gruyter, 2022), 241.

One way in which Hasmonean ideology is apparent occurs in the role of language in Babel and in the call of Abram. The rewritten character of Babel in the book of *Jubilees* straddles both clear engagement with the biblical text as well as at least one major divergence. Already at the beginning of the narrative of Babel, the phrasing from Genesis 11:1 is absent.[30] When the divine perspective is offered in *Jubilees* 10:22, the narrative highlights the oneness and unity of action, but this recasting of Genesis 11:1 and 11:6 omits phrasing that such oneness relates in any way to a lip, tongue, or language. Any such phrasing from Genesis 11:1 is altogether absent, and the Ethiopic carries over only the "one people" terminology from Genesis 11:6. The effect is that for *Jubilees*, multilingualism was already in existence, and the narrator does not understand the story to evoke in any fashion an etiology for multiple languages in the world.[31]

The strategy at play in the absence of this notice is not simply a facet of rewritten biblical interpretation, in which later authors attempt to rewrite or reposition elements of the Bible for the sake of clarity or dealing with contradictions.[32] *Jubilees* is not trying to take the notice of "one lip," understood as monolingualism, out of the narrative, since Genesis 10 in the Hebrew already has a notice (from P) of the spread of languages. There is a more fundamental attempt to relate the Tower of Babel to the following episode in the call of Abram, but for fundamentally political reasons.[33] This instance involves one of the two main ways that ancient interpreters dealt with putting these passages into conversation with one another, in this case writing language, understood to have been in some fashion part of the Tower of Babel, even if not as the advent of multilingualism, into the call of Abram.

If not as an origin myth of multilingualism, then, an explanation is required for how language functions in the Tower of Babel for *Jubilees*, and how this text makes such a function meaningful in the call of Abram. For *Jubilees*, Babel did not represent the loss of monolingualism in the face of multilingualism as divine judgment. Instead, the result of divine wrath on the

---

30   For a discussion, see Sherman, *Babel's Tower Translated*, 104–106.

31   Sherman, *Babel's Tower Translated*, 105.

32   The literature on rewritten Scripture is vast. See, most recently, Molly M. Zahn, *Genres of Rewriting in Second Temple Judaism: Scribal Composition and Transmission* (Cambridge: Cambridge University Press, 2020).

33   Schniedewind, *A Social History of Hebrew*, 170–171.

plain of Shinar entailed the loss of the language of creation, namely Hebrew.[34] The disappearance of this language from the world meant that creation itself was incomplete, as was any knowledge kept in books written in Hebrew. Yet the retelling of the Tower of Babel in *Jubilees* does not make this absence of Hebrew explicit as a consequence of God's judgment. The text instead offers an ambiguous assessment: there is no statement beginning the retelling of the episode to correspond to Genesis 11:1, but the result of God's disdain at the tower and city was, indeed, confusion of speech. God confused the languages of humankind at Babel, and from then all nations spread with their own languages. This notice does not mean that humans spoke only one language prior; rather, some have argued that the advent of multilingualism for *Jubilees* occurs earlier, after the expulsion from Eden.[35] It could be that *Jubilees* is claiming that after Babel, these distinct languages were no longer intelligible, or perhaps that simply the one language at Babel (though others existed) was split and confused.[36] In any case, excising the note about the spread of nations from Babel according to languages also resolves a tension in the biblical text: it much more clearly and concisely demonstrates how the notices in the Table of Nations in Genesis 10 were actually the consequence of Genesis 11. In this, *Jubilees* demonstrates that its concern in recasting the biblical narrative in light of Priestly law in Leviticus also shapes how it is sensitive to Priestly rhetoric elsewhere, and how such rhetoric relates to non-Priestly material.

The note that Hebrew was lost at Babel occurs later in the call of Abram. The presentation of Abram's youth in *Jubilees* is a complex web of interpretive backgrounds, some of which seem to draw from exegetical motifs from within Judaism and some of which seem also to be a function of wider cultural influence from both the Hellenistic and Babylonian streams of tradition.[37] In this recasting of Abram's youth, the text portrays him as coming to a conclusion that is the mirror image of what the Babelites attempt: human contrivances to reach or image the divine is idolatry. Like God destroying the tower and toppling it over, Abram smashes the idols of his homeland in Ur. He arrives at the exact opposite conclusion of the tower

---

34   Sherman, *Babel's Tower Translated*, 116–117.

35   Sherman, *Babel's Tower Translated*, 105.

36   J. T. A. G. M. van Ruiten, *Primeval History Interpreted: The Rewriting of Genesis 1–11 in the Book of Jubilees*, JSJSupp 66 (Boston: Brill, 2000), 348.

37   van Ruiten, *Abraham in the* Book of Jubilees: *The Rewriting of Genesis 11:26–25:10 in the* Book of Jubilees *11:14–23:8*, JSJSupp 161 (Boston: Brill, 2012).

and city builders, namely that all control of the world and events therein result from divine direction, not human initiative. As a result, God not only promises Abram land, descendants, and a great reputation, all backed with a privileged relationship to the deity, but God also reveals to Abram the Hebrew language. This revelation gives Abram access to his father's books, written in Hebrew but unintelligible to anyone since Hebrew was lost at Babel. Language became a part of Abram's call in an intricate and foundational framework that ties this pivotal moment explicitly with Babel, even if such a connection involves the detail of Hebrew as a lost language that is itself absent from the biblical text.

The loss and recovery of Hebrew indicates a deep fissure between humanity and divinity in *Jubilees*. Hebrew was the language of revelation itself, as indicated in Abram's father's books, sitting dormant with no one who could understand them, and thus who could understand what God was saying to humankind.[38] The loss of Hebrew was the hiatus of revelation.[39] In this fashion, language functions not simply as an independent feature or detail but rather as indicative of how divinity and humanity do or do not relate to one another. The Babelites were not granted access to the divine, certainly not on their own terms, and for their transgression, God shut off any revelation at all with the departure of Hebrew. Underlying the period between Hebrew as a lost and then a found language was a complete absence of revelation, a link forged again in the call of Abram. Subtle claims to authority in revelation can also be seen in this episode: any party with ties to Hebrew as a divinely appointed language could also claim a sort of divinely mandated establishment and claim particular insight into divine revelation, which, in the context of the second century BCE production of *Jubilees*, bolstered Hasmonean claims to rule in Jerusalem.[40]

Uncovering Hasmonean ideology, how it imputes its own politics into the retelling of the Tower of Babel, and how Babel and Abram relate, on the one hand, and, on the other, the interpretation of the biblical passage itself exposes

---

38   Sherman, *Babel's Tower Translated*, 117.

39   Sherman rightly labels it a "(momentary) eclipse of sacred tradition" (*Babel's Tower Translated*, 113).

40   See the insightful discussion in Sherman, and the bibliography of Rubin and David Goldblatt on the uses of Hebrew and aspects of ancient Jewish Nationalism, *Babel's Tower Translated*, 118–119.

a number of factors. The biblical story is no less political than the retelling in *Jubilees* (though functioning for different ends than the Hasmonean text), but taking language out of Babel in Genesis 11:1–9 makes it more evident how the problems of Babel are resolved in call of Abram. For *Jubilees*, the pivot of Babel as problem to Abram as solution offered a platform for the revitalization of the Hebrew language told as an episode of crisis when it was lost to a moment of a new beginnings with God when it was revealed again. Though the actual use of language in coinage and inscriptions in the Hasmonean period bears the marks of the extensively multilingual environment in which the Maccabees came to power, this rhetoric stamps the use of Hebrew and its revival in the Maccabean reign with all the divine approval that Abram's initial election called to mind.[41] The problem of foreign interference in Jerusalem and foreign language in Greek culture and dominance was met with Hasmonean ideology of using Hebrew symbolically to communicate new, nationalistic hopes.

This tactic clearly demonstrates how useful the connection of Babel to Abram's call was for Hasmonean ideology in the second century BCE.[42] It is not simply that God revealed Hebrew to Abram but that it was lost in a preceding, godless situation marked by human initiative to usurp divine privilege. The Maccabees would also take on elements of Greek and Roman culture over time and act in ways that countered traditional positions and beliefs in Jerusalem, combining offices of priest and king, which defied the biblical distinction between them (coming as they do from distinct tribes— Levites were connected to priesthood and Judahites were kings from the line of David).[43] But for the sake of casting off Greek rule, this appeal to Hebrew and biblical mythology in Babel and the call of Abram served a host of rhetorical ends for the Maccabean dynasty.

Even in antiquity, then, the Tower of Babel was a locus of interpretive energy for the sake of a current political situation. As another example,

---

41 For an overview of issues of Hebrew and the "trilingual" context of the Hasmoneans, see Dongbin Choi, *The Use and Function of Scripture in 1 Maccabees*, LSTS 98 (New York: T&T Clark, 2021), 44–45 n. 67.

42 Schniedewind, *A Social History of Hebrew*, 170–171.

43 See Numbers 18, in which the priests should be from the sons of Aaron, though according to Deuteronomy 18, any Levite could be a priest. In either scenario, the Priestly lineage is distinct (from Levi ultimately) than that of the kings. See 2 Samuel 7 for the divine promise to David, from the tribe of Judah, that one of his descendants will always be on the throne in Jerusalem.

Josephus labeled Nimrod as a tyrant in the sense of classical political theory as found in Plato.[44] Moreover, the same chronological issues examined above in the *L.A.B.* led Josephus, in his retelling of biblical stories, to place the Tower of Babel and events at Shinar prior to the spread of groups as described in his retelling of the Table of Nations, demonstrating how the issues of chronology and contemporaneous politics manifest in other ancient sources in the interpretation of Babel are on display in Josephus's writings.[45] Yet understanding Genesis 11:1–9 as a narrative about languages made its connection to Abram complicated. The Maccabean ideology of a revitalized Hebrew provided the historical means and backgrounds against which a literary connection could be forged between the stories, pivoting between political activity against the Israelite God (so Babel and the Seleucids) and in service to God (Abram and the Maccabees).

TARGUMIC TECHNIQUES, COMMUNAL IDENTITY AT QUMRAN, AND MAPPING THE CURE OF BABEL:
Abram and the Holy Language Recovered in the Eschaton

The other major interpretive strategy for relating Babel to Abram when Babel is understood to be a narrative about language is to delay the solution to Babel. In this mode, Abram's call answers some questions and solves some problems inherent in the events at Babel (such as human hubris and how divinity and humanity relate in the call of Abram), but it pushes the resolution of language and multilingualism into the future. Multilingualism is a feature of humanity

---

44 See Sherman and his engagements with Feldman's analysis in *Babel's Tower Translated*, 176–177.

45 For Josephus's retelling of the Babel episode, see Sherman, *Babel's Tower Translated*, 153–194. For an incisive study on how Josephus's own historical context and the events of the war in Judea influenced his retelling of Babel, see Sabrina Inowlocki, "Josephus' Rewriting of the Babel Narrative (Gen 11:1–9)," *JSJ* 37 (2006): 169–191. Louis Feldman argues that there is nonetheless a typically Greek framing of the events at Babel in terms of the rhetoric of hubris ("Josephus' Commentary on Genesis," *JQR* 72 [1981]: 129–130). For an analysis of the relationship between *L.A.B.*, Josephus, and rabbinic sources pertaining to the Tower of Babel, see Feldman, "Josephus' *Jewish Antiquities* and Pseudo-Philo's *Biblical Antiquities*," in *Josephus, the Bible, and History*, ed. Louis H. Feldman and Gohei Hata (Detroit: Wayne State University Press, 1989), 62–63. Note especially Feldman's comments on *L.A.B.* and the rabbis and how these sources connect Abram and Babel.

that originates in divine judgment at Babel, and therefore is something that will be solved as an eschatological reckoning. At least for one interpretation of a manuscript from the Dead Sea Scrolls, it may even have been the contemporaneous community's self-perception that this particular Jewish sect had a role to help solve it.

The targumim and the aforementioned text discovered at Qumran provide insights into this second mode of use of the Tower of Babel, in which language remains a facet of world history that both testifies to the divine judgment at Babel and provides hope for a renewed connection to God through the holy tongue of Hebrew. If both the targumim and Qumran texts display this hoped-for use of language to remedy the problem of Babel, they do so in distinct ways. For the targumim, the renewal of universal use of Hebrew in the eschaton remains on the horizon. With respect to the community at Qumran, some scholars have identified their use of Hebrew as a self-reflective marker to convey their unique relationship to God, placing the eschatological moment in their present, contemporaneous identity.

The targumic translations of the Hebrew Bible into Aramaic contain a variety of exegetical layers that not only render parts of the Hebrew but, to varying degrees, implicitly encode or explicitly state interpretative traditions in the biblical text itself.[46] The Targum Neofiti, which presents the Pentateuchal text in Aramaic translation, makes such interpretive decisions with respect to the Tower of Babel episode, clarifying the otherwise obscure language in the Masoretic Text of Genesis 11:1–9. Alongside Neofiti, other translations, such as Pseudo-Jonathan and Onkelos, also render the Tower of Babel story to include interpretive traditions about language and history. Each not only crafts Genesis 11:1–9 in a way to make the story explicitly about language but also renders Abram's call as a reversal of rebellion. Since language does not feature in Abram's call in these translations, the targumic traditions then project the resolution of the problem posed by multilingualism (as a sign of divine curse) into a future era, typically identified in prophetic discourse in Zephaniah 3:9. Each case, then, demonstrates the manner in which Abram functions as a partial solution to Babel, and the other part of the solution appears in a distinct era, a contrast to the reading proposed here for the

---

46   Some targumim, such as Onkelos, are more "literal," and others more expansive. See Paul Flesher and Bruce Chilton, *The Targums: A Critical Introduction* (Waco, TX: Baylor University Press, 2011), 9.

biblical text itself in which the entirety of the problems of Babel find their solution in Abram's call.

Targum Onkelos, which often adheres more closely to the biblical text than other targumim, translates the idioms in Genesis 11:1 in a manner that diverges from the grammar of the Hebrew Bible. Where Genesis 11:1 in the Hebrew has "one lip," the Targum Onkelos uses *lishan khad*, a more explicit reference to "tongue," as in language. Even further diverging from the Masoretic Text, the second phrase in the Hebrew, a notoriously ambiguous and difficult plural *devarim akhadim*, appears instead as an easier, more readily recognizable and understandable *memallel khad*, which can mean "one speech," "one tongue," or "one pronunciation." Any of these renderings clearly relates to the understanding of the story as a narrative about language, and one in which God confuses language specifically (retaining *lishan*, "tongue," in Genesis 11:6, 7, and 9). Despite the slight alteration of Genesis 11:1–9 in phrasing in order to make clearer that the narrative concerns language, Targum Onkelos otherwise adheres closely to the grammar and phrasing of the Masoretic Text in the call of Abram. The juxtaposition of Babel and Abram as subsequent narratives in accordance with the biblical sequence relates them as problem to solution, though, in contrast to other targumic traditions, the relationship is not explicit in Targum Onkelos. Yet the change in phrasing in Genesis 11:1 is still notable. Typically, the targumic traditions translate "lip" (*safah*) with *memallel*, and "tongue," *lashon*, with Aramaic *lishan*. Other examples include Ezekiel 3:6 and Isaaiah 28:11, where the Hebrew terms *safah* and *lashon* appear as the Aramaic *memallel* and *lishan* respectively.[47]

Other targumic translations similarly use this phrasing and expand on its interpretive possibilities. These translations, Targum Pseudo-Jonathan and Targum Neofiti, employ the same phrasing in Genesis 11:1 to frame the story as one not only of hubris against the divine but one in which humanity went from speaking the same language to speaking different languages. Whereas the Targum Onkelos does not specify which language the people spoke, Pseudo-Jonathan and Neofiti make explicit that the language prior to the confusion of tongues was the holy language, or language of the Temple, Hebrew (*bilshan bet qudshah*). If Hebrew functioned in such a meaningful

---

47   For more on the linguistic issues of ממלל, קלילן, and לשון in Aramaic in this passage, see Grossfeld, *Targum Neofiti I: An Exegetical Commentary to Genesis* (Brooklyn, NY: Sepher-Hermon Press, 2000), 123.

sense prior to Babel, and since these targumic traditions do not connect Abram's call to recapturing the holy tongue, then these Aramaic renderings leave the door open for a future restoration of the holy language as part of the reversal of Babel, signifying the ultimate reconciliation between divinity and humanity (whereas the curse of Babel signified a major breach). Such an application of language to a repaired relationship appeared in the targumic traditions to the prophetic text, particularly in Zephaniah 3:9. This verse in its Aramaic renderings contains phraseology strikingly reminiscent of the Targum Onkelos on Genesis 11:1.[48]

A particular detail in some of the targumim for Genesis 11:1 subtly, if also significantly, draws the Tower of Babel narrative into conversation with the call of Abram as oppositions. For example, Targum Pseudo-Jonathan employs an additional phrase to the twofold notice in Genesis 11:1 that the world had one language, and one that makes explicit the theme of unity of action and intent explored elsewhere as a central thrust to these idioms. In addition to one language and one speech, Pseudo-Jonathan appends these phrases with the notice that the world also had "one advice" (*'iṭā' khedā'*). Though some manuscripts of Neofiti add this notice, most do not, and the modern edition of Neofiti excludes this addition in the main line of transition of this targum. Yet Targum Neofiti includes a note in the call of Abram absent from Pseudo-Jonathan, namely in Genesis 12:3, that the nations will be blessed by Abram's "merit" (*zekhut*). The Fragmentary Targumim contain both: the builders of Babel have a singular counsel, and Abram's blessing to the nations would be according to his merit.

The role of Abram's merit in the targumic traditions, especially Neofiti, has been well documented and contains insight into interpretations that clarify a number of aspects of biblical exegesis, including elements in the Gospels.[49] Yet the triangulation of these notices about the counsel of Babel and merit of

---

48 As Sherman notes, there are no interpretive traditions in the targumim in Genesis 11:1–9 that are not also in Genesis Rabbah (*Babel's Tower Translated*, 291 n. 6). As a result, he excludes the targumic traditions from his book. For the purposes of the analysis above, the phrasing in the targumim both demonstrate how Genesis 11:1–9 was transformed into a passage about language and how these phrasings were employed later in the targum to the Minor Prophets as a way to imagine a future solution to the problem of multilingualism at Babel. In this fashion, the targumim make the problem and solution part of biblical rhetoric itself between a mythic tragedy of multilingualism that ruptured the relationship between divinity and humanity.

49 Craig E. Morrison, "The 'Hour of Distress' in *Targum Neofiti* and the 'Hour' in the Gospel of John," *CBQ* 67 (2005): 590–603.

Abram are important, as they set forth the contrast between the two episodes as problem (Babel) to solution (call of Abram). Traditions existed in Targum Neofiti and the Fragmentary Targums in which this "advice" is of the nations in Genesis 15:11 ("the kingdoms of the earth, when they conspired with advice"), which is contrasted with the "purity" of Abraham ("in the purity of Abram their father"). In Neofiti to Genesis 15:11, the contrast to Abram's merit is evil advice from the nations, a phrasing containing the related root to Pseudo-Jonathan's "advice" in Genesis 11:1. Naturally, the noun "advice," *'iṭā'* and related *'iṣā'* have a variety of valences, not all bad or nefarious. For example, Aḥīqar was called a "wise scribe and master of good counsel (*'iṭṭā' ṭābtā'*)."[50] Rather, it is the specific contrast in the Abram story and its use in the Tower of Babel that make the term more significant for the analysis here. Seen in this light, the advice in Genesis 11:1 and the merit or purity of Abram's call in Genesis 12:3 are explicitly laid in opposition to one another in God's revelation to Abram in Genesis 15:11. Taken together, the additional statement of the earth having "one counsel" in Genesis 11:1 in Pseudo-Jonathan sets this situation in direct opposition to the call of Abram, as problem to solution made clear in Neofiti to Genesis 15:11.[51]

If the call of Abram and the covenant ceremony in Genesis 15:11 provided one avenue to contrast the builders at Babel with the patriarch and his relationship to God, it also left the issue of language unresolved. As one could imagine, the issue of language was a major feature of the translation of Genesis 11:1–9 in the targumim. Pseudo-Jonathan and the Fragmentary Targum identify the language as the tongue spoken from the beginning, specified in Pseudo-Jonathan as the holy language and in Neofiti as the language spoken in the Temple.[52]

---

50   Note also Deuteronomy 32:28, in which evil doers and oppressors can ruin "good counsel" (עיטין טבן).

51   Interestingly, Nimrod in the Targum Pseudo-Jonathan, much like the Syriac interpretation in Ephrem and Ishodad, flees the cities of southern Mesopotamia such as Babel in Genesis 10:11. Targum Pseudo-Jonathan in this verse claims that Nimrod did so because he wanted no part in the counsel that was forming in the generation of division (עיטת דרא דפלוגתא). In this interpretive trajectory, the contrast exists between Abram and Nimrod, on the one hand, and the counsel of the generation of division, on the other.

52   See Smelik's argument that the eschatological dimensions of the phrasing לשׁון הקודשׁ are a secondary extension of the primary, and more limited, designation of the phrase as liturgical and pertaining to the Temple more properly (*Rabbis, Language*

The resulting activity of construction that the builders propose could not have been further from the language appropriate for God's Temple. According to these translations, the builders wanted to make an idol on top of the tower for worship, and with a sword in its hand no less. This mention of a sword emphasizes how improper such worship was envisioned to be. God had prohibited not only idols but also altars hewn by the sword (Exodus 20:23–25 in the Masoretic Text). This implement of war against the divine held in the hands of an idol, then, could have multiple aspects of violation of the human and divine realm: the idol with a sword not only signified something of a war against God, but in the context of worship, is also a direct violation of how altars should be constructed. Add to these factors the use of the holy language, specified as the language used in the Temple, and it becomes clear just how aggressively the Babelites acted against God.

This holy language would be fractured into seventy languages, one for each nation and one for each angel with God according to the targumic translations.

> Then the Memra of the LORD was revealed over the city, and with him were the seventy angels corresponding to the seventy nations. And each one, the language of his people and the mark of its writing were in his hand. And he scattered them from there over the face of all the earth into seventy languages, and each did not know what his neighbor was saying. And they were killing each other, so they stopped building the city.

This detail of the post-Babel situation makes explicit the reading strategy of Genesis 10 and 11 together. The Table of Nations was thought to have seventy to seventy-two nations listed, and by placing this notice in the targumic text to Genesis 11:8, it relates the overlapping chronology of the chapters in the final form of the biblical text. The angels created on the second day of the world according to the targum to Genesis 1:26 were presumably the heavenly hosts involved. Biblical warrant exists for this connection in Qumran manuscripts and the Septuagint to Deuteronomy 32:8 and 32:43.[53]

---

and *Translation in Late Antiquity* [New York: Cambridge University Press, 2013], 42–99, esp. 45–51).

53   See also Deuteronomy 4:19; Psalm 82; Daniel 10:12–13, and 20–21.

It should be noted that the targumim do envision a situation in which nation and language have one-to-one correspondence in the same sense that it will constitute a political sense of identity in the modern nation-state. The triangulation between nation, angel, and language represents the attempt to address a textual puzzle. As will become clear, the solution to the problem of multilingualism in the Aramaic translations appears in prophetic discourse in Zephaniah 3:9. The problem is severe, as the Targum Pseudo-Jonathan claims that the polyglot situation led to violence ("they were killing each other"), but the solution was not in the activities of the nation—as will be the case in the nation-state—but rather in an eschatological, future hope for reconciliation between God and human grounded in universal discourse in the holy language.

The Targum Jonathan to Zephaniah 3:9 identifies in the biblical text an oblique reference not to a pure language but specifically to a "chosen" one. This identification then could provide a future vision in which the reversal of Babel occurs with the unified condition, divinely approved this time, of all people speaking this elected language, presumably Hebrew.

Then I will restore to all the nations one pure/chosen speech.

The connection between "pure" in the Masoretic Text of Zephaniah 3:9 and "chosen" in Targum Jonathan occurs in a secondary meaning of the root *b-r-r* (the primary meaning is "pure"). In 1 Chronicles 7:40 and 16:41, the passive participle *berurim* means "chosen, selected."[54] In this sense, the Targum Jonathan may be connecting Zephaniah 3:9 to a return to a pre-Babel situation in which the "chosen language" returns as a part of the prophetic vision of an ideal future. Connecting Genesis 11:1–9 with Zephaniah 3:9 in interpretive tradition was perhaps also strengthened by the lexical overlaps

---

54 So Kevin J. Cathcart and Robert P. Gordon state regarding this phrasing in the targum:

> For the expression *mmll ch-d* see g. Onq. Gen 11:1, describing conditions before Babel. MT *brwrh* ("pure") is represented by another possible nuance of BH *brr* I ("choose"; cf. 1 Chr 7:40; 16:41); so also Syr, Vg, Aq, Theod. *Tg.*, by its paraphrasing of the MT, may be suggesting a return to the situation before Babel when "the whole earth had one language and few words" (Gen 11:1)."

See Cathcart and Gordon, *The Targum of the Minor Prophets*, The Aramaic Bible 14 (Wilmington, DE: Michael Glazier, 1989), 172 n. 23.

between the passages, involving seven words ("name," "all of them," "call," "lip," "people," "one," and "LORD").[55]

A fragmentary manuscript from Qumran makes the connection between the Tower of Babel, Zephaniah 3:9, and the holy language (or, language of the Temple), even if other aspects of the manuscript and its significance for broader Jewish beliefs at the time remain obscure.

> [. . .]confused
> [. . .]to Abraham
> [. . .]forever, for he
> [. . .]read the holy language (or, language of the Temple)
> [. . .]"for I will give] purified lip(s) to the peoples"

Other traditions connect these passages as well, such as the Midrash Tanhuma. But in the Qumran text, 4Q464, the initial editors not only spied the first mention of a *lashon haqodesh*, or "holy language," in Jewish texts but also an apocalyptic expectation due to the citation of Zephaniah 3:9 ("[for I will give] purified lip(s) to the peoples") and likely reference to the Tower of Babel (*niblat*, or "confused," evoking the biblical *b-l-l*) that this language carried an end-of-days status, and not merely a historical description of Hebrew as the language of the Temple but a reversal of the curse of Babel. The editors saw in this phrase something of vital importance for the linguistic identity of the community that produced this text, an importance that other scholars have explored in more theoretical terms. One scholar has argued that 4Q464 contains beliefs regarding Hebrew's status as a language preserved for the "end of days," and through writing in a dialect of Hebrew (Qumran Hebrew) this sect was signaling its relationship to God and ability to converse with the angelic realm.[56] For another scholar, the use of this dialect signaled that Hebrew for those at Qumran functioned as an "anti-language," a marker of communal identity against more dominant norms.[57]

---

55   Ho, *The Targum of Zephaniah*, 357.

56   So the passage in *Jubilees* is relevant here as another datum for this community, since Hebrew in *Jubilees* 11 preserves divine secrets revealed by angels. Steven Weitzman, "Why Did the Qumran Community Write in Hebrew?," *JAOS* 119 (1999): 35–45.

57   William H. Schniedewind, "Qumran Hebrew as an Antilanguage," *JBL* 118 (1999): 235–252; "Linguistic Ideology in Qumran Hebrew," in *Diggers at the Well: Proceedings of a Third International Symposium on the Hebrew of the Dead Sea Scrolls and*

Both theses have been subject to much debate recently, and it is beyond the scope of this chapter and book to address how, or whether, Hebrew functioned in specific ways amongst the sect responsible for much of the Dead Sea Scrolls.[58] For the purposes of the argument that the Tower of Babel and call of Abram act as problem to solution, and for the purposes of exploring how ancient interpreters explored this relationship in light of the reading of the Tower of Babel as it pertains to language, a number of features of this Qumran manuscript are notable. First, the manuscript is tantalizingly detailed enough to connect Abram, Babel, and Zephaniah 3:9 in a manner that appears also in the targumic material. Abram functions as some sort of counterpart to Babel, and Zephaniah 3:9 provides a vision of a time in which an elect/selected language or dialect, presumably of Hebrew, is a sign of such a reversal of Babel, whether as a future prediction or historical event embedded in the call of Abram itself. For the targumim, Abram's call does not resolve the issue of language, meaning that this feature of Babel awaits future fulfillment as described in Zephaniah 3:9 in the targumic rendering. Similarly, the Qumran community may have seen itself as a fulfillment of such expectations, at least in one interpretation: they are both elect like Abram and their use of Hebrew signals their role in the reversal of Babel.

At the same time, the manuscript is frustratingly fragmentary and incomplete. It could equally be the case that the triangulation of Babel, Abram, and the citation of Zephaniah 3:9 was a historical claim, much like *Jubilees*. The manuscript is simply too damaged to know one way or the other. Indeed, it has been suggested that the reference to Zephaniah 3:9 in 4Q464 should be brought into "the orbit of the episode at hand," namely the connection between Abram and Babel. In this manner, the citation of Zephaniah

---

Ben Sira, ed. Takamitsu Muraoka and John F. Elwolde, STDJ 36 (Leiden: Brill, 2000), 245–255.

58   Eibert Tigchelaar has argued against Schniedewind's notion of Hebrew at Qumran as an "anti-language" in "Sociolinguistics and the Misleading Use of the Concept of Anti-Language for Qumran Hebrew," in *The Dead Sea Scrolls and the Study of the Humanities: Method, Theory, Meaning: Proceedings of the Eighth Meeting of the International Organization for Qumran Studies (Munich 4–7 August, 2013)*, ed. Pieter B. Hartog, Alison Schofield, and Samuel I. Thomas, STDJ 125 (Boston: Brill, 2018), 195–206. Popović argues against Weitzman's theory in "Multilingualism, Multiscripturalism, and Knowledge Transfer in the Dead Sea Scrolls and Greaco-Roman Judea," in *Sharing and Hiding Religious Knowledge in Early Judaism, Christianity, and Islam*, Judaism, Christianity, and Islam—Tension, Transmission, Transformation 10 (Boston: De Gruyter, 2018), 49–50.

functions like a *pesher*, or commentary, to the relationship between Babel, Abram, and Hebrew as the holy language. Given connections elsewhere in 4Q464 to *Jubilees*, according to one theory, we should see this Qumran fragment differently than the initial editors proposed.[59]

Notable for this discussion is the manner in which these traditions use Abram in juxtaposition to Babel, as a solution to a problem. If Targum Jonathan and 4Q464 do point to future eschatological visions of solving the problem of Babel, Abram's call is a partial solution, since it does not overtly involve language. That aspect of Babel awaits a future fulfillment, perhaps even in the contemporaneous community that employs the holy language. If the manuscript describes a historical connection in Abram's life, the components of 4Q464 are still relevant, but are aligned with the strategy evident in *Jubilees*, in which Abram's call involved the renewed use of Hebrew, but as a historical and not eschatological detail (buttressed by Zephaniah 3:9 as a prooftext). Even if 4Q464 reflected engagement with the same ideas as in *Jubilees*, and thus the connection between Babel, Abram, and Zephaniah 3:9 functioned as a reference to Hebrew at the call of Abram, it would still be a relevant triangulation for contemporaneous communal identity. This conclusion would simply align 4Q464 with the reading of *Jubilees* offered above.

---

59 So Poirier argues

> It may be said that 4Q464 falls within the "rewritten Bible" genre. Considering that the text appears to rewrite portions of *Jubilees*, however, it would be more accurate to describe it as "rewritten *rewritten* Bible." The text appears to use biblical prooftexts to explain or justify *Jubilees*'s expansions of Genesis. The quotation from Zeph 3 functions in this way: the reference to "turning to the people a pure language" is merely a justifying prooftext for an otherwise unscriptural episode in *Jubilees*'s account of Abraham's life. In keeping with the way in which prooftexts typically function, the operative echoes really have little to do with either the authorial or the popular meaning of Zephaniah: the eschatological perspective of Zeph 3:9 is not at all operative. Rather, it is the case of a religiously Hebrew-speaking community finding a scriptural node for the story, appearing in *Jubilees*, of the divine redispensation of Hebrew to Abraham.

John C. Poirier, "'4Q464': Not Eschatological," *Revue de Qumrân* 20 (2002): 586–587; Eshel and Stone, "An Exposition on the Patriarchs (4Q464) and Two Other Documents (4Q464ᵃ and 4Q464ᵇ)," *Le Muséon* 105 (1992): 243–264; "The Holy Tongue in the Last Days in the Light of a Fragment from Qumran," *Tarbiz* 62 (1992–1993): 169–177 (Hebrew); "4QExposition of the Patriarchs," in *Qumran Cave 4, vol. XIV: Parabiblical Texts, Part 2*, ed. Magen Broshi, et al., DJD 19 (Oxford: Clarendon Press, 1995), 215–230.

THE GENESIS RABBA, THE "GENERATION OF
SEPARATION," AND THE CALL OF ABRAM

The exegetical traditions in the ancient rabbinic commentary Genesis Rabba and their significance for unpacking how Babel was viewed in antiquity have already been discussed in extensive detail in other studies. One passage in particular, however, is revealing with respect to the issue of how Babel and Abram were thought to relate to one another.[60] Much like *Biblical Antiquities*, one finds a passage in which Abram is present, or at least directly addressed, on the plains of Shinar. In Genesis Rabba 38.6.2, Rabbi Eleazar and Yohanan debate the meaning of the term *devarim akhadim* in Genesis 11:1, offering a number of solutions including "of the same possessions" and other such renderings. One suggestion provides a particularly interesting way in which Babel and Abram are related as problem to solution:

> Another interpretation: those who spoke sharp words (*devarim khadim*) against (Deuteronomy 6:4) the LORD our God who is unique/one, and against (Ezekiel 33:24) Abraham who was unique/one in the land. They said: "This Abraham is a barren mule and cannot produce offspring." Against the LORD our God they said "He has no right to choose the celestial spheres for himself and assign us to the terrestrial realm! But come, let us build a tower for ourselves, and let us build an idol on its top, and we will put a sword in its hand, and it will appear to wage war against Him!

In this passage, the rabbis connect *akhad* with *khad*. Both mean "one," the former in Hebrew and the latter in Aramaic. Moreover, *khad* can also mean "sharp," in the sense of a "sharp word" or insult. Further, the Babelites insult "unique" characters in the process, namely God and Abram, providing another play on *akhad*, "*one*," as "unique." This lexeme is attached to God most famously in Deuteronomy 6:4 and to Abraham as unique in Ezekiel

---

60   Such a bringing together of Abram and Babel was not always the case in "main-line" rabbinic thought. As Lipton argues, much of rabbinic thought attempts to keep Abram "far away from Babel's building site." She claims that the complex manner in which the creation of nations, nationalism, and the evils that such a state evokes necessitated, for the most part, keeping Abram away from the site of Babel. See Lipton, "The Reluctant Brick Maker," 1077.

33:24. In other words, such a connection, and the multiple plays on *akhad*, could be seen to have textual warrant from the Bible itself.

The basis of the insults both play on the call of Abram, even though one is directed to Abram himself and the other, as is consistent with the theme in the Primeval History, against the divine. Specifically, the derogatory comments toward Abram target his inability to have children. To mock him, the Babelites will create their own name for themselves, all of which creates a contrast that will be reversed. Though initially impotent, God will ultimately give Abram a great name and many descendants while God will foil the activities and construction of the builders of the Tower of Babel.

Noteworthy is the manner in which the rabbis argue that Abram is directly insulted, as though the Babelites know the patriarch. This direct insult calls to mind the strategy of *Biblical Antiquities*: since the chronology of Genesis 10 to Genesis 12 is so complicated, one might argue that Abram himself was present at Babel. Such a strategy has the advantage of directly juxtaposing Babel as problem to Abram as solution, a direct juxtaposition that has textual, chronological license. Notably, however, this way of approaching the two stories makes the idiom of Genesis 11:1 decidedly nonlinguistic in nature. The interpretation involves insulting words directed at God and the divinely chosen. In configuring how Abram and Babel are related, this particular textual connection in Genesis Rabba takes language in the sense of distinct linguistic dialects out of the scenario. Naturally, this is not to argue that the rabbis did not see the world as unilingual, only to become multilingual in the event of Babel. They clearly did, as evidenced in a number of occasions in the Genesis Rabba.

While many other passages from the Genesis Rabba could be, and have been, analyzed for their underlying ideologies of language and how they viewed the problem of Babel, this particular interpretation puts the events in Genesis 11:1–9 in direct relation to the life of Abram. In this example, there is an attempt to relate Abram as a solution to the problem directly, and language does not feature at all as part of that particular interpretation. Instead, the rabbis pick up on themes already noted in the source-critical examination: the Babelites mock the divine-human boundary, and they mock God's elected individual whom God chose as his means for relating to humanity. Moreover, they insulted Abram in such a way, according to this rabbinic interpretation, that calls to mind how they functioned as mirror opposites to the call of the patriarch himself.

THE QUR'AN AND ISLAMIC EXEGESIS:
On the Relationship between Egyptian Pyramids and a Mesopotamian Tower

That Babel represented an opposition to the divine and other holy characters would have significance for Islamic traditions as well, written in the centuries following the compilation of the Genesis Rabba around 500 CE or so. The two main references to the Tower of Babel in the Qur'an appear in the following *sūrah*s, or chapters:[61]

> Q Al-Qasas 28:38: Pharaoh said, "O [members of the] elite! I do not know of any god that you may have besides me. Hāmān, light for me a fire over clay, and build me a tower so that I may take a look at Moses's God, and indeed I consider him to be a liar!"

> Q Ghafir 40:36–37: Pharaoh said, "O Hāmān! Build me a tower so that I may reach the routes—the routes of the heavens—and take a look at the God of Moses, and indeed I consider him a liar." The evil of his conduct was thus presented as decorous to Pharaoh, and he was kept from the way [of God]. Pharaoh's stratagems only led him into ruin.

The nature of the Qur'an as a document differs greatly from the more narrative-driven framework of the Hebrew Bible. Yet the Qur'an often appeals to the biblical stories, though in a way that allows for changes to occur in order to adhere to a prophetology in the Qur'an that resolves in Muhammad.[62] As such, the nature of the problem of Babel and its solution does not entail

---

61 For a translation of these passages (as used above) and a brief selection of Islamic commentary on them, see Brannon Wheeler, *Prophets in the Quran: An Introduction to the Quran and Muslim Exegesis* (New York: Continuum, 2002), 188–190.

62 For the prophetology in the Qur'an, see Sidney Griffith, *The Bible in Arabic: The Scriptures of the "People of the Book" in the Language of Islam*, Jews, Christians, and Muslim from the Ancient to the Modern World (Princeton, NJ: Princeton University Press, 2013). Note the similar way in which the Hebrew Bible functions in the New Testament relative to Jesus. For other studies on the relationship between the Bible and the Qur'an, see Gabriel Said Reynolds, *The Qurʾān and Its Biblical Subtext*, Routledge Studies in the Qurʾan 10 (New York: Routledge, 2010); Emran El-Badawi, *The Qurʾān and the Aramaic Gospel Traditions*, Routledge Studies in the Qurʾan (New York: Routledge, 2014); Gabriel Said Reynolds, *The Qurʾān and the Bible: Text and Commentary* (New Haven, CT: Yale University Press, 2018).

the same narrative pivot between the tower and the call of Abram as in the Hebrew Bible.

In fact, the story of the Tower of Babel is quite different in the Qur'an and is located in Egypt. Though Islamic interpretation included stories about Nimrod constructing a tower in Babil, and condemnation that resulted in the spread of languages (the original being Syriac in some traditions), the only appearance of a story with clear reference to the biblical Babel (with a structure reaching heaven as an affront to God) in the Qur'an itself appears in *sūrah* 28:38 and 40:36–37. A constellation of different stories and characters from the Bible appears in seemingly random configuration. A closer examination, however, reveals that this grouping of biblical references has pre-Islamic basis in interpretive history (many of which have been noted previously, though another datum will be added). Such a shift also influences how Islamic interpreters understand the relation between Babel and Abram, or Ibrahim in Arabic.[63]

The setting for the tower narrative, in Egypt, involves Pharaoh confronting Musa (Arabic for Moses) over the nature of God. Whereas Musa had a revelation from God, Pharaoh desires to build a structure high enough to see God for himself, evoking the motivations of overreach into the divine realm from the biblical passage. In *sūrah* 28, Musa has confronted Pharaoh with "clear signs" from Allah, an act established with divine blessing founded on God's revelation of himself to Musa.[64] In response, Pharaoh sets a plan to see God for himself, constructing a pyramid that could reach into the heavenly realm, thereby offering Pharaoh a platform and means for breaching into the heavens, whether God was ready or not.

The resonances with the biblical story of the Tower of Babel are clear, although the characters are different. It is not difficult to understand how the characters could have been switched over time. Pharaoh is an archetypal, evil

---

63   Note al-Ṭabarī, who states that the languages spread from the events at Babel as an almost traumatic, fear-like response to God's destruction of the tower (William M. Brinner, *The History of al-Ṭabarī: An Annotated Translation, Volume II: Prophets and Patriarchs* [Albany: State University of New York Press, 1987], 108). Other traditions include the note that Noah's descendants were already speaking eighty distinct languages when they came off of the ark (Marianna Klar, *Interpreting al-Tha ʿlabī's Tales of the Prophets: Temptation, Responsibility and Loss* [New York: Routledge, 2009], 180).

64   The connection here with Muhammad and divine approval is evident, as the only sign of Muhammad's station as a prophet from Allah was the Qur'an in "clear" Arabic. A series of clear signs were offered in salvation history in Islamic thought.

gentile ruler who attempted to oppress God's people, a dire situation that led to God revealing himself to Moses at the burning bush at Sinai.[65] Musa, like the biblical Moses, was a figure whom God approached to inaugurate a new phase of divine relation to the human realm. The resemblances to Nimrod, also an archetypal evil ruler, and Abraham, also called by God (at least in later biblical interpretation) in the wake of oppressive acts of Nimrod, in biblical legends are manifest.[66]

Other features of the stories connect them in both general and, at least in one example, concrete ways. First, there is a common setting of a figure chosen by God who has to navigate a foreign king in a foreign land. Tales from Egypt and Mesopotamia have been linked on a variety of grounds in this manner, as in the story of Joseph and Tobit.[67] They bring to the fore how someone who has a relationship to God endures in hardship. Indeed, concrete details of the Exodus in the Bible and the Tower of Babel connected the narratives as ones of oppressive work out of which God revealed himself to Moses and Abram. The apocalypse Third Baruch identifies in the work of the Tower the same oppression that featured in the construction of Pharaoh's pyramids.[68] Just as the Exodus narrative also highlighted the role of pregnant Hebrew women in the face of Pharaoh's oppression, so the author of Third Baruch includes the detail that the oppression of constructing the Tower of Babel entailed forcing pregnant women to continue work (one of whom gave birth and carried the child in her apron, all while continuing to build the tower). Though the biblical text does not ascribe such oppression to the building of the Tower, one can see how the connection between passages appeared founded on this theme of forced labor. In only Genesis 11:3 and Exodus 1:14 are the materials for construction of an edifice detailed as *khomer* ("mortar") and *levenah* ("bricks"). Given the oppression of the building of the pyramid, given the

---

65 Note, however, that it is J in which this revelation occurs from the sky in a parallel manner to God's call of Abram in Genesis 12:1–3. Note also that the burning bush (סנה) in Hebrew may have originally referred to סיני, Sinai the mountain itself.

66 See Bakhos, "A Migrating Motif: Abraham and his Adversaries in *Jubilees* and al-Kisā ī," *Mizan: Journal for the Study of Muslim Societies and Civilizations* 2 (2017): 1–17; Yishai Kiel, "Abraham and Nimrod in the Shadow of Zarathustra," *JR* 95 (2015): 35–50.

67 See Joseph, Tobit, Esther, and the theme of Jews in foreign courts in relation to Haman's role in the Qur'an in Adam J. Silverstein, *Veiling Esther, Unveiling Her Story: The Reception of a Biblical Book in Islamic Lands* (New York: Oxford University Press, 2018), 31.

68 See the discussion in Sherman, *Babel's Tower Translated*, 195–215.

divine displeasure involved in both, and given how God approaches a new figure for a new relationship in the wake of each (Abram and Moses), then it makes sense to see in Genesis 11:1–9 aspects of forced labor and oppression as well.

These comments are by way of showing that pre-Islamic interpretive traditions existed that drew elements of Babel and the Exodus to one another. It is not entirely surprising, then, that the Qur'an would place the construction of a building for the purposes of encroaching on the divine realm in Egypt with Pharaoh. What might be more surprising is the appearance of Haman, the evil henchman of the book of Esther, functioning in *sūrah* 28 and 40 as a sort of right-hand-man to Pharaoh. The character in the Bible served in the court of the Persian king Ahasuerus in the fifth century BCE, but has been dislocated in both space and time to Egypt during Musa's life centuries prior. Good arguments exist for understanding the Haman of the Bible and of the Qur'an as not only the same character but both as, in a sense, a common literary *topos* of ancient Near Eastern literature.[69] In other words, the issue is not how Haman got from the biblical story of Esther set in Persia to Egypt in the Qur'an set during the life of Musa. Rather, the question is how Haman-like characters function across ancient Near Eastern texts. In this sense, Haman is like Nādān in the story of *Aḥīqar*. Aḥīqar, according to the story set even earlier in seventh-century BCE Assyria, had the wisdom to construct a tower that could reach to the heavens. Nādān attempts to frame Aḥīqar for the charge of treason against the Assyrian king Esarhaddon, though while in prison, Aḥīqar persuades the executioner not to kill him. Nādān, in later traditions of the story preserved in Syriac, announces to Pharaoh that Aḥīqar is dead. Pharaoh uncovers the plot by writing to the Assyrian king that the Egyptian ruler would like to build a tower for Esarhaddon, one that would extend to the heavens. Knowing that only Aḥīqar could perform such a feat, Nādān's plot is revealed when Aḥīqar completes the structure.

Many aspects of this literary comparison merit further comment, but the correlation demonstrates how both the biblical texts and qur'anic material participate in the same, larger context of telling such narratives. Haman in this sense is an evil henchman, who appears six times in the Qur'an performing a similar function, heralding evil acts against the divine. In parallel manner, giants in the Hebrew Bible often appear as harbingers of disaster, and a

---

69   For the following arguments, see Silverstein, "Hāmān's Transition from Jāhiliyya to Islām," *Jerusalem Studies in Arabic and Islam* 34 (2008): 285–308.

number of interpretive traditions likewise transport or conflate archetypal evil characters, such as Nimrod, Sennacherib, Nebuchadnezzar, and Titus.[70] Notably, however, the qur'anic rendering of a tower to defy the heavens lacks any mention of language or the advent of multilingualism at all. Thus any feature of God's plan to address this hubris similarly does not entail details of a linguistic nature. Instead, in the Qu'ran human culture diversifies, including language, after humans overpopulate in a single area and need to spread out when disputes begin to arise (*sūrah* 10:19). From this natural process, languages also diversify, though the nations that result from this are said to be a product of divine plan (*sūrah* 49:13).

Though seemingly different stories, the qur'anic use of the Tower of Babel, despite being set in Egypt with Haman, Pharaoh, and Musa as principal characters and without any mention of multilingualism, shares the same principles as the biblical episode. Indeed, later Islamic interpreters such as al-Ṭabarī, a famous scholar in the ninth and tenth centuries CE of qur'anic exegesis—or *tafsīr*—who was also well versed in biblical literature, would retell the confrontation between Ibrahim and Nimrod, like Musa and Pharaoh, in ways that more closely resembled the biblical story of Babel. In a series of plotting against God, which included a failed attempt to tie four eagles to a chest in which Nimrod sat to try to fly into the heavens, Nimrod built a tower in order to gaze at God. God upends the structure by the foundations, sending pieces of the tower crumbling to the ground, though other interpretive traditions specify that it was Gabriel's wings that actually struck the tower. Al-Ṭabarī then adds a detail that does not feature in the Qur'an: the punishment on Nimrod's activity resulted in the dispersion of people over the earth, including the division of the original language into seventy-three tongues. Notably, al-Ṭabarī identifies the original language of creation with Syriac, not Arabic, a tradition well ensconced in a variety of Near Eastern traditions and one that shows up in Islamic hadith.[71] Yet al-Ṭabarī also clarifies how Ibrahim ends up speaking Hebrew, a development explained on the basis of the verb "to cross over" (*'avar* in Hebrew/*'abara* in Arabic) and Abraham's crossing of the Euphrates to escape Nimrod. This physical movement over the Euphrates mirrored an accompanying linguistic development resulting

---

70 See the arguments and bibliography in Boyd, "Sennacherib's Successor: Titus and Anti-Roman Rhetoric in TgJon to Isa. 10:32," *AS* 17 (2019): 67–86.

71 For this story, see M. J. Kister, *Concepts and Ideas at the Dawn of Islam* (New York: Routledge, 2016), 119, 140.

in Hebrew. The denouement of linguistic evolution is that Nimrod, seeking to find and kill Ibrahim, is not able to identify him. His henchmen come upon Ibrahim, but do not recognize him, since he no longer spoke Syriac but instead spoke Hebrew.

Other traditions, such as preserved in Thaʿlabī, recognize that Ibrahim spoke Hebrew (and label him as "a Hebrew"), though identify Ishmael as "an Arab" who spoke Arabic. Yet Thaʿlabī, in an almost reversal of Babel-esque confusion, claims that:

> It is said that when Abraham began to build the House, Ishmael would hand him the stones. While Abraham was a Hebrew, Ishmael was an Arab, but God instilled in each of them the language of the other. Abraham would say: "Give me a *kayn*," meaning: "Give me a stone," and Ishmael would say: "Here, take it." The two of them built the Kabah from five mountains: Mount Sinai, the Mount of Olives, Mount Lebanon, and al-Judr, while its foundations were built of Mount Hira. When at last only one stone was needed, Ishmael went to look for it. When he came back, he saw that Abraham had already set the stone in its place. "Father," he said: "who brought you this stone?" He said to him: "Someone brought it to me who did not want me to depend on you." Then Abraham said to Ishmael: "Bring me a beautiful stone which I may place in the corner so that it will be a sign to Mankind." But Mount Abu Qubays called out to him: "Abraham, I have something for you that has been entrusted to me for safekeeping; here it is, take it." So Abraham took the Black Stone from Mount Abu Qubays and set it in its place.[72]

This tradition is worth quoting in entirety because of (1) the role of multi-lingualism that (2) is overcome in a pivotal moment of construction that (3) attests to the construction of the Kabah in a divinely sanctioned plan, all of which makes this story an almost Babel in reverse. If the proposal that Jacob at Bethel in Genesis 28 was an Israelite response to Babel was unconvincing, a better case can be made for this Islamic tradition, whether its function as a reverse Babel is overt and intentional or whether it is simply a facet of subli-mated tradition. In the latter case, resonances of Babel in reverse are simply a feature of genre, not intentional literary echoes. Nonetheless, the fact that

---

72   Thaʿlabī, ʿArāʿis Al-majālis Fī Qiṣaṣ Al-anbiyā, Or, Lives of the Prophets, trans. William M. Brinner, Studies in Arabic Literature 24 (Boston: Brill, 2002), 149.

language difference is overcome to construct the most holy spot in Islamic thought where the divine and human meet is notable for its evocation of themes of the Tower of Babel story, though set in reverse.

The point here for the discussion of the Tower of Babel in interpretive history is that Islamic traditions also demonstrate how tower narratives relate to an Abram-like figure as a sort of problem-to-solution literary pivot. In the Qur'an, language does not feature at all in the tower story, but the called figure (Musa) represents the true line of prophetology and connection to the divine against the hubris of Pharaoh. In some Islamic traditions, as in al-Ṭabarī, Nimrod and the tower at Babil look closer to traditions engaging directly with the Bible, and language reappears as a feature, not unlike *Jubilees*. For both, Hebrew becomes a language with historical importance in the figure of Abram. The hubris of Babil is a problem, which requires a solution in the lives of the prophets, and to the degree that language functions as a detail in the retelling of the tower, it is reconnected to the life of Abram in a manner that demonstrates how Abram functions as a contrast to Nimrod.

BRINGING BIBLICAL CRITICISM AND RECEPTION HISTORY INTO CONVERSATION:
How an Interpretation of Genesis 11:1–9 without Language Makes Sense of Ancient Exegesis

Some of the ways in which Genesis 11:1–9 has been understood as a problem to be overcome have been presented in the foregoing. Eco refers to the intellectual and political perspective of this passage as multilingualism representing, in some fashion, a "wound" that needs to be healed. A more robust account of the cultural, social, and political implications of this reading of the Tower of Babel remains to be addressed, particularly in the context of the modern nation-state. If multilingualism was an abiding problem of humanity, and if the call of Abram did not solve it, then it still needs to be solved. If, however, there is nothing left to resolve from Babel after the call and life of Abram in a new reading of the passage, then there is no role for the nation or nation-state to leverage Babel as a metaphor or story for political action.

For the purposes of investigating ancient biblical interpretation and traditions, a closer look at how the Hebrew Bible frames the Tower of Babel as a problem underscores the need for later readers to apply solutions to the issues reflected in Genesis 11:1–9. The problems in the Tower of Babel also function as symptoms that have plagued humanity since creation, an observation built upon the source-critical presentation of the Primeval History. The point in this presentation is not only to demonstrate a connection between Genesis 11:1–9 and Genesis 12:1–3 (both belonging to J) but to show how Abraham functions as a solution to the problem posed by Babel in its entirety.

The survey of selected ancient sources functions as a prelude, highlighting the pivotal relationship between Babel and Abram, in order to explore more fully Abram as the solution to Babel in the reception history of Genesis 11:1–9. More specifically, two interpretive trajectories were traced in relating Babel, understood both as an act of hubris/rebellion and as an etiology for the spread of multilingualism, to Abram: (1) either the call of Abram in Genesis 12 reverses the curse of Babel in terms of the divine/human relationship but the solution to multilingualism is projected far into the eschatological future (to which, in some sense, Abram's call is connected as a foretaste or starting point perhaps); or (2) the call of Abraham serves as a solution to both the problem of human rebellion and the advent of multilingualism. These aspects of reception history were examined in order to display how a reading of Genesis 11:1–9 in which language is not a part of the narrative creates a more coherent sense of the relationship between Babel as a problem and Abraham as a solution.

One more general aspect of reception history of these texts could be offered by way of bridging the divide between these disciplines. The stories of Abram's youth, smashing idols and confronting his father and Nimrod, abound in interpretive traditions, and speak to an underlying question about what Abram was doing to deserve a call from God. Nothing about his youth is told at all in the Bible, and the voice that commands him to leave his family makes all the more pronounced the silence about his youth. In light of the argument of this book about the Tower of Babel, this gap in Abram's biography that has haunted interpreters for centuries is real and intentional. When seen as connected passages uniting a problem in the Tower of Babel to solution in the life of Abram, the thesis argued that Genesis 11:1–9, and especially the idioms in 11:1 and 11:6, are entirely about hubris and the assumption that human leaders can control affairs and political alliances takes on new importance. J presents these alliances as a constant problem in the Primeval History. Genesis 12:1–3 is the ultimate solution: an election without any warning, preconditions, or actions on the part of humanity. Such a gap bothered ancient interpreters, but can be understood to be an intentional feature of the biblical text. The divinely arbitrary decision, top-down, to begin a relationship with Abram provides an apt literary contrast to the events in Genesis 11:1–9.

The objective is not to pit ancient biblical interpretation against historical critical scholarship, one reigning supreme over the other. Ancient interpreters worked with a redacted Pentateuch and did not have the cultural context to conceive of it in any other way. Nor did they have access to comparative materials from the ancient Near East. Instead, highlighting how interpreters in the reception history of Genesis 11:1–9 flagged aspects of this narrative that found their resolution in the call of Abram or were projected beyond Abram provides avenues for identifying in these ancient interpretations the same elements that need to be accounted for in a new understanding of the Tower of Babel. Ancient exegetes were aware of the intricate connection between these two passages. Even if the meaning of the Tower of Babel without language diverges from their understanding of the passage, the interpretation that the story is not about language benefits greatly from the many ways in which premodern commentators on the passage observed the relationship between Genesis 11:1–9 and 12:1–3. As they argued, Abram's call serves as the antidote to the problem of Babel, though understanding Genesis 11:1–9 without language necessarily reworks how Abram's call functions both in relation to Babel and also on its own terms. Indeed, this reconfigured relationship between Babel and Genesis 12:1–3 not only creates a coherent interpretation between these passages when Babel is no longer understood as an etiology of the spread of languages but also brings to the fore key features of the call of Abram that would occupy significant intellectual energy in the writings of thinkers in Judaism, Christianity, and Islam. The fact that a number of interpretive traditions over time, including Islamic traditions, struggled to relate how Abram as a solution to Babel could address, or not, the abiding issue of multilingualism highlights how this very feature of the biblical text needs to be explored more. In this manner, the history, philology, and source-critical approaches to Genesis 11:1–9, in some fashion, have been brought to bear on aspects of the reception history of this text and how it relates to the call of Abram.

Indeed, the same characteristics that pre-modern exegetes identified as essential features connecting Babel and Abram can find a cogent explanation when Babel is not understood as an etiology for the spread of languages. Abram, in this fashion, does not need to be cast as the speaker of Hebrew as the long-lost language to reverse Babel. Similarly, pertaining to the second group of ancient interpretations in which Abram does not heal the wound of multilingualism, Abram does not reverse only part of the curse of Babel thereby necessitating an alternate mode of overcoming the problem of multilingualism projected into the eschatological future. Rather, in the interpretation offered here, in which the Tower of Babel is not a story about language, all the problems that Babel presents find their resolution in the call of Abram. The examples above display the manner in which reception history aids an exploration of the connection between Genesis 11:1–9 and Genesis 12:1–3 as problem and solution respectively.

CHAPTER 6

Babel in America

"If only God would again inspire your Highness, the idea which had the goodness to determine that I be granted 1200 ecus would become the idea of a perpetual revenue, and then I would be as happy as Raymond Lull, and perhaps with more reason . . . For my invention uses reason in its entirety and is, in addition, a judge of controversies, an interpreter of notions, a balance of probabilities, a compass which will guide us over the ocean of experiences, an inventory of things, a table of thoughts, a microscope for scrutinizing present things, a telescope for predicting distant things, a general calculus, an innocent magic, a non-chimerical cabal, a script which all will read in their own language; and even a language which one will be able to learn in a few weeks, and which will soon be accepted amidst the world. And which will lead the way for the true religion everywhere it goes."[1]

---

1 Gottfried Wilhelm Leibniz, Letter to the Duke of Hanover, 1679. For more on the nature of the symbolic language "in which all truth of reason would be reduced to a kind of calculus" and which would be "very easy to learn without any dictionaries," see his letter to Nicolas Remond, January 10, 1714 (*Philosophical Papers and Letters: A Selection Translated and Edited, with an Introduction by Leroy E. Loemker, Volume II* [Chicago: University of Chicago Press, 1956], 1063).

REIMAGINING BABEL IN MODERNITY:
A Look Back and a Return to the Sixteenth and Seventeenth Centuries (and Beyond)

As is clear by now, the story of the Tower of Babel in Genesis 11:1–9 was not an etiology or mythological explanation of multilingualism, at least in its earliest phases. Though, as elsewhere in J, an etiology occurs in the narrative (in this case, for the name of Babylon, *b-b-l*, because God confuses, *b-l-l*, the otherwise unified plans of humans), the origin story does not pertain to languages. Instead, the idioms usually translated as being about the spread and diversification of languages are actually political phrases that have particular importance in the light of Neo-Assyrian imperial ideology. The ambition of this empire changed the landscape of the ancient Near East. Yet this change did not occur in a vacuum. The Neo-Assyrians leveraged the political currency of their forebears, the Middle Assyrian empire (as well as other, even older, imperial centers). They borrowed terminology from their predecessors, simultaneously hearkening back to the glory of former kingdoms and innovating on their rhetoric to communicate distinctively Neo-Assyrian propaganda. Additionally, their unprecedented expansion created new historical situations that required new ways to perpetuate, communicate, and perform royal ideology. Assyrian scribes helped to sponsor and manufacture this rhetoric. They crafted the means to communicate both to Assyrians and especially to subjugated and governed populations within the reach of the power of the Neo-Assyrian king, the benefits of obeying the terms of Assyrian oversight and governance, and, perhaps most importantly, the inevitable doom awaiting rebellious factions.

This historical context, beginning especially in 744 BCE with the ascent of Tiglath-Pileser III to the throne, provides much of the background for the composition of Genesis 11:1–9. The intent in sketching this historical background is not to identify the specific Neo-Assyrian king in whose reign the story was composed and who may or may not have inspired its creation. The events in the reign of Sargon II and how they were understood in late eighth- and early seventh-century Assyrian and Babylonian scribal texts, however, are particularly tempting as historical canvases against which themes in the Tower of Babel story appear in strong relief. Scribes at this time had a variety of mechanisms for creating counter-texts and talking back to the royal center. Perhaps most significantly for a reinterpretation of the Tower of

Babel, Neo-Assyrian rhetoric of imperial consolidation might be reflected in the biblical text, particularly the contrast between good governance, in which the king imposes "one mouth," and treason, in which other, non-Assyrian political entities impose "one mouth" on each other.

Yet to reinterpret a story is to re-examine its constituent parts. An analysis of Genesis 11:1–9 was offered, seeking to incorporate theoretical and philological observations. Crucial to the argument was a narratological observation, namely that the narrator and the divine agent have the same perspective on the problem at hand, but use slightly different phrasing. An exploration of how the narrator and divine actor relate, then, clarifies otherwise obscure locutions in Genesis 11:1 and Genesis 11:6. Focalization and perspective as narratological categories prove to be particularly helpful in this regard. Further, this philological and narratological examination underscores that the Tower of Babel is not a story concerning the advent of multilingualism but relates instead to issues of authority and governance, to who has the power to unify and fragment political entities.[2] As such, this analysis demonstrates that Genesis 11:1–9 on its own can be translated, interpreted, and understood apart from a reference to languages and, as a self-contained unit and narrative, does not contain an etiology of multilingualism.

Naturally, the episode at Babel is not self-contained and has a narrative context. Reconstructing literary context is an act of interpretation, and an interpretation of the Tower of Babel in light of recent developments in the study of the compilation of the Pentateuch was illuminating regarding the meaning and function of the passage in a larger narrative, namely J. Specifically, the philological and historical conclusions were put into conversation with the Neo-Documentary approach to the Pentateuch. This approach is advantageous for a variety of reasons, not least of which is that the goal of this mode of analysis of Genesis through Deuteronomy is not only to find out what literary sources may underlie the final form of the Pentateuch but

---

2   As a hypothetical aside, in the biblical imagination ancient Israelites help to construct foreign cities and building projects, from Egypt in the book of Exodus, to Babylon in Jeremiah and Ezekiel, to Persia in the book of Esther. In Jeremiah and Ezekiel, the prophets indicate that people of different languages will surround the former inhabitants of Jerusalem in exile, yet this new multilingual environment was not thought to be an impediment toward building projects. See chapter 3 for these references. In this fashion, it would not necessarily be the case in the biblical imagination that multilingualism in the traditional interpretation of Genesis 11:1–9 would result in the cessation of building activities.

also to demonstrate why the final form looks the way it does. Regarding the former, a new interpretation of the Tower of Babel makes better sense of the call of Abram, especially in the context of the J source. An account of this source consistent with Neo-Documentarian goals to explain the Bible as it exists demonstrates how Genesis 11:1–9 became a story about the multiplication of languages.

This thesis has explanatory power, not least because the influence of the Bible in history and in the modern world functions at the level of the edited book. Though many different traditions contain varied Bibles, the Tower of Babel exerted its influence on religious traditions as part of an edited, compiled, and accepted biblical text in religious communities. This influence made itself present with regard to the manner in which the call of Abram was understood as the antidote to the Tower of Babel. In this fashion, a new reading of the Tower of Babel can be put into conversation with reception history, not as though the latter is a distraction from the "original" intent of the narrative. Rather, later interpreters dealt with many of the same features of the text, and a new interpretation can indicate the significance of the features that led ancient exegetes in a variety of directions.

The reception history of this passage, then, is not a distraction to the study of the Tower of Babel; however, the understanding of the Tower of Babel as a story about the spread of multilingualism, which has shaped ancient and modern religious communities, was the product of the compilation of the sources of the Pentateuch. Yet the reverberating effects of this story do not exist because of scholarly reconstructions but rather because of the transmission and interpretation of the compiled text. The way in which language and politics shape human history often occurs because of the manner in which the belief in one universal, pure language functions in society. No foundational text, whether explicitly or implicitly, has served this role more than Genesis 11:1–9. The Tower of Babel has been an animating narrative to identify multilingualism as a social ill. Indeed, the reversal of this episode has been understood as a politically mediated cure. The discussion, then, picks up where it left off in the introduction, exploring the intellectual legacy of the Tower of Babel in society and politics into the twenty-first century.

What follows, however, is not a simple intellectual history. Two vital issues become transparent. The inherently political nature of Genesis 11:1–9 cannot be denied. Indeed, the politics that might lie behind the passage are also an integral part of the text itself. As such, the political edge of the Tower of Babel story and all it implies are inseparable aspects of the text itself and cannot be removed from it. In this manner, the foregoing historical-critical examinations are not intended to undermine the political nature of the narrative but rather seek to emphasize that Genesis 11:1–9 is essentially a political story and that its enduring message remains one with implications for political systems. That the narrative has been put to use in politics is, generally speaking, not an issue.

At the same time, while the essentially political nature of the story should be affirmed, how it has been used in the realm of politics should also be interrogated. In this fashion, the connection between language, state, and political action based on supposed biblical justification is an issue that merits further consideration. For this reason, the intellectual history of Genesis 11:1–9 traced earlier began in earnest in the seventeenth century CE as a prelude to the political and cultural context in which the beliefs about the Tower of Babel, statecraft, and language merged in America's early history in the eighteenth century CE. As a bookend and as a conclusion to the application of historical-critical readings of the Hebrew Bible in the context of current issues, this intellectual history picks up in the late-medieval but more specifically early-modern period. Where relevant for showing how modern interpretations of the story are innovations of specifically sixteenth-century CE and later concerns, texts and thinkers appear again in the following from antiquity to bring the contrast of modernist applications of Genesis 11:1–9 to the nation-state in sharp relief from other historic understandings of the passage. The focus on the sixteenth century CE and following periods in Europe sets the stage again for the reception of ideas about language and the state in the twenty-first-century CE America. The goal is to show that the specific twenty-first-century CE readings of the Tower of Babel having to do with language and politics arose not from a reading of the text that always was. Rather, with one crucial exception in antiquity, they arose from a specific, modern issue of statehood and language. When current uses of the narrative are understood as a *novum* of the modern era, the function of the Tower of Babel in nationalistic discourse and in current debates regarding immigration can be better understood.[3] In this fashion, the academic study

---

3   For more on the absence of ethnolinguistic nationalism in antiquity and the rise of the concept of "national languages" in the era of the nation-state, see Thomas Paul Bonfiglio, *Mother Tongues and Nations: The Invention of the Native Speaker*, Trends

of the Hebrew Bible can be put into a corrective conversation with the uses of the Bible in the public sphere.

THE TOWER OF BABEL AND LANGUAGE:
The Underpinnings of a Nationalistic Narrative

To frame the following examination of the function of this story in the current century, a return to 1679 is insightful, the same year that Athanasius Kircher wrote his *Turris Babel*. The century witnessed both the fear and possibilities inherent in a new, modern nationalism that also expressed itself in transnational terms.[4] In this fashion, Leibniz's epigraph above provides an excellent illustration of how a unified, universal language (as in the pre-Babel condition) and nationalism converge. It offers a launching pad for a critical assessment of the manner in which the political imagination, explicitly or implicitly, has used the traditional interpretation of the Tower of Babel in societal crises. Indeed, what Leibniz experienced personally and as part of his larger historical context has intriguing parallels to the idea of Babylon as a theopolitical concept and construct in American cultural, religious, and political rhetoric.

Though Leibniz nowhere mentions the Tower of Babel explicitly in his 1679 letter to the Duke of Hanover, the ideas therein about language demonstrate a concern to reverse the effects of Babel, understood as the root of multilingualism.[5] The letter reveals personal fears, as his benefactor had died and he was appealing to new sources of revenue to conduct his research. The Thirty Years War left Germany fractured and created a sense of urgency behind constructing a nationalistic endeavor, including the German language, partly inspired by Luther's Bible and partly through fanciful reconstructions of the

---

in Linguistics 226 (New York: DeGruyter Mouton 2010). See especially pages 41–62 for the lack of such ideology in antiquity. Bonfiglio traces the history well, but does not mention the Tower of Babel generally or its role politically in this regard in the volume.

4 For nationalism during this period and explorations of the significance of language in light of such nationalism, see Eco, *The Search for the Perfect Language*, 95–103.

5 For Leibniz, the cure was not a reversal to a lost language of Adam, which was "irredeemably lost," but instead the construction of a new perfect language (Eco, *The Search for the Perfect Language*, 86). Leibniz proposed a language that contained all knowledge, past and future, embedded within its symbols.

German language as a purer, and older, language than others in the world.[6] The relationship between these transnational connections and conflicts, on the one hand, and the resulting need to appeal to national identity through language, on the other, found wide intellectual acceptance in the seventeenth, eighteenth, and nineteenth centuries, demonstrated in this example of Leibniz. Indeed, Leibniz highlights the dual issues of globalization and nationalism through language. These tensions that emerge between globalization and nationalism and the manner in which language generally and biblical authority specifically cast a political vision in light of the Tower of Babel, then, can be seen in remarkable detail in the history of modernity through the twentieth century.[7]

Leibniz's thoughts on language and overcoming the perceived problems inherent in diversity through the construction of a "perfect" language display well the manner in which the Tower of Babel functions both as a mirror and as a lens.[8] As a mirror, the Tower of Babel serves as a narrative against which social pundits, intellectuals, and politicians gauge their own communities,

---

6 Eco, *The Search for the Perfect Language*, 100.

7 These tensions would not cease with the passing of time between Leibniz and the twenty-first century. The traditional interpretation of the Tower of Babel has allowed those in power to shape identity in nationalistic terms that frame the attachment to language as ideologically loaded, leveraging in explicit and implicit ways a biblical story to craft narratives of belonging, fear, and hope. Naturally, other passages in the Bible lend themselves toward dialect, language, identity, and the labeling of insiders and outsiders. The famous *shibboleth* episode in Judges 12:6 and passages such as Nehemiah 13:23–25 demonstrate how language could function as key for identity. Given the patently political nature of the Tower of Babel passage and its function in the traditional interpretation as an origin story of multilingualism, and given its coinage as a term that associates language, divine judgment, and the frustration of politically unified action, the cultural, political, philosophical, and artistic idea of an original, pure *Ursprache* arguably would not exist as it does if Genesis 11:1–9 were understood differently. Naturally, many other cultures had legends about language and primordial times, as well as etiologies exploring how multilingualism came to exist. Arno Borst extensively documented such stories in his multivolume work (*Der Turmbau von Babel*). No story has carried such lasting weight in so many spheres of society (art, literature, politics, etc.) as the Tower of Babel. In this fashion, the power of the Tower of Babel, understood as an etiology for the dangers and condemnation apparent in multilingualism, cast its long shadow not only in early modernity to the twentieth century but, as Erin Runions has argued (and as examined more below), Babylon generally and its tower specifically continue to haunt US political discourse.

8 For the use of language as a mirror and lens, see these categories in Guy Deutscher, *Through the Looking Glass: Why the World Looks Different in Other Languages* (New York: Metropolitan Books, 2010).

identifying societal ills against the metric of language ideology and the purported downside of diversity that would otherwise demolish a sense of national identity.[9] Leibniz, in the epigraph above, implies such beliefs about multilingualism; for him, a universal language would lead to "true religion everywhere it goes," as though the current state of affairs without such a language represents falsehood and a deficiency in the human condition. The narrative in Genesis 11:1–9 is well suited as a proof text for such sentiments. It is the first story in the biblical account in which anything remotely like a political entity acts in concert, all other previous actors being named as individuals or, as in Cain's genealogy, as tribes that construct cities and produce cultural artifacts like music. We see in the story what we want to see, its influence enduring over time as an episode involving, principally in the popular, intellectual, political, and artistic imagination, a tower. In reality, however, the tower appears in Genesis 11:4–5, a total of two times in the passage. In contrast, the building of the city is actually more prominent in the narrative, appearing not only in Genesis 11:4–5 but in Genesis 11:8 as part of the final summation of the event.

Yet the tower has been the consistent focus of the story's interpretive history, revealing how readerly imagination operates. The visual and spectacular excites the mind and, for us no less than ancient Judeans witnessing the ziggurat of Etemenanki in Babylon in the sixth century BCE, the concrete aspects of a passage are what draws our attention to it. Naturally, cities and urban features could equally capture the attention of scribes and interpreters. Nonetheless, the tower stands out (so to speak!) as a detail that demands explanation, especially given the fact that other ancient historians, such as Herodotus, made it a feature of their narratives, extolling the larger-than-life nature of Babylon in terms that indicate the centrality of its ziggurat.[10]

Different and perhaps more cogent and comprehensive interpretive possibilities emerge when focus is drawn away from architecture, structure, and a direct correlation to an obvious monumental feature of the southern Mesopotamian landscape and pointed toward rhetorical worlds and references

---

9   See, for example, Tristan Major's volume, in which he examines the role of Genesis 10–11, and the significance of the geography and number of seventy-two languages and nations therein, on Anglo-Saxon identity in Late Antiquity and the Middle Ages (*Undoing Babel: The Tower of Babel in Anglo-Saxon Literature*, Toronto Anglo-Saxon Series [Toronto: University of Toronto Press, 2018]).

10   For more on Herodotus's description, see George, "The Tower of Babel: Archaeology, History and Cuneiform Texts."

that might underlie the production of Genesis 11:1–9. When this shift occurs, another understanding, one that does not identify in the passage an etiology for the spread of languages, can explain more features of the text. Moreover, such an understanding demonstrates how the text, in J, functions within its source discourse. In this fashion, there is a vital component to the story that is political, yet not in the same manner that some interpreters of the story, in the traditional understanding, use it, at least not in the context of the rise of the modern nation-state. But its political nature is undeniable. As such, the narrative is perfectly suited to function as a mirror into which successive generations gaze and assess how they have developed. This inherently political story combined with the traditional interpretation about language has served as a particularly effective narrative of nationalism. Political power brokers and their constituents alike have used it to generate a variety of questions about statehood and identity, particularly whether or not there is too much or too little diversity, too much multilingualism, or, if it is part of the divine plan, too little multilingualism. In these issues posed by the traditional interpretation, the tower is symptomatic of something about society, and, in times of nationalistic fervor, the mirror can reveal points of stress, fractured identities, and other features that highlight social fears and perceived dangers.

THE TOWER OF BABEL GAZES BACK:
The Art and Ideology of Genesis 11:1–9

Indeed, the manner in which the Tower of Babel plays into societal solipsism appears most tangibly in the history of artistic depiction of the structure itself.[11] Artistic renderings of the Tower of Babel became increasingly popular in the medieval period, and these renderings were subject to interpretation such that the structure often looked like the advances in architecture that prevailed in whatever locality and time period was responsible for the depiction.[12] As artists rendered the tower over time, it morphed from a structure that matched the relative dimensions of large monuments in contemporaneous society to larger and larger edifices as building practices and materials

---

11   For more on the artistic renderings of the Tower of Babel through time, see Helmut Minkowksi, *Vermutungen über den Turm zu Babel* (Freren: Luca, 1991).

12   Rannfrid Thelle, *Discovering Babylon*, SHANE (New York: Routledge, 2019), 27–28.

made taller and taller towers imaginable.[13] In all of these representations, especially in illustrated Bibles from the eleventh to the sixteenth centuries CE, the process of building included the techniques that were current in the artist's own period. In most cases, the tower was quadratic, the act of building was the focus of the image, and "human figures are represented as Europeans in local dress style."[14] Particularly notable is the Morgan Bible from around 1250 CE in this regard. The Tower of Babel appears in the upper right-hand corner of an illustration in it, constructed from "hewn stone" with technologies current in the thirteenth century CE, such as the wheel and crane to move heavy objects, and the actors themselves appear in medieval garb.

The four scenes in the full panel on this illustrated page do not evoke the image of language with the story of Babel but do contain negative associations, as the construction of the tower is juxtaposed in the upper half with Noah's drunkenness. Moreover, the placement of scenes from Abram's life below on the same page also create an association: Abram is in some sense the antidote of the world gone wrong in Noah's day and in the time of the building of the Tower of Babel. The scene of kings capturing Lot from Genesis 14 is particularly appropriate in conjunction with Genesis 11. These are the only two chapters in the Bible to mention Shinar. Moreover, the interpretation of Amraphel in Genesis 14 as Nimrod had ancient currency (though this explicit connection is not made in the Morgan Bible specifically).[15]

The Tower of Babel image proliferates in the 1300s and later, at which point it is put to uses other than decoration in biblical manuscripts and churches.[16] Within this period, depictions of the structure changed along with

---

13   Thelle, *Discovering Babylon*, 28.

14   Thelle, *Discovering Babylon*, 27–32 (quotes at 27 and 32, respectively).

15   See the rabbinic etymology of Amraphel's name as derived from the verb אמר, "to say," and פל, the imperative form of נפל, "to fall," which would mean something like "He said, 'make (him) fall!'" or "'He said, 'Cast (him) down!'" The sense is that Amraphel's name is linked to stories about Nimrod who issued the command to cast Abram into fire.

16   Thelle, *Discovering Babylon*, 32. Even after this period, as Liverani notes, the artistic depiction of the Tower of Babel becomes much more frequent, especially in the seventeenth and eighteenth centuries, an important observation given the arguments below about the use of this narrative for propaganda related to the modern nation-state (*Imagining Babylon: The Modern Story of an Ancient City*, trans. Ailsa Campbell, SANER 11 [Boston: DeGruyter, 2016], 13–14).

Europe's changing contact with the non-Western world. During this time, the non-Western world expanded and altered European sensibilities about what the structure and actors could look like. In particular, the fourteenth-century fresco in the baptistery of St. John in Padua, Italy, displays this move in rendering the narrative in art. The artist, Giusto de Menabuoi, presents Nimrod in non-European (and therefore "othering") fashion. The manifold significance of the fresco is notable: not only does this depiction begin to show the structure as something other than European but the Tower, for the first time in European art, looks more like a ziggurat, or pyramid, in shape.[17] This opening of the world and of the image of Babylon allowed for the possibility to render the scene as something other than European, paving the way for more historical attempts to portray Genesis 11:1–9. Indeed, by the sixteenth century, artists began to focus on the ancient and foreign aspects of the tower, showing features that were not part of the immediate, contemporary architectural design.[18]

Even with this shift, however, the depictions of the tower served contemporary debates, often for the purpose of scoring political points. Kircher would represent a move to "get it right," but even here, as seen in his work in *Arca Noae*, his motives were polemical. His projects were an attempt to defend the Jesuit reading of the Bible from deviant Protestant interpretations, a defense based on as much historical information as was available. For example, between the mid-sixteenth century and mid-seventeenth century CE in the Netherlands, both the depictions of the Tower of Babel based on ancient Greek sources (such as Herodotus) as well as based on ancient Roman sources and designs were available to artists. The sixteenth century portraits by Pieter Bruegel the Elder and Lucas van Valckenborch display the round, colosseum type of structure so prominent in Roman architecture. Indeed, the decision seems to be intentional, and the layout influenced almost all subsequent artistic renditions of the tower in early modern Europe. The square style of Maarten von Heemskerck's 1569 painting *The Tower of Babel*, which

---

17 Thelle, *Discovering Babylon*, 32–33.
18 Thelle, *Discovering Babylon*, 35. Note also Liverani's discussion of the manner in which the city becomes more a part of the landscape, which was an important component of art at the time ("portraits of cities") and is consistent with the biblical narrative in Genesis 11:1–9 (in which the city is mentioned three times, whereas the tower is mentioned only twice). See Liverani's discussion of Johann Fischer von Erlach's *Spectacula Babylonica* (1721–1723), *Imagining Babylon*, 14–15.

more closely approximated to actual ziggurat designs, was also ignored in favor of the more Roman, colosseum style.[19]

The intentionality of the Roman representation of the Tower of Babel reflected, like a mirror, the Protestant critique of Catholicism and, at the same time, functioned like a lens in portraying and categorizing Rome as a Babel of sorts.[20] For Protestants in the Netherlands, the institution of the Roman Catholic Church functioned like a Tower of Babel: an ecclesiastical edifice attempting to reach heaven by human endeavor. The concerted effort and the one language (mediated through sanctioned Latin services and translation of the Bible) was fragmented through divine action. The result was a divided landscape of church authority, one that Catholics might have viewed as a confused mess while Protestants could appeal to the divine legitimation of the many-splendored church existence. With it came a multitude of tongues into which the Bible was translated, further sanctioning the multilingual landscape. In this fashion, the rise of the vernacular as a vehicle for communicating divine revelation in the Bible also put a positive interpretation of the post-Babel realm into which Protestantism emerged after God's judgment of a corrupt, late-medieval Catholic institution.[21]

REBUILDING BABEL, REVERSING THE CLOCK:
The Science of History, Language, and National Identity

Indeed, the rise in nationalism in the sixteenth and seventeenth centuries and the focus on the connection between nation-state and language coincide with the tail end of these artistic renderings. Here, the correlation between interpretations of the Tower of Babel, artistic renderings of the narrative, and arguments pertaining to religion, politics, and the rise of the modern nation-state merged. Leibniz provides an excellent example of an intellectual who both reacted against this sort of reading and yet shows a clear immersion

---

19   Thelle, *Discovering Babylon*, 34–35, 45. Since modern archaeology would not begin until the mid nineteenth century, the historical correspondence of the Mesopotamian styles might not have been as accessible.

20   Thelle, *Discovering Babylon*, 46.

21   Thelle, *Discovering Babylon*, 46. The result was not, however, a celebration of post-Babel circumstances, as shown below.

in contemporary assumptions about language, nationalism, and a pre-Babel connection to a politically defined pure tongue.[22]

An example in which art and intellectual theory merge appears in the same period (sixteenth and seventeenth centuries CE) in the Dutch republic. While artists during this century painted the Tower of Babel as simultaneously ancient yet cast in features that pertained to their current political and religious situations, other Dutch intellectuals were theorizing that Flemish (in the dialects they knew in the sixteenth century) was related to the original, perfect language. In 1569 Goropius Becanus argued that a direct genealogical line existed between the inhabitants of Antwerp, through the Cimbri (an ancient Germanic tribe that fought Rome in the late second century BCE), to the descendants of Japheth.[23] The connection between the line of Japheth and "gentiles" generally had, in some measure, biblical basis in Genesis 10:5:

> From these, the coasts of the nations (*goyim*) spread out by their land, each according to its language, according to their clans, by their nations.

One could also translate the first clause as "from these, they spread out to the coasts of the nations," understanding "coasts of the *goyim*" as an adverbial accusative. The interpretation of the passage came to mean not "nations" generally but gentiles specifically.[24] As such, many nations found ways to justify in this verse a movement of Noah's descendants to Europe. If, then, the line of Japheth migrated to Europe, each descendant with their "language," and if this line migrated prior to the construction of Babel (particularly since Nimrod, as leader of the city and tower construction, was not from the line of Japheth), it was possible to argue that some European language might be the direct descendant of the perfect, original language. In this context,

---

22   See Eco for Leibniz's critiques of some of the endeavors to posit local vernaculars as part of an *Ursprache* or pure dialect (*The Search for the Perfect Language*, 100).

23   Eco, *The Search for the Perfect Language*, 96–97.

24   Eco, *The Search for the Perfect Language*, 95. See also, for Genesis 10 and the connection to Europe, the article cited below, Philip S. Alexander, "Jerusalem as the *Omphalos* of the World: On the History of a Geographical Concept," *Judaism* 46 (1997): 147–158. For more on Noah Webster's use of this verse and the Tower of Babel in Genesis 11 to construct a Germanic lineage and sense of Eurocentric superiority of languages in his dictionary work, see Thomas Paul Bonfiglio, *Race and the Rise of Standard American*, Language, Power, and Social Process 7 (New York: Mouton de Gruyter, 2002), 82.

Becanus claimed that the dialect of Flemish from Antwerp was the heir of that language, attempting to prove this connection through demonstrating the monosyllabic nature of Flemish, the phonological "richness" of the language, and etymological explorations that became the object of intellectual ridicule.[25] Despite this ridicule, Becanus's ideas were influential into the seventeenth century CE, and the "Flemish thesis," attempting to connect Dutch (sometimes called "Teutonic") to Hebrew, or at least some pre-Babel language that did not suffer the wound of confusion (and debasement) of Babel, had defenders even into the nineteenth century CE.[26]

This Eurocentric view even had a basis in a map that allowed interpreters to connect biblical chronology to the concept that a European language was the original, perfect mode of communication prior to the events at Babel. In the post-flood movement of humanity, the genealogy of Japheth found an interpretation that landed this patriarch and his descendants in the realm of gentiles generally and, according to the second-century BCE book *Jubilees*, in Europe specifically. While *Jubilees* itself never became authoritative in Western Christianity, many of the concepts therein, including its map of the world, survived in intellectual and religious discourse, even if the book was never canonized in the sense that it was in Ethiopic Christianity. The relationship between the map and the rhetoric of *Jubilees*, itself drawn from the Table of Nations in Genesis 10, created a bridge between the spread of humanity and how Europe viewed itself.[27] Indeed, even if not a map in the technical sense, the intellectual background of this connection appeared in Isidore of Seville's famous T-O map, which itself was the basis for the medieval Hereford *mappa mundi*.[28] This mapping of Noah's descendants and the belief that the perfect language was perhaps retained in the European sphere proved to be a perfect fit with the artistic depiction and intellectual discourse surrounding the Tower of Babel in the sixteenth and subsequent centuries.[29]

---

25   Eco, *The Search for the Perfect Language*, 97.

26   Eco, *The Search for the Perfect Language*, 97.

27   Alexander, "Jerusalem as the *Omphalos* of the World," 149–151. See also Alexander, "Geography and the Bible (Early Jewish)," in *ABD*, 2: 982.

28   Alexander, "Jerusalem as the *Omphalos* of the World," 153–155.

29   As Eco claims regarding the theses of a Eurocentric pure, original, and perfect language that survived the "wound" of Babel,

   Such nationalistic hypotheses are comprehensible in the seventeenth and eighteenth centuries, when the larger European states began to take form, posing the problem of which of them was to be supreme on the continent. In

The relationship between language and state and the function of the Tower of Babel in constructing this intellectual and political picture had a specific historical context, which was not the same as the context of the production of these texts. The Tower of Babel narrative was crafted not to support the needs of the state but rather as a response to state-as-empire making claims on Israel and Judah. It was not a narrative to create a map of identity in the service of supremacy lost and regained but rather to critique a specific claim of supremacy itself.

With the biblical grounding of Genesis 10:5 and the ability to draw a lineage from Japheth to Germanic, Celtic, or Gothic tribes, a variety of Euro-centric positions crystalized in the late-medieval and early-modern period. Swedish and, perhaps most influentially, German have been documented as languages with ardent defenders to the claim that they somehow had a genetic connection to the original language lost at Babel.[30] While proponents of the theory that German was somehow a primordial language existing prior to the confusion of Genesis 11:1–9 were already propounding their theories in the fourteenth century CE, the religious and political significance of German as a chosen, ancient, and pure language became a special topic of examination beginning in the sixteenth century CE with the Reformation and Luther's translation of the Bible.[31] The vernacularization of the Bible through its translation in local dialects, dialects identified with the rise of the nation-state in the sixteenth century CE, sanctioned the architects of politics in early modern Europe to think of the relationship between identity, nationalism, and language in theological terms of chosen-ness or election. This special status could then even be projected back into primordial times and justified in the present through a particularly political line of argumentation.[32] This

---

this period, spirited claims to originality and superiority arise no longer from the visionary quest for universal peace, but—whether their authors realized this or not—from concrete reasons of state.

Eco, *The Search for the Perfect Language*, 102.

30 Eco, *The Search for the Perfect Language*, 98–99.
31 Eco, *The Search for the Perfect Language*, 100.
32 As Eco puts it,

German had remained in a state of perfection because Germany had never been subjected to the yoke of a foreign ruler. Lands that had been subjected had inevitably adapted their customs and language to fit those of the victor. This was also the opinion of Kircher. French, for example, was a mix of Celtic, Greek and Latin. The German language, by contrast, was richer in terms than

argument was, naturally, not new. Ishodad of Merv made similar statements on language-mixing and political power in the eighth century CE. What changed in the sixteenth century CE was the sanctioning of this connection through the particularly nationalistic use of the Tower of Babel as a biblical (and, therefore, authoritative) narrative that portrayed the historical circumstances of the "wound" of multilingualism. The passage provided the framework for reverse engineering of the curse through the nation-state.[33]

As seen above in art, during this same period, increased trade and missions to the Far East also challenged European conceptions of language and nation constructed through the biblical framework. Indeed, as missionaries landed in China, they found a civilization that far predated the biblical history they knew, meaning that the Chinese language and writing must have existed prior to the fall in Eden or the collapse of the Tower of Babel.[34] As such, theories about how Egyptian hieroglyphs, Chinese characters, and Amerindian pictographs related to one another began to appear.[35] The concept of devolution was prominent: Kircher proposed that Noah brought Egyptian hieroglyphs to China after the flood, and that Amerindian pictographs were a further devolution and degrading of this ancient script.[36] The scale thus was concocted along these lines: if a symbolic, image-oriented writing stood for not only a picture in the world but a deeper, more abstract principle and concept, it would represent a more esoteric, ancient, and authentic form of conveying knowledge through pictures.[37] The Egyptian hieroglyph was

---

Hebrew, more docile than Greek mightier than Latin, more magnificent in its pronunciation than Spanish, more gracious than French, and more correct than Italian.

Eco, *The Search for the Perfect Language*, 99.

33 As explored in chapter 1 of this book, the reverse engineering had as its model the "wound" of the fall, which was healed in the election of individuals to dwell "in" Jesus as the messiah (or Christ). For the political sphere, the wound of Babel would be reversed in the saving actions of the nation-state, which provided identity for its inhabitants to dwell "in" it as a safe haven of identity.

34 Eco, *The Search for the Perfect Language*, 91–92.

35 See particularly an analysis of Kircher's theory relating these writing systems in Eco, *The Search for the Perfect Language*, 160–162.

36 Kircher claimed that the particularly "pagan" Amerindian communities also reflected this devolved religious conception in their writing system (Eco, *The Search for the Perfect Language*, 162). This concept of "devolution" and the superiority of earlier, supposedly pristine literature, writing, and religion appears full-fledged in the Romantic historicism of Wellhausen (Machinist, "The Road Not Taken," 469–531).

37 For Kircher's monumental works on Egyptian and Chinese, see, respectively, his *Oedipus Aegyptiacus* (1652–1655) and his *China monumentis, qua sacris qua*

believed to convey not only pictures but such esoteric knowledge, with the Chinese characters signifying more of a direct, nonesoteric relationship to the natural world. At the bottom of the spectrum was the Amerindian pictograph, whose representation of the natural world was so simple and direct as not to evoke any deeper realms of thought.[38] The date of the Chinese writing system, however, indicates how European contact with the world would challenge narratives and create the sense of urgency to find new ways to maintain the relationship between history, biblical mythology, the nation, and language.

At the end of this history and into the nineteenth-century beginnings of modern archaeology, the influence of the story of Babel in Genesis 11 held firm, a symbol of the nationalistic self to be rediscovered among the mass of multilingual confusion. In the early nineteenth century, the first artifacts from Mesopotamia appeared in Europe, making Babylon known and visible on its own terms and not as a refraction of biblical and classical sources. In the decades preceding the first excavations of Assyria in the 1840s and the decipherment of Akkadian in 1857, Claudius Rich of the East India Company, who had lived in Baghdad, introduced objects from ancient Mesopotamia to Great Britain.[39] Though these objects did not go on public display at the British Museum until 1836, the physical look and representation of Assyria and Babylon began to make themselves known. However, the Bible did not recede from view entirely: in 1818 a Bible from America displayed in its illustrations two cuneiform tablets and the Tower of Babel. As one scholar remarks, the cuneiform tablets were "perfectly rendered."[40]

Artistic and intellectual discourse concerning the Tower of Babel during this time of the rediscovery of the ancient Near East nonetheless still served the desire to create a sense of nationalism in modern terms, despite the increasing cultural and historical knowledge of the context in which the

---

profanis, nec non variis naturae & artis spectaculis, aliarumque rerum memorabilium argumentis illustrata (1667).

38 Eco, *The Search for the Perfect Language*, 159–161.

39 See Mogens Trolle Larsen, *The Conquest of Assyria*, 9–10.

40 Thelle, 64. The illustrated Bible is from the Brattleboro Bible, held in the Beineke Museum at Yale. See also Paul C. Gutjahr, *An American Bible: A History of the Good Book in the United States* (Stanford: Stanford University Press, 1999), 60, 62; Benjamin Foster, "The Beginnings of Assyriology in the United States," in Stephen Holloway (ed.), *Orientalism, Assyriology and the Bible*, HBM 10 (Sheffield: Sheffield Phoenix Press, 2007), 46. For a history of the tablets in the illustration and how they were brought to America, see William B. Dinsmoor, "Early American Studies of Mediterranean Archaeology," *Proceedings of the American Philosophical Society* 87 (1943): 100. Dinsmoor claims that these were the first tablets brought to America.

text was produced. The Tower of Babel, with all it entailed, was a perfect text for such purposes and reflected like a mirror the particular concerns of the nation-state. At the forefront of the themes that make themselves evident (in the traditional understanding of this passage), and particularly suitable for nationalistic discourse, is language. America was not immune to this larger cultural project. Indeed, the idea of language in the construction of political identity and the role of the Tower of Babel in that construction were at the forefront of the cultural project. Yet Genesis 11:1–9, historically, source-critically, and philologically, does not contain an etiology for the advent of multilingualism and spread of languages. In one sense, proponents of the Tower of Babel as a symbol of language purism and its application to the modern nation-state generally (and America specifically) are not likely to heed this sort of analysis. Indeed, there are other passages in the Hebrew Bible, most notably Nehemiah 13:23–25, that would seem to justify such a nationalistic use of language. Even without viewing Genesis 11:1–9 as a reaction to specifically Neo-Assyrian political rhetoric and without a source-critical framework, the translation of "lip"/*safah* as "language" on its own presents problems. As such, even in a synchronic reading, a good justification exists for understanding the Tower of Babel as a story about something other than the advent of multilingualism. Although the compilation of the Pentateuch encourages this interpretation, it does not necessitate it. In this manner, even those who do not ascribe to diachronic critical frameworks of the biblical text could still benefit from the arguments herein and re-evaluate their understanding and any nationalistic applications of this passage.

BABEL AS A LENS THROUGH WHICH TO VIEW AND CONSTRUCT OTHERS

Perhaps beyond its usefulness as a mirror, one of the major reasons for maintaining and promoting the traditional interpretation of Genesis 11:1–9 in the context of modern political debates is the way in which the narrative functions as a lens. In the understanding of the Tower of Babel as a story about the political dangers of multilingualism, the focus has often been on the pre-confusion state as a destination for social return. The post-Babel world is part of society that is cast off, the validity of which is denied, whereas the "one language" state of affairs in the pre-Babel society is a state to be emulated. The emulation does not involve the hubris or acts of the builders of the tower and city but rather the reversal of multilingualism as an act of divine judgment.

In seeing oneself in the narrative, the creation of an "other" is also inevitable. The act of seeing others through the story is not a "window" in the sense of transparency but rather a lens in which the act of analysis appears. Language difference is a sign of not belonging to the national project of reversing the curse of Babel (or healing "the wound" as Eco would phrase it). The belief that Egyptian hieroglyphs represented a perfect symbolic system attached to divine mysteries of the original Adamic language entailed a corresponding judgment on other symbolic writing systems as "less" perfect in various degrees in seventeenth- and eighteenth-century intellectual discourse. It is not simply that Egyptian hieroglyphs were a symbolic representation of a perfect language but that Chinese or Amerindian symbolic/pictographic writing systems were "less" so. The nationalistic drive for identifying one's language as "original" or "perfect" stood in contrast to others, understood as devolved and poor reflections of something better, signs of the post-Babel state of confusion and divine judgment. The relationship between state and language, then, involved the presence of multilingualism as a social barometer, gauging the relative success and failures of the nationalistic process by the extent of assimilation into the language (and, presumably, culture as well) of choice.

The function of the lens of the Tower of Babel, in which the story creates an "other," appears in the influence of the British artist John Martin's painting *The Fall of Babylon* on the Scottish artist James Fergusson's *The Monuments of Nineveh Restored*.[41] A caption containing Fergusson's image on the cover of the 1853 publication of Austin Henry Layard's archaeological discoveries suggested that his rendering was based on his own eyewitness account, sketching his restoration based on the ruins that he himself observed.[42] There is no indication, however, that Fergusson ever actually saw the ruins of Nineveh or Nimrud.[43] Indeed, the similarities between Martin's painting, finished in 1835,

---

41   For more on Martin, see Liverani, *Imagining Babylon*, 18–19.

42   The caption reads "A view of the Palaces of Nimrud from a sketch by James Fergusson."

43   Thelle, *Discovering Babylon*, 53–55. See Bahrani's article and the theory of "history in reverse," in which later values and artistic sensibilities frame (if not determine) historical claims and narratives ("History in Reverse: Archaeological Illustration and the Reconstruction of Mesopotamia," in *Historiography in the Cuneiform World*,

and the work by Fergusson, finished eighteen years later, are striking, with the orientation and layout of each appearing to be dramatically overlapping.[44]

The effect of association, particularly as Fergusson's painting adorned Layard's first English publication of archaeological finds from Mesopotamia, is remarkable. Martin's depiction of the fall of Babylon fused a number of themes from a variety of time periods into one scene, in which many of the associations of the orient in the nineteenth century merged. Babylon appears decadent, foregrounding over-satiation at Balshazzar's feast. The Tower of Babel sits prominently in the distance, enshrouded by clouds and struck by lightning. The scene evokes decadence to the point that the crowds have a look of immoderation to them. Martin created these epically disastrous landscapes for Babylon as well as Nineveh (the latter finished in 1828), but the portrait of Babylon's judgment seems to have especially influenced Fergusson's depiction of Nimrud.[45] Though Fergusson's landscape reconstruction of Nimrud had none of the immediate signs of downfall and judgment that were patent in Martin's *Judgment of Babylon*, the presence of extensive similarities between the two indicates that the situation of one (Babylon) could easily appear in the other (Nimrud). Indeed, while Martin's Babylon undergoes dramatic judgment as part of the portrayal, one could then identify in Fergusson's Nineveh the opulence and decadence that immediately preceded its doom.

By placing Fergusson's painting (which evoked so clearly and strongly Martin's depiction of the fall of Babylon) on Layard's English publication of the early archaeology of Mesopotamia, the artistic rendering and Orientalist perceptions of the rise and downfall of Mesopotamia was cast on the actual history of the area. It did not matter that the texts were soon to allow scholars of the region to write the history of ancient Assyria and Babylon in terms and categories constructed by the Assyrians and Babylonians themselves (however

---

eds. Tzvi Abusch et al., Proceedings of the XLVth Recontre Assyriologique Internationale [Bethseda, MD: CDL Press, 2001], 15–28).

44   As Liverani states, Martin was aware of the embellishments in his own paintings and commented on them openly. He stated regarding his Mesopotamian paintings rendering Babylon: "the style of architecture, particularly of the Egyptian on the one hand, and of ancient Indian on the other, has been invented as the most appropriate for a city situation between the two countries, and necessarily in frequent intercourse with them" (as cited in Liverani, *Imagining Babylon*, 19). Liverani observes that Nebuchadnezzar's reputation in classical sources as conqueror of Egypt and India may have given rise to this sort of idea.

45   Thelle, *Discovering Babylon*, 55.

much those ancient perspectives were refracted through the methods and perspectives of modern historians). This example demonstrates a process known as "history in reverse," in which, in the words of one scholar, "artistic sensibilities from a particular epoch have come to interpret new historical knowledge."[46] In this fashion, Martin's Babylon represents a non-Western "other," an Orientalist construct of exoticism and decadence that Fergusson then mapped on to other realms of Mesopotamia (such as Nineveh to the north). Placing Fergusson's painting on the cover of Layard's publication, the first of its kind in English, then frames the history of that region in terms determined already by artistic conceptions.[47] In this manner, Martin and Fergusson both participated in the Orientalist fantasizing of the East, creating an "other" with negative associations that then became a framing picture of the region and its history through the placement of art in Layard's work. The associations created a lens that focuses the eye on the epic decadence and downfall of the Tower of Babel.

LANGUAGE, NATIONALISM, AND BABEL:
An Absent History and Modern Construct

The intellectual currents of the seventeenth, eighteenth, and nineteenth centuries, and the manner in which these currents used Babel as a mirror and lens, found fertile ground in the history of the United States. Even in America, where the idea that English (or the American version of it) was an original or perfect language was never seriously considered, language and nationalism merged such that Babel became a category in which the political project found both a mirror and a lens.[48] The belief in the "chosen" state of America extends to the language that, it is perceived, should identify it. English in the American vision thus is not an original or perfect language but a chosen language for the American political project. Any deviation is an acceptance of divine curse, and multilingualism is a symptom of this deeper disease. The political nature of Genesis 11:1–9 gains new purchase

---

46 Thelle, *Discovering Babylon*, 55.

47 Liverani, *Imagining Babylon*, 35.

48 A notable exception is Noah Webster, who argued that American English could be attached historically to the sons of Noah prior to the events in Babel. See the reference in Bonfiglio cited below.

in light of a new interpretation. The issue is not whether or not the Tower of Babel is a story with political importance. The political significance of the passage is inherent. The issue pertains to the sort of political message the Tower of Babel narrative endorses: linguistic purism to retain divine (and imperial) favor, or, as a response to imperial claims, undermining those claims and arguing for an alternate organizing order for one's own society. While both interpretations can operate as a way to promote a sense of self and political order attached to national identity, the former (traditional) interpretation seeks to maintain and support the claims of empire, whereas the latter responds negatively to illegitimate claims to authority and, even if the denouement of the narrative results in the call of a patriarch who founds a nation, identifies the legitimacy of authority beyond the nation-state. In other words, the use of the Tower of Babel as a category for the former (linguistic purism in service of empire) undermines the latter understanding (Genesis 11:1–9 as a reaction against imperial claims) of the passage. It is this latter interpretation that is best justified historically, philologically, and linguistically. Moreover, devoid of language, the analysis demonstrates how subsequent interpreters struggled to understand the call of Abram as an antidote to Babel, how a new interpretation of Genesis 11:1–9 makes better sense of the transition out of Primeval History in the biblical text, and how this transition itself was crafted in a manner to undermine imperial claims on the southern Levant.

The Tower of Babel, understood as a mirror and a lens into and through which cultures gaze to assess themselves and form perceptions of others, became a major tool of nationalism beginning in the sixteenth century. There is perhaps only one major exception to this timeline. In the mid second century BCE, the author of the book of *Jubilees*, possibly to combat the similar issues that the author of 1 Maccabees addresses in 1 Maccabees 1:11, rewrote biblical narratives from the beginning of the world to the Exodus.[49] The author of *Jubilees* did so in order to demonstrate the illegitimacy of entering into covenants with, and joining the legal world of, the gentiles. As *Jubilees* rewrites history to depict the law as valid from the beginning of time, the book defuses any arguments that the law and covenant happened only subsequently in Israel's history. In other words, *Jubilees* constructs an argument against the idea that the covenant was historically contingent

---

49 James VanderKam, *Jubilees 1–21*, Hermeneia (Minneapolis: Fortress Press, 2018), 40.

(since it happens chronologically in the Hebrew Bible well after the creation of the world).[50] It was feared that this implication could mean that other covenant relationships were an option.[51] The author of 1 Maccabees 1:11 likewise states that

> In those days lawless men came forth from Israel, and misled many, saying "Let us go and make a covenant with the Gentiles round about us, for since we separated from them many evils have come upon us."

The concern is with Jews who have cast off the law ("lawless men who came forth from Israel") and who see the call of Abram out of the nations and the subsequent covenant at Sinai (which marks Israel as distinct) as bad omens, signaling the cause of the many evils that have come upon them. In contrast, both the author of 1 Maccabees and the author of *Jubilees* made arguments otherwise, championing a sense of peoplehood under the banner of the Hasmoneans.

As examined already, the author of *Jubilees* casts the call of Abram as the antidote to the Tower of Babel, a common trope in ancient Jewish literature. Distinctly, however, the retelling in *Jubilees* 12:25–27 includes the belief that Abram, as part of curing the wound of Babel, was miraculously taught Hebrew. According to one scholar, aside from *Jubilees* 12:25–27 and Syncellus, "the idea that the Hebrew language revived with Abram is not found in the ancient Jewish sources."[52] It has been argued that this reading of the relationship between Babel and Abram in the Hasmonean period was a call to nationalism *via* the resurrection of Hebrew as an important language for an autonomous Jewish state.[53] Thus, this example displays a connection between state, language, and the Tower of Babel (as well as Abram as the antidote to the Tower of Babel) in a vaguely analogous manner as was unique to the modern period beginning in the sixteenth century CE.

---

50   For more on issues of creation and covenant in *Jubilees* and other Second Temple Jewish texts, see Ari Mermelstein, *Creation, Covenant, and the Beginnings of Judaism: Reconceiving Historical Time in the Second Temple Period*, Supplements to the Journal for the Study of Judaism 168 (Boston: Brill, 2014).

51   VanderKam, *Jubilees 1–21*, 40.

52   VanderKam, *Jubilees 1–21*, 458.

53   See, for example, the excellent analysis in Schniedewind, *A Social History of Hebrew*, 170–171.

Yet the situation in the Hasmonean dynasty differs from the story of language, nationalism, and the use of the Tower of Babel presented in modernity. The Hasmoneans themselves never made a language policy of exclusive Hebrew usage in the same manner that European nation-states, beginning especially in the seventeenth century CE, promoted their national languages to the expense of others. Indeed, while the Maccabees initially minted Hebrew coinage as a sign of national pride, they did so alongside coins with Greek, and later used the latter language exclusively in their currency.[54] Moreover, there are inscriptions that the Hasmoneans sponsored written in Aramaic. This observation demonstrates that while Hebrew was a special, symbolic language of a renewed autonomous Jewish state, and while the Hasmoneans perhaps promoted the language initially to gain support against the Greek overlords, this example in *Jubilees* 12:25–27 was never in service to nationalism in the same manner in which Babel would function in modernity.[55]

The historical picture, then, appears clear. The issue is not the importance of language for national identity. Such a symbolic relationship between language and state has always been a feature of the political landscape in human history (though the elimination of other languages to the exclusion of using the prestigious dialect as a way of enculturating immigrants is perhaps a more modern feature).[56] The competition between Sumerian and Akkadian scribes in the mid-to late third millennium BCE shows how the use of language was central to the project of state identity and power.[57]

---

54   For more, see Eyal Regev, *The Hasmoneans: Ideology, Archaeology, Identity*, Journal of Ancient Judaism Supplements 10 (Göttingen: Vandenhoeck & Ruprecht, 2013), 218; Samuel Rocca, *Herod's Judea: A Mediterranean State in the Classical World*, TSAJ 122 (Tübingen: Mohr Siebeck, 2008), 244.

55   Other Jewish groups, such as the Qumran community, promoted Hebrew for important religious and political uses (perhaps as a way to define themselves against other groups). This example, however, is also distinct from the modern, nationalistic employment of the Tower of Babel to justify language as a measure of state and national support. For more on Qumran and Babel, and the debates regarding Hebrew at Qumran, see chapter 5.

56   It was the case that the Akkadian scribal education could be used as a tool of enculturation in the Neo-Assyrian empire, but this practice was not a means destroying the use of foreign dialects within its own territory. For more on Assyrian perspectives on the benefits and positives of diversity, see Jessie DeGrado, "King of the Four Corners: Diversity as a Rhetorical Strategy of the Neo-Assyrian Empire," *Iraq* 81 (2019): 1–19.

57   The competition did not result in the exclusion of either language completely, as Sumerian retained its status as a scholarly language in scribal education and literary and scientific texts.

The writing of vernacular languages such as Hebrew in the ninth century BCE was also a political act, and the literature written in these vernaculars (Hebrew inscriptions no less than the Hebrew Bible itself) helped to support, if not create, the very political entities that this literature was crafted to address. Thus, the issue is not that language and national/political identity are a product of modernity and modern nation-states. That connection has always been there and cannot be ascribed as a feature (at least in the general sense) of the modern context.

Nor is the issue of the use of the Bible in the political realm a product of modernity. Ever since the so-called conversion of Constantine, the Bible has been a constant feature of political action and justification in the Christian West.[58] The situation was similar in the East. In Ethiopia the emperor Ezana II converted to Christianity between 323 and 327 CE and made the Axumite kingdom a Christian kingdom as a result (preceding the official Christianization of the Roman empire by Theodosius II in 380 CE).[59] In doing so, the coinage in Ethiopia shifted from acknowledging Maḥrem, the traditional god of Ethiopian religion, to citations of the Psalms and the book of Matthew. Augustine's appeal to the Bible with respect to the policy of limited toleration and occasional harassment of Jewish populations in Christian territories became, in some manner, the basis of official doctrine in Christendom until the expulsion of Jewish populations from Spain in 1492 CE.[60] The Reformation and Enlightenment, while drastically changing the nature of the Bible and how it was read once it was put into vernacular translations, in no sense

---

58   For the complexities of the use of the Bible during the third and fourth centuries BCE and the issue of Constantine's conversion, see Robin Lane Fox, *Pagans and Christians in the Mediterranean World: From the Second Century AD to the Conversion of Constantine* (New York: Knopf, 1987), 544–545, 609–681; David L. Dungan, *Constantine's Bible: Politics and the Making of the New Testament* (Minneapolis: Fortress Press, 2007).

59   See Aaron M. Butts, "Ethiopic Christianity, Syriac Contacts with," in *Gorgias Encyclopedic Dictionary of the Syriac Heritage*, eds. Sebastian P. Brock et al. (Piscataway, NJ: Gorgias Press, 2011), 148; Edward Ullendorff, *The Bible and Ethiopia*, Schweich Lectures (London: British Academy, 1968).

60   See the analysis of Augustine's use of Psalm 59:12 and his "witness doctrine" in John Efron, Steven Weitzman, and Mattias Lehmann, *The Jews: A History*, 2nd ed. (New York: Pearson, 2014), 180; Paula Fredriksen, *Augustine and the Jews: A Christian Defense of Jews and Judaism* (New Haven, CT: Yale University Press, 2010), 304. As such, Augustine's perspectives on issues relating to the Bible and politics, as examined below with his thoughts on language and nation, are extremely important when making historical narratives.

abandoned the political importance of the text. The foundational sense in which the Bible was supposed to frame Western society culturally and politically survived the "secularization" of the scriptural text when it began to be studied as any other historical document.[61] When people who claimed to be connected (whether by name or in reality) to religious traditions stemming from the Bible began to take and maintain imperial power in the fourth century CE, the Bible became an ever-present part of sustaining claims to nation and empire.[62]

Thus, the connection between languages and nations was itself not a *novum* of the early modern nation-state, as the aforementioned use of Akkadian and Sumerian in the late third-millennium southern Mesopotamian city-states suggests. Sumerian city-states used Sumerian, and a language competition with Akkadian seems to have taken place until Sumerian city-states died out and the language became a dead, scribal language.[63] Indeed, in Late Antiquity, the Table of Nations in Genesis 10 and the story of the Tower of Babel in Genesis 11 provided a biblical basis for theorizing the relationship between language and nation. In this fashion, Augustine offered sustained reflections on the relationship between language and polity.[64] He hypothesized that the number of languages that appeared after Babel numbered seventy-two (or seventy-three): "Seventy-three, or rather, as calculation will show, seventy-two nations and as many languages came into being on earth." In other words, for Augustine, there were seventy-two nations, each with a distinct language, in the post-Babel situation. The number seventy-two itself was derived from the *recapitulo* process of interpretation, in which Augustine made the calculation based

---

61 Jonathan Sheehan has called attention to the ways in which the Bible survived the vicissitudes of historical and religious movements because these movements developed a secular appreciation of the text. Sheehan names this phenomenon "The Enlightenment Bible." Jonathan Sheehan, *The Enlightenment Bible: Translation, Scholarship, Culture* (Princeton, NJ: Princeton University Press, 2007).

62 See Bonfiglio's book cited above.

63 See Christopher Woods, "Bilingualism, Scribal Learning, and the Death of Sumerian," in *Margins of Writing, Origins of Cultures*, ed. Seth L. Sanders, OIS 2 (Chicago: Oriental Institute of the University of Chicago, 2006), 91–120.

64 The legalization of Christianity and then promotion of Christianity perhaps politically encouraged sustained thought along these lines, though there is, perhaps, a difference in degree and not kind with earlier Christian thinkers before Constantine, who also reflected on language.

on the spread of nations already present prior to Genesis 11 in the Table of Nations in Genesis 10.[65]

Augustine then explored the relationship between the seventy-two nations themselves and distinct languages, but through a scheme of historical evolution in which the multiplication of nations outpaced the multiplication of languages.[66] He hypothesized that "the number of nations increased much stronger than the number of languages; for in Africa, too, we have heard of very many barbarous nations/tribes which have only one language among them." Historical experiences during Augustine's own days demonstrated that while an intricate connection existed between language and nation, there was not a simple relationship of one language to one nation and vice versa. Here, contemporary observation of language and nationhood functioned as vital frameworks through which historical claims were made. Augustine was aware that in Africa, many people of many nations spoke a "barbaric" language. Scholars have argued that this "barbaric" language that dominated much of Africa was not Punic, which Augustine never labelled as "barbaric," but rather a Libyan language, perhaps "paleo-Berber."[67] From his perspective, the fact

---

65 For more on Augustine's *recapitulo* as a reading and interpretive strategy, see Denecker, *Ideas on Language in Early Latin Christianity*, 99–101. The discussion regarding the number of languages in the post-Babel world was a long-standing issue prior to Augustine. For example, Filastrius believed there to have been seventy-five languages, though he does not make his calculations clear. Clement of Alexandria also posited seventy-five languages resulting from the dispersion and confusion at Babel. Pacian did not connect the number of languages at the advent of multilingualism to the narrative in Genesis 11:1–9 explicitly, but nonetheless claimed that God "has arranged His language resources into 120 tongues." Jerome provided an upper limit for these discussions, when he claimed that 72,000 languages emerged from Babel, connecting his interpretation to Deuteronomy 32:8, in which the number of angels (an exceedingly high number) and the number of nations are correlated. For Jerome, the connection to seventy-two may have been significant as it became the standard, putatively biblical, count, more than the degree to which seventy-two was magnified. For these examples, see Denecker, *Ideas on Language in Early Latin Christianity*, 108–110.

66 Augustine modified the initial suggestion of seventy-three languages to seventy-two, noting that Heber and Peleg were part of the same nation and unit, and should, therefore, be counted as one (Denecker, *Ideas on Language in Early Christianity*, 111).

67 Denecker, *Ideas on Language in Early Latin Christianity*, 112; Claude Lepelley, "Témeoignages de saint Augustin sur l'ampleur et les limites de l'usage de la langue punique dans l'Afrique de son temps. Briand-Ponsart," in *Indentités et culture dans l'Algérie antique* (Rouen: Publications des Universités de Rouen et du Havre, 2005), 128–129.

that so many African peoples from different nations would speak the same language meant that nations must have multiplied at a much faster pace than language.[68] The point for the purposes of the argument here, however, is that Augustine's analysis of language and nationhood, and the manner in which he related those concepts to Genesis 10–11 as the historical, religious, and intellectual map for charting the political devolution of humanity, was distinct from the early modern discussions of the same issues of language, nationhood, and the Tower of Babel. Even for such a politically influential figure as Augustine,[69] the solution to multilingualism was not political reverse engineering or the selection of a language as the chosen primordial dialect to which all members of a polity must adhere (though he certainly claimed, like most—though not all—intellectuals of his time, that Hebrew was this primordial language). The uses of the Tower of Babel and the claims its interpreters made to support the efforts of the nation-state in conducting such reverse engineering, then, are quite far removed from Augustine and other ancient interpreters.

In fact, despite the connection between nation and language, and despite the lamentable situation that Augustine identifies in the post-Babel multilingualism, even more lamentable for him are the (seemingly necessary from Augustine's vantage point) measures that authorities need to take in order to keep multilingualism in check for the sake of political order and communication. So, for example, Augustine writes with regard to the dominance of Latin in the Roman Empire and its benefits that

> It is true that the Imperial City has imposed on subject nations not only her yoke but also her language, as a bond of peace and society, so that there should be no lack of interpreters but a great abundance of them. But how many great wars, what slaughter of men, what outpourings of human blood have been necessary to bring this about![70]

For Augustine, the political measures are lamentable. Although they offer peace and stability to society, he in no way pretends that such measures offer

---

68   Denecker, *Ideas on Langauge in Early Latin Christianity*, 111.

69   Augustine was influential in the Latin West, though, for a variety of reasons (not least of which was Augustine's lack of knowledge of Greek), he was not considered influential (and, in many ways, was reviled) in the Byzantine East. See Brown, who states that "some leading figures of the Christian Greek world barely noticed him" (*Augustine of Hippo*, 464).

70   Denecker, *Ideas on Language in Early Latin Christianity*, 134.

a solution to the curse of Babel. Indeed, the quote indicates more, not fewer, interpreters with the spread of the imperial language because he never imagined that the political advantages of such measures would be at the expense of local dialects. Instead, for Augustine, multilingualism was a badge that demonstrated not a problem for the nation-state to overcome but rather the power of the unity wrought through the Holy Spirit and the Gospel.[71] For him, as for other intellectuals in Late Antiquity, multilingualism might have been a sign of a wound, but the events of Pentecost transformed that wound into a multicolored robe of sorts that displayed the transcendent scope of Christianity across national and linguistic lines.[72] Whatever disadvantages were inherent in multilingualism, and whatever the perception of the Tower of Babel as the cause of this lamentable situation, the cure for the "wound" of multilingualism for Augustine and the thinkers following him in Late Antiquity and in the Middle Ages was not a politically engineered counteracting through linking Genesis 11:1–9, nationhood, and language. Rather, the solution was the Pentecost, in which language distinctions were not obliterated but, instead, were affirmed through a spiritual unity in the Christian belief in the Holy Spirit.[73]

Augustine's reflections on the relationship between language, nation, and the events in Genesis 10–11 became, in many ways, the authoritative foundation for examining these issues in the centuries to come. Scholars in the wake of Augustine betray clear indications of indebtedness to his thought. Augustine's student Quodvultdeus claimed that "the languages . . . now dispersed over the earth created separate nations, each [nation] with its own language."[74] Claudius Marius Victorius likewise noted the connection, claiming that the tower builders congregated together since language and national allegiance consolidates in accordance to likeness: "everyone accommodates to whom he understands, and joins that person to himself; the overall affinity perishes, and language defines nation; they are dispersed in equal groups and hasten to lands that are scattered over various regions."[75] He employed an analogy from the world of birds, that color and voice, much

---

71 Denecker, *Ideas on Language in Early Latin Christianity*, 139.
72 Denecker, *Ideas on Language in Early Latin Christianity*, 139–142.
73 See also Jerome's appraisal of linguistic diversity along these lines (Denecker, *Ideas on Language in Early Latin Christianity*, 138–139).
74 Denecker, *Ideas on Language in Early Latin Christianity*, 112.
75 Denecker, *Ideas on Language in Early Latin Christianity*, 113.

like appearance and language, attract birds to one another in their grouping as also in nations.[76]

As in so many respects with Augustine's views, Isidore of Seville provided a summary and consolidation of Augustine's thoughts on language. He affirmed Augustine's number of nations arising from the post-Babel situation: "the elderly men [from Num. 11], over whom the Holy Spirit came, symbolize the seventy-two languages over the nations spread over this world, from which many believers have received the grace of the Holy Spirit."[77] Isidore also reflected on the relationship between language and nation in a similar fashion as Augustine: "We have treated languages first, and then nations, because nations arose from languages, and not languages from nations."[78] Isidore gives priority to language over nations, though "languages and 'nations' cannot exist without each other, or cannot be defined without reference to each other. . . . Only as a consequence of this linguistic diversification (into seventy-two languages, that is), people started clustering with those who happened to speak the same language as they did, and thus formed 'nations.'"[79] While the interrelatedness is apparent in Isidore, he nonetheless ascribes to language the formative matrix for nation-building. Regarding the initial situation after God's judgment at Babel, Isidore says that "at the outset there were as many languages as there were nations, and then more nations than languages, because many nations sprang from one language."[80]

There is a sense in these foregoing comments that language forges nationhood, and not vice versa. This thesis is an inversion of Max Weinreich's

---

76   See also Avitus of Vienne, who claimed that "everyone joins himself to the words he is able to understand, and every nation follows the new languages" (Denecker, *Ideas on Language in Early Latin Christianity*, 113).

77   Denecker, *Ideas on Language in Early Latin Christianity*, 114.

78   Denecker, *Ideas on Language in Early Latin Christianity*, 115.

79   Denecker, *Ideas on Language in Early Latin Christianity*, 116.

80   Other ancient, non-Christian Greek thinkers debated whether language came first and then society, laws, and political action, or vice versa. See Gera, *Ancient Greek Ideas on Speech, Language, and Civilization*, 10, 127–147. For Christian thinkers, the Bible controlled the chronology of how interpreters viewed the relationship. Adam gave the animals names, and Eve spoke as well in Eden prior to any other events, and the cultural and urban developments in the genealogy in Genesis 4 came later. Moreover, given that Babel was the precipitating event for the spreading of nations, nation-building could follow the advent of multilingualism or be coterminous in the very moment of the advent of multilingualism, but it could not precede multilingualism.

sentiment that a language is nothing but a dialect with an army or navy.[81] Weinreich here implies that the nation, bestowed with arms and a sense of attachment to dialect, controls the definition, if not the very creation and construction, of a language. The distinction between Quodvultdeus, Victorius, and Isidore, on the one hand, and Weinreich, on the other, is real and symptomatic of the distinction in the use of the Tower of Babel between antiquity and modern politics. For the latter, the nation-state is primary and shapes all else, including its relationship to language. The distinction thus marks a political context in which the nation can engineer a language policy with Genesis 10–11 as its manual and map for pressing "reverse."[82] In this sense, this line of interpretation represents an innovation and *novum*, and not the Bible as always read and applied in society. The contrast demonstrates a point that will become clearer later. Indeed, the manner in which modern politicians employ this passage represents a particular modern concern and is far removed from not only the ancient context of the passage's production but also its application until the modern era.[83]

---

81 Dani Byrd and Toben H. Mintz claim that Weinreich popularized, but did not invent, this maxim (*Discovering Speech, Words, and Mind* [Malden, MA: Wiley-Blackwell, 2010], 72).

82 For Augustine, the empire can use language to unify (to a certain degree) its subjects, but this is not the same claim as found in modern sources.

83 This is not to argue that, in general, all modern thinkers viewed the creation of language as a simple byproduct of (and as a step subsequent to) political action and identity. Philip Pettit has argued that Hobbes claimed that the invention of language made incorporation possible, giving in some sense primacy of language itself as a technological invention allowing for politics (*Made with Words: Hobbes on Language, Mind, and Politics* [Princeton, NJ: Princeton University Press, 2009], 115–140). I claim above that while ancient and modern thinkers both ascribe to language the framework from which political incorporation arises, each offers drastically distinct solutions to the perceived problems of multilingualism, the distinction attributable to the project of the modern nation-state. See Tuska Benes's comments that "for Herder, language and a shared cultural legacy organically gave birth to a nation" (*In Babel's Shadow: Language, Philology, and the Nation in Nineteenth Century Germany*, Kritik [Detroit, MI: Wayne State University Press], 40). Indeed, language had a shaping function to the cultural legacy of a people, which became the bedrock of nationhood. For Herder, linguistic diversity was bound up in the idea that each nation had a language that was a receptacle of its own culture and history, but such ideas also gave a one-to-one framework of a language and a nation that made it difficult to theorize how multilingualism and diversity could exist within the same nationalistic project (Benes, *In Babel's Shadow*, 44–45; see the comments on dialect and language in Schmeller and Grimm, Benes, *In Babel's Shadow*, 128–137).

By contrast, while multilingualism was for the most part thought of as lamentable and a sign of curse in antiquity, the cure was not identified in the workings of governments and political identity.[84] Rather, the solution for these Christian thinkers appears in an eschatological event in the transcendence of the Gospel and the diversity of the early Christian movement. In fact, multilingualism could be thought of as a badge as sorts, a sign of honor that the message could transcend such diversity. In this manner, a Joseph-like logic makes itself apparent: what humans have wrought through their own hubris (multilingualism as a divine curse), God has woven into a tapestry of blessing through the salvific acts of Jesus and the Spirit.[85] This blessing became manifest in the post-Pentecost period as the Jesus movement spread throughout the world without obliterating the linguistic distinctions of the nations now engrafted into the divine covenant (to use Paul's phasing in Romans 9–11).

What never appears before the modern nation-state, however, is a suggestion that the nation that took its identity in a dialect should engineer a political solution of language purity, in which the nation crafted its language as either the proto/pristine language or chosen language as the basis upon which all members of the polity are measured. In other words, the pre-modern period does not contain a trace of the nationalistic drive to reverse-engineer Babel. While a variety of languages served official usages, whether Akkadian, Aramaic, Greek, Latin, or Arabic, none of them functioned in the political imagination as a standard against which others were legislated as a matter of political purity using Babel as an authoritative narrative. If Herodotus

---

84   There are at least three occasions, however, in which Augustine identifies multilingualism as a positive for society. See also below. In the first, Augustine notes the positive effects of multilingualism in an early writing, which may borrow more from non-Christian ("pagan") sources than his later works. Such pagan sources viewed multilingualism as a good trait in society. The second also relates to this pagan context. Augustine gave a sermon, likely to a majority non-Christian audience, in which he again extols the benefits of multilingualism in society. On the third occasion, Augustine praises multilingualism when he discusses the advantages of knowing many languages for biblical interpretation. The latter use of multilingualism could itself be seen as a positive only in light of a prevailing negative situation, namely the abiding curse of Babel, which Augustine focuses on so much elsewhere. Denecker, *Ideas on Language in Early Latin Christianity*, 145–147. See also the positive understandings of multilingualism for government and negotiations in early Christianity, Denecker, *Ideas on Language in Early Latin Christianity*, 185.

85   Denecker, *Ideas on Language in Early Latin Christianity*, 139–142.

discussed the mixed forms of language of the Scythians, or if Nehemiah 13 contains a decidedly negative evaluation of mixed languages, it is not because their own dialect was somehow conceived as a basis for persecuting or legislating against speakers of other languages.[86] Specifically in the realm of the use of the Bible in the political sphere, the story in Genesis 11:1–9 does not function until the modern nation-state as a narrative containing a curse to be overcome through political means of language policy. For Augustine and other ancient interpreters, passages like Acts 2 and Pentecost demonstrated that the Gospel cut through multilingualism, but no language policy in the political realm, no matter how lamentable language diversity might be, was proposed.

Juxtaposing the uses to which the story has been put with the historical-critical and reception history analyses of the passage, political claims utilizing the Tower of Babel to construct a nationalist ideology based around language make at least two historical mistakes. The narrative is not about language. Additionally, even when understood as being about language, the use of the passage politically to justify the promotion of a language to reverse the curse of Babel is exclusively a modernist project. As argued above, the convergence of language, nation, and the biblical text generally in the sixteenth century appears to be an innovation of modernity.[87] Interest in the Tower of Babel specifically thrived in this century. The issue examined here is when the Tower of Babel functioned to justify the state, nationalism, language ideology, and imperial expansion in the context of the political uses and abuses of the Bible generally. The sixteenth century CE appears to be a launching pad for this form of interpretation and provides an intellectual context in which America emerged and highlighted this discourse in the eighteenth century. In this fashion, this political use of the Tower of Babel in which the nation could engineer a language policy based on this passage is a *novum* and

---

86 Gera notes that discussions of language in the golden age of Kronos in Greek sources never identify the language spoken as Greek, though, as she observes, this absence may itself indicate an assumption that such a language was assumed to be Greek without having to specify (*Ancient Greek Ideas on Speech, Language, and Civilization*, 21). If the rhetoric of Nehemiah 13 might suggest legislation against non-Hebrew speakers, the reality, as evidenced at Elephantine with Aramaic manuscripts, in Nehemiah 8:8, and in the Aramaic letters in Ezra, was surely more complicated.

87 The increasing numbers of artistic renderings of the Tower of Babel beginning in the sixteenth century confirms the importance of this narrative during this period of nation-building. See the Liverani citation above.

innovation of modernity, and this use speaks to specifically modern political and economic sensibilities.

BABYLON AS A THEO-POLITICAL CATEGORY

Yet, despite the use of the Tower of Babel to support nationalism through language, even Babylon generally and the Tower of Babel specifically have a complex, nonlinear use in political discourse. The historical survey above supports this nonlinearity, particularly in the writings of Augustine. On at least three occasions, he refers to multilingualism positively. Generally speaking, multilingualism could be argued to be a badge of the transcendent growth of Christianity.[88]

This aspect of the many uses of Babylon in literature, film, and politics has been examined, highlighting the staying power of Babylon in a variety of media.[89] The power of the Tower of Babel, understood as an etiology for the dangers and condemnation apparent in multilingualism, cast its long shadow not only in early modernity to the twentieth century but Babylon generally and its tower specifically continue to haunt US political discourse. As has been commonly observed, appeal to biblical authority has a particular persuasiveness and power in American culture. In times of national stress and fears stemming from globalization, citing passages from the Bible to shore up identity ("us") relative to others ("them") is a way not only to promote nationalism and national identity but also to do so while simultaneously engaging in globalized markets (thereby encouraging transnational movements) and yet holding those same global cultural interactions in suspicion. This dynamic relationship between globalization and nationalism has a particularly strong backing in light of the biblical picture of Babylon, which is both an object of scorn (most often) and an object of fascination and care (less often).[90] Indeed, the Tower of Babel episode, sitting as it does between the universal Primeval

---

88   See note above.

89   Runions, *The Babylon Complex*. Her use of the Bible for critical theory ("Critical Biblical Studies") applied to history, politics, and culture was recently the focus of an entire issue of *The Bible & Critical Theory*, each contributor taking a part of Runions's approach and applying it to a topic in media or politics. None of the contributions addressed the Tower of Babel.

90   See especially Runions's reading of Babylon in Jeremiah (*The Babylon Complex*, 14–15).

History in Genesis 1–11 and the beginnings of the story of the nation of Israel in Genesis 12, has been a particularly important passage for those who think about, and legislate how, nations and globalism interact.

As such, Babylon and the Tower of Babel have functioned as theo-political categories. In particular, the traditional view of the narrative as concerning the origins of multilingualism as a divine curse functions as a political category to achieve political ends, especially in the wake of globalism and population movements, leading to increased immigration in many countries. Babylon and its tower stand for a host of images that, in turn, political power brokers employ or suppress in order to enact their respective political visions (be it by conservatives or neoliberals, equally bound by market-driven forces).[91] Nationalist fears that multilingualism in America is diagnostic of (if not the root cause for) the downfall of the nation have resulted in the use of the Tower of Babel to express these phobias. This sort of analysis is more relevant than ever given the use of the passage in the political sphere.

Yet this political leveraging of the Bible fails to account for the composition and reception of the Tower of Babel in two key ways. In the time in which it was composed, Genesis 11:1–9 was not a story concerning the advent of multilingualism generally, much less a curse attached to social polyglossia. In addition, this sort of political and national manufacturing of identity founded on attachment to a language is a particularly novel and innovative use of the Tower of Babel.[92] Regarding the first point, one might argue that the traditional religious understanding and interpretation handed down over time that informs theo-political action is more important and authoritative than historical-critical concerns. This argument fails on two counts. The semantics of the passage in Genesis 11:1–9, what the words themselves mean, even as a passage translated on its own terms, do not necessitate an interpretation of the story about language, which leads to the question that the tradition might be incorrect, even in the final form of the Hebrew Bible. As another consideration, a commitment to the traditional interpretation of the passage as a chain of authority upon which one forms theo-political commitments means that the second point above regarding the history of interpretation of the passage should prevent the political employment of the Tower of Babel story for nationalistic ends. The perception of language, nation, and Genesis

---

91 Runions, *The Babylon Complex*, 2.
92 For Noah Webster's attempt to trace American English to the pre-Babel period with the sons of Noah, see Bonfiglio, *Race and the Rise of Standard American*, 84–85.

11:1–9 as relevant for the creation of political policy, particularly as it relates to immigration, is an innovation of modernity and not how the passage was always understood.

THE FEAR OF BABEL IN THE WAKE OF 2001

Nonetheless, the use of the Tower of Babel as a political category in light of issues of diversity, immigration, and language policy has had particular power in the wake of September 11, 2001. If Babylon generally has proven to be a remarkably elastic, if not convenient, category for political, economic, and religious thought, then the Tower of Babel particularly functions similarly. This function entails the twofold scheme elaborated above, in which the tower is both a mirror and lens. Particularly in the wake of September 11, 2001, America experienced a tragedy that awakened it to the Middle East in a manner that sparked both curiosity and fear. While the Gulf War of 1990 perhaps placed Iraq on the mental, political, and religious map of American consciousness, the successes of this conflict served as reassurance of American dominance globally (defined in particularly American-centric terms). The events of September 11, however, meant that such conflicts were no longer exclusively "over there," but could also land "here" as well.

Other scholars have shown perceptively the manner in which September 11 reframed popular and political imaginings of religion and threats to identity.[93] For example, the rise of zombie movies since September 11 is a monster-making strategy of dealing with fears of Muslim communities and immigration, in much the same way that Bram Stoker's Dracula dealt with fear of Jewish communities.[94] Stereotypes of Jews included large noses and the desire to take money and to suck non-Jewish economies dry; the description of Dracula as having a large nose and as a blood-sucking, wealthy vampire played on these fears. These stereotypes were given concrete attachment to their Jewish targets when Bela Lugosi played Dracula while wearing a Star of David.[95] So also zombie movies, which were produced with

---

93   See, for example, Bruce Lincoln, *Holy Terrors: Thinking about Religion after September 11*, 2nd ed. (Chicago: University of Chicago Press, 2006).

94   For zombies, September 11, and the manner in which Muslims have been made into monsters, see Arjana, *Muslims in the Western Imagination* (New York: Oxford University Press, 2014), 165–183 (chapter titled "The Monsters of September 11").

95   Arjana, *Muslims in the Western Imagination*, 122–129.

a noticeable increase after 9/11, played on the image of invasive, almost-human figures (usually browned in color) who mindlessly feed on innocent victims, calling to mind immigrant terrorists from the Middle East killing random people.

The horrendous attacks on the Twin Towers on 9/11 led some cultural and political commentators to employ the Tower of Babel as a critique of the global economic enterprises that the towers represented, offering a mirror to excessive capitalistic values.[96] Yet outlasting these criticisms were the increased awareness and fear by some in America of the Middle East. Any immigration that threatened a perceived identity became a topic of concern. The Latino presence in America that was understood as a benefit of a global economy in the 1990s became part of the larger threat spurred by the terrorist attack, even as the sources of these perceived threats through immigration were from entirely different migrant groups.[97] In each case, Genesis 11:1–9 served as a category of alarm when national identity was threatened. As such, the Tower of Babel has become a particularly effective lens through which to construct and identify "others."

BABEL'S TOWER AND RESURGENT NATIONALISM AFTER 2016

As the first political narrative of group action in the Bible, and one in which unity was lost by divine curse resulting in (at least in the traditional interpretation) multilingualism and diversity, the Tower of Babel has become increasingly popular in nationalist, political rhetoric, particularly as language has become a badge for national identity and concerted action. On May 14, 2018, the Southern Poverty Law Center reported that a group called ProEnglish visited the Trump White House on January 23, 2018, to discuss

---

96 See the analysis in Tim Gauthier, *9/11 Fiction, Empathy, and Otherness* (New York: Lexington Books, 2015), 112.

97 Observe, for example, the rhetoric that the migrant caravans coming from Latin American countries also had in their midst terrorists from the Middle East who want to attack the United States. The pastor Carl Gallups, a frequent speaker at Trump rallies in 2016, declared these caravans to be a sign of divine judgment against the United States, invoking the story of the Tower of Babel as evidence that such globalism and diversity is not "biblical." See his comments in https://www.patheos.com/blogs/dispatches/2018/11/29/gallups-refugee-caravan-is-gods-judgment-on-america/.

initiatives for making English the national language of the United States.[98] ProEnglish has existed as a group since 1994, but has recently made its political activity more public and aggressive. They introduced legislation in 2017 to the House of Representatives, sponsored by Steve King from Iowa, titled the English Language Unity Act.[99] They operate at the state level in thirty-two states, and the executive director Stephen Guschov said in an interview with Breitbart news that "we don't want to see America become a new Tower of Babel."[100]

These fears of immigration and outsiders threatening national identity have played out not only in the arena of special interest groups like ProEnglish but even in the platform of the Republican presidential nominee Pat Buchanan, a former speechwriter for Ronald Reagan.[101] In 2012 Buchanan criticized then President Obama for many of his policies, frequently invoking the Tower of Babel to cast a negative tone on immigration without linguistic

---

98   https://www.splcenter.org/hatewatch/2018/01/26/anti-immigrant-hate-group-proenglish-visits-white-house.

99   https://www.congress.gov/bill/115th-congress/house-bill/997.

100   https://proenglish.org/2018/12/12/breitbart-news-features-proenglish-on-siriusxm-patriot/.

101   Academia has also been prone to creating schemes of "domestications" of immigrant languages on American English as a way to promote nationalism. No less a figure than Einar Haugen, an early theorist of language contact, stated in the beginning of his *Ecology of Language*:

> America's profusion of tongues has made her a modern Babel, but a Babel in reverse. City and countryside have teemed with all accents of Europe and the rest of the world, yet America has never swerved from the Anglo-Saxon course set by her founding fathers. In the course of a century and a half the United States has absorbed her millions and taught them her language more perfectly than Rome taught the Gauls and the Iberians in centuries of dominion. Oriental and African, Spaniard and Frenchman, Jew and Gentile have all been domesticated, and this without leaving any serious impression on American English.

See *Ecology of Language*, Language Science and National Development (Stanford: Stanford University Press, 1972), 1. For an analysis of this quote, see Bonfiglio, *Race and the Rise of Standard American*, 138–139. One could also note Thomas Bailey Aldrich's 1892 poem published in the *Atlantic Monthly*, expressing fears of immigration and using the Tower of Babel to stoke such fears: "Wide open and unguarded stand our gates, / And through them presses a wild motley throng / . . . / Flying the Old World's poverty and scorn; / These bringing with them unknown gods and rites, / Those, tiger passions, here to stretch their claws. / In street and alley what strange tongues are these, / Accents of menace alien to our air, / Voices that once the Tower of Babel knew! O Liberty, white Goddess! is it well / To leave the gates unguarded?"

assimilation to English.[102] This immigration agenda has long been an issue for Buchanan, in which he frequently proposed actions that connect national identity and political cohesion. His agenda, however, was not mere reform but rather the implementation of a language policy by appealing to polyglossia in America as a sign of divine displeasure.[103] The Tower of Babel, as an etiology for the multiplication of languages and political divisiveness, functioned as proof that such multilingualism was evidence of God's curse and reflected the doomed state of America if action was not taken. While Buchanan's own presidential nominations in 1996 and in 2000 did not succeed (and were short-lived generally), he stumped for the eventual nominee Donald Trump, continuing his appeal to the Tower of Babel in exclaiming that Trump would end the Bush presidents' policies of more relaxed immigration.[104] Indeed, in discussing this reversal, he frequently invoked the Tower of Babel on his website as a biblical warning against multilingualism and diversity in a nation.[105]

As a recent analysis on the website Politico has argued, and as Buchanan himself has maintained, he lost the primaries, but the election of Trump in 2016 meant that his ideas, in effect, won.[106] Trump's platform issues represented a reboot of Buchanan's own positions twenty years prior. The former supports a preference given to English as a national language, as Buchanan has repeatedly argued and pushed for in legislation.[107] Buchanan continues to have a foothold in the Trump administration, as when Buchanan wrote a letter titled "Declare an Emergency" in order to urge the president to make such a declaration to get the funding to build a wall, the purpose of which is putatively to stem the

---

102   See, for example, the uses of the Tower of Babel with respect to immigration, language, and diversity in his book *State of Emergency: The Third World Invasion and Conquest of America* (New York: St. Martin's Griffin, 2006), 13, 162, and 246.

103   See his 2012 interview with Charlie Rose, transcript here: https://www.realclearpolitics.com/video/2012/02/21/pat_buchanan_we_are_becoming_a_tower_of_babel.html.

104   https://buchanan.org/blog/buchanan-trumps-rise-is-rejection-of-quarter-century-of-bush-republicanism-124847. The link also cites a 2008 piece in which Buchanan connected Bush-era immigration policies with America's decline into a "Tower of Babel."

105   See the many links: https://buchanan.org/blog/?s=Tower+of+Babel.

106   https://www.politico.com/magazine/story/2017/04/22/pat-buchanan-trump-president-history-profile-215042. See also more recently https://theweek.com/articles/853163/how-pat-buchanan-made-president-trump-possible.

107   https://www.vox.com/2019/1/14/18181897/trump-pat-buchanan-column-tweet.

inflow of illegal immigration.[108] Even when he does not explicitly invoke the Tower of Babel, the episode appears frequently on his website in columns that warn of the downfall of democracy and national identity in America, a downfall that has its root cause in immigration, loss of national unity, and the related promotion of diversity by Democrats.[109] For Buchanan, the Tower of Babel functions as a battle cry. Appeal to it stokes fears that the traditional interpretation of the story calls to mind, in which multilingualism and diversity are emblematic of a divine curse on a nation. Its relevance to American politics goes unquestioned given its presence in the Bible.[110]

Seemingly more innocuous, but playing on the same fears by use of the Tower of Babel, Bobby Jindahl penned a piece for the *Wall Street Journal* in which he connected diversity, promoted by Democrats, and the Tower of Babel.[111] Jindahl does not invoke language as a category for his critique but clearly demonstrates that the society that Democrats would like to create, emphasizing diversity as a self-evident value, would in essence make us another Tower of Babel. The use of the passage is not neutral but rather plays on a link between diversity and the downfall of a nation.

As seen from antiquity to modernity, the Tower of Babel is more than a political metaphor. Rather, for some particularly in the modern era into the twenty-first century, their interpretation acts as a roadmap in which they seek to engineer a particular kind of society through the nation-state. The passage has an inherently political context for its production. This dimension cannot and should not be divorced from its interpretation. Moreover, its placement in the editing of the Pentateuch indicates a possible, though by no means necessary, interpretation as pertaining to language diversity and the spread of nations. On the other hand, the story was not actually about language in its original production, nor is it necessarily interpreted as such, even in the

---

108   https://buchanan.org/blog/memo-to-trump-declare-an-emergency-135677?doing_
      wp_cron=1564588936.9655640125274658203125.

109   See link above where "Tower of Babel" is a search item on his website.

110   Many recent examples of this sort of use of the Bible in the modern American political sphere could be cited, such as Jeff Sessions's argument that Romans 13 invoked the "law" of nations as sovereign (even though Paul uses "authority" with respect to governing authorities and reserves the use of "law," νομος, later for the "law of love"). See Margaret Mitchell's analysis: https://divinity.uchicago.edu/sightings/apostle-and-ag. Scott Pruitt, in dismantling the Environmental Protection Agency's governing board, likewise used a passage from Joshua 24:14–15 as some fashion of biblical justification for his actions.

111   https://www.wsj.com/articles/the-roots-of-political-polarization-1541111248.

compiled Pentateuch. Moreover, the idioms in Genesis 11:1 and 11:6 that have given rise to the understanding of the passage about language were actually idioms pertaining to governance and legitimation (or lack thereof) to unify in political action. The implications of the distinction between the uses of the passage in current political debates and the historical and philological arguments for a new reading of Genesis 11:1–9 have far-reaching consequences.

AMERICA'S GHOST:
Why the Tower of Babel Still Haunts Us

Many other examples from print and online sources could be adduced in which the Tower of Babel functions as a call to political action for language and immigration reform. The instances above suffice to demonstrate the manner in which the story from the Bible, viewed as a narrative about politics and language, has become a rallying cry for nationalism. The history of the passage in America shows how deeply entrenched the story has been in political debates in the United States.

The narrative still fascinates us for a variety of reasons. The first is the obvious legacy of the Bible generally in American identity. The stories therein have been mapped onto the public consciousness through a variety of means. The presence of the Bible as a symbol in American consciousness also makes it ripe for politicians and power brokers in conveying their platform issues, providing motivation to broadcast their message with religious significance that can, simultaneously, achieve a desired goal. The second reason involves the very nature of Genesis 11:1–9. It is an inherently political story, and one that functions in a particular manner within both the J source and the compiled Torah as well. But if the enduring legacy and relevance of the story appears in popular, artistic, and political domains, this persistence also further props up the traditional associations with language and diversity. What these interpretations get wrong in how they have been employed in politics is that they play into the hegemonic and imperialist agendas that the story was crafted to dismantle.

Indeed, a recent announcement from the Creation Museum in Kentucky lies at this very convergence of the centrality of the Bible in American culture and abiding social and political issues.[112] In addition to other offerings,

---

112   https://www.christianitytoday.com/news/2021/july/tower-of-babel-ark-encounter-ky-ken-ham-answers-genesis.html.

perhaps most famously their life-sized model of Noah's ark, this museum is hoping to open within a few years a replica of the Tower of Babel (though how close it will reach to the heavens has yet to be disclosed). The museum itself is famous for its devotion to a particular understanding of the Bible and defending its literal interpretation. The founder, Ken Ham, writes for a website called "Answers in Genesis," advertising the apologetic nature of his approach.[113] Alongside the clear devotion to the Bible in attempting to prove that the Tower of Babel story happened in history, the museum has also advertised a political concern as a motivation for this attraction: to "tackle racism issues, showing how all people groups have developed from one biological race."[114] Yet in attempting to solve a real political issue of inequality, the museum plays into the hands of the very mechanisms that give rise to racism, namely the theory that there is a biological basis to the concept of race. As many studies have pointed out, "the concept of race has no genetic or scientific basis."[115] Attempting to leverage a biblical passage like Genesis 11:1–9 for the purposes of racial history on the basis of a biological explanation of a story about the origins of nations and languages, no matter how laudable their motivations, situates the museum's attraction in a long history of politics, religion, language, and race. At the same time, this example underscores how real, powerful, and potentially dangerous readings of the Tower of Babel can be for addressing issues in society through devotion, if not misplaced obsession, with a particular reading of the Bible.

FOMENTING DISCONTENT:
The Tower of Babel, Political Reimaginings, and New Possibilities with New Interpretations

Even ever-present images and common conceptions that Genesis 11:1–9 brings to mind can, on a careful reading of the passage, be more complicated than assumed. For example, despite the common label (used also in this book) of

---

113 https://answersingenesis.org/tower-of-babel/what-did-the-tower-look-like/.

114 https://www.patheos.com/blogs/thefreethinker/2021/07/ken-ham-plans-to-add-a-tower-of-babel-to-his-ark-encounter/.

115 For more on the science as well the political uses of "whiteness" with reference to Rome, as well as this quote above from Craig Venter (one of the leading scientists involved in sequencing the human genome), see https://aeon.co/essays/colonialism-is-built-on-the-rubble-of-a-false-idea-of-ancient-rome.

"The Tower of Babel," the presence of the tower as the main focus of the passage is as much a function of an association between Babylon and ziggurats, an aspect that is both a part of the biblical text but also further connected in extrabiblical descriptions such as Herodotus's account of E-temen-anki. Yet the city has as much, if not more, of a focus in the narrative than the tower. If such a dual focus on tower and city led some scholars to propose that two originally distinct oral tales have been interwoven into the same text, when viewed as part of a uniform composition, a striking detail emerges: the tower is mentioned twice, while the city appears three times. Such a numerical distinction may not at first appear significant, yet the tower is a feature that appears only prior to God's judgment. When the narrator says that the people leave off building, the focus is on the city, not the tower, which is not mentioned at all after the descent for divine judgment.

The issue is that we have not made the most sense of the passage as we could, and part of the obstacle is when accepted meanings and uses of a narrative prevent us from seeing it anew. The focus on the city in Genesis 11:1–9, when viewed through the lens of events in eighth-century BCE Mesopotamia, is a vital aspect for understanding the divine concern. Given the long shadow that Assyria cast on the Levant since Tiglath-Pileser III inaugurated renewed attempts to control the western territories in 744 BCE, and given the Assyrian push to consolidate and maintain this control through the seventh century BCE, Genesis 11:1–9 makes sense as a counter-text to imperial claims. In this fashion, the reading proposed in this book (based on historical, linguistic, philological, and source-critical analyses) is of a piece with interpretations proposed for another biblical source, E, and its legal collection.[116]

Reimagining Genesis 11:1–9 in this fashion then underscores how incompatible the meaning derived from the passage is from certain uses of the narrative in the traditional interpretation in modern politics. The clearly stated objectives of political power brokers in invoking Babel often involve the desire to maintain national unity for the sake of politically concerted action to the point of assimilating, dominating, and colonizing

---

116 See David Wright, *Inventing God's Law: How the Covenant Code of the Bible Used and Revised the Laws of Hammurabi* (New York: Oxford University Press, 2009), 350–351. For the features of the Covenant Code identified in Wright's 2009 book as part of the E source, see Wright, "The Covenant Code Appendix (Exodus 23:20–33), Neo-Assyrian Sources, and Implications for Pentateuchal Study," in *The Formation of the Pentateuch: Bridging the Academic Cultures of Europe, Israel, and North America*, eds. Jan C. Gertz et al., FAT 111 (Tübingen: Mohr Siebeck, 2016), 47–86.

others in the name of nationalism. Yet the exact opposite political point was the impetus behind the composition of Genesis 11:1–9. When Genesis 11:1–9 is viewed as a critique of imperial claims to unify and govern beyond its divine right (and, in essence, overstepping its authority into the divine realm), the use of this passage to defend and prop up American power fails to be a legitimate use of the passage based on any connection to its historical context of production. No matter how much politicians might claim to speak and act on behalf of God's interests, in light of its composition in the eighth century BCE, Genesis 11:1–9 exists as an abiding critique of overextended claims to authority in human governance. Any such use of the Tower of Babel for the sake of constructing linguistic purity in the service of the nation-state is a reading that is only possible after the sixteenth century CE. In other words, such interpretations are a modern construct, and cannot be said to be historic or biblical in the sense that either word is typically meant.

How could a new interpretation, one attuned to historical contexts of production, critical theories of the growth of the text, and examinations of the semantics of the words therein, function in modern political discourse? On the one hand, this sort of prescriptive vision for the use of the Bible in the public sphere is not part of the historical-critical investigation of biblical texts.[117] On the other hand, in arguing that the interpretation proposed in this book is incompatible with (and undermines) the use of the passage in much modern political discourse, I hope to pave the way for more responsible and historically sensitive uses of the Bible in public domain for those who continue to seek significance and meaning in it. Just as it is not sufficient to argue what Genesis 11:1–9 does not mean but rather one should put forward a better, more satisfactory meaning, so it is not sufficient to make an argument for how the passage should not be used in political and public discourse without also opening the way for more accurate, constructive, and responsible appeals to the Bible to build a more equitable society.

---

117   See, for example, John Barton's use of E. D. Hirsch's categories of "meaning" versus "significance" (also discussed in chapter 2). Biblical criticism, for Barton, has traditionally been about meaning; in other words, the historical and contextual sense of a passage in its composition and not how significant it has been in religious or other communities in the history of interpretation. See Barton, *The Nature of Biblical Criticism*, 86–87.

(ALMOST) CONCLUDING THOUGHTS:

On the Uses and Abuses of the Bible in the Public Sphere,
or Dismantling the Tower Brick by Brick by Refining
the Solution to the Problem of Babel

This book contains evidence for (and the implications of) the thesis that the Tower of Babel is not about language. This thesis entails a reconfigured hypothesis of what it is about, and this hypothesis helps us to see how all the issues in Babel are resolved, in some manner, in Abram's call. In particular, a new interpretation of Genesis 11:1–9 explains why Abram's election appears to be arbitrary and random, a feature of the biblical text that greatly exercised the imaginations of Jewish and Islamic exegetes. Abram naturally needs to live up to the calling, and the story does not end.[118] Nonetheless, the first passage (Babel) pivots to the second (Abram) as from problem to solution. Historical-critical examinations provided the underpinnings for determining what the narrative in Genesis 11:1–9 is about, and for how this narrative functioned in relation to the call of Abram in both the Hebrew Bible and in reception history. Ancient interpreters related Abram's call to Babel, and when Abram's call did not include the language aspect (as it does in *Jubilees*), then the resolution to the problem of language and multilingualism in Babel was projected into a future time.

The political and intellectual history through modernity also demonstrates how the interpretation of Babel as the advent of multilingualism through divine curse means that, given perceptions of multilingualism as a problem for the nation-state, Babel still represents a problem to be overcome for many. Yet, as argued in this book, all of the issues presented at Babel, as a crescendo of divine-human boundary-crossing, find their resolve in the call of Abram. Not only is the story not about the advent of multilingualism (certainly in its pre-canonical context and, one could argue, also in the canonical setting) but the main thrust of the idioms in Genesis 11:1, 6, and 7 concerns where authority lies and the situatedness of proper governance. This understanding of these verses, along with the long-observed themes of hubris and transgressing into the divine sphere in Genesis 11:1–9, mean that the main problems presented in this story find their resolution in Abram's call. Language is not a feature of Abram's call in Genesis 12 because it was not a feature of the problem in

---

118   For the various tests that Abraham encounters in the Pentateuchal sources as part of the "promise," see Baden, *Promises of the Patriarchs*, 22, 97, and 122.

Genesis 11:1–9. As such, the interpretive moves in *Jubilees* 12 (reconstructing language as a part of Abram's call) and other ancient sources (plotting a future resolution in which everyone will speak the holy tongue) address prominent issues in one reading of the canonical text, but are not required in order to relate Babel as problem to Abram as solution.

The modern political constructions of multilingualism as a problem and Babel as the map highlighting the originary moment for this problem, then, are misplaced. Such anxieties about the relationship between language and nationhood are not featured in the biblical text, nor does such an understanding correctly assess the problem that Babel presents in the Bible and where the solution lies (Abram's call and not political engineering in the modern nation-state). It is this key insight that helps to put biblical criticism in a corrective, and hopefully constructive, conversation with modern political issues affecting real people in the world.

Epilogue

Much of this book was written during a pivotal time in American history. Many claimed that the end of the Trump administration would hearken a return to an imagined sense of pride about the nation, one that was inclusive, science-based, and founded on the principles of equality and diversity. As many historians pointed out, this "return" was oriented more toward an imagined ideal than a reality for many minorities. What could America return to as a sign of former, better angels if eight years of a Black president encouraged so much white nationalism to surface? The cancer of racism and nativism has always been present, and any hope that Barack Obama's presidency would cause discrimination to yield was quickly tempered in the days, months, and years that followed in Trump's inauguration. Some commentators even saw in Biden's inauguration and new administration the neoliberal specter of a white, male leader at the helm, once again sparking fears about the fate of the country only two weeks after an insurrection. Lurking behind the claim of Biden's record mandate that he garnered the most votes in American history was the fact that second place to that title belonged to Trump in the same election. It was difficult to tell whether Trump's America belonged to the past or the future.

Religious advocates for the latter option gathered in Washington, DC to protest Trump's loss in the 2020 election. Titled the Jericho March, the rally featured a number of religious symbols and rituals derived from the Bible, as the name "Jericho March" might suggest. Some scholars have demonstrated that such biblical engagements were more selective, drawing from a few key elements and passages of the Bible while ignoring many others. Despite claims to peaceful motivation, commentators have shown how the very title and biblical context that it evokes could easily be used to generate motivations for violent action. All one has to do was read between the lines, and perhaps the January 6 insurrection was not such a surprising outcome.

The Tower of Babel was present in the rhetoric of the day of the Jericho March, albeit as a sky-high edifice also found, perhaps not too subtly, between the lines. At one point in the rally, Eric Metaxas, a self-styled Christian intellectual who routinely flaunts his Yale undergraduate degree, and who doggedly has supported Trump and Trump's policies, addressed the crowd. He stirred the faithful with the proclamation "Yeshua ha-Mashiach," Hebrew for "Jesus (is) the Messiah." Clearly Metaxas knows some Hebrew, which made his next statement eye-raising. He stated that "Hallelujah is American for 'Praise the Lord'!"

Undoubtedly Metaxas is aware that *hallelujah* is Hebrew, an awareness signaled in the preceding "Yeshua ha-Mashiach." Yale-educated, he also knows, very likely, that American is not a language but rather a dialect of English. Yet the use of language, politics, nationalism, and religion in this example displays, in some fashion, the shadow of Babel in much modern discourse. In one sentence, Metaxas elevates a dialect to a national language and sanctifies it by making a claim that a lexeme in Biblical Hebrew can now, in his political moment and for his political cause, be "American" and have an inner-language gloss as "Praise the Lord."[1]

Dictionaries will not rewrite entries based on Metaxas's linguistic classification and etymology. But this move underscores the power that language, politics, and religion can have when merged. Even if not explicitly cited, one can see the shadows of Babel cast over much of modern politics. The fusion of these realms of politics, language, and religion that form the foundation of much modern thought and framework for how especially many people in America think of their identities has been a trademark of the use and employments of Genesis 11:1–9. A critical understanding of this passage, an investigation into how it has been interpreted, and insight into what those interpretations reveal about the modern obsession with nation, language, and religion reflected in and refracted through interpretation of this passage seem as important as ever, even with a new administration in the White House.

The tower casts its long shadow even in the economic realm, as the bastion of global capitalism, Amazon has designed its new headquarters in Virginia in a structure that looks strikingly like Pieter Brugel the Elder's depiction of the Tower of Babel. The resemblance has been noted, even if the tensions of economic globalism, transnationalism, and cosmopolitanism, on the one

---

1   See   Rod   Dreher's   coverage,   https://twitter.com/roddreher/status/133779367
3057210370.

hand, and regional and nationalistic thought, on the other, apparent in the traditional applications of the biblical passage and evident in Amazon's marketplace activities, have not.[2] Recent commentary has also highlighted how digital systems of thought, whether Amazon in commerce or social media platforms, have simultaneously created more intelligent systems producing vast amounts of information while also creating a tribalism, leading to confusion and the general dumbing-down of society. As testimony to the malleability of the passage, the Tower of Babel has been evoked as the story in human history that most encapsulates the possibilities and dangers of the current cultural moment.[3]

And the dangers are real. In the annual tradition at an art grounds in Russia called Nikola-Lenivets, a wooden structure is constructed and then burned to the ground. The construction selected for 2022 was the Tower of Babel, which was built and then burned on March 6, less than two weeks after Russia launched its invasion of Ukraine on February 24.[4] The significance of the display, and why the Tower of Babel was chosen for the year, provoked endless commentary, much like the biblical passage itself. One could view the use of the Tower of Babel in light of the political and humanitarian crisis of the conflict in the Ukraine as a reflection of the hubris of attempting to force unity, which would inevitably collapse under the weight of overweening ambition in Putin's invasion. The politics of language of the war also comes to mind, as Ukrainian is closely related to Russian yet distinct enough that many bilingual Ukrainians began to cease using Russian because of the invasion.[5] The creators of the structure explained that their intention was

---

2 https://www.washingtonpost.com/dc-md-va/2021/02/02/amazon-arlingon-head-quarters-helix/.

3 See Jonathan Haidt's piece in https://www.theatlantic.com/magazine/archive/2022/05/social-media-democracy-trust-babel/629369/. Russell Moore wrote a response to Haidt's article in which Moore argued that fragmentation was not the problem of Babel but rather the wrong sorts of unification. The fragmentation, for Moore, was divinely ordained and led to the call of Abram. https://www.christianitytoday.com/ct/2022/april-web-only/russell-moore-tower-babel-evangelical-unity-fragmentation.html.

4 Though, as argued in chapter 3, the tower according to the Bible was a completed structure, the Russians artists purposefully did not complete their rendition of it prior to burning it in an attempt to mimic the common perception that the tower was left incomplete.

5 https://www.washingtonpost.com/world/2022/04/12/ukrainians-abandon-russian-language/.

to call to mind the conflict that emerged from the global world order in the wake of the Covid-19 pandemic.[6] In any case, the passage clearly speaks to the politics of our day, for ill or for good. Hoping to steer the artistic act in the latter direction, the creators highlighted that the burning happened on March 6, a Sunday known as Forgiveness Sunday in Orthodox Christianity. In the wake of the invasion of Ukraine, the artists reinterpreted the use of Babel for the annual ritual as a means to call to mind the dangers of discord, to emphasize the longing for reconciliation, and to promote peace.[7]

Understanding the Tower of Babel, what it has symbolized in the past, and how it continues to speak to the present is, to put it mildly, important. A better grasp on the narrative historically and its reception over time may not provide an immediate salve to the world's problems. But it at least highlights how immensely relevant this story is, and why it offers enduring glimpses into something of human nature. The issues surrounding the interpretation of Genesis 11:1–9, the projection of all that the narrative is thought to entail in politics and economics, and how best to read the passage in light of critical theories will be with us for quite some time. Confronting the possibility, then, that even such a ubiquitous story as this one may still be poorly understood is an opportunity to examine our most entrenched assumptions about how we read and how interpretations of the Bible and the creation of a better world can go hand in hand.

---

6 https://archi.ru/events/19542/maslenica-v-nikola-lenivce.

7 https://www.instagram.com/p/CajkhMpgHRv/?utm_source=ig_embed&ig_rid=8305c69d-8898-42f9-832e-421d71ec1522.

Bibliography

Ackerman, Susan. *When Heroes Love: The Ambiguity of Eros in the Stories of Gilgamesh and David*. New York: Columbia University Press, 2005.

Al-Fouadi, A. H., and T. A. Madhloom. "Bassetki Statue with an Old Akkadian Royal Inscription of Naram-Sin of Agade." *Sumer* 32 (1976): 63–77.

Albenda, P. "Dur-Sharrukin, the Royal City of Sargon II, King of Assyria," *BCSMS* 38 (2003): 5–13.

Albertz, Rainer. "The Recent Discussion of the Formation of the Penateuch/Hexateuch." *HS* 59 (2018): 65–92.

Alexander, Philip S. "Geography and the Bible (Early Jewish)." In *Anchor Bible Dictionary, Volume 2*, edited by D. N. Freedman, 977–988. New York: Doubleday, 1992.

———. "Jerusalem as the *Omphalos* of the World: On the History of a Geographical Concept." *Judaism* 46 (1997): 147–158.

Alter, Robert. *The Art of Biblical Narrative*. 2nd revised and updated edition. New York: Basic Books, 2011.

Amit, Yairah. *Reading Biblical Narratives: Literary Criticism and the Hebrew Bible*. Minneapolis: Fortress Press, 2001.

Anderson, Gary. *Christian Doctrine and the Old Testament: Theology in the Service of Biblical Exegesis*. Grand Rapids, MI: Baker Academic, 2017.

Arjana, Sofia. *Muslims in the Western Imagination*. New York: Oxford University Press, 2014.

Arnold, Bill. "The Holiness Redaction of the Primeval History." *ZAW* 129 (2017): 483–500.

Aster, Shawn Zelig. "Transmission of Neo-Assyrian Claims of Empire to Judah in the Late Eighth Century BCE." *HUCA* 78 (2007): 1–44.

———. *Reflections of Empire in Isaiah 1–39: Responses to Assyrian Ideology*. ANEM 19. Atlanta: SBL Press, 2017.

Aster, Shawn Zelig, and Avaham Faust, ed. *The Southern Levant under Assyrian Domination*. University Park, PA: Eisenbrauns, 2018.

Bach, Johannes. "Royal Literary Identity under the Sargonids and the Epic of Gilgameš." *WO* 50 (2020): 318–338.

Baden, Joel S. *J, E, and the Redaction of the Pentateuch*. FAT 68. Tübingen: Mohr Siebeck, 2009.

———. "The Tower of Babel: A Case Study in the Competing Methods of Historical and Modern Literary Criticism." *JBL* 128 (2009): 209–224.

———. "The Morpho-Syntax of Genesis 12:1–3: Translation and Interpretation." *CBQ* 72 (2010): 223–237.

———. "Deuteronomic Evidence for the Documentary Theory." Pages 327–344 in *The Pentateuch: International Perspectives on Current Research*. Edited by Thomas B. Dozeman, Konrad Schmid, and Baruch J. Schwartz. FAT 78. Tübingen: Mohr Siebeck, 2011.

———. *The Composition of the Pentateuch: Renewing the Documentary Hypothesis*. AYBRL. New Haven, CT: Yale University Press, 2012.

———. *The Promise to the Patriarchs*. New York: Oxford University Press, 2013.

———. *The Historical David: The Real Life of an Invented Hero*. New York: HarperOne, 2013.

———. "'His Tent': Pitched at the Intersection of Orthography and Source Criticism." Pages 283–290 in *"Like ʾIlu Are You Wise": Studies in Northwest Semitic Languages and Literatures in Honor of Dennis G. Pardee*. Edited by Humphrey Hardy, Joseph Lam, and Eric Reymond. Chicago: Oriental Institute Press, 2022.

Baden, Joel S., and Candida Moss. *Reconceiving Infertility: Biblical Perspectives on Procreation and Childlessness*. Princeton, NJ: Princeton University Press, 2015.

Bagg, Ariel M. "Palestine under Assyrian Role: A New Look at the Assyrian Imperial Policy in the West." *JAOS* 133 (2013): 119–144.

———. "Assyria and the West: Syria and the Levant." Pages 268–274 in *A Companion to Assyria*. Edited by Eckart Frahm. Blackwell Companions to the Ancient World. Hoboken, NJ: John Wiley & Sons, 2017.

Bahrani, Zainab. "History in Reverse: Archaeological Illustration and the Reconstruction of Mesopotamia." In *Historiography in the Cuneiform World*, edited by Tzvi Abusch et al., 15–28. Proceedings of the XLVth Recontre Assyriologique Internationale. Bethseda, MD: CDL Press, 2001.

Bakhos, Carol. "A Migrating Motif: Abraham and His Adversaries in *Jubilees* and al-Kisāʾī." *Mizan: Journal for the Study of Muslim Societies and Civilizations* 2 (2017): 1–17.

Bal, Mieke. *On Story-Telling: Essays in Narratology*. Edited by David Jobling. Foundations and Literary Facets. Sonoma, CA: Polebridge Press, 1991.

———. *Narratology: Introduction to the Theory of Narrative*. 4th edition. Toronto: University of Toronto Press, 2017.

Barton, John. *The Nature of Biblical Criticism*. Louisville, KY: Westminster John Knox Press, 2007.

Beaulieu, Paul-Alain. "Nebuchadnezzar's Babylon as World Capital." *Journal for the Canadian Society of Mesopotamian Studies* 3 (2008): 5–12.

———. "Aspects of Aramaic and Babylonian Linguistic Interaction in First Millennium BC Iraq." *Journal of Language Contact* 6 (2013): 358–378.

———. *A History of Babylon, 2200 BC–AD 75*. Chichester, UK: John Wiley & Sons, 2018.

———. "What's in a Name? Babylon and Its Designations throughout History." *Journal for the Canadian Society of Mesopotamian Studies* 17 (2019): 29–37.

Benes, Tuska. *In Babel's Shadow: Language, Philology, and the Nation in Nineteenth Century Germany*. Kritik. Detroit, MI: Wayne State University Press, 2008.

Berlejung, A. "Living in the Land of Shinar: Reflections on Exile in Genesis 11:1–9?" Pages 89–111 in *The Fall of Jerusalem and the Rise of Torah*. Edited by Peter Dubovský, Dominik Markl, and Jean-Pierre Sonnet. FAT 107. Tübingen: Mohr Siebeck, 2016.

Berlin, Adele. *Poetics and Interpretation of Biblical Narrative*. Winona Lake, IN: Eisenbrauns, 1994.

Berlin, Adele, and Marc Brettler. "Psalms." Pages 1265–1435 in *The Jewish Study Bible*. Edited by Adele Berlin and Marc Zvi Brettler. 2nd edition. New York, 2014.

Blenkinsopp, Joseph. *Abraham: The Story of a Life*. Grand Rapids, MI: Eerdmans, 2015.

Bloch, Yigal. *Alphabet Scribes in the Land of Cuneiform: Sēpiru Professionals in Mesopotamia in the Neo-Babylonian and Achaemenid Periods*. Gorgias Studies in the Ancient Near East 11. Piscataway: Gorgias Press, 2018.

Block, Daniel I. "The Role of Language in Ancient Israelite Perceptions of National Identity." *JBL* 103 (1984): 321–340.

Bloom, Harold. *Ruin the Sacred Truths: Poetry and Belief from the Bible to the Present*. Cambridge, MA: Harvard University Press, 1991.

Bohak, Gideon. *Ancient Jewish Magic*. New York: Cambridge University Press, 2011.

Bonfiglio, Thomas Paul. *Mother Tongues and Nations: The Invention of the Native Speaker*. Trends in Linguistics 226. New York: De Gruyter Mouton, 2010.

———. *Race and the Rise of Standard American*. Language, Power, and Social Process 7. New York: Mouton de Gruyter, 2002.

Borger, Rykle. *Beiträge zum Inschriftenwerk Assurbanipals: die Prismenklassen A, B, C = K, D, E, F, G, H, J und T sowie andere Inschriften*. Wiesbaden: Harrassowitz Verlag, 1996.

Borst, Arno. *Der Turmbau von Babel: Geschichte der Meinungen über Ursprung und Vielfalt der Sprachen und Völker.* 4 vols. Stuttgart: A. Hiersemann, 1957–1963.

Boyd, Samuel L. "Exodus 21:35 and the Composition and Date of the Covenant Code." *WO* 48 (2018): 9–23.

———. "Sargon's Dūr-Šarrukīn Cylinder Inscription and Language Ideology: A Reconsideration and Connection to Genesis 11:1–9." *JNES* 78 (2019): 87–111.

———. "Sennacherib's Successor: Titus and Anti-Roman Rhetoric in TgJon to Isa. 10:32." *AS* 17 (2019): 67–86.

———. "Place as Real and Imagined in Exile: Jerusalem at the Center of Ezekiel." Pages 1–27 in *Next Year in Jerusalem: Exile and Return in Jewish History.* Edited by Leonard J. Greenspoon. Studies in Jewish Civilization. West Lafayette, IN: Purdue University Press, 2019.

———. "The Flood and the Problem of Being an Omnivore." *JSOT* 43 (2019): 163–178.

———. "Applied Ritual: The Application of Blood and Oil on Bodies in the Pentateuchal Sources." *BI* 29 (2021): 120–147.

———. *Language Contact, Colonial Administration, and the Construction of Identity in Ancient Israel: Constructing the Context for Contact.* HSM 66. Boston: Brill, 2021.

Braun-Holzinger, Eva. "Darstellungen der Suḫäer und Weiterer Nachbarn der Assyrer im 9. JH. 1. Teil." *Iraq* 80 (2018): 35–62.

Breidbach, Olaf, and Michael T. Ghiselin. "Athanasius Kircher (1602–1680) on Noah's Ark: Baroque 'Intelligent Design' Theory." *Proceedings of the California Academy of Sciences* 57 (2006): 991–1002.

Briggs, Richard S. "The Book of Genesis." In *A Theological Introduction to the Pentateuch: Interpreting the Torah as Christian Scripture*, edited by Richard S. Briggs and Joel N. Lohr, 19–50. Grand Rapids, MI: Baker Academic, 2012.

Brinkman, J. A. "Sennacherib's Babylon Problem: An Interpretation." *JCS* 25 (1973): 89–95.

———. *Prelude to Empire: Babylonian Society and Politics, 747–626 B.C.* Occasional Publications of the Babylonian Fund 7. Philadelphia, PA: Babylonian Fund, University Museum, 1984.

Brinner, William M. *The History of al-Ṭabarī: An Annotated Translation, Volume II: Prophets and Patriarchs.* Albany: State University of New York Press, 1987.

Brown, Peter. *Augustine of Hippo: A Biography.* 2nd ed. Berkeley: University of California Press, 2000.

Buchanan, Pat. *State of Emergency: The Third World Invasion and Conquest of America*. New York: St. Martin's Griffin, 2006.

Budge, E. A. W., and L. W. King. *The Annals of the Kings of Assyria: The Cuneiform Texts with Translations, Transliterations, etc., from the Original Documents in the British Museum, Volume 1*. London: Trustees of the British Museum, 1902.

Butts, Aaron M. "Ethiopic Christianity, Syriac Contacts with." In *Gorgias Encyclopedic Dictionary of the Syriac Heritage*, edited by Sebastian P. Brock et al., 148–153. Piscataway, NJ: Gorgias Press, 2011.

Byrd, Dani, and Toben H. Mintz. *Discovering Speech, Words, and Mind*. Malden, MA: Wiley-Blackwell, 2010.

Carr, David M. *The Formation of the Hebrew Bible: A New Reconstruction*. New York: Oxford University Press, 2011.

———. *Holy Resilience: The Bible's Traumatic Origins*. New Haven: Yale University Press, 2014.

———. "Strong and Weak Cases and Criteria for Establishing the Post-Priestly Character of Hexateuchal Material." Pages 19–34 in *The Post-Priestly Pentateuch: New Perspectives on its Redactional Development and Theological Profiles*. Edited by Federico Giuntoli and Konrad Schmid. FAT 101. Tübingen: Mohr Siebeck, 2015.

———. *The Formation of Genesis 1–11: Biblical and Other Precursors*. New York: Oxford University Press, 2020.

Carroll, Lewis. *Alice in Wonderland and Through the Looking Glass*. Hertfordshire: Wordsworth Classics, 1993.

Cassuto, Umberto. *A Commentary on the Book of Genesis*. Translated by Israel Abrahams. Jerusalem: Magnes, 1992.

Cathcart, Kevin J. "The Earliest Contributions to the Decipherment of Sumerian and Akkadian." *CDLJ* (2011): 1–12.

Cathcart, Kevin J., and Robert P. Gordon. *The Targum of the Minor Prophets*. The Aramaic Bible 14. Wilmington, DE: Michael Glazier, 1989.

Chatman, Seymour. *Story and Discourse: Narrative Structure in Fiction and Film*. Ithaca, NY: Cornell University Press, 1978.

Choi, Dongbin. *The Use and Function of Scripture in 1 Maccabees*. Library of Second Temple Studies 98. New York: T&T Clark, 2021.

Cline, Eric H. *1177 B.C.: The Year Civilization Collapsed*. Princeton, NJ: Princeton University Press, 2014.

Clines, David J. A. "The Significance of the 'Sons of God' Episode (Genesis 6:1–4) in the Context of the 'Primeval History' (Genesis 1–11)." *JSOT* 13 (1979): 33–46.

Cogan, M. *Bound for Exile: Israelites and Judeans under Imperial Yoke, Documents from Assyria and Babylonia*. Jerusalem: Carta Handbook, 2013.

———. "The Author of Ashurbanipal Prism A (Rassam): An Inquiry into his Plan and Purpose, with a Note on His Persona." *Orient* 49 (2014): 69–83.

———. *The Raging Torrent: Historical Inscriptions from Assyria and Babylon Relating to Ancient Israel.* 2nd ed. Jerusalem: Carta Handbook, 2015.

———. "Restoring the Empire: Sargon's Campaign to the West in 720/719 BCE." *IEJ* 2 (2017): 151–167.

Cranfield, C. E. B. *The Epistle to the Romans: Volume 1.* ICC. New York: T&T Clark, 2001.

Crawford, Sidnie White. *The Text of the Pentateuch.* Boston: De Gruyter, 2022.

Crisostomo, Jay. "'Recount for Me the Spell of Nudimmud' . . . yet again." *JAOS.* Forthcoming.

Dalley, S. "Nineveh, Babylon and the Hanging Gardens: Cuneiform and Classical Sources Reconciled." *Iraq* 56 (1994): 45–58.

———. "Babylon as a Name for Other Cities including Nineveh." Pages 25–34 in *Proceedings of the 51st Recontre Assyriologique Internationale 2005.* Edited by R. D. Biggs, J. Myers, and M. T. Roth. SAOC 62. Chicago: Oriental Institute, 2008.

———. *Myths from Mesopotamia: Creation, The Flood, Gilgamesh, and Others.* Oxford: Oxford University Press, 2008.

Davies, R. R. "The Peoples of Britain and Ireland 1100–1400: IV. Language and Historical Mythology." *Transactions of the Royal Historical Society* 7 (1997): 1–24.

Day, John. "The Tower and City of Babel Story (Genesis 11.1–9): Problems of Interpretation and Background." In *From Creation to Babel: Studies in Genesis 1–11,* 166–188. LHB/OTS 592. New York: Bloomsbury, 2013.

———. *From Creation to Babel: Studies in Genesis 1–11.* LHB/OTS 592. New York, 2013.

———. "The Table of Nations in Genesis 10." Pages 163–187 in *From Creation to Abraham: Further Studies in Genesis 1–11.* LHB/OTS 726. New York: T&T Clark, 2022.

———. "In Search of Nimrod: Problems in the Interpretation of Genesis 10:8–12." Pages 188–206 in *From Creation to Abraham: Further Studies in Genesis 1–11.* LHB/OTS 726. New York: T&T Clark, 2022.

DeGrado, Jessie. "King of the Four Corners: Diversity as a Rhetorical Strategy of the Neo-Assyrian Empire." *Iraq* 81 (2019): 1–19.

———. "Syrian Fashion, Assyrian Style: Clothing Syro-Anatolia in Ninth-Century BCE Assyrian Art." *American Journal of Archaeology* 125 (2021): 479–504.

Denecker, Tim. *Ideas on Language in Early Latin Christianity: From Tertullian to Isidore of Seville*. Supplements to Vigiliae Christianae 142. Boston: Brill, 2017.

Dershowitz, Idan. "Man of the Land: Unearthing the Original Noah." *ZAW* 128 (2016): 357–373.

Deutscher, Guy. *Through the Looking Glass: Why the World Looks Different in Other Languages*. New York: Metropolitan Books, 2010.

Dewrell, Heath. "Textualization and the Transformation of Biblical Prophecy." Pages 95–106 in *Scribes and Scribalism*. Edited by Mark Leuchter. The Hebrew Bible in Social Perspective. New York: T&T Clark, 2021.

Dillmann, August. *Die Bucher Numeri, Deuteronomium, und Joshua*. Kurzgefasstes exegetisches Handbuch zum Alten Testament 13. Leipzig: S. Hirzel, 1886.

Dinsmoor, William B. "Early American Studies of Mediterranean Archaeology." *Proceedings of the American Philosophical Society* 87 (1943): 70–104.

Doak, Brian. *The Last of the Rephaim: Conquest and Cataclysm in the Heroic Ages of Ancient Israel*. Ilex 7. Boston: Ilex Foundation, 2012.

Douglas, Mary. "Poetic Structure in Leviticus." Pages 239–256 in *Pomegranates and Golden Bells: Studies in Biblical, Jewish, and Near Eastern Ritual, Law, and Literature in Honor of Jacob Milgrom*. Edited by David P. Wright, David Noel Freedman, and Avi Hurvitz. Winona Lake, IN: Eisenbrauns, 1995.

Dungan, David L. *Constantine's Bible: Politics and the Making of the New Testament*. Minneapolis: Fortress Press, 2007.

Düring, Bleda. *The Imperialisation of Assyria: An Archaeological Approach*. New York: Cambridge University Press, 2020.

Ebeling, E., B. Meissner, and E. F. Weidner. *Die Inschriften der Altassyrischen Könige*. AOBib 1. Leipzig: Quelle & Meyer, 1926.

Eco, Umberto. *The Search for the Perfect Language*. Making of Europe. Cambridge, MA: Blackwell, 1994.

Efron, John, Steven Weitzman, and Mattias Lehmann. *The Jews: A History*. 2nd ed. New York: Pearson, 2014.

El-Badawi, Emran. *The Qur'ān and the Aramaic Gospel Traditions*. Routledge Studies in the Qur'an. New York: Routledge, 2014.

Elayi, Josette. *Sargon II, King of Assyria*. Archaeology and Biblical Studies 22. Atlanta: SBL Press, 2017.

Enns, Peter. "Pseudo-Solomon and His Scripture: Biblical Interpretation in the Wisdom of Solomon." Pages 389–414 in *A Companion to Biblical Interpretation in Early Judaism*. Edited by Matthias Henze. Grand Rapids, MI: Eerdmans, 2012.

Ephrem. *St. Ephrem the Syrian: Selected Prose Words*. Edited by Kathleen Mcvey. Translated by Edward G. Mathews, Jr. and Joseph P. Amar. Fathers of the Church 91. Washington, DC: Catholic University of America Press, 1994.

Eshel, E., and M. Stone. "An Exposition on the Patriarchs (4Q464) and Two Other Documents (4Q464ª and 4Q464ᵇ)." *Le Muséon* 105 (1992): 243–264.

———. "The Holy Tongue in the Last Days in the Light of a Fragment from Qumran." *Tarbiz* 62 (1992–1993): 169–177 (Hebrew).

———. "4QExposition of the Patriarchs." Pages 215–230 in *Qumran Cave 4, vol. XIV: Parabiblical Texts, Part 2*. Edited by Magen Broshi et al. DJD 19. Oxford: Clarendon Press, 1995.

Faber, Alice. "Phonetic Reconstruction." *Glossa* 15 (1981): 233–262.

———. "Semitic Sibilants in an Afro-Asiatic Context." *JSS* 29 (1984): 189–224.

———. "Akkadian Evidence for Proto-Semitic Affricates." *JCS* 37 (1985): 101–107.

Fales, F. Mario. "Between Archaeology and Linguistics: The Use of Aramaic Writing in Painted Characters on Clay Tablets of the 7th Century BCE." Pages 139–160 in *XII Incontro Italiano di linguistica camito-semitica (afroasiatica)*. Edited by M. Moriggi, Medioevo romanzo e orientale. Colloqui 9. Soveria Mannelli: Rubbettino, 2007.

———. "Multilingualism on Multiple Media in the Neo-Assyrian Period: A Review of the Evidence." *SAAB* 16 (2007): 95–122.

———. "On *Pax Assyriaca* in the Eighth-Seventh Centuries BCE and Its Implications." Pages 17–35 in *Isaiah's Vision of Peace in Biblical and Modern International Relations: Swords into Plowshares*. Edited by Raymond Cohen and Raymond Westbrook. Culture and Religion in International Relations. New York: Palgrave Macmillan, 2008.

———. "New Light on Assyro-Aramaic Interference: The Assur Ostracon." Pages 189–204 in *Camsemud 2007: Proceedings of the 13th Italian Meeting of Afro-Asiatic Linguistics: Held in Udine, May 21st-24th, 2007*. Edited by Frederick Mario Fales and Giulia Francesca Grassi. HANE/M 10. Padova: S.A.R.G.O.N., 2010.

———. "Su un passo di Sargon e la "Torre di Babele." Pages 149–166 in *"Suadìti?" Scritti di amici e colleghi in memoria di Francesco Aspesi*. Edited by Vermondo Brugnatelli and Leonardo Magini. Studi Camito-Semitici 9. Milano: Centro Studi Camiti-Semitici.

Faust, Avraham. "Settlement, Economy, and Demography under Assyrian Rule in the West: The Territories of the Former Kingdom of Israel as a Test Case." *JAOS* 135 (2015): 765–789.

Feldman, Liane. *The Story of Sacrifice: Ritual and Narrative in the Priestly Source*. FAT 141. Tübingen: Mohr Siebeck, 2020.

———. "Josephus' Commentary on Genesis." *JQR* 72 (1981): 121–131.

———. "Josephus' *Jewish Antiquities* and Pseudo-Philo's *Biblical Antiquities*." Pages 59–80 in *Josephus, the Bible, and History*. Edited by Louis H. Feldman and Gohei Hata. Detroit: Wayne State University Press, 1989.

Findlen, Paula. *Athanasius Kircher: The Last Man Who Knew Everything*. New York: Routledge Press, 2004.

———. "The Janus Faces of Science in the Seventeenth Century: Athanasius Kircher and Isaac Newton." In *Rethinking the Scientific Revolution*, edited by M. J. Osler, 221–246. New York: Cambridge University Press, 2000.

Finkel, Irving. *The Ark before Noah: Decoding the Story of the Flood*. London: Hodder & Stoughton, 2014.

Finn, Jennifer. *Much Ado about Marduk: Questioning Discourses of Royalty in First Millennium Mesopotamian Literature*. SANER 16. Boston: De Gruyter, 2017.

Flesher, Paul, and Bruce Chilton. *The Targums: A Critical Introduction*. Waco, TX: Baylor University Press, 2011.

Floyd, Michael H. "Review: Weltreich und "eine Rede": Eine neue Deutung der sogenannten Turmbauerzählung (Gen. 11,1–9) by Christoph Uehlinger." *JBL* 111 (1992): 321–323.

Fludernik, Monika. *An Introduction to Narratology*. New York: Routledge, 2009.

Fokkelmann, Jan. *Narrative Art in Genesis: Specimens of Stylistic and Structural Analysis*. 2nd edition. Sheffield: JSOT Press, 1991.

Foster, Benjamin. "The Beginnings of Assyriology in the United States." In *Orientalism, Assyriology and the Bible*, edited by Stephen Holloway, 44–73. HBM 10. Sheffield: Sheffield Phoenix Press, 2007.

Fox, Robin Lane. *Pagans and Christians in the Mediterranean World: From the Second Century AD to the Conversion of Constantine*. New York: Knopf, 1987.

Frahm, Eckart, ed. *A Companion to Assyria*. Hoboken, NJ: John Wiley & Sons, 2017.

———. "Nabû-Zuqup-Kēnu, das Gilgameš-Epos, und der Tod Sargons II." *JCS* 51 (1999): 73–90.

———. "Countertexts, Commentaries, and Adaptations: Politically Motivated Responses to the Babylonian Epic of Creation in Mesopotamia, the Biblical World, and Elsewhere." *Orient* 45 (2010): 3–33.

———. "A Sculpted Slab with an Inscription of Sargon II Mentioning the Rebellion of Yau-bi 'di of Hamath." *AoF* 40 (2013): 42–54.

———. "The Neo-Assyrian Period (ca. 1000–609 BCE)." Pages 176–183 in *A Companion to Assyria*. Edited by Eckart Frahm. Blackwell Companions to the Ancient World. Hoboken, NJ: John Wiley & Sons, 2017.

Frayne, Douglas. *Old Babylonian Period (2003–1595 B.C.)*. RIME 4. Toronto: University of Toronto Press, 1990.

Fredriksen, Paula. *Augustine and the Jews: A Christian Defense of Jews and Judaism*. New Haven, CT: Yale University Press, 2010.

Fried, Lisabeth S. "The High Places (Bāmôt) and the Reforms of Hezekiah and Josiah: An Archaeological Investigation." JAOS 122 (2002): 437–465.

Friedman, R. E. *The Disappearance of God: A Reverent Investigation of Three Divine Mysteries*. Boston: Little, Brown, 1995.

Fuchs, Andreas. *Die Inschriften Sargons II. aus Khorsabad*. Göttingen: Cuvillier Verlag, 1994.

Fyler, John M. "Language Barriers." *Studies in Philology* 112 (2015): 415–452.

Gauthier, Tim. *9/11 Fiction, Empathy, and Otherness*. New York: Lexington Books, 2015.

Genette, Gérard. *Narrative Discourse*. Translated by Jane E. Lewin. Oxford: Blackwell, 1980.

———. *Narrative Discourse Revisited*. Translated by Jane E. Lewin. Ithaca, NY: Cornell University Press, 1988.

George, Andrew. *The Babylonian Gilgamesh Epic: Introduction, Critical Edition and Cuneiform Texts, Volume 1*. New York: Oxford University Press, 2003.

———. "The Tower of Babel: Archaeology, History and Cuneiform Texts." *AfO* 51 (2005/2006): 75–95.

Gera, Deborah Levine. *Ancient Greek Ideas on Speech, Language, and Civilization*. New York: Oxford University Press, 2003.

Gertz, Jan C. "Babel im Rücken und das Land vor Augen: Anmerkungen zum Abschluß der Urgeschichte und zum Anfang der Erzählungen von den Erzeltern Israels." Pages 9–34 in *Die Erzväter in der biblischen Tradition*. Edited by Anselm C. Hagedorn and Henrik Pfeiffer. BZAW 400. Berlin: De Gruyter, 2009.

———. "The Formation of the Primeval History." Pages 107–136 in *The Book of Genesis: Composition, Reception, and Interpretation*. Edited by Craig A. Evans, Joel N. Lohr, and David L. Peterson. VTSup 152. Boston: Brill, 2012.

———. *Das erste Buch Mose (Genesis): Die Urgeschichte Gen 1–11*. Das Alte Testament Deutsch, Neues Göttinger Bibelwerk 1. Göttingen: Vandenhoeck & Ruprecht, 2018.

———. "Genesis in Form and Tradition Criticism Today." Pages 53–74 in *The Cambridge Companion to Genesis*. Edited by Bill T. Arnold. Cambridge Companions to Religion. New York: Cambridge University Press, 2022.

Gertz, Jan C., Konrad Schmid, and Markus Witte, ed. *Abschied vom Jahwisten: Die Komposition des Hexateuch in der jüngsten Diskussion*. BZAW 315. Berlin: Walter de Gruyter, 2002.

Gesundheit, Shimon. *Three Times a Year: Studies on Festival Legislation in the Pentateuch*. FAT 82. Tübingen: Mohr Siebeck, 2012.

———. "Philology and Theory: Exodus 12:21–27 as a Case Study." *VT* 70 (2019): 414–425.

Giorgetti, Andrew. "The 'Mock Building Account' of Genesis 11:1–9: The Polemic against Mesopotamian Royal Ideology." *VT* 64 (2014): 1–20.

———. "Building a Parody: Genesis 11:1–9, Ancient Near Eastern Building Accounts, and Production-Oriented Intertextuality." PhD Diss., Fuller Theological Seminary, 2017.

Godwin, Joscelyn. *Athanasius Kircher: A Renaissance Man and the Quest for Lost Knowledge*. London: Thames & Hudson, 1979.

———. *Athanasius Kircher's Theatre of the World: The Life and Work of the Last Man to Search for Universal Knowledge*. Rochester, VT: Inner Traditions, 2009.

Gordis, Daniel. "The Tower of Babel and the Birth of Nationhood." *Azure* (2010): 19–36.

Götze, Albrecht. *Old Babylonian Omen Texts*. Yale Oriental Series 10. New Haven: Yale University Press, 1947.

Grabbe, Lester. *A History of the Jews and Judaism in the Second Temple Period, Vol. 1: Yehud, A History of the Persian Province of Judah*. LSTS 47. New York: T&T Clark, 2004.

Grafton, Anthony. "Kircher's Chronology." In *Athanasius Kircher: The Last Man Who Knew Everything*, edited by Paula Findlen, 171–187. New York: Routledge, 2004.

Grayson, A. Kirk. *Assyrian Rulers of the Third and Second Millennia BC (To 1115 BC)*. RIMA 1. Toronto: University of Toronto Press, 1987.

———. *Assyrian Rulers of the Early First Millennium BC I (1114–859 BC)*. RIMA 2. Toronto: University of Toronto Press, 1991.

Greenstein, Edward. *Job: A New Translation*. New Haven, CT: Yale University Press, 2019.

Griffith, Sidney. *The Bible in Arabic: The Scriptures of the "People of the Book" in the Language of Islam*. Jews, Christians, and Muslim from the Ancient to the Modern World. Princeton: Princeton University Press, 2013.

Grossfeld, Bernard. *Targum Neofiti I: An Exegetical Commentary to Genesis*. Brooklyn, NY: Sepher-Hermon Press, 2000.

Gunkel, Hermann. *Genesis*. Translated by Mark E. Biddle. 3rd ed. Macon, GA: Mercer University Press, 1997.

Gunn, David M., and Danna Nolan Fewell. *Narrative in the Hebrew Bible*. London: Oxford University Press, 1993.

Gutjahr, Paul C. *An American Bible: A History of the Good Book in the United States*. Stanford: Stanford University Press, 1999.

Gzella, Holger. *A Cultural History of Aramaic: From the Beginnings to the Advent of Islam*. HdO 111. Boston: Brill, 2015.

———. "Aramaic Sources." Pages 117–132 in *A Companion to the Achaemenid Persian Empire*. Edited by Bruno Jacobs and Robert Rollinger. 2 volumes. Blackwell Companions to the Ancient World. Hoboken, NJ: Wiley Blackwell, 2021.

Harper, G. Geoffrey, *"I Will Walk Among You": The Rhetorical Function of Allusion to Genesis 1–3 in the Book of Leviticus*. BBRSup 21. University Park, PA: Eisenbrauns, 2019.

Harper, Robert Francis. *Assyrian and Babylonian Letters Belonging to the Kouyunjik Collections of the British Museum*. 14 vols. Chicago: University of Chicago Press, 1892–1914.

Harshav, Benjamin. *Explorations in Poetics*. Stanford: Stanford University Press, 2007.

Haugen, Einar. *Ecology of Language*. Language Science and National Development. Stanford: Stanford University Press, 1972.

Haynes, Stephen R. *Noah's Curse: The Biblical Justification of American Slavery*. New York: Oxford University Press, 2002.

Hendel, Ronald. "Review: Weltreich und "eine Rede": Eine neue Deutung der sogenannten Turmbauerzählung (Gen. 11,19) by Christoph Uehlinger." *CBQ* 55 (1993): 785–787.

———. "Genesis 1–11 and Its Mesopotamian Problem." In *Cultural Borrowings and Ethnic Appropriations in Antiquity. Oriens et Occidens*, edited by Erich S. Gruen, 23–36. Studien zu antiken Kulturkontakten und ihrem Nachleben 8. Stuttgart: F. Steiner, 2005.

———. "Historical Context." Pages 51–81 in *The Book of Genesis: Composition, Reception, and Interpretation*. Edited by C. A. Evans, J. N. Lohr, and D. L. Peterson. VTSup 152. Boston: Brill, 2012.

———. "Sex, Honor, and Civilization in Genesis 1–11." Pages 129–147 in *With the Loyal You Show Yourself Loyal: Essays on Relationships in the Hebrew Bible in Honor of Saul M. Olyan*. Edited by Tracy M. Lemos, Jordan D. Rosenblum, Karen B. Stern, and Debra S. Ballantine. Atlanta: SBL, 2021.

———. "How Old is the Hebrew Bible? A Response to Konrad Schmid." *ZAW* 133 (2021): 361–370.

Hiebert, Theodore. *Landscape of the Yahwist: Nature and Religion in Early Israel*. New York: Oxford University Press, 1996.

———. "The Tower of Babel and the Origins of the World's Cultures." *JBL* 126 (2007): 29–58.

Himmelfarb, Martha. *Ascent to Heaven in Jewish and Christian Apocalypses*. New York: Oxford University Press, 1993.

Hirsch, E. D. *Validity in Interpretation*. New Haven, CT: Yale University Press, 1967.

———. "Meaning and Significance Reinterpreted." *Critical Inquiry* 11 (1984): 202–225.

———. "Past Intentions and Present Meanings," *Essays in Criticism* 33 (1984): 79–98.

Ho, Ahuva. *The Targum of Zephaniah: Manuscripts and Commentary*. Studies in the Aramaic Interpretation of Scripture 7. Boston: Brill, 2009.

Hobbes, Thomas. *Memoirs of Literature: Containing a Large Account of Many Valuable Books, Letters and Dissertations upon Several Subjects, Miscellaneous Observations, etc., Vol. III*. London: R. Knaplock, 1722.

Hom, Mary Katherine Y. H. "' . . . A Mighty Hunter before YHWH': Genesis 10:9 and the Moral-Theological Evaluation of Nimrod." *VT* 60 (2010): 63–68.

Huehnergard, John. "What is Aramaic?" *ARAM* 7 (1995): 261–282.

Hunger, Herman. *Astrological Reports to Assyrian Kings*. SAA 8. Helsinki: Helsinki University Press, 1992.

Hurowitz, Victor Avigdor. "In Search of Resen (Genesis 10:12): Dūr-Šarrukīn?" Pages 511–524 in *Birkat Shalom: Studies in the Bible, Ancient Near Eastern Literature, and Post-Biblical Judaism Presented to Shalom M. Paul on the Occasion of His Seventieth Birthday*. Edited by Chaim Cohen et al. Winona Lake, IN: Eisenbrauns, 2008.

Inowlocki, Sabrina. "Josephus' Rewriting of the Babel Narrative (Gen 11:1–9)." *Journal for the Study of Judaism in the Persian, Hellenistic, and Roman Period* 37 (2006): 169–191.

Jacobson, Howard. "Biblical Interpretation in Pseudo-Philo's *Liber Antiquitatum Biblicarum*." Pages 180–201 in *A Companion to Biblical Interpretation in Early Judaism*. Edited by Matthias Henze. Grand Rapids, MI: Eerdmans, 2012.

Jahn, Manfred. *Narratology 2.3: A Guide to the Theory of Narrative*. Online publication, http://www.uni-koeln.de/~ame02/pppn.pdf.

Jean, Charles-F. *Lettres Diverses*. Archives Royales de Mari 2. Paris: Imprimerie Nationale 1950.

Karlsson, Mattias. *Relations of Power in Early Neo-Assyrian State Ideology*. SANER 10. Boston: De Gruyter, 2016.

Karmi, Shlomo. עם אחד ושפה אחת: תחיית הלשון העברית בראייה בין תחומית, קורות ומקורות. Tel Aviv: Ministry of Defense, 1997.

Kass, Leon. "What's Wrong with Babel?," *The American Scholar* 58 (1989): 41–60.

Kaufman, Stephen. *The Akkadian Influences on Aramaic*. AS 19. Chicago: University of Chicago Press, 1974.

Kawashima, Robert. "*Homo Faber* in J's Primeval History." *ZAW* 116 (2004): 483–501.

———. "Sources and Redaction." Pages 47–70 in *Reading Genesis: Ten Methods*. Edited by Ronald Hendel. New York: Cambridge University Press, 2010.

Keen, Suzanne. *Narrative Form*. 2nd edition, revised and expanded. New York: Palgrave Macmillan, 2015.

Kelly, Joseph Ryan. "Does God Command and Punish in the Garden of Eden?," *VT* (2021): 1–22.

Kertai, David. *The Architecture of Late Assyrian Royal Palaces*. New York: Oxford University Press, 2015.

Kiel, Yishai. "Abraham and Nimrod in the Shadow of Zarathustra." *JR* 95 (2015): 35–50.

Kikawada, Isaac. "The Shape of Genesis 11:1–9." Pages 18–32 in *Rhetorical Criticism: Essays in Honor of James Muilenburg*. Edited by Jared J. Jackson and Martin Kessler. PTMS 1. Pittsburg: Pickwick, 1974.

Kikawada, Isaac, and Eric W. Heese. "Jonah and Genesis 11–1." *Annual of the Japanese Biblical Institute* 10 (1984): 3–19.

Kister, M. J. *Concepts and Ideas at the Dawn of Islam*. New York: Routledge, 2016.

Klar, Marianna. *Interpreting al-Tha ʿlabī's Tales of the Prophets: Temptation, Responsibility and Loss*. New York: Routledge, 2009.

Knohl, Israel. "Nimrod, Son of Cush, King of Mesopotamia, and the Dates of P and J." Pages 45–52 in *Birkat Shalom: Studies in the Bible, Ancient Near Eastern Literature, and Post-Biblical Judaism Presented to Shalom M. Paul on the Occasion of His Seventieth Birthday*. Edited by Chaim Cohen et al. Winona Lake, IN: Eisenbrauns, 2008.

Koenig, Jean. *L'Herméneutique analogique du Judaïsme antique*. VTSup 33. Leiden: Brill, 1982.

Konai, Theodore bar. *Liber Scholiorum (Seert Version)*. Edited by Edidit Addai Scher. CSCO. Scriptores Syri series 2 volume 65. Lovanii: E. Peeters, 1960.

———. *Liber Scholiorum (Seert Version)*. Translated by Robert Hespel and René Draguet. CSCO. Scriptores Syri 187. Lovanii: E. Peeters, 1981.

Kratz, Reinhard G. *The Composition of the Narrative Books of the Old Testament*. London: T&T Clark, 2005.

———. "The Analysis of the Pentateuch: An Attempt to Overcome Barriers in Thinking." *ZAW* 128 (2016): 529–561.

Kugel, James. *Traditions of the Bible*. Cambridge, MA; Harvard University Press, 1998.

Kugel, James L., and Rowan A. Greer. *Early Biblical Interpretation*. Library of Early Christianity 3. Philadelphia: Westminster John Knox, 1986.

Kuhrt, Amélie. *The Ancient Near East, c. 3000–330 BC: Volume I.* Routledge History of the Ancient World. New York: Routledge, 1997.

———. *The Ancient Near East, c. 3000–330 BC: Volume II.* Routledge History of the Ancient World. New York: Routledge, 1997.

Kwa, Chunglin. *Styles of Knowing: A New History of Science from Ancient Times to the Present.* Translated by David McKay. Pittsburgh: University of Pittsburgh Press, 2011.

LaCocque, Andrew. "Whatever Happened in the Valley of Shinar? A Response to Theodore Hiebert." *JBL* 128 (2009): 29–41.

Laessøe, J. "A Prayer to Ea, Shamash, and Marduk, from Hama." *Iraq* 18 (1956): 60–67.

Lam, Joseph. "Review of *The Composition of the Pentateuch: Renewing the Documentary Hypothesis.*" *JNES* 72 (2013): 308–309.

Lambdin, T. O. *Introduction to Biblical Hebrew.* New York: Scribner, 1971.

Lambert, W. "Assyrien und Israel." Pages 265–277 in *Theologische Realenzyklopädie 4.* Edited by Gerhard Krause and Gerhard Müller. Berlin: De Gruyter, 1979.

Landman, Yael. "On Lips and Tongues in Ancient Hebrew." *VT* 66 (2016): 66–77.

Lanfranchi, Giovani B., and Simo Parpola. *The Correspondence of Sargon II, Part II: Letters from the Northern and Northeastern Provinces.* State Archives of Assyria 5. Helsinki: Helsinki University Press, 1990.

Larsen, Mogens Trolle. *The Conquest of Assyria: Excavations in an Antique Land, 1840–1860.* New York: Routledge, 1996.

Lauinger, Jacob. "Esarhaddon's Succession Treaty at Tell Tayinat: Text and Commentary." *JCS* 64 (2012): 87–123.

———. "The Neo-Assyrian *adê*: Treaty, Oath, or Something Else?" *ZABR* 19 (2013): 99–115.

Lauinger, Jacob, and Stephen Batiuk. "A Stele of Sargon II at Tell Tayinat." *ZA* 105 (2015): 54–68.

Leow, Rachel. *Taming Babel: Language in the Making of Malaysia.* New York: Cambridge University Press, 2016.

Lepelley, Claude. "Témeoignages de saint Augustin sur l'ampleur et les limites de l'usage de la langue punique dans l'Afrique de son temps. Briand-Ponsart." In *Indentités et culture dans l'Algérie antique,* 127–153. Rouen: Publications des Universités de Rouen et du Havre, 2005.

Lester, Mark. "The Material Transmission of Tradition in Deuteronomy." PhD Diss., Yale University, 2020.

Levenson, Jon D. *Creation and the Persistence of Evil: The Jewish Drama of Divine Omnipotence.* 2nd edition. Princeton: Princeton University Press, 1994.

———. *Inheriting Abraham: The Legacy of the Patriarch in Judaism, Christianity, and Islam.* Princeton: Princeton University Press, 2012.

Levin, Christoph. "The Yahwist: The Earliest Editor in the Pentateuch." *JBL* 126 (2007): 209–230.

Levin, Y. "Nimrod the Mighty, King of Kish, King of Sumer and Akkad." *VT* 52 (2002): 350–366.

Levinson, Bernard. *"The Right Chorale": Studies in Biblical Law and Interpretation*. Winona Lake, IN: Eisenbrauns, 2011.

Leibniz, Gottfried Wilhelm. *Philosophical Papers and Letters: A Selection Translated and Edited, with an Introduction by Leroy E. Loemker, Volume II*. Chicago: University of Chicago Press, 1956.

Lie, A. G. *The Inscriptions of Sargon II*. Paris: P. Geuthner, 1929.

Lim, Jeehyum. *Bilingual Brokers: Race, Literature, and Language as Human Capital*. New York: Fordham University Press, 2017.

Lincoln, Bruce. *Holy Terrors: Thinking About Religion after September 11*. 2nd edition. Chicago: University of Chicago Press, 2006.

———. *Apples and Oranges: Experiments in, on, and with Comparison*. Chicago: University of Chicago Press, 2018.

Lincoln, Bruce, and Cristiano Grottenelli. "Theses on Comparison." Pages 121–130 in *Gods and Demons, Priests and Scholars: Critical Explorations in the History of Religions*. Chicago: University of Chicago Press, 2012.

Lipiński, Edward. *Semitic Languages: Outline of a Comparative Grammar*. OLA 80. Leuven: Peeters, 1997.

Lipton, Diana. "The Reluctant Brick Maker: Babel and Abram in Pseudo-Philo and Bereshit Rabbah." Pages 1065–1078 in *Ve-ʾEd Yaʿaleh (Gen 2:6): Essays in Biblical and Ancient Near Eastern Studies Presented to Edward L. Greenstein, Volume 2*. Edited by Peter Machinist, et al. Atlanta: SBL Press, 2021.

Liverani, Mario. *Imagining Babylon: The Modern Story of an Ancient City*. Translated by Ailsa Campbell. SANER 11. Boston: De Gruyter, 2016.

———. *Assyria: The Imperial Mission*. MC 21. Winona Lake, IN: Eisenbrauns, 2017.

———. *Historiography, Ideology and Politics in the Ancient Near East and Israel*. Edited by Niels Peter Lemche and Emanuel Pfoh. Changing Perspectives 5. New York: Routledge, 2021.

Luzzatto, Samuel David. *The Book of Genesis: A Commentary*. Translated by Daniel A. Klein. Northvale, NJ: Jason Aronson, 1998.

Lyon, David G. *Keilschrifttexte Sargons, Königs von Assyrien (722–705 v Chr.):Nach den Originalen*. Leipzig: J. C. Hinrichs, 1883.

Machinist, P. "The Assyrians and Their Babylonian Problem: Some Reflections." *Jahrbuch des Wissenschaftskolleg zu Berlin* (1984–1985): 353–364.

———. "Assyrians on Assyria in the First Millennium B.C." Pages 77–104 in *Anfänge politischen Denkens in der Antike*. Edited by K. Raaflaub. Schriften des Historischen Kollegs Kolloquien 24. Munich, 1993.

————. "The Road Not Taken: Wellhausen and Assyriology." Pages 469–531 in *Homeland and Exile: Biblical and Near Eastern Studies in Honour of Bustenay Oded*. Edited by Gershon Galil, Markham Geller, and Alan Millard. VTSup 130. Leiden: Brill, 2009.

Major, Tristan. *Undoing Babel: The Tower of Babel in Anglo-Saxon Literature*. Toronto Anglo-Saxon Series. Toronto: University of Toronto Press, 2018.

Malcolm, Noel. "Private and Public Knowledge: Kircher, Esotericism, and the Republic of Letters." In *Athanasius Kircher: The Last Man Who Knew Everything*, edited by Paula Findlen, 297–310. New York: Routledge, 2004.

Mankowski, Paul V. *Akkadian Loanwords in Biblical Hebrew*. HSS 47. Winona Lake, IN: Eisenbrauns, 2000.

Mastjnak, Nathan. "Prestige, Authority, and Jeremiah's Bible." *JR* 98 (2018): 542–558.

May, Natalie N. "Gates and Their Functions in Mesopotamia and Ancient Israel." Pages 77–121 in *The Fabric of Cities: Aspects of Urbanism, Urban Topography and Society in Mesopotamia, Greece and Rome*. CHANE 68. Boston: Brill, 2014.

Mermelstein, Ari. *Creation, Covenant, and the Beginnings of Judaism: Reconceiving Historical Time in the Second Temple Period*. Supplements to the Journal for the Study of Judaism 168. Boston: Brill, 2014.

Meshel, Naphtali S. "Food for Thought: Systems of Categorization in Leviticus 11." *HTR* 101 (2008): 203–229.

Meyers, Carol. *Rediscovering Eve*. New York: Oxford University Press, 2013.

Mindlin, M., M. J. Geller, and J. E. Wansbrough, eds. *Figurative Language in the Ancient Near East*. London: University of London, School of Oriental and African Studies, 1987.

Minets, Yuliya. *The Slow Fall of Babel: Languages and Identities in Late Antique Christianity*. New York: Cambridge University Press, 2022.

Mitchell, Margaret M. "On Comparison, and Calling the Question." Pages 95–110 in *The New Testament in Comparison: Validity, Method and Purpose in Comparing Traditions*. Edited by J. M. G. Barclay and B. G. Wright. New York: T&T Clark, 2020.

Moore, Karl, and David Lewis. "Entrepreneurs of the Aegean." Pages 114–144 in *The Origins of Globalization*. Routledge International Studies in Business History. New York: Routledge, 2009.

Morrison, Craig E. "The 'Hour of Distress' in *Targum Neofiti* and the 'Hour' in the Gospel of John." *CBQ* 67 (2005): 590–603.

Morrow, William. "Resistance and Hybridity in Late Bronze Age Canaan." *RB* 115 (2008): 321–339.

——. "'To Set the Name' in the Deuteronomic Centralization Formula: A Case of Cultural Hybridity." *JSS* 55 (2010): 365–383.

Moss, Yonatan. "The Language of Paradise: Hebrew or Syriac? Linguistic Speculations and Linguistic Realities in Antiquity." In *Paradise in Antiquity: Jewish and Christian Views*, edited by Markus Bockmuehl and Guy G. Strousma, 120–137. New York: Cambridge University Press, 2010.

Muffs, Yochanan. "Who Will Stand in the Breach? A Study of Prophetic Intercession." Pages 9–48 in *Love and Joy: Law, Language, and Religion in Ancient Israel*. New York: Jewish Theological Seminary of America, 1992.

Murphy, Frederick. *Pseudo-Philo: Rewriting the Bible*. New York: Oxford University Press, 1993.

Nellen, Henk, and Piet Steenbakkers. "Biblical Philology in the Long Seventeenth Century." In *Scriptural Authority & Biblical Criticism in the Dutch Golden Age: God's Word Questioned*, edited by Dirk van Miert et al, 16–57. New York: Oxford University Press, 2017.

Nissinen, Martti. *Homoeroticism in the Biblical World*. Minneapolis: Fortress Press, 1998.

Noegel, Scott. ed. *Puns and Pundits: Wordplay in the Hebrew Bible and Ancient Near Eastern Literature*. Bethesda, MD: CDL Press, 2000.

——. *Wordplay in Ancient Near Eastern Texts*. ANEM 26. Atlanta: SBL Press, 2021.

Noll, Mark A. *America's Book: The Rise and Decline of a Bible Civilization, 1794–1911*. New York: Oxford University Press, 2022.

Novotny, Jamie, and Joshua Jeffers. *The Royal Inscriptions of Ashurbanipal (668–631 BC), Aššur-etel-ilāni (630–627 BC), and Sîn-šarra-iškun (626–612 BC), Kings of Assyria, Part 1*. RINAP 5/1. University Park, PA: Eisenbrauns, 2018.

Oded, B. *Mass Deportations and Deportees in the Neo-Assyrian Empire*. Wiesbaden: L. Reichert, 1979.

——. "The Settlements of the Israelite and the Judean Exiles in Mesopotamia in the 8th–6th Centuries BCE." Pages 91–103 in *Studies in Historical Geography and Biblical Historiography: Presented to Zechariah Kallai*. Edited by Gershon Galil and Moshe Weinfeld. VTSup 81. Boston: Brill, 2000.

——. גלות ישראל ויהודה באשור ובבל. Ḥefah: Pardes, 2010.

Orlov, Andrei A. *The Enoch-Metatron Tradition*. TSAJ 107. Tübingen: Mohr Siebeck, 2005.

Pardee, Dennis. "Review: Weltreich und "eine Rede": Eine neue Deutung der sogenannten Turmbauerzählung (Gen. 11,1–9) by Christoph Uehlinger." *JNES* 53 (1994): 220–221.

Parker, Grant. "Environmental Perspectives on Ancient Communication." Pages 3–22 in *Mercury's Wings: Exploring Modes of Communication in the Ancient*

World. Edited by F. S. Naiden and Richard J. A. Talbert. New York: Oxford University Press, 2017.

Patton, Kimberly C., and Benjamin C. Ray, eds. *A Magic Still Dwells: Comparative Religion in the Postmodern Age*. Berkeley: University of California Press, 2000.

Pearce, Laurie. "*Sepīru* and ᴸᵁA.BA: Scribes of the Late First Millennium." Pages 355–368 in *Languages and Cultures in Contact: At the Crossroads of Civilization in the Syro-Mesopotamian Realm*. Edited by K. Van Lerberghe and G. Voet. OLA 96. Leuven: Peeters, 1999.

Perron, Paul. *Narratology and Text: Subjectivity and Identity in New France and Québécois Literature*. Toronto Studies in Semiotics and Communication. Toronto: University of Toronto Press, 2003.

Peters, J. P. "Tower of Babel at Borsippa." *JAOS* 41 (1921): 157–159.

Pettit, Philip. *Made with Words: Hobbes on Language, Mind, and Politics*. Princeton, NJ: Princeton University Press, 2009.

Pippin, Tina. *Apocalyptic Bodies: The Biblical End of the World in Text and Image*. New York: Routledge, 1999.

Podany, Amanda. *Brotherhood of Kings: How International Relations Shaped the Ancient Near East*. New York: Oxford University Press, 2010.

Poirier, John C. "'4Q464': Not Eschatological." *Revue de Qumrân* 20 (2002): 583–587.

Pongratz-Leisten, Beate. "Toponyme als Ausdruck assyrischen Herrschaftsanspruchs." Pages 325–343 in *Ana šadî Labnāni lū allik: Beiträge zu altorientalischen und mittelmeerischen Kulturen, Festschrift für Wolfgang Röllig*. Edited by Beate Pongratz-Leisten, Hartmut Kühne, and Paolo Xella. AOAT 247. Neukirchen-Vluyn: Neukirchener Verlag, 1997.

———. *Religion and Ideology in Assyria*. SANER 6. Boston: De Gruyter, 2015.

Popović, Mladen. "Multilingualism, Multiscripturalism, and Knowledge Transfer in the Dead Sea Scrolls and Greaco-Roman Judea." Pages 46–71 in *Sharing and Hiding Religious Knowledge in Early Judaism, Christianity, and Islam*. Judaism, Christianity, and Islam—Tension, Transmission, Transformation 10. Boston: De Gruyter, 2018.

Quick, Laura. *Deuteronomy 28 and the Aramaic Curse Tradition*. Oxford Theology and Religion Monographs. New York: Oxford University Press, 2018.

Radner, K. "Assyrische *ṭuppi adê* als Vorbild fur Deuteronomium 28,20–44?" Pages 351–378 in *Die deuteronomistischen Geschichtswerke: Redaktions- und religionsgeschichtliche Perspektiven zur"Deuteronomismus"-Diskussion in Tora und Vorderen Propheten*. Edited by Markus Witte et al. BZAW 365. New York: De Gruyter, 2006.

————. "Neo-Assyrian Treaties as a Source for the Historian: Bonds of Friendship, the Vigilant Subject, and the Vengeful King's Treaty." Pages 309–328 in *Writing Neo-Assyrian History: Sources, Problems, and Approaches*. Edited by G. B. Lanfranchi, R. Mattila, and R. Rollinger. SAAS 29. Helsinki: The Neo-Assyrian Text Corpus Project, 2019.

Ramos, Melissa. *Ritual in Deuteronomy: The Performance of Doom*. Ancient World. London: Routledge, 2021.

Ramsey, Paul J. "The War against German-American Culture: The Removal of German-Language Instruction from the Indianapolis Schools, 1917–1919." *Indiana Magazine of History* 98 (2002): 285–303.

Rapp, Jr., Stephen H. "The Georgian Nimrod." Pages 188–216 in *The Armenian Apocalyptic Tradition: A Comparative Perspective. Essays Presented in Honor of Professor Robert W. Thomson on the Occasion of His Eightieth Birthday*. Studia in Veteris Testamenti Pseudepigrapha 25. Boston: Brill, 2014.

Ravid, Liora. "The *Book of Jubilees* and Its Calendar—A Reexamination." *DSD* 10 (2003): 371–394.

Regev, Eyal. *The Hasmoneans: Ideology, Archaeology, Identity*. Journal of Ancient Judaism Supplements 10. Göttingen: Vandenhoeck & Ruprecht, 2013.

Rendtorff, Rolff. *Das überlieferungsgeschichtliche Problem des Pentateuch*. BZAW 147. Berlin: De Gruyter, 1977.

————. *The Problem of the Process of Transmission in the Pentateuch*. Translated by John J. Scullion. JSOTSup 89. Sheffield: Sheffield Academic, 1977.

Reymond, Eric. *Nimrodia*. New Texture, 2018.

Reynolds, Gabriel Said. *The Qur'ān and Its Biblical Subtext*. Routledge Studies in the Qur'an 10. New York: Routledge, 2010.

————. *The Qur'ān and the Bible: Text and Commentary*. New Haven, CT: Yale University Press, 2018.

Richelle, Matthieu. "Was the Tower of Babel Really Left Unfinished? Genesis 11:5 in Light of Hebrew Syntax, the Septuagint, and Jewish Reception." *Semitica* 63 (2021): 125–139.

Ricks, Thomas E. *First Principles: What America's Founders Learned from the Greeks and Romans and How That Shaped Our Country*. New York: Harper, 2020.

Roberts, Kathleen Glenister. *Alterity and Narrative: Stories and the Negotiation of Western Identities*. Negotiating Identity. Albany: State University of New York Press, 2007.

Robinson, Andrew. *Cracking the Egyptian Code: The Revolutionary Life of Jean-François Champollion*. New York: Oxford University Press, 2012.

Rocca, Samuel. *Herod's Judea: A Mediterranean State in the Classical World*. TSAJ 122. Tübingen: Mohr Siebeck, 2008.

Römer, Thomas Christian, et al., ed. *A Farewell to the Yahwist? The Composition of the Pentateuch in Recent European Interpretation.* SBLSymS 34. Atlanta: SBL Press, 2006.

Rosenberg, David, and Harold Blook. *The Book of J.* New York: Grove Weidenfeld, 1990.

Rowland, Ingrid D. *The Ecstatic Journey: Athanasius Kircher in Baroque Rome.* Chicago: University of Chicago Press, 2000.

Runions, Erin. *The Babylon Complex: Theopolitical Fantasies of War, Sex, and Sovereignty.* New York: Fordham University Press, 2014.

———. "Empire's Allure: Babylon and the Exception to Law in Two Conservative Discourses." *JAAR* 77 (2009): 680–711.

Sanders, Seth L. *The Invention of Hebrew.* Traditions. Urbana: University of Illinois Press, 2009.

Sandys-Wunsch, John. "Early Old Testament Critics on the Continent." In *Hebrew Bible/Old Testament: The History of Its Interpretation II: From the Renaissance to the Enlightenment,* edited by Magne Sæbø, 971–984. Göttingen: Vandenhoeck & Ruprecht, 2008.

Santini, Marco. "Languages, Peoples, and Power: Some Near Eastern Perspectives." *Chatreššar* 4 (2021): 5–39.

Sardo, Domenico Lo. *Post-Priestly Additions and Rewritings in Exodus 35–40.* FAT.2 119. Tübingen: Mohr Siebeck, 2020.

Schama, Simon. *The Story of the Jews: Finding the Words, 1000 BC–1492 AD.* New York: Ecco, 2014.

Schmid, Konrad. *The Old Testament: A Literary History.* Translated by Linda M. Maloney. Minneapolis: Fortress Press, 2012.

———. "How to Identify a Persian Period Text in the Pentateuch." Pages 101–118 in *On Dating Biblical Texts to the Persian Period: Discerning Criteria and Establishing Epochs.* Edited by Richard J. Bautch and Mark Lackowski. FAT 2.101 Tübingen: Mohr Siebeck, 2019.

———. "A Neo-Documentarian Manifesto: A Critical Reading." *JBL* 140 (2021): 461–479.

Schneider, Tammy. *An Introduction to Ancient Mesopotamian Religion.* Grand Rapids, MI: Eerdmans, 2011.

Schniedewind, William. "Qumran Hebrew as an Antilanguage." *JBL* 118 (1999): 235–252.

———. "Linguistic Ideology in Qumran Hebrew." Pages 245–255 in *Diggers at the Well: Proceedings of a Third International Symposium on the Hebrew of the Dead Sea Scrolls and Ben Sira.* Edited by Takamitsu Muraoka and John F. Elwolde. STDJ 36. Leiden: Brill, 2000.

———. *How the Bible Became a Book.* New York: Cambridge University Press, 2004.

———. "Aramaic, the Death of Written Hebrew, and Language Shift in the Persian Period." Pages 137–147 in *Margins of Writing, Origins of Cultures.* Edited by Seth L. Sanders. OIS 2. Chicago: Oriental Institute of the University of Chicago, 2006.

———. *A Social History of Hebrew: Its Origins through the Rabbinic Period.* AYBRL. New Haven, CT: Yale University Press, 2013.

———. "Scribal Education in Ancient Israel and Judah into the Persian Period." Pages 11–28 in *Second Temple Jewish Paideia in Context.* Edited by Jason M. Zurawski and Gabriele Boccaccini. BZNW 228. Berlin: De Gruyter, 2017.

Schroeder, Otto. *Keilschrifttexte aus Assur Historischen Inhalts: Zweites Heft.* Wissenschaftliche Veröffentlichung der Deutschen Orient-Gesellschaft 37. Leipzig: J. C. Hinrichs, 1922.

Schwartz, Baruch. "The Priestly Account of the Theophany and Lawgiving at Sinai." Pages 103–134 in *Text, Temples, and Traditions: A Tribute to Menahem Haran.* Edited by Michael V. Fox, et al. Winona Lake, IN: Eisenbrauns, 1996.

———. "What Really Happened at Sinai?," https://www.thetorah.com/article/what-really-happened-at-mount-sinai.

———. "Does Recent Scholarship's Critique of the Documentary Hypothesis Constitute Grounds for Its Rejection?" Pages 3–16 in *The Pentateuch: International Perspectives on Current Research.* Edited by Thomas B. Dozeman, Konrad Schmid, and Baruch Schwartz. FAT 78. Tübingen: Mohr Siebeck, 2011.

———. "How the Compiler of the Pentateuch Worked: The Composition of Genesis 37." Pages 264–278 in *The Book of Genesis: Composition, Reception, and Interpretation.* Edited by Craig A. Evans, Joel N. Lohr, and David L. Peterson. VTSup 152. Boston: Brill, 2012.

———. "Leviticus." Pages 193–266 in *The Jewish Study Bible.* Edited by Adele Berlin and Marc Z. Brettler. 2nd edition. New York: Oxford University Press, 2014.

Seebaß, H. *Genesis 1. Urgeschichte (1,1–11,26).* Neukirchen-Vluyn: Neukirchener, 1996.

Segal, Alan F. *Sinning in the Hebrew Bible: How the Worst Stories Speak for its Truth.* New York: Columbia University Press, 2012.

Sheehan, Jonathan. *The Enlightenment Bible: Translation, Scholarship, Culture.* Princeton: Princeton University Press, 2007.

Shell, Marc. "Babel in America: Or, the Politics of Language Diversity in the United States." *Critical Inquiry* 20 (1993): 103–127.

Sherman, Phillip Michael. *Babel's Tower Translated: Genesis 11 and Ancient Jewish Interpretation.* Biblical Interpretation 117. Boston: Brill, 2013.

Silverstein, Adam J. "Hāmān's Transition from Jāhiliyya to Islām." *Jerusalem Studies in Arabic and Islam* 34 (2008): 285–308.

———. *Veiling Esther, Unveiling Her Story: The Reception of a Biblical Book in Islamic Lands.* New York: Oxford University Press, 2018.

———. "Monoglot 'Standard' in America: Standardization and Metaphors of Linguistic Hegemony." In *The Matrix of Language: Contemporary Linguistic Anthropology,* edited by D. Brenneis and R. H. S. Macaulay, 284–305. Oxford: Westview, 1996.

Ska, Jean Louis. *Introduction to Reading the Pentateuch.* Translated by Sr. Pascale Dominique. Winona Lake, IN: Eisenbrauns, 2006.

Smelik, Willem. *Rabbis, Language and Translation in Late Antiquity.* New York: Cambridge University Press, 2013.

Smith, J. Z. "In Comparison a Magic Dwells." Pages 23–33 in *Imagining Religion: From Babylon to Jonestown.* Chicago: University of Chicago Press, 1982.

———. *Drudgery Divine: On the Comparison of Early Christianities and the Religions of Late Antiquity.* Chicago: University of Chicago Press, 1994.

Soden, Wolfram von. *Akkadisches Handwörterbuch.* 3 volumes. Wiesbaden: Harrassowitz, 1965–1981.

Sommer, Benjamin. "Dating Pentateuchal Texts and the Dangers of Pseudo-Historicism." Pages 85–108 in *The Pentateuch: International Perspectives on Current Research.* Edited by Thomas B. Dozeman, Konrad Schmid, and Baruch J. Schwartz. FAT 78. Tübingen: Mohr Siebeck, 2011.

Spinoza, Benedictus de. *Theological-Political Treatise.* Edited by Jonathan Israel. Translated by Michael Silverthorne and Jonathan Israel. Cambridge Texts in the History of Philosophy. New York: Cambridge University Press, 2007.

Staal, Frits. "Oriental Ideas on the Origin of Language." *JAOS* 99 (1979): 1–14.

Stackert, Jeffrey. "The Holiness Legislation and Its Pentateuchal Sources: Revision, Supplementation, and Replacement." Pages 187–204 in *The Strata of the Priestly Writings: Contemporary Debate and Future Directions.* Edited by Sarah Shectman and Joel S. Baden. Zürich: TVZ, 2009.

———. "Compositional Strata in the Priestly Sabbath: Exodus 31:12–17 and 35:1–3." *JHS* 11 (2011): article 15.

———. *A Prophet Like Moses: Prophecy, Law, and Israelite Religion.* New York: Oxford University Press, 2014.

———. "How Priestly Sabbaths Work: Innovation in Pentateuchal Priestly Ritual." Pages 79–111 in *Ritual Innovation in the Hebrew Bible and Ancient Judaism.* Edited by Nathan MacDonald. BZAW 468. Boston: De Gruyter, 2016.

———. *Deuteronomy and the Pentateuch*. AYBRL. New Haven, CT: Yale University Press, forthcoming.

Stackert, Jeffrey, and Jeremy Shipper. "Blemishes, Camouflage, and Sanctuary Service." *HeBAI* 2 (2013): 458–478.

Stager, Lawrence E. "Forging an Identity: The Emergence of Ancient Israel." Pages 90–131 in *The Oxford History of the Biblical World*. Edited by Michael D. Coogan New York: Oxford University Press, 2001.

Stern, Ephraim. *Archaeology of the Bible, Volume II*. ABRL. New York: Doubleday, 2001.

Sternberg, Meir. *The Poetics of Biblical Narrative: Ideological Literature and the Drama of Reading*. ISBL. Bloomington: Indiana University Press.

Stevens, Daniel Gurden. "The Tower of Babel: History in Picture." *The Biblical World* 41 (1913): 185–189.

Steymans, Hans Ulrich. "Deuteronomy 28 and Tell Tayinat." *Verbum et Ecclesia* 32 (2013): 1–13.

Stolzenberg, Daniel. "Four Trees, Some Amulets, and the Seventy-two Names of God: Kircher Reveals the Kabbalah." In *Athanasius Kircher: The Last Man Who Knew Everything*, edited by Paula Findlen, 149–169. New York: Routledge, 2004.

———. *Egyptian Oedipus: Athanasius Kircher and the Secrets of Antiquity*. Chicago: University of Chicago Press, 2013.

Strawn, Brent. "Comparative Approaches: History, Theory, and the Image of God." Pages 117–142 in *Method Matters: Essays on the Interpretation of the Hebrew Bible in Honor of David L. Peterson*. Edited by Joel M. LeMon and Kent Harold Richards. RBS 56. Atlanta: Society of Biblical Literature, 2009.

———. https://global.oup.com/obso/focus/focus_on_towerbabel/.

Strong, John T. "Shattering the Image of God: A Response to Theodore Hiebert's Interpretation of the Story of the Tower of Babel." *JBL* 124 (2008): 625–34.

Telfer, Charles K. *Wrestling with Isaiah: The Exegetical Methodology of Campegius Vitringa (1659–1722)*. Reformed Historical Theology 38. Göttingen: Vandenhoeck & Ruprecht, 2016.

Tha 'labī, Abu Ishaq. *'Arā 'is Al-majālis Fī Qiṣaṣ Al-anbiyā, Or, Lives of the Prophets*. Translated by William M. Brinner. Studies in Arabic Literature 24. Boston: Brill, 2002.

Thelle, Rannfrid. *Discovering Babylon*. SHANE. New York: Routledge, 2019.

Thompson, R. C. *The Reports of the Magicians and Astrologers of Nineveh and Babylon in the British Museum: The Original Texts, Printed in Cuneiform Characters*. Luzac's Semitic Text and Translation Series 6–7, 2 vols. London: Luzac, 1900.

Thureau-Dangin, F. *Tablettes d'Uruk à l'usage des prêtres du Temple d'Anu au temps des Séleucides*. Musée du Louvre, Département des antiquités orientales, Textes cunéiformes, 6. Paris: P. Geuthner, 1922.

Tigchelaar, Eibert. "Sociolinguistics and the Misleading Use of the Concept of Anti-Language for Qumran Hebrew." Pages 195–206 in *The Dead Sea Scrolls and the Study of the Humanities: Method, Theory, Meaning: Proceedings of the Eighth Meeting of the International Organization for Qumran Studies (Munich 4–7 August, 2013).* Edited by Pieter B. Hartog, Alison Schofield, and Samuel I. Thomas. STDJ 125. Boston: Brill, 2018.

Toepel, Alexander. "The Cave of Treasures." In *Old Testament Pseudepigrapha: More Noncanonical Scriptures, Volume 1,* edited by Richard Bauckham, James R. Davila, and Alexander Panayotov, 531–584. Grand Rapids, MI: Eerdmans, 2013.

Toorn, K. van der, and P. W. van der Horst. "Nimrod Before and After the Bible." *HTR* 83 (1990): 1–29.

Touber, Jetze. *Spinoza and Biblical Philology in the Dutch Republic, 1660–1710.* New York: Oxford University Press, 2018.

Tov, E. *Textual Criticism of the Hebrew Bible.* 3rd edition. Minneapolis: Fortress Press, 2012.

Tropper, Josef, and Rebecca Hasselbach-Andee. *Classical Ethiopic: A Grammar of Gǝ'ǝz.* LANE 10. University Park, PA: Eisenbrauns, 2021.

Tyson, Craig W., and Virginia R. Hermann. *Imperial Peripheries in the Neo-Assyrian Period.* Louisville: University Press of Colorado, 2018.

Uehlinger, Christoph. *Weltreich und "eine Rede": Eine neue Deutung der sogenannten Turmbauerzählung (Gen 11, 1–9).* OBO 101. Göttingen: Vandenhoeck & Ruprecht, 1990.

Ullendorff, Edward. *The Bible and Ethiopia.* Schweich Lectures. London: British Academy, 1968.

Van de Mieroop, Marc. "Literature and Political Discourse in Ancient Mesopotamia: Sargon of Assyria and Sargon of Agade." Pages 327–339 in *Munuscula Mesopotamica: Festschrift für Johannes Renger.* Edited by Barbara Böck, Eva Cancik-Kirschbaum, and Thomas Richter. AOAT 267. Munster: Ugarit-Verlag, 1999.

———. *A History of the Ancient Near East, ca. 3000–323 BC.* 3rd ed. Blackwell History of the Ancient World. Malden, MA: Wiley Blackwell, 2015.

Van der Kooij, A. *Die Alten Textzeugen des Jesajabuches: Ein Beitrag zur Textgeschichte des Alten Testaments.* OBO 35. Göttingen: Vandenhoeck & Ruprecht, 1981.

———. "The City of Babel and Assyrian Imperialism: Genesis 11:1–9 Interpreted in the Light of Mesopotamian Sources." Pages 1–18 in *Congress Volume Leiden 2004.* Edited by André Lemaire. VTSup 109. Leiden: Brill, 2006.

Van Rooy, R. "'Πόθεν οὖν ἡ τοσαύτη διαφωνία;' Greek Patristic Authors Discussing Linguistic Origin, Diversity, Change and Kinship." *Beiträge zur Geschichte der Sprachwissenschaft* 23 (2013): 21–54.

Van Ruiten, J. T. A. G. M. *Primeval History Interpreted: The Rewriting of Genesis 1–11 in the* Book of Jubilees. JSJSupp 66. Boston: Brill, 2000.

———. *Abraham in the* Book of Jubilees: *The Rewriting of Genesis 11:26–25:10 in the* Book of Jubilees *11:14–23:8*. JSJSupp 161. Boston: Brill, 2012.

Vanderhooft, David. "Babylon as Cosmopolis in Israelite Texts and Achaemenid Architecture." *HeBAI* 9 (2020): 41–61.

VanderKam, James. *The Book of Jubilees*. CSCO 511. Leuven: Peeters, 1989.

———. "The Origins and Purposes of the *Book of Jubilees*." Pages 4–16 in *Studies in the* Book of Jubilees. Edited by M. Albani, J. Frey, and A. Lange. TSAJ 65. Tübingen: Mohr Siebeck, 1997.

———. "Recent Scholarship on the Book of Jubilees." *CBR* 63 (2008): 405–431.

———. *Jubilees 1–21*. Hermeneia. Minneapolis: Fortress Press, 2018.

Vanstiphout, Herman. *Epics of Sumerian Kings: The Matter of Aratta*. WAW 20. Atlanta: SBL Press, 2003.

Vayntrub, Jacqueline. *Beyond Orality: Biblical Poetry on Its Own Terms*. The Ancient World. New York: Routledge, 2019.

Vile, John R. *The Constitutional Convention of 1787: A Comprehensive Encyclopedia of America's Founding*. Rev. 2nd ed. Clark, NJ: Talbot Publishing, 2016.

Voogt, Alex de, and Irving Finkel, ed. *The Idea of Writing: Play and Complexity*. Boston: Brill, 2010.

Von Rad, Gerhard. *Genesis*. OTL. Philadelphia: Westminster, 1972.

Walker, Joel. "The Legacy of Mesopotamia in Late Antique Iraq: The Christian Martyr Shrine at Melqi (Neo-Assyrian Milqia)," *ARAM* 18–19 (2006–2007): 483–508.

Waltke, Bruce, and M. O'Connor. *An Introduction to Biblical Hebrew Syntax*. Winona Lake, IN: Eisenbrauns, 1990.

Weidner, Ernst. *Die Inschriften Tukulti-Ninurtas I. und seiner Nachfolger*. Reprint. Archiv für Orientforschung Beiheft 12. Osnabrück: Biblio Verlag, 1970.

Weitzman, Steven. "Why Did the Qumran Community Write in Hebrew?" *JAOS* 119 (1999): 35–45.

Wenham, Gordon. *Genesis 1–15*. WBC 1. Waco, TX: Word Books, 1987.

Westermann, Claus. *Genesis 1–11: A Commentary*. Translated by John J. Scullion. Continental Commentaries. Minneapolis: Augsburg Publishing House, 1984.

Wheeler, Brannon. *Prophets in the Quran: An Introduction to the Quran and Muslim Exegesis*. New York: Continuum, 2002.

Williamson, H. G. M. "Review: *Wrestling with Isaiah: The Exegetical Methodology of Campegius Vitringa (1659–1722)*." *JTS* 69 (2018): 225–228.

Winckler, Hugo. *Die Keilschrifttexte Sargons: Nach der Papierabklatschen und originalen.* 2 vols. Leipzig: E. Pfeiffer, 1889.

Winitzer, Abraham. "Etana in Eden: New Light on the Mesopotamian and Biblical Tales in Their Semitic Context," *JAOS* 133 (2013): 441–465.

———. "Assyriology and Jewish Studies in Tel Aviv: Ezekiel among the Babylonian *literati.*" Pages 163–216 in *Encounters by the Rivers of Babylon: Scholarly Conversations between Jews, Iranians and Babylonians in Antiquity.* Edited by Uri Gabbay and Shai Secunda. TSAJ 160. Tübingen: Mohr Siebeck, 2014.

Witte, M. *Die biblische Urgeschichte.* BZAW 265. Berlin: De Gruyter, 1998.

Woods, Christopher. "Bilingualism, Scribal Learning, and the Death of Sumerian." In *Margins of Writing, Origins of Cultures,* edited by Seth L. Sanders, 91–120. OIS 2. Chicago: Oriental Institute of the University of Chicago, 2006.

Worthington, Martin. *Principles of Akkadian Textual Criticism.* SANER 1. Berlin: De Gruyter, 2012.

Wright, David. *Inventing God's Law: How the Covenant Code of the Bible Used and Revised the Laws of Hammurabi.* New York: Oxford University Press, 2009.

———. "The Covenant Code Appendix (Exodus 23:20–33), Neo-Assyrian Sources, and Implications for Pentateuchal Study." In *The Formation of the Pentateuch: Bridging the Academic Cultures of Europe, Israel, and North America,* edited by Jan C. Gertz et al., 47–86. FAT 111. Tübingen: Mohr Siebeck, 2016.

Younger, Lawson K. "The Deportation of the Israelites." *JBL* 117 (1998): 201–227.

———. "The Assyrian Economic Impact on the Southern Levant in the Light of Recent Study." *IEJ* 65 (2015): 179–204.

Zahn, Molly M. *Genres of Rewriting in Second Temple Judaism: Scribal Composition and Transmission.* Cambridge: Cambridge University Press, 2020.

Zakovitch, Yair. "'God Said One Word, I Heard Two': Ambiguous Expressions in Biblical Literature." Pages 98–100 in *'I Will Utter Riddles from Ancient Times': Riddles and Dream-Riddles in Biblical Narrative.* Tel Aviv: Am Oved, 2005.

———. *Jacob: Unexpected Patriarch.* Jewish Lives. New Haven, CT: Yale University Press, 2012.

Zevit, Ziony. *What Really Happened in the Garden of Eden?* New Haven, CT: Yale University Press, 2013.

Zoref, Arye. "The Influence of Syriac Bible Commentaries on Judeo Arabic Exegesis as Demonstrated by Several Stories from the Book of Genesis." *SCJR* 11 (2016): 1–18.

WEBSITES

http://kircher.stanford.edu/

https://www.patheos.com/blogs/dispatches/2018/11/29/gallups-refugee-caravan-is-gods-judgment-on-america/

https://www.splcenter.org/hatewatch/2018/01/26/anti-immigrant-hate-group-proenglish-visits-white-house

https://www.congress.gov/bill/115th-congress/house-bill/997

https://proenglish.org/2018/12/12/breitbart-news-features-proenglish-on-siriusxm-patriot/

https://www.realclearpolitics.com/video/2012/02/21/pat_buchanan_we_are_becoming_a_tower_of_babel.html

https://buchanan.org/blog/buchanan-trumps-rise-is-rejection-of-quarter-century-of-bush-republicanism-124847

https://buchanan.org/blog/?s=Tower+of+Babel

https://www.politico.com/magazine/story/2017/04/22/pat-buchanan-trump-president-history-profile-215042

https://theweek.com/articles/853163/how-pat-buchanan-made-president-trump-possible

https://www.vox.com/2019/1/14/18181897/trump-pat-buchanan-column-tweet

https://buchanan.org/blog/memo-to-trump-declare-an-emergency-135677?doing_wp_cron=1564588936.9655640125274658203125

https://divinity.uchicago.edu/sightings/apostle-and-ag

https://www.wsj.com/articles/the-roots-of-political-polarization-1541111248

https://www.washingtonpost.com/world/2022/04/12/ukrainians-abandon-russian-language/

https://archi.ru/events/19542/maslenica-v-nikola-lenivce

https://www.instagram.com/p/CajkhMpgHRv/?utm_source=ig_embed&ig_rid=8305c69d-8898-42f9-832e-421d71ec1522

https://www.theatlantic.com/magazine/archive/2022/05/social-media-democracy-trust-babel/629369/

https://www.washingtonpost.com/dc-md-va/2021/02/02/amazon-arlingon-headquarters-helix/

https://www.christianitytoday.com/ct/2022/april-web-only/russell-moore-tower-babel-evangelical-unity-fragmentation.html

Subject Index

Index of Modern Authors

Index of Passages